Lessons in Educational Equality

Lessons in Educational Equality

SUCCESSFUL APPROACHES TO INTRACTABLE PROBLEMS AROUND THE WORLD

EDITED BY

JODY HEYMANN

and

ADÈLE CASSOLA

OXFORD
UNIVERSITY PRESS

OXFORD
UNIVERSITY PRESS

Oxford University Press, Inc., publishes works that further
Oxford University's objective of excellence in research,
scholarship, and education.

Oxford New York
Auckland   Cape Town   Dar es Salaam   Hong Kong   Karachi
Kuala Lumpur   Madrid   Melbourne   Mexico City   Nairobi
New Delhi   Shanghai   Taipei   Toronto

With offices in
Argentina   Austria   Brazil   Chile   Czech Republic   France   Greece
Guatemala   Hungary   Italy   Japan   Poland   Portugal   Singapore
South Korea   Switzerland   Thailand   Turkey   Ukraine   Vietnam

Copyright © 2012 by Jody Heymann and Adèle Cassola

Published by Oxford University Press, Inc.
198 Madison Avenue, New York, New York 10016
www.oup.com

Oxford is a registered trademark of Oxford University Press, Inc.

Library of Congress Cataloging-in-Publication Data

  Lessons in educational equality: successful approaches to intractable problems
around the world/edited by Jody Heymann and Adèle Cassola.
    p. cm.
  Includes bibliographical references and index.
  ISBN 978-0-19-975501-1 (hardcover)
  1. Educational equalization. 2. Equality. I. Heymann, Jody, 1959- II. Cassola, Adèle.
  LC213.L47 2012
  379.2'6—dc22   2011012564

9 8 7 6 5 4 3 2 1

Printed in the United States of America on acid-free paper

*To Benjamin Heymann Brewer and Mary Ann Buttigieg,
and all those who commit a part of their lives
to teaching in the hardest settings.*

Contents

Part 5   APPLYING LESSONS ACROSS GEOGRAPHY

Acknowledgments

When Jody created the Institute for Health and Social Policy, she hoped that the Institute would be defined by its focus on addressing inequities and by its commitment to initiatives that bridge the gap between research and policy, between evidence and action. While this was her hope from the outset and is reflected in the founding mission statement of the Institute, no organization can even begin to chip away at this kind of goal without the deep contributions of many. We are indebted to the academic leadership at McGill for fostering the university as a place where this kind of global, evidence-based research is supported and translated into action. In particular, we are grateful for the support in launching this from Heather Munroe-Blum, Anthony Masi, Denis Therien, Rich Levin, and Chris Manfredi.

Funded by the generous support of the Max Bell Foundation, and with matching funds from McGill University, the Institute launched as its first major initiative a program on *Moving from Evidence to Effective Public Policy*. This program has as its core three elements: (1) conferences to bring together top researchers, policy-makers, and program staff from around the world seeking to address seemingly intractable problems; (2) a fellowship program in which fellows coming from a broad range of disciplines travel around the world to conduct in-depth studies of successful policies and programs; and (3) an effort to bring together the best expertise to write about how the research evidence can be translated into policies and programs that work. The problems that this initiative has addressed have included ameliorating the conditions faced by the working poor, increasing civic participation among marginalized populations, and improving the environmental economy. In 2008 and 2009, the initiative focused on addressing educational equity.

In 2008, eight Policy Fellows travelled the globe to examine initiatives that were promoting access, quality, and equity in education for marginalized groups. Their work was made possible by the exceptional direction and guidance of Tinka Markham Piper, Magda Barrera, and Jennifer Proudfoot, along with partners running programs around the world who generously shared their experiences and wisdom. The Fellowship team was instrumental in identifying promising initiatives that are increasing educational equity around the world, facilitating Fellows' travel to and research about these programs, and helping them translate their findings into concrete recommendations to inform the work of policy-makers and practitioners around the world.

The leap from research to recommendations greatly benefitted from the work of a dedicated team that brought together leading experts on educational equity from around the world at a global conference hosted at McGill University in 2009. Ceyda Turan, Jennifer Proudfoot, Melanie Benard, and Elisheva Bouskila worked tirelessly to bring together a unique group of leading international policy and aca-demic experts and educational practitioners who would not normally have the opportunity to discuss their diverse perspectives on equity issues face to face. This volume, which aims to move the debates begun at the conference into proposals for action, would not have come together without the invaluable contributions of Parama Sigurdsen and Gonzalo Moreno and the countless insights and thought-provoking questions of other Institute staff members.

Being surrounded by bright and creative coworkers and classmates has been a constant source of joy and learning for Adèle and Jody. Adèle is particularly grateful to Leanna Eaton, Anne Game, and Maria Vamvalis for teaching her that, with enough determination, imagination, and heart, global inequities can be addressed—and for providing her first opportunities to do so.

Jody's and Adèle's lives, like so many of our lives, were transformed by class-room teachers. If Jody were to tell the story of what each gave, the personal thanks in the acknowledgments would be longer than this book, so we'll need to stick with three to stand for the rest. Cecile Brault grew up in a gritty immigrant neigh-borhood in Chicopee, Massachusetts. Although she taught her native French to high school students, including Jody, with passion, even more influential was the passion she brought to showing them that they both could make a difference in the world and had a responsibility to. Harvey Fineberg's and Richard Zeckhauser's influence as research supervisors was equally profound. When some professors preferred to teach tidy problems that were more readily solved, they were willing to advise on complex, nearly impossible ones that matter. The implicit lesson that these challenges were addressable and worth taking on was not lost on Jody.

Jody's oldest son, Ben, began teaching last year in a special-needs high school in a particularly poor district in the South Bronx, in New York. The students bring creativity, questions, and strength; they also bring as many challenges to school, as life has brought them. Many students have barely learned to read before enter-ing the high school. Deeply affected by drugs and gang activity, the school screens for weapons at the entrance and has a security force in the hallways. Together with committed veteran teachers and other teaching fellows, Ben is working to figure out how to achieve the most learning with his students, day in and day out, in a setting where the odds are often stacked against it. As we edited and wrote for this volume, Jody was inspired by Ben's work and the humor, insights, courage, and commitment he brought to it.

Adèle's grandmother, Mary Ann, began teaching primary school in Malta shortly after World War II broke out. In the years that followed, amid immense hardship, she continued to teach her students in the classroom and in bomb shelters so that their education would not be interrupted by the war. The commitment that she and her colleagues showed to teaching throughout heavy air raids that devastated the country is a testament to the courage of all those who brave hostile conditions within and outside of the classroom, in order to bring education to children who would otherwise be left on the margins. This book is dedicated to Ben and Mary Ann and to all those who commit a part of their lives to teaching in the hardest settings—without their imagination, resilience, strength, and extraordinary efforts, we would not be able to achieve a true chance at education for all.

About the Editors

Jody Heymann is the founding director of McGill University's Institute for Health and Social Policy. An internationally renowned researcher on health and social policy, Heymann holds a Canada Research Chair in Global Health and Social Policy. She has authored and edited over 190 publications, including *Profit at the Bottom of the Ladder* (Harvard Business Press, 2009), *Raising the Global Floor* (Stanford University Press, 2009), *Trade and Health* (McGill Queens University Press, 2007), *Forgotten Families* (Oxford University Press, 2006), *Healthier Societies* (Oxford University Press, 2006) and *Unfinished Work* (New Press, 2005). Deeply committed to translating research into policies and programs that will improve individual and population health and well-being, Heymann has worked with leaders in North American, European, African, and Latin American governments, as well as with a wide range of intergovernmental organizations including the World Health Organization, the International Labor Organization, UNICEF, and UNESCO.

Heymann established and leads the WoRLD Global Data Centre, the first global initiative to examine social policy in all 193 UN nations. As part of this effort, the WoRLD Education Initiative is bringing together the vast range of globally collected data on children's educational outcomes with each country's corresponding educational policies. Using global data from UNESCO and the UN Special Rapporteur on the Right to Education, and countries' constitutional and legal guarantees of free and compulsory education, the WoRLD Education Initiative provides a comprehensive source of data on educational policy, practice, and progress around the globe. From 2008 to 2010, Heymann chaired an initiative on Educational Inequalities that brought together students and experts from around the world to examine successful programs and develop policy recommendations for practitioners and decision-makers. As part of this initiative, Policy Fellows carried out fieldwork on five continents. In 2011–2012, Heymann chairs the World Economic Forum's Global Agenda Council on Education Systems.

Adèle Cassola conducts comparative research at McGill University's Institute for Health and Social Policy on how education policy and legal rights affect the life chances of marginalized populations. As part of the WoRLD Global Data Centre research team, she leads an initiative analyzing the protections established in the constitutions of all UN member states across a number of life contexts in which discrimination can occur, including education, work, health, family, and political and civic participation. Her commitment to finding practical strategies to improve the well-being of vulnerable groups previously led her to conduct research with the Plan Institute for Caring Citizenship in Vancouver and the Centre for Research on Inner City Health in Toronto. She also spent several years developing and implementing youth education initiatives with the non-governmental organization War Child Canada. Cassola received her B.A. in peace and conflict studies from the University of Toronto and her M.Sc. in sociology from the London School of Economics.

About the Authors

Jessica Ball is a professor in the School of Child and Youth Care at the University of Victoria, Canada, and director of the Centre for Early Childhood Research and Policy. She is also the principal investigator of an interdisciplinary program of research on the cultural nature of child and family development. Ball has conducted research and program evaluation and development projects for the Open Society Foundation, the Aga Khan Foundation Canada, and UNESCO. She spent a dozen years in Southeast Asia working with community service agencies and government ministries on research and service programs involving all levels of education. She is the author or co-author of over 100 journal articles and book chapters and three books, including *Supporting Indigenous Children's Development: Community-University Partnerships* (University of British Columbia Press, 2006). She has created and taught courses for universities in North America, Asia, Africa, and the Middle East. Ball received her M.A. in developmental psychology, Ph.D. in clinical psychology, and M.P.H. in international health from the University of California, Berkeley.

Koli Banik is an education specialist at the Education for All – Fast Track Initiative (EFA FTI) Secretariat. Banik coordinates the Secretariat's work on issues of educational inclusion and equity, and works with FTI partner countries to ensure that issues of disabilities are addressed in country education sector plans. Prior to joining the FTI Secretariat, Banik worked for the Population Council, World Bank, American Friends Service Committee, and local non-governmental organizations in India. Banik has extensive field experience working with the disabled community in India and Vietnam, and is a member of the UNAIDS Inter-Agency Task Team on Education and United Nations Girls' Education Initiative. Banik has a Ph.D. in international education from the University of Maryland, College Park, and an M.A. in social work from the University of Pennsylvania.

Carol Benson is an experienced educator, researcher, and consultant in educational development with a focus on language issues in multilingual societies.

Based at Stockholm University in Sweden, where she teaches higher education pedagogy, Benson also pursues interests in European regional and minority languages in education. She has worked as a consultant in formal education on issues such as teacher education and curriculum development and in non-formal education on projects promoting literacy and gender equity in Asia, Latin America, and Africa. Her recent work includes consulting with the Ministry of Education and Training in Vietnam and UNICEF to design and pilot bilingual schooling in three minority languages and Vietnamese. Benson holds a Ph.D. in social sciences and comparative education from the University of California, Los Angeles.

Ebony Bertorelli is a research associate with the Global Health Diplomacy Initiative at McGill University, where she conducts research, training, and advisory projects concerning global policy-making and negotiation processes in the areas of trade and health, health and foreign policy, global health governance, and globalization and health. Bertorelli has held fellowships at the Institute for Health and Social Policy, during which the work for this volume was conducted, and the Institute for the Study of International Development. She holds a B.A. from the University of British Columbia in political science and film and an M.A. from McGill University in the comparative politics of the developing world.

Aneel Brar is an international development researcher and practitioner interested in post-conflict development, capacity building, organizational development, and education. Most recently, Brar was a Research Award Recipient with Canada's International Development Research Centre, where he helped develop a capacity-building program to strengthen research organizations in Africa, Asia, and Latin America. Brar conducted the research for the present volume as a Policy Fellow with McGill University's Institute for Health and Social Policy. He also worked with the Institute on the WoRLD Global Data Centre database of poverty-related legislation from around the world. He completed his M.A. in political science at McGill University, and his B.A. in political science and B.Sc. in biology at the University of Calgary.

North Cooc is a doctoral student at the Harvard Graduate School of Education studying quantitative policy analysis in education. His research explores how home and school factors affect the enrollment and experiences of minority students in special education. He is especially interested in how parental expectations, cultural beliefs, and school policies influence the decisions of parents of children with special needs in the United States and Japan. Prior to his doctoral studies, Cooc worked in educational research in Washington, D.C., where he conducted evaluations and studies of out-of-school time programs, early literacy initiatives, and youth development and arts programs. He also spent 2 years teaching junior high school English in rural Japan. Cooc holds an Ed.M. in international education policy from Harvard and a B.A. in history and Japanese from the University of California, Berkeley.

Marie Duru-Bellat is professor of sociology of education at Sciences-Po (Paris Institute of Political Science) and a researcher at the Observatory of Sociological Change, Paris. She leads research on gender and social inequalities in schools, assessing their importance and their evolution. She also analyses school processes, such as the impact of tracking and of socially and academically mixed classes and schools. She has consulted on educational issues and reforms with the Centre d'Analyse Stratégique, Cour des Comptes and UNESCO's International Institute for Educational Planning, among others. Duru-Bellat has published widely on education and inequality, including most recently *Education and Equity: International Perspectives on Theory and Policy* (Vol. 3; Dordrecht, Springer, 2007), *Le mérite contre la justice* (Presses de Sciences Po, 2009), and *Les sociétés et leur école* (Seuil, 2010).

Serge Ebersold is professor of sociology and Head of Research at the Higher Education and Research Institute for Teacher Training and Research for Special Needs Education. He coordinates an OECD project looking at pathways students with disabilities follow to tertiary education and employment and was formerly an analyst with the OECD's Directorate for Education. Prior to joining the OECD, he was a professor at the University of Strasbourg, where he taught disability sociology for 15 years and conducted research on persons with disabilities' education and employment opportunities. He also collaborated with the European Commission on comparing disability policies within the European Union, was involved in the World Health Organization's revision process of the International Classification of Disability, and participated actively in analysis conducted by the European Agency for Development in Special Needs Education. He has published several books on opportunities for persons with special needs and their families in the realms of citizenship, education, and employment, including *Parents et professionnels face au dévoilement du handicap* (Eres, 2007), *Le Temps des servitudes: La famille à l'épreuve du handicap* (Presses universitaires de Rennes, 2005), and *Disability in Higher Education* (OECD, 2003).

Peter Evans worked, from 1989 until his recent retirement, as a senior analyst at the OECD with responsibility for work carried out on children at risk and those with special educational needs. He previously worked with the Department of Special Education at the University of London's Institute of Education, where he ran courses for teachers of children with learning difficulties. After directing a research project on curriculum development for children with learning difficulties for the Department of Education and Science in the United Kingdom, he became head of the Department of Child Development and Educational Psychology at the Institute of Education at the University of London. He has published some 20 books on educational issues for children with disabilities, including *Students with Disabilities, Learning Difficulties and Disadvantages in the Baltic States, South Eastern Europe and Malta: Educational Policies and Indicators* (OECD, 2009), *Disability in Higher Education* (OECD, 2003), and *"Special Care" Provision: The Education of*

Children with Profound and Multiple Learning Difficulties (NFER-Nelson, 1987). He has traveled extensively, studying special education systems in both OECD and non-OECD countries. Evans studied psychology and anthropology at the University of London and completed his Ph.D. in mental handicap at the University of Manchester.

Merle Froschl has more than 35 years of experience in education and publishing. As co-director of the Educational Equity Center at FHI 360, she provides leadership and oversight to projects that include curriculum development, professional development, parent education, research and evaluation, and coalition-building. Since the 1970s, she has developed curricular and teacher training models in the field of educational equity. Froschl is a nationally known speaker on issues of gender equity and equality of opportunity in education and is co-author of *Supporting Boys' Learning: Strategies for Teacher Practice, Pre-K-Grade 3* (Teachers College Press, 2010). From 1982 to 2004, Froschl was co-founder and co-director of Educational Equity Concepts, a nonprofit organization that promoted bias-free learning regardless of gender, race/ethnicity, disability, or level of family income. She holds a B.S. in journalism from Syracuse University and is a graduate of the Institute for Not-for-Profit Management, Columbia University.

Jodut Hashmi is a doctoral student at the Harvard Graduate School of Education, where she studies college access and success policies. Prior to graduate school, Hashmi worked as an assistant director with the United States Advisory Committee on Student Financial Assistance, where she co-authored several Congressional reports on college textbook affordability, community college transfer, and the provision of early financial aid information to low-income students. Hashmi has served as a Teach For America corps member in St. Louis, Missouri, where she was a seventh-grade mathematics teacher in an international studies middle school. Hashmi received her M.A. in international education policy from the Harvard Graduate School of Education and her B.A. in policy analysis and management from Cornell University.

Clyde Hertzman is director of the Human Early Learning Partnership at the University of British Columbia; Canada Research Chair in Population Health and Human Development, and professor in the School of Population and Public Health. He serves as principal investigator of the Provincial Early Child Development Mapping Unit and the Child & Youth Developmental Trajectories Research Unit, and the Population Health and Learning Observatory. Nationally, Hertzman is a fellow of the Experience-based Brain and Biological Development Programme and the Successful Societies Programs of the Canadian Institute for Advanced Research. Hertzman has played a central role in creating a framework that links population health to human development, emphasizing the special role of early childhood development as a determinant of health. His research has contributed to international, national, provincial, and community initiatives for healthy child development. Hertzman is the recipient of the Canadian Institutes of Health Research 2010 Michael Smith Prize in Health Research, Canada's Health Researcher of the Year, and the Canadian Institute of Child Health (CICH) 2010 National Child Day Award.

Emily Hertzman is a Ph.D. candidate in the Department of Anthropology at the University of Toronto. Hertzman is currently conducting ethnographic field research about mobility, migration, and ethnicity in West Kalimantan, Indonesia. She has worked as a research assistant and a coordinator of international projects at the Human Early Learning Partnership at the University of British Columbia, where she conducted research and produced communications that promote knowledge about early child development measurement and monitoring in an international context. Between 2005 and 2008, she was a member of the Organizational Hub of the Knowledge Network for Early Child Development, which was part of the World Health Organization's Commission on Social Determinants of Health. She holds a B.A. and an M.A. in sociocultural anthropology from the University of British Columbia.

Lori Irwin is the former deputy director of the Human Early Learning Partnership at the University of British Columbia. As part of her role as deputy director, Irwin leads the work of the early child development mapping team, which uses tools such as the Early Development Instrument for data gathering. Irwin consults nationally with a team of researchers on population health measurement using the Early Development Instrument. Her research interests include investigating the various child, family, and community factors that influence children's early development and learning. She is also helping to develop a child rights monitoring framework for early child development for the United Nations Committee on the Rights of the Child. She completed a Ph.D. in nursing and a postdoctoral fellowship in early child development, learning, and population health at the University of British Columbia.

Brittany Lambert is a researcher at McGill University's Institute for Health and Social Policy, where she works on several education- and children-related initiatives as part of the WoRLD Global Data Centre team. As a graduate student, Lambert participated in the Institute's Policy Fellowship Program and traveled to Bolivia to conduct research on how intercultural bilingual education is reducing educational inequalities for Indigenous students. This research later became the basis for her contribution to this book. Lambert holds an M.A. in political science from McGill University and a B.A. in international studies and modern languages from the University of Ottawa.

Maureen Lewis is economic advisor in the World Bank Africa Region's Human Development Department. She was formerly Chief Economist for Human Development and Advisor to the Vice President for Human Development, a Senior Fellow at the Center for Global Development, and previously managed a group of policy analysts and project managers in the area of human development in the World Bank's Eastern Europe and Central Asia region. Lewis spent 10 years working on Latin America and the Caribbean at the World Bank and at The Urban Institute. She has published dozens of articles in peer-reviewed journals on education and health policy, and has a special focus on gender issues in education. She earned her Ph.D. at Johns Hopkins University.

Marlaine Lockheed is a sociologist of education with 40 years of experience advising governments, donor agencies, and private organizations on reforms for education quality, gender equity, and school effectiveness. During her 20 years at the World Bank, she served as interim Education Director, managed a group of policy analysts and project managers in the area of human development in the World Bank's Middle East and North Africa region, and directed a group of evaluation researchers in the World Bank Institute. Prior to joining the World Bank, she was a principal research sociologist at Educational Testing Service in Princeton, New Jersey, where she directed research on gender equity. She is author of several books, including the internationally recognized *Improving Primary Education in Developing Countries* (Oxford University Press, 1991) and over 150 journal articles and research reports. She has served on the boards of numerous professional associations and scientific journals and has also taught at Harvard, Stanford, Princeton, and University of Texas. She holds a Ph.D. in international development education from Stanford University.

Mokubung Nkomo is the director of the Center for Diversity and Social Cohesion and professor in the Faculty of Education at the University of Pretoria, South Africa. He has served as the chair of the South African Qualifications Authority, the South African Senior Certificate Council, and currently chairs the Education Sector Committee of the South African National Commission of UNESCO. Prior to joining the University, he was executive director of education and training at the Human Sciences Research Council. He was the director of the South Africa Partnership Programme at the New School for Social Research in New York City, after serving as a professor at the University of North Carolina-Charlotte. He is the author of *Student Culture and Activism in Black South African Universities* (Greenwood Press, 1984), editor of *Pedagogy of Domination: Toward a Democratic Education in South Africa* (Africa World Press, 1990), and co-editor of three books, including *Within the Realm of Possibility: From Disadvantage to Development at the University of the North and the University of Fort Hare* (HSRC Press, 2006).

Laura Pilozzi-Edmonds is currently completing a medical degree at McGill University. As an undergraduate student, she took part in the Institute for Health and Social Policy Fellowship Program, for which she travelled to Tanzania to conduct research on gender equity in the education system. During this research, she came across a ground-breaking program at the University of Dar es Salaam aimed at increasing gender equity in engineering, which became the focus of her research and the basis of her contribution to this book. Laura is now concentrating on finishing her medical studies and plans to continue research on the social determinants of health in the future. She holds a BA. Sc. from McGill University, where she completed a major concentration in biomedical science and minor concentrations in African studies and social studies of medicine.

Robert Prouty is the head of the Education for All – Fast Track Initiative (EFA FTI) Secretariat, a global partnership of donor and developing countries, multilateral institutions, and civil society groups based at the World Bank in Washington, D.C. Since its creation in 2002, EFA FTI has grown steadily and now endorses the education sector plans of 43 developing countries around the world. Prouty specializes in classroom issues and learning outcomes. He lived for 10 years in rural areas of the Democratic Republic of the Congo (formerly Zaire) and Rwanda and speaks three African languages. Much of his career has been focused on education issues in francophone West Africa. He holds a Ph.D. in educational administration with an emphasis on African studies from Michigan State University and has taught at the primary, secondary, and university levels.

Fernando Reimers is the Ford Foundation Professor of International Education and Director of the International Education Policy Program at the Harvard Graduate School of Education. He teaches courses on the relationship between education policy, democratic citizenship, and instructional improvement. His current research in Brazil and Mexico focuses on the impact of education policy, education leadership, and teacher professional development on literacy competencies, citizenship, and advanced cognitive skill. He is also evaluating a cross-national project to foster democratic citizenship skills and civic education in Chile, Colombia, Guatemala, the Dominican Republic, Mexico, and Paraguay. He has published numerous books and articles on international education and development, and has worked as an advisor to governments and international development institutions in several countries in Asia, Latin America, and the Middle East. He is a member of the Council of Foreign Relations, a Fellow of the International Academy of Education, Chair of the World Economic Forum's Global Agenda Council on Education, and Member of the Middle East and North Africa Advisory Group of the World Economic Forum, as well as a member of the United States National Commission for UNESCO.

Arjumand Siddiqi is assistant professor at the University of Toronto's Dalla Lana School of Public Health and an associate member of the Canadian Institute of Advanced Research Program on Successful Societies. Her research utilizes a cross-national comparative perspective to understand the consequences of social welfare policies for inequalities in health and developmental outcomes. Siddiqi was formerly assistant professor at the University of North Carolina Gillings School of Global Public Health, and a Faculty Fellow of the Carolina Population Center. She was a member of the World Health Organization's Commission on Social

Determinants of Health Knowledge Hub on Early Child Development, and has consulted for several international agencies, including the World Bank and UNICEF. Siddiqi received her Ph.D. in social epidemiology from Harvard University.

Barbara Sprung is co-director of the Educational Equity Center at FHI 360. She has over 40 years of experience in early childhood education, as a teacher and as an innovator of programs and materials to promote equality of opportunity for children regardless of gender, race/ethnicity, disability, or level of family income. From 1982 to 2004, Sprung was co-founder and co-director of Educational Equity Concepts, a national nonprofit organization whose mission was to create bias-free programs and materials beginning in early childhood. Sprung has written extensively about equity in education, including most recently *Supporting Boys' Learning: Strategies for Teacher Practice, Pre-K–Grade–3* (Teachers College Press, 2010), and is a nationally known speaker on issues of gender equity, teasing and bullying, early science equity, and inclusion. She is the recipient of the 2011 Bank Street College Alumni Association Award. Sprung holds an M.S. in child development from the Bank Street College of Education, and is a graduate of Columbia University's Institute for Not-for-Profit Management.

Deepa Srikantaiah is a consultant with the Education for All–Fast Track Initiative Secretariat, which is hosted by the World Bank in Washington, D.C. Srikantaiah's doctoral research examined the integration of indigenous knowledge, or non-Western knowledge systems, in education and health development. Srikantaiah has worked as a senior research associate with the Center on Education Policy in Washington, D.C., where she led a project examining the impact of accountability policies on curriculum and instruction in the United States. She has also worked as a consultant at the World Bank, and has been an adjunct faculty member at the University of Maryland. Srikantaiah received her Ph.D. in international education policy from the University of Maryland, College Park.

Ziba Vaghri is the director of the International Research and Initiatives Program at the University of British Columbia's Human Early Learning Partnership. Vaghri spent her early career working internationally as a pediatric nurse. Her current interest is in monitoring early child development at the population level in diverse parts of the world. Vaghri is also a member of a team working on the development of a framework for monitoring child rights in early childhood for the UN's Committee on the Rights of the Child. She completed a Ph.D. in human nutrition with a special focus on pediatric nutrition at the University of British Columbia.

Lessons in Educational Equality

1

Ending Educational Exclusion

JODY HEYMANN AND ADÈLE CASSOLA

Alicia was raised in South Central Los Angeles. The neighborhood was better known for urban blight than for opportunity. By the time Alicia was school-age, the city had changed the *barrio*'s name to South Los Angeles, hoping to reduce the stigma. But the school system still lagged far behind any affluent district. Plagued by many of the same problems as other junior high school students in areas of concentrated poverty, to succeed at school, Alicia would have to find a way through the gangs and schoolyard violence; through overcrowded classrooms with poor infrastructure, few supplies, and outdated textbooks, and classes taught by under-resourced and frustrated teachers.[1] Fewer than 45% of her Latino peers in the Los Angeles Unified School District would graduate from high school.[2] Her problems were not unique. In the United States, only 55.5% of Latino students graduate from high school,[3] yet they are the fastest growing population of children in the country.[4] By 2030, 30% of the country's youth are projected to be Latino.[5]

Disparities run deep in the United States. In spite of the country's reputation for having many of the best universities in the world, American youth lag behind when it comes to university education. Only 57% of those who entered a 4-year postsecondary program in 2001 obtained a degree within 6 years of enrollment, compared to an average 70% completion rate among Organisation for Economic Co-operation and Development (OECD) countries for comparable cohorts. When taking into account American students who don't even begin tertiary education and those who begin but fail to complete, one finds that only a minority of Americans graduate with a college or university degree. In 2008, just 37% of college-aged youth in the United States could expect to graduate from a 4-year tertiary program. Thirteen OECD countries registered higher graduation rates, including 63% in Finland and 57% in Iceland and Slovakia.[6]

The consequences of falling behind in education for the lives of American girls and boys, men and women, and for the country as a whole have become increasingly grave. With the rapid globalization of communications, transportation, and the economy over the past three decades, jobs have increasingly become mobile.

Manufacturing jobs that allow a decent standard of living with only a high school education were among the first to leave the United States.[7] Manufacturing employment has shrunk by 33% since 2001, with over 5.6 million jobs lost between January 2001 and January 2010.[8] The jobs that remain for those with a high school education have seen their wages and benefits erode dramatically. For the country as a whole, it has become increasingly clear that the only path to effective competition that will allow anything like a sustained quality of life requires a highly skilled, knowledgeable workforce that can compete for higher salaries.

Mahmood was born half a world away in Pakistan. His family immigrated to East London. Like millions of immigrants, their move was motivated by the desire to find better opportunities for their children. Although his parents sought opportunity, Mahmood saw a school system in which students in the so-called "public schools" (referred to as private in most countries because they require a fee) were approximately 40 percentage points more likely to get the exam results needed to get into top universities[9,10] and six times as likely to attend these universities compared to those in state-run schools.[11] Compared to students in state schools who qualify for a free meal, those who attend public schools are 3.5 times as likely to achieve the highest grades and nearly 22 times as likely to attend a top university.[12] Even if Mahmood became one of the few who managed to succeed on the exams, he was unlikely to be able to afford to attend. In 2010, amid a global recession, the British government announced 30% cuts in real, inflation-adjusted terms for universities by 2012–2013, which are expected to lead to dramatic increases in tuition fees.[13]

Zitha was born the same year a new South Africa was born. Growing up in post-apartheid South Africa, she would have the chance that her parents and grandparents never had to attend desegregated schools. Apartheid South Africa had offered her parents neither an education nor the kind of jobs that would allow them to exit poverty. Their hopes for Zitha's future were completely intertwined with what they imagined would be the future of a South Africa where race did not determine all chances. But, by the time Zitha reached high school in 2008, only 56.6% of black South Africans who made it to the end of secondary school were passing their school-leaving exams,[14] and only 12% of the relevant age cohort was enrolled in university.[15] The school system remained highly unequal, with large disparities in total (private plus public) spending per pupil between formerly "white" and formerly "black" schools. Three-quarters of the top-performing schools in terms of pass rates on high school leaving exams were formerly designated as "white" or "Indian" schools, whereas those formerly designated as "black"—84% of which still had a student population that was 100% black South African—had pass rates that were predominantly in the bottom three quintiles.[16] On top of its continuing educational problems, the country faced economic growth rates that lagged behind other emerging middle-income economies, high inflation, an unstable exchange rate, a shortage of skilled labor, and one of the highest rates of income inequality in the world.[17] With minimum wages that were higher than China's,

South Africa could only hope to attract jobs by providing an educated workforce. Yet, only 15% of the university-age population in South Africa was enrolled in tertiary education compared to 23% in China,[18] and less than 1% of the population over the age of 25 had completed tertiary education, compared to 4% of the same age group in China.[19] These conditions contributed to the fact that a staggering 23% of the South African population was unemployed,[20] with unofficial estimates placing the unemployment rate as high as 40%.[21] Like educational attainment, joblessness was not distributed equally: Only 5% of the white population was unemployed, compared to 29% of the black population, with its apartheid-driven concentration of lower-skilled labor.[22]

   Lessons in Educational Equality addresses the urgent questions: How bad are the disparities within and between countries? And, are there effective and affordable ways to address them? Written for teachers, parents, principals, policy-makers and advocates concerned about improving education in their own countries, and individuals who worry about global inequalities and realize that addressing educational inequities is central to any answer, *Lessons in Educational Equality* brings together leading innovators in education from around the world. *Lessons in Educational Equality* also reports on a unique series of global case studies that focused on understanding which educational programs around the world have been particularly effective at addressing inequity and improving educational outcomes.

Global Efforts in Education

The global story to date on education is a good news, bad news one. The good news is that, over the past 20 years, the world has repeatedly committed to ensuring that all children receive an education. In 1990, the global community gathered at the World Conference on Education for All (EFA) in Jomtien, Thailand, to adopt the six EFA goals, which focused on improving educational access, quality, and equity from early childhood to adulthood.[23] Ten years later, in Dakar, Senegal, 164 governments and partner organizations reaffirmed their commitment to these goals and adopted a framework for achieving them by 2015. Although international commitments to universal and equitable education had been expressed in numerous conventions from the 1948 Universal Declaration of Human Rights (UDHR) to the 1989 Convention on the Rights of the Child (CRC), the EFA goals brought unprecedented attention, focus, and momentum to education.

   When world leaders met to name global priorities in 2000, education remained one of the top commitments. The second Millennium Development Goal (MDG) was set as achieving universal primary education. Moreover, the need for greater equity was highlighted in the third MDG, which called for ending disparities between girls and boys in education. The setting of the goals, backed by substantial international and national commitments made to them, has led to marked increases in how many children are enrolled in primary school. In 2008, 52 million more children were enrolled in primary school compared to 1999. In South and West Asia, the number of children excluded from primary education dropped by half and enrollment rates in sub-Saharan Africa increased by a third between 1999 and 2008.[24] The gap in girls' and boys' education has also narrowed since the EFA and MDG targets were adopted. The proportion of out-of-school children who are girls declined from 58% to 53% between 1999 and 2008, and recently 97 girls enrolled in primary school for every 100 boys.[25] It is clear that national and global commitments can make a difference. That's the good news.

But, the gaps in achieving these goals remain substantial: 67 million children were still not in primary school in 2008, and recent slowing of progress in enrollment further threatens reaching the EFA and MDG targets of all children attending primary school by 2015.[26] Globally, more than 30% of those enrolled in low-income countries do not finish primary school.[27] In sub-Saharan Africa, where nearly one in four primary-aged children is not in school, an estimated 10 million leave school each year before finishing the primary level.[28] An estimated 90% of children with disabilities in developing countries are not enrolled in school, and globally, a third of out-of-school children have a disability.[29] The goal of gender parity in primary and secondary education was set to be achieved by 2005, but girls still form a disproportionate share of children who are out-of-school in some regions, and these excluded girls are less likely than their male peers to enroll in formal schooling.[30] In sub-Saharan Africa and the Arab states, less than 93 girls per 100 boys are enrolled at the primary level; in Afghanistan, the Central African Republic, and Chad, this number drops to fewer than 75 girls for every 100 boys.[31] In Yemen, just over 20% of out-of-school girls are expected ever to enroll, compared to 64% of out-of-school boys; a similar gap exists in Pakistan, where 38% of girls and 73% of boys who are out of school are likely to enroll.[32] Twelve million girls in sub-Saharan Africa are not expected to ever step foot inside a classroom, compared to 7 million boys.[33]

Critically, not only are the EFA and MDG goals not on track to be met, but they were modest to begin with. To have a serious chance of exiting poverty, let alone of reaching their full potential, children need more than a primary school education. The MDGs ignore the 74 million secondary school-aged children who are not enrolled and the millions more who leave school without obtaining a meaningful education.[34] They also fail to make educational quality a priority at a time when just 30% of grade 6 students in Malawi, Namibia, and Zambia have attained basic math skills, fewer than 50% of grade 3 students in the Dominican Republic, Ecuador, and Guatemala can read a simple text and find clearly stated information within it, and many millions more globally complete primary school without attaining basic literacy and numeracy skills.[35] Inequalities across social and economic groups are just as dramatic as across gender. Yet, no global targets were set to ensure that all youth complete secondary education, that disparities based on income or disability would disappear, and that children would have an equal chance regardless of their race, ethnicity, religion, or linguistic group.

As a result, the disparities are devastating. Globally, Indigenous children and those from ethnic, racial, and linguistic minority groups have less chance at an education than the rest of the population.[36] In the United States, the out-of-school rate among the African American population is double that of Caucasians.[37] Differences in educational attainment between Indigenous and non-Indigenous children are severe in Guatemala, Peru, Cambodia, and Laos, among other countries: In Guatemala, for instance, speaking the Indigenous language Q'eqchi' at home is associated with twice the probability of being in the lowest fifth of the population when it comes to years of schooling attained.[38] In Bolivia, children who speak Indigenous languages at home attain between 2 and 4 years of schooling fewer than their Spanish-speaking peers.[39] Immigrant children in the OECD whose home language differs from the language of instruction have been found to achieve at lower levels than their peers in primary and secondary school.[40]

Children with disabilities are among the most disadvantaged groups when it comes to educational participation, with disparities between them and their nondisabled peers greater than gaps based on other demographics in many countries.[41] In 13 developing countries, children with disabilities are less likely than their peers to attend school even when individual, household, and community conditions are taken into account.[42] Children with disabilities in Bolivia, Cambodia, Colombia, Indonesia, Jamaica, Mongolia, South Africa, and Zambia have school attendance rates ranging from 20 to 50 percentage points lower than their peers who are not identified as having a disability.[43] Enrollment rates for children with disabilities aged 7 to 15 in Moldova and Romania are 39 percentage points and 34 percentage points lower than for children without disabilities, respectively.[44] In South Africa, studies show that, on average, children with disabilities complete fewer than 4 years of education.[45]

How Committed Are Countries?

If world leaders have made a commitment to primary education for all but not more, it would be reasonable to ask how committed countries are to ensuring education for all their citizens beyond primary school. There are many different ways to measure such a commitment, but one fundamental way is to examine whether the right to education is seen as a central enough part of belonging to a country to be embodied in its constitution. We examined the right to education in the constitutions of 191 UN member states. One hundred and twenty one of these countries guarantee the right to education to all citizens. Twenty-eight countries guarantee the right to higher education to all citizens, and 15 of these countries guarantee this right to all residents. An additional 18 countries aspire to protect the right to higher education for all citizens. In short, although the goal of providing all with the right to education is aspired to across most countries of the world, the right to higher education remains far behind.

Moreover, in practice, huge disparities exist between and within countries based on income in who obtains education. Children in Germany are ten times more likely to enroll in secondary school than children in Niger.[46] This is not an isolated example. Children in 11 high-income countries have a better chance of attaining tertiary education than those in 15 lower-income countries do of finishing primary school.[47] The disparities within countries can be just as devastating. Children from more affluent families have a better chance of receiving an education than do their peers from poorer households in both high- and low-income countries. In the United States, 17% of low-income youth of secondary school age are out of school, compared to 5% of youth from higher-income households.[48] Children from the poorest fifth of the population in the Middle East and North Africa are over four times less likely to be in school than are their peers from the most affluent fifth; in Bolivia, Burkina Faso, Chad, Ethiopia, Mali, and Niger, the poorest children are two to three times less likely to be in school than are those from the richest households.[49] In 22 low-income countries, the poorest quintile of the population achieves 5 fewer years of schooling on average than the richest fifth.[50]

Feasible Solutions

Lessons in Educational Equality is the product of a multiyear effort to examine: How feasible is it to find solutions to national and global inequities in education? In seeking to answer this fundamental question, we brought together academics, educators, individuals running programs, those teaching students from within schools and outside of them, and other stakeholders from around the world. As they met together, they sought the best ways to address inequities from preschool through graduate school. We also ran an initiative which examined programs in every region of the world that might bring innovative approaches to addressing inequalities. To these programs, we sent Policy Fellows who interviewed teachers, program directors, students, government officials, and community members; observed classroom interactions, extracurricular programs, and teacher training sessions; analyzed policy documents; and examined student outcomes.

Both from the expert meetings and from the in-depth case studies, the clear answer to the question of whether feasible solutions exist is yes. Although there is little doubt that the constraints countries face differ, it was equally clear that important lessons could be applied from one country to the next. Just as some of the best medical solutions to tough problems have come from low-income countries and been applied in high-income countries, it was clear that countries in

Africa could teach solutions to countries in Europe, and countries in North America had solutions to offer to Asia.

Lessons in Educational Equality reports these findings. The first section examines approaches to increasing access and quality outcomes for groups at the university level. We begin at the most advanced level of education because we believe it is critical to change all our aspirations. Not since the 19th century has it been enough to hope that all children would have a primary school education. Without a doubt, in the 21st century, all youth need access to a university education if they are truly going to have equal chances in the workforce. Although we begin with university education, both to highlight the need for increasing equity at this level and its achievability, it is clear that equal outcomes in university education will only be achieved once there are more equitable outcomes in secondary education. The book goes on to look at what can be done to improve equity at the secondary level. Likewise, the outcomes of secondary education depend on primary, and the outcomes of primary on preschool. Each of these is addressed by a section in turn.

In examining these themes, this volume brings together leading members of academia, national and global research organizations, and international organizations, including UNESCO, the World Health Organization's Commission on Social Determinants of Health, the OECD, the World Bank, and the Education for All Fast Track Initiative. They have experience and expertise in South, Central, and North America; Southeast Asia; Western and Eastern Europe; North Africa; the Middle East; and sub-Saharan Africa. They design, lead, implement, and monitor programs, advise governments, non-governmental organizations (NGOs), and international agencies, and work with and within communities to improve the educational chances of girls, boys, children with disabilities, Indigenous groups, linguistic and ethnic minorities, poor children, and other marginalized populations.

Their findings highlight what could work to transform education globally. For example, statistics show that gender segregation by field of study is a common challenge for gender equity in universities in high- and low-income countries alike, with serious implications for equity in employment and income. Chapter 3 details how the Special Pre-Entry Program (SPEP) at the University of Dar-es-Salaam in Tanzania is improving women's representation and performance in engineering and technology programs. Since 2004, the program has provided 8 weeks of subsidized, supplemental training in engineering, mathematics, chemistry, and communications to girls whose secondary school grades prevent them from being admitted directly to the College of Engineering and Technology (CoET). In its first year, the program more than doubled the percentage of girls enrolled in the CoET (from 7.7% to 15.5%). By the program's fourth year, nearly a quarter of engineering students were women, SPEP students were achieving at the same level as their male and female peers, and instructors were unable to distinguish between SPEP students and those who had been admitted directly.

A continent away, Finland's secondary school students register the second highest scores among OECD countries on Programme for International Student Assessment (PISA) tests of academic achievement. The country also has the smallest percentage of low-performing pupils in Europe, with only 1.7% of students performing at the lowest levels on reading tests, compared to an OECD average of 5.7%. Finally, Finland registers the smallest variation in reading scores, and students' achievement is not strongly tied to their socioeconomic status or their school.[51] Chapter 5 describes how the Finnish school system equalizes students' chances by intervening to address difficulties at multiple levels. First, a teacher or teacher's assistant provides individualized help to a struggling student within the classroom. If necessary, a special educational needs teacher works one-on-one with the student to provide support in specific subject areas. Every effort is made to keep students who are experiencing difficulties in the same classrooms with their peers and their regular teacher. Although 20% of high school students receive extra help, only those with complex learning challenges, or fewer than 2% of students, attend separate schools. Importantly, a fourth level of intervention is implemented for children who are disadvantaged because of their home situation. School professionals partner with social workers, psychologists, and housing and health representatives to address the problems that might prevent these students from achieving well in school.

Although a strong net of supports guarantees top outcomes in Finland, many low-income countries are still struggling to provide even the most basic quality educational opportunities to all children. India has one of the world's largest primary school-aged populations, with roughly 210 million children between the ages of 6 and 14. Although the country has made huge strides in primary enrollment, providing quality education to all children remains a challenge. Chapter 8 describes how the educational NGO Pratham partnered with two state governments and thousands of community members to implement a quality initiative targeting marginalized learners. Between 2006 and 2008, Pratham trained over 140,000 teachers, mobilized more than 97,000 community volunteers,[52] and engaged over 2.5 million students in 55,613 schools in the states of Himachel Pradesh (HP) and Uttar Pradesh (UP). Pratham's emphasis on participatory learning and monitoring student progress produced measurable results. In UP, one of India's poorest states, with below-average literacy rates, the *Nai Disha* quality initiative improved learning achievement among children at the lowest learning levels. In the pilot year, the percentage of grade 1 students in participating schools who were unable to recognize letters and basic words, and the percentage that could not recognize numbers from 1 to 20, both dropped by close to 50 percentage points. The initiative also produced a nearly 20 percentage point increase in the number of grade 2 students who could read basic stories and a nearly 30 percentage point increase in the number of children who could add or subtract with numbers ranging from 1 to 100 in its pilot year.

Children's chances at an equal education can be diminished by their home language, family income, ethnicity, and other factors that, in a fair world, would have no effect on opportunity. Chapter 10 describes how one of the poorest countries in South America increased the educational chances of its disadvantaged Indigenous population through a national commitment to home-language learning. Bolivia's 5-year Intercultural Bilingual Education pilot project reached 30 school districts, including 14 in rural areas, and engaged 400 teachers. Under this system, children learned to read and write in their home language before Spanish was gradually integrated into the curriculum. Between 1997 and 2002, enrollment rates in mainly Indigenous areas rose by 13% and drop-out rates fell by 4%. Thirty-five percent of Indigenous students participating in IBE achieved satisfactory scores on national evaluations of arithmetic and literacy, compared to 19% who were not in IBE schools. Indigenous children in IBE schools were half as likely to be categorized as "at risk" based on these results than their non-IBE peers. Importantly, IBE students also achieved higher grades in Spanish grammar than did those attending schools where Spanish was the language of instruction. IBE also reduced gender disparities in achievement. The program's success led the government to adopt the program as official state policy in 1994, expanding it beyond the three most-spoken Indigenous languages to include smaller linguistic groups. By 2002, the program was engaging 192,238 students and 9,028 teachers in 2,899 schools.

Gaps in school readiness open up even before programs like Pratham's quality initiatives or Bolivia's primary school innovations reach grade 1 students. Universal early childhood education is therefore one of the key contributors to equity throughout the school life course and beyond. Chapter 11 describes how Cuba's focus on early childhood education has contributed to child development and health outcomes that are among the best in the world, high rates of primary and secondary school retention, and higher than average test scores among third- and fourth-grade students compared to other Latin American countries. Between 1983 and 2003, Cuba's *Educa a Tu Hijo* (Educating Your Child) network provided early childhood care and education services to more than 800,000 families. The government continued its investment in this far-reaching program even when the country experienced economic difficulties in the early 1990s. Through this system, children participate in at least 104 development sessions before they are 2 years old and between 162 and 324 sessions from the ages of 3 to 5. The program is implemented by 52,000 teachers, physicians, and other professionals, along with a support team of 116,000 additional staff, students, and volunteers, with strong involvement from local governments. Only 13% of children who participated in the program entered school without satisfactory motor and social-personal skills and cognitive development, making them less vulnerable to reaching school age unprepared than children in Canada and Australia.

Like many Indigenous and ethnic minority populations worldwide, Canada's Aboriginal people historically have had less access to quality preschool, affecting their school outcomes. Chapter 13 shows how community-driven initiatives, in partnership with universities and governments, are increasing equity for this group from early childhood to tertiary education. The federally funded Aboriginal Head Start (AHS) program enables Aboriginal host agencies to implement early childhood programs for young children within their communities. Host communities are given significant autonomy to determine program characteristics, the majority of staff is Aboriginal, and most programs are either conducted in an Aboriginal language or include some exposure to one. Currently, 140 AHS programs reach 4,500 Aboriginal children in urban centers and large communities in remote areas. An additional 9,100 children living on reserves are enrolled in AHS programs. Children who participate in at least 1 year of AHS are less likely to repeat a grade in primary school and more likely to experience improved health, literacy, self-esteem, and school readiness. To support these efforts, the First Nations Partnership Program at the University of Victoria has increased Indigenous capacity in early childhood care and education (ECCE) through university- and community-generated curricular content taught by university instructors and Indigenous Elders. The program has achieved the highest rate of completion for Indigenous students in 1-year certificate and 2-year diplomas nationally. In these teacher training programs, 151 Indigenous students earned ECCE credentials; 95% of these returned to their communities; 65% initiated programs for children, and 21% joined existing initiatives. Over 11% went on to pursue a university degree.

Chapter 7 documents how governments in low- and middle-income countries are beginning to make progress for children with disabilities, the largest out of school population, in response to global incentives. By 2005, 50% of countries submitting Education Sector Plans (ESP) to the Education for All Fast Track Initiative (FTI) had developed or were developing an education strategy for children with disabilities, compared to just 16% only 4 years earlier. This increase in commitment resulted from a stronger focus on children with disabilities in the ESP appraisal guidelines, including requests for data on their participation and achievement in education. Cambodia has made educating children with disabilities a national priority. The country's ESP outlines a detailed strategy to improve access and quality in primary education, which gained approval and funding from the FTI. Lesotho has committed to constructing 1,000 new classrooms with disability- and gender-sensitive infrastructure. This comes on top of the government's existing measures to promote equity, including awarding 19,200 scholarships to children with disabilities and other disadvantaged children in 2008.

The Gains To Be Reaped

If we are able to build on these and other successes to improve access to and quality of schooling for *all* children and youth, the gains will be great for individuals completing more school and the countries in which they live. These dramatic gains will reverberate in employment, income, health and other aspects of life.

Globally, individuals who have attained a secondary or tertiary education are less likely to be unemployed than their peers with fewer years of schooling.[53] Men in OECD countries who have completed secondary school have unemployment rates approximately half those of their less-educated peers, and individuals who have attained a tertiary education have employment rates on average 9 percentage points higher than those who have only completed upper secondary schooling.[54] In Brazil, Malaysia, and Paraguay, among others, completion of higher levels of education significantly increases women's and men's likelihood of being employed.[55] Education is also an important contributor to equity in employment. In OECD countries, women who have not completed secondary school are 23 percentage points less likely to be employed than their male counterparts who did not complete this level of schooling, whereas women who have attained higher education are only 10 percentage points less likely to be employed than men who have received the same level of education.[56] In ten low- and middle-income countries, women with a primary education or lower were, on average, 40 percentage points less likely to be employed than were men with the same level of education. With completion of upper secondary schooling, this gap decreased to 28 percentage points; completion of a tertiary-level program reduces the gap in employment between men and women to 15 percentage points.[57]

Increased educational attainment is strongly associated with higher individual income. A study of 13 countries found that, even taking into account educational quality, each additional year of schooling completed raised individuals' incomes by nearly 5%;[58] in the Philippines[59] and Chile,[60] even stronger effects of additional years of schooling on income have been documented. Even when identical twins are raised in the same household, one twin's additional year of education has been found to increase his or her wages relative to his or her sibling by 9% to 16%.[61] Importantly, completing tertiary education can have a strong effect on income relative to completing upper secondary school: In Indonesia, men who have completed tertiary schooling earn 82% more than those who have completed upper secondary education; in Paraguay, the difference is nearly 300%. Similar results were found for women in Indonesia and Brazil.[62]

The economic benefits of education are reaped on a national scale as well. Cross-national studies demonstrate that higher average national levels of schooling are associated with higher aggregate economic growth.[63] A study of 50 countries estimated that increasing average educational attainment by 1 year could lead to a 0.37% increase in gross domestic product (GDP) annually.[64] According to a 2010 OECD study, an increase in PISA scores of 0.25 standard deviations by 2030 could increase aggregate OECD GDP by $1.4 trillion per year.[65] Reducing inequalities in education also reaps substantial economic gains. Data from 65 low- and middle-income, and transition countries suggest that addressing gender inequity in upper secondary education could yield $92 billion annually in GDP growth.[66]

With increased education, individuals experience better overall health,[67] mental health,[68] memory capacity,[69] healthy life expectancy,[70] and mortality rates.[71] Adults in the United States report better self-rated health the higher their educational attainment;[72] a study of 22 European countries found that men and women who had completed upper secondary or higher education were two to three times more likely to report good health than were their less-educated peers.[73] In Switzerland,[74] the United Kingdom,[75] Austria,[76] and South Korea,[77] increased years of education has been associated with declining risk of mortality for both men and women; in Bangladesh, a similar connection was found between increased education and women's mortality rates.[78]

The health benefits of education, as well as the disadvantages of a lack of schooling, persist across generations. Parents who have received more schooling are more likely to be healthy and to have healthy children than are their less-educated peers.[79] Increased parental education is associated with lower infant and under-5 mortality rates,[80] increased immunization rates,[81] better height-and-weight-for-age,[82] and decreased risk of malnutrition.[83] Mothers' completion of secondary school or higher appears to be particularly important for their children's health and survival.[84]

Individuals who have attained more years of schooling have higher rates of civic and political participation, including a higher tendency to vote.[85] Increased education has been linked with a greater probability of engaging in forms of electoral participation in East Asia[86] and North America.[87] A 30-year-old individual who had completed tertiary education in Canada had a 66% likelihood of voting, compared to a 37% likelihood for an individual who had not finished secondary school.[88] Similar results were found in a study of voter participation in the United States.[89] Higher rates of education also positively affect participation rates in political associations, civic organizations, political parties, and other forms of civic engagement in Argentina, Chile, Mexico, Peru,[90] and India.[91] Data from 25 countries demonstrated that completing higher levels of schooling also increases individuals' likelihood of nonformal political participation.[92]

This book is about the concrete ways in which we can move toward a world where all children reap the benefits of a quality education. National governments and international institutions have targeted education for all—and many have demonstrated the remarkable progress that can be made when political will combines with practical savvy. But the targets of universal primary education—without mention of either the educational quality or higher levels of education needed in the global economy—remain far too low. The extraordinary leaders who have come together in this volume present wide-ranging, innovative approaches to ensuring that all children, regardless of gender, ethnicity, income, disability or learning difference, receive all the quality education they need.

NOTES

1. Blume, H. (2010, April 5). A chance at redemption: Jefferson High hopes to turn things around. So does one of its students. *Los Angeles Times*. Retrieved January 5, 2011,

http://articles.latimes.com/2010/apr/05/local/la-me-jefferson5–2010apr05; Landsberg, M. (2009, June 22). Two students, two schools–and a world of difference 20 miles apart. *Los Angeles Times*. Retrieved January 5, 2011, http://articles.latimes.com/2009/jun/22/local/me-11thgrade22/4

2. The Education Trust West. (2008). *Raising the roof: Explore California public school data (Los Angeles Unified School District)*. Retrieved January 10, 2011, http://rtr.edtrustwest.org/grad_rates.php

3. Editorial Projects in Education, Diplomas Count. (2010). Graduating by the number: Putting data to work for student success. Special issue. *Education Week, 29*(34), 24.

4. Population Division, U.S. Census Bureau. (2008, August 14). Table 7. *Projected change in population size by race and Hispanic origin for the United States: 2000 to 2050 (NP2008-T7)*. Retrieved January 4, 2011, http://www.census.gov/population/www/projections/summarytables.html; Population Division, U.S. Census Bureau. (2008, August 14). Table 20. *Projections of the Hispanic population (any race) by age and sex for the United States: 2010 to 2050 (NP2008-T20)*. Retrieved January 4, 2011, http://www.census.gov/population/www/projections/summarytables.html; Population Division, U.S. Census Bureau. (2008, August 14). Table 14. *Projections of the non-Hispanic white alone population by age and sex for the United States: 2010 to 2050 (NP2008-T14)*. Retrieved January 4, 2011, http://www.census.gov/population/www/projections/summarytables.html; Population Division, U.S. Census Bureau. (2008, August 14). Table 15. *Projections of the black alone population by age and sex for the United States: 2010 to 2050 (NP2008-T15)*. Retrieved January 4, 2011, http://www.census.gov/population/www/projections/summarytables.html; Population Division, U.S. Census Bureau. (2008, August 14). Table 17. *Projections of the Asian alone population by age and sex for the United States: 2010 to 2050 (NP2008-T17)*. Retrieved January 4, 2011, http://www.census.gov/population/www/projections/summarytables.html; Population Division, U.S. Census Bureau. (2008, August 14). Table 16. *Projections of the American Indian and Alaska Native alone population by age and sex for the United States: 2010 to 2050 (NP2008-T16)*. Retrieved January 4, 2011, http://www.census.gov/population/www/projections/summarytables.html; Population Division, U.S. Census Bureau. (2008, August 14). Table 18. *Projections of the Native Hawaiian and other Pacific Islander alone population by age and sex for the United States: 2010 to 2050 (NP2008-T18)*. Retrieved January 4, 2011, http://www.census.gov/population/www/projections/summarytables.html

5. Population Division, U.S. Census Bureau. (2008, August 14). Table 12. *Projections of the population by age and sex for the United States: 2010 to 2050 (NP2008-T12)*. Retrieved January 4, 2011, http://www.census.gov/population/www/projections/summarytables.html; Population Division, U.S. Census Bureau. (2008, August 14). Table 20. *Projections of the Hispanic population (any race) by age and sex for the United States: 2010 to 2050 (NP2008-T20)*. Retrieved January 4, 2011, http://www.census.gov/population/www/projections/summarytables.html

6. OECD. (2010). *Education at a Glance 2010: OECD Indicators* (pp. 58, 79). Paris: OECD Publications.

7. Bureau of Labor Statistics. (2011, January 7). Table B-3. *Average hourly and weekly earnings of all employees on private nonfarm payrolls by industry sector, seasonally adjusted*. Retrieved January 12, 2011, http://www.bls.gov/news.release/empsit.t19.htm; Helper, S., & Wial, H. (September 2010). Strengthening American manufacturing: A new federal approach, Brookings Institute Metropolitan Policy Program, (pp. 1–3). Retrieved January 5, 2011, http://www.brookings.edu/~/media/Files/rc/papers/2010/0927_great_lakes/0927_great_lakes_papers/0927_great_lakes_manufacturing.pdf

8. Bureau of Labor Statistics. (2011). *Employment, hours, and earnings from the current employment statistics survey (national): Manufacturing*. Retrieved January 5, 2011, http://data.bls.gov/pdq/SurveyOutputServlet?series_id=CES3000000001&data_tool=XGtable

9. When including public school students who took the General Certificate of Secondary Education (GCSE) exams as well as those who took the International GCSEs, the percentage of public school students obtaining top grades in 2010 registers at 93.1%. Only 54.8% of state school students obtained top grades in the GCSEs, indicating a gap of nearly 40 percentage points between state school and public school students. The International GCSE curriculum

was not available in state schools before September 2010, so there is no comparable cohort of state school students who also took the International GCSE. In addition, 60% of public school students achieved scores of A or above on their GCSEs, compared to a national average of 22.6%. In the school year 2005–2006, public school students were 51 percentage points more likely to achieve top grades compared to state school students who qualified for a free meal. See Williams, R. (2010, September 4). One in three GCSEs taken at private schools earned an A or A+. *The Guardian*. Retrieved January 6, 2011, http://www.guardian.co.uk/education/2010/sep/04/third-gcses-private-top-grades; The Sutton Trust. (December 2010). *Responding to the new landscape for university access*. Retrieved January 5, 2011, http://www.sutton-trust.com/public/documents/access-proposals-report-final.pdf; University of Cambridge International Examinations. (2010, June 21). Cambridge welcomes IGCSE funding announcement for state schools. Retrieved January 31, 2011, http://www.cie.org.uk/news/features/detail?feature_id=31796)

10. Williams, R. (2010, October 21). State school pupils do better at GCSE. *The Guardian*. Retrieved January 6, 2011, http://www.guardian.co.uk/education/2010/oct/21/state-pupils-do-better-at-gcse

11. The Sutton Trust. (2010). *Responding to the new landscape*, p. 14.

12. Ibid.

13. Baker, S., & Jump, P. (2010, December 20). Grant letter reveals extent of cuts. *Times Higher Education*. Retrieved January 10, 2011, http://www.timeshighereducation.co.uk/story.asp?storycode=414645; Vasagar, J., Shepherd, J., & Stratton, A. (2010, November 3). Elite universities welcome flexibility to triple students' fees. *The Guardian*. Retrieved January 12, 2011, http://www.guardian.co.uk/education/2010/nov/03/universities-welcome-flexbility-triple-fees

14. Nkomo, M., personal communication, February 2, 2011. Based on data drawn from the South African Department of Basic Education's *National Senior Certificate Database*, 2008–2009.

15. Department of Education. (2009). *Trends in education macro-indicators: South Africa* (p. 12). Retrieved January 10, 2011, http://www.info.gov.za/view/DownloadFileAction?id=114966

16. OECD. (2008). *Reviews of national policies for education: South Africa* (p. 203). Paris: OECD Publications.

17. OECD. (2008). *OECD economic surveys: South Africa economic assessment*. Paris: OECD Publications.

18. UNESCO. (2010). *Education for All Global monitoring report 2010: Reaching the marginalized* (pp. 374, 378). Oxford: Oxford University Press.

19. Barro, R., & Lee, J. W. (2010). China: Educational attainment for total population; and South Africa: Educational attainment for total population. Barro-Lee Educational Attainment Dataset. Retrieved January 10, 2011, http://www.barrolee.com/

20. Statistics South Africa. (2009, July 28). *Quarterly labor force survey: Quarter 2 (April to June)*. Retrieved January 11, 2011, http://www.statssa.gov.za/news_archive/press_statements/QLFS-Q2–2009%20Press%20Release.pdf

21. IRIN News. (2009, January 21). South Africa: For richer or for poorer. *IRIN humanitarian news and analysis*. Retrieved January 12, 2011, http://www.irinnews.org/Report.aspx?ReportId=82499

22. OECD. (2008). *South Africa economic assessment*, p. 97.

23. UNESCO. (2008). *Education for All Global monitoring report 2008: Education for All by 2015: Will we make it?* (p. 13). Oxford: Oxford University Press.

24. UNESCO. (2011). *Global monitoring report 2011: The hidden crisis*, (p. 1). Paris: UNESCO.

25. Ibid., pp. 43, 73.

26. Ibid., pp. 1, 6.

27. Ibid., p. 40.

28. Ibid., p. 47.

29. UNESCO. (2011). *Children with disabilities*. Retrieved January 13, 2011, portal.unesco.org/education/en/ev.phpURL_DO=DO_TOPIC&URL_SECTION=201.html

30. UNESCO. (2011). *Global monitoring report 2011*, p. 43.

31. Ibid., pp. 73, 307.
32. UNESCO. (2010). *Global monitoring report 2010*, p. 60.
33. Ibid.
34. UNESCO. (2011). *Global monitoring report 2011*, p. 54.
35. UNESCO. (2010). *Global monitoring report 2010*, p. 106.
36. Ibid.
37. Ibid., p. 10.
38. Ibid., p. 151.
39. Ibid., p. 146
40. Christensen, G., & Stanat, P. (2007). *Language policies and practices for helping immigrants and second-generation students succeed*. Washington, DC: Migration Policy Institute/ Bertelsmann Stiftung; Schnepf, S.V. (2004). *How different are immigrants? A cross-country and cross-survey analysis of educational achievement*. Bonn/Southampton: University of Southampton, Southampton Statistical Sciences Research Institute (S3RI)/Institute for the Study of Labor (IZA).
41. Filmer, D. (2008). Disability, poverty, and schooling in developing countries: Results from 14 household surveys. *World Bank Economic Review*, 22(1), 141–163.
42. Ibid.
43. Ibid.
44. Mete, C. ed. (2008). *Economic implications of chronic illness and disability in Eastern Europe and the former Soviet Union* (p. 21). Washington, DC: World Bank.
45. Loeb, M., Eide, A. H., et al. (2008). Poverty and disability in eastern and western Cape Provinces, South Africa. *Disability and Society*, 23(4), 311–321.
46. UNESCO. (2010). *Global monitoring report 2010*, pp. 368–370.
47. UNESCO. (2009). *Education for All Global monitoring report 2009: Overcoming inequality: Why governance matters* (p. 73). Oxford: Oxford University Press.
48. UNESCO. (2010). *Global monitoring report 2010*, p. 155.
49. UNESCO Institute for Statistics. (2005). *Children out of school: Measuring exclusion from primary education* (pp. 84-86). Montreal: UNESCO Institute for Statistics.
50. Data drawn from Demographic and Health Surveys and Multiple Indicator Cluster surveys on eighty developing countries and analyzed in UNESCO. (2010). *Education for All Global monitoring report 2010*.
51. OECD. (2010). *PISA 2009 results: What students know and can do*. Paris: OECD Publishing. Retrieved January 11, 2011, http://www.pisa.oecd.org/dataoecd/34/60/46619703.pdf
52. Pratham. (2008). *Read India Annual Report 2007–2008* (p. 23). Retrieved July 18, 2011, http:// pratham.org/images/Read%20India%20Annual%20Report%202007-2008%5B1%5D.pdf
53. Hanushek, E. A., & Woessmann, L. (2007). The role of educational quality for economic growth. World Bank Policy Research Work Paper no. 4122. Washington, DC: World Bank; Hanushek, E. A., & Luque, J. A. (2002). Efficiency and equity in schools around the world. NBER Working Paper no. 8949. Cambridge, MA: National Bureau of Economic Research; Hanushek, E. A., & Woessmann, L. (2007). *Education quality and economic growth*. Washington DC: World Bank; UNESCO. (2004). *Education for All Global monitoring report 2005: The quality imperative*. Paris: UNESCO.
54. OECD. (2008). *Education at a glance 2008: OECD Indicators* (pp. 144–148). Paris: OECD.
55. UNESCO Institute for Statistics & OECD. (2002). *Financing education: Investments and returns*. Paris: UIS/OECD.
56. OECD. (2008). *Education at a glance 2008*, p. 144.
57. UNESCO Institute for Statistics & OECD. (2002). *Financing education*, p. 178.
58. Hanushek, E. A. & Zhang, L. (2009). Quality-Consistent estimates of international schooling and skill gradients. *Journal of Human Capital, 3*(2), 107–143.
59. UNESCO Institute for Statistics & OECD. (2002). *Financing education*, p. 37.
60. Ibid., p. 37.
61. Ashenfelter, O., & Krueger, A. B. (1994). Estimates of the economic return to schooling from a new sample of twins. *American Economic Review, 84*(5), 1157–1173; Ashenfelter, O., &

Rouse, C. (1998). Income, schooling, and ability: evidence from a new sample of identical twins. *Quarterly Journal of Economics, 113*, 253–284.

62. UNESCO Institute for Statistics & OECD. (2002). *Financing education*, p. 37.
63. Ibid.
64. UNESCO. (2009). *Global Monitoring Report 2009*, p. 30.
65. The study estimated that the gains would amount to $115 trillion between 2010 and 2090, or approximately $1.4 trillion per year. OECD. (2010). *The high cost of low educational performance* (p. 27). Paris: OECD Publishing.
66. Plan International. (2008). *Paying the price: The economic cost of failing to educate girls* (p. 8). Surrey: Plan Ltd.
67. Ross, C. E., & Wu, C. L. (1995). The links between education and health. *American Sociological Review, 60*(5), 719–745.
68. Feinstein, L., Sabates, R., et al. (2006). Measuring the effects of education on health and civic engagement: 4. What are the effects on health? In Desjardins, R. & Schuller, T. (eds). *Measuring the Social Outcomes of Learning*. Copenhagen: OECD.
69. Ramos, M. (2007). Impact of socioeconomic status on Brazilian elderly health. *Revista de Saude Publica, 41*(4), 616–624.
70. Bossuyt, N., Gadeyne, S., et al. (2004). Socio-economic inequalities in health expectancy in Belgium. *Public Health, 188*(1), 3–10.
71. Feinstein, Sabates, et al. (2006). Measuring the effects.
72. Ross & Wu. (1995). The links between education and health.
73. von dem Knesebeck, O., & Geyer, S. (2007). Emotional support, education and self-rated health in 22 European countries. *BMC Public Health, 7*, 272–278.
74. Feinstein, Sabates, et al. (2006). Measuring the effects.
75. Ibid.
76. Doblhammer, G., Rau, R., et al. (2005). Trends in educational and occupational differentials in all-cause mortality in Austria between 1981/82 and 1991/92. *Wiener Klinische Wochenschrift, 117*(13–14), 468–479.
77. Khang, Y.-H., Lynch, J. W., et al. (2004). Health inequalities in Korea: Age- and sex-specific educational differences in the 10 leading causes of death. *International Journal of Epidemiology, 33*(2), 299–308.
78. Hurt, L.S., Ronsmans, C., et al. (2004). Effects of education and other socioeconomic factors on middle age mortality in rural Bangladesh. *Journal of Epidemiology and Community Health, 58*(4), 315–320.
79. Heaton, T. B., Forste, R., Hoffmann, J. P., & Flake, D. (2005). Cross-national variation in family influences on child health, *Social Science & Medicine, 60*(1), 97–108; Kravdal, O. (2004). Child mortality in India: The community-level effect of education. *Population Studies, 58*(2), 177–192; Lindelow, M. (2008). Health as a family matter: Do intra-household education externalities matter for maternal and child health? *Journal of Development Studies, 44*(4), 562–585; Feinstein, Sabates, et al. (2006). Measuring the effects; Shehzad, S. (2006). The determinants of child health in Pakistan: An economic analysis. *Social Indicators Research, 78*(3), 531–556; Mashal, T., et al. (2008). Factors associated with the health and nutritional status of children under 5 years of age in Afghanistan: Family behaviour related to women and past experience of war-related hardships. *BMC Public Health, 8*, 13.
80. Agha, S. (2000). The determinants of infant mortality in Pakistan. *Social Science & Medicine, 51*(2), 199–208; Al-Mazrou, Y. Y., Alhamdan, N. A., Alkotobi, A. I., Nour, O.E.M., & Farag, M. A. (2008). Factors affecting child mortality in Saudi Arabia. *Saudi Medical Journal, 29*(1), 102–106; Arntzen, A., & Andersen, A.M.N. (2004). Social determinants for infant mortality in the Nordic countries, 1980–2001. *Scandinavian Journal of Public Health, 32*(5), 381–389; Bhalotra, S., & van Soest, A. (2008). Birth-spacing, fertility and neonatal mortality in India: Dynamics, frailty, and fecundity. *Journal of Econometrics, 143*(2), 274–290; Bhargava, A. (2003). Family planning, gender differences and infant mortality: Evidence from Uttar Pradesh, India. *Journal of Econometrics, 112*(1), 225–240; Burgard, S. A., & Treiman, D. J. (2006). Trends and racial differences in infant mortality in South Africa. *Social Science &*

Medicine, 62(5), 1126–37; Demeer, K., Bergman, R., & Kusner, J. S. (1993). Sociocultural determinants of child-mortality in southern Peru – Including some methodological considerations. *Social Science & Medicine, 36*(3), 317–331; Fay, M. et al. (2005). Achieving child-health-related millennium development goals: The role of infrastructure. *World Development, 33*(8), 1267–1284; Fernandez, A.W.H., Giusti, A. E., & Sotelo, J. M. (2007). The Chilean infant mortality decline: Improvement for whom? Socioeconomic and geographic inequalities in infant mortality, 1990–2005. *Bulletin of the World Health Organization, 85*(10), 798–804; Frey, R. S., & Field, C. (2000). The determinants of infant mortality in the less developed countries: A cross-national test of five theories. *Social Indicators Research, 52*(3), 215–234; Gokhale, M. K., et al. (2004). Female literacy: The multifactorial influence on child health in India. *Ecology of Food and Nutrition, 43*(4), 257–278; Jahan, S. (2008). Poverty and infant mortality in the Eastern Mediterranean region: A meta-analysis. *Journal of Epidemiology and Community Health, 62*(8), 745–751; Kandala, N. B., & Ghilagaber, G. (2006). A geo-additive Bayesian discrete-time survival model and its application to spatial analysis of childhood mortality in Malawi. *Quality & Quantity, 40*(6), 935–957; Kiros, G. E., & Hogan, D. P. (2001). War, famine and excess child mortality in Africa: the role of parental education. *International Journal of Epidemiology, 30*(3), 447–455; Mogford, L. (2004). Structural determinants of child mortality in sub-Saharan Africa: A cross-national study of economic and social influences from 1970 to 1997. *Social Biology, 51*(3–4), 94–120; Pena, R., Wall, S., & Persson, L. A. (2000). The effect of poverty, social inequity, and maternal education on infant mortality in Nicaragua, 1988–1993. *American Journal of Public Health, 90*(1), 64–69; Sastry, N. (2004). Trends in socioeconomic inequalities in mortality in developing countries: The case of child survival in Sao Paulo, Brazil. *Demography, 41*(3), 443–464; Schell, C. O., et al. (2007). Socioeconomic determinants of infant mortality: A worldwide study of 152 low-, middle-, and high-income countries. *Scandinavian Journal of Public Health, 35*(3), 288–297; Sharifzadeh, G. R., Namakin, K., & Mehrjoofard, H. (2008). An epidemiological study on infant mortality and factors affecting it in rural areas of Birjand, Iran. *Iranian Journal of Pediatrics, 18*(4), 335–342; Ssewanyana, S., & Younger, S. D. (2008). Infant mortality in Uganda: Determinants, trends and the Millennium Development Goals. *Journal of African Economies, 17*(1), 34–61; Yassin, K. M. (2000). Indices and sociodemographic determinants of childhood mortality in rural upper Egypt. *Social Science & Medicine, 51*(2), 185–197.

81. Bondy, J. N., Thind, A., Koval, J. J., & Speechley, K. N. (2009). Identifying the determinants of childhood immunization in the Philippines. *Vaccine, 27*(1), 169–175; Briscoe, J. (1991). Underlying and proximate determinants of child health - The Cebu Longitudinal Health and Nutrition Study. *American Journal of Epidemiology, 133*(2), 185–201; Desai, S., & Alva, S. (1998). Maternal education and child health: Is there a strong causal relationship? *Demography, 35*(1), 71–81; Gyimah, S. O. (2006). Cultural background and infant survival in Ghana. *Ethnicity & Health, 11*(2), 101–120; Huq, M. N., & Tasnim, T. (2008). Maternal education and child healthcare in Bangladesh. *Maternal and Child Health Journal, 12*(1), 43–51; Semba, R. D., de Pee, S., Sun, K., Sari, M., Akhter, N., & Bloem, M. W. (2008). Effect of parental formal education on risk of child stunting in Indonesia and Bangladesh: A cross-sectional study. *Lancet, 371*(9609), 322–328.

82. Boyle, M. H., Racine, Y., Georgiades, K., Snelling, D., Hong, S. J., Omariba, W., et al. (2006). The influence of economic development level, household wealth and maternal education on child health in the developing world. *Social Science & Medicine, 63*(8), 2242–2254; Chen, Y. Y., & Li, H. B. (2009). Mother's education and child health: Is there a nurturing effect? *Journal of Health Economics, 28*(2), 413–426; Fedorov, L., & Sahn, D. E. (2005). Socioeconomic determinants of children's health in Russia: A longitudinal study. *Economic Development and Cultural Change, 53*(2), 479–500; Glewwe, P. (1999). Why does mother's schooling raise child health in developing countries? Evidence from Morocco. *Journal of Human Resources, 34*(1), 124–159; Gokhale, M. K., et al. (2004). Female literacy: The multifactorial influence on child health in India. *Ecology of Food and Nutrition, 43*(4) 257–278; Female literacy; Rahman, A., & Chowdhury, S. (2007). Determinants of chronic malnutrition among preschool children in Bangladesh. *Journal of Biosocial Science, 39*(2), 161–173; Semba et al. (2008). Effect of parental

formal education on risk of child stunting in Indonesia and Bangladesh: A cross-sectional study. *Lancet, 371*(9606), 322–328.

83. Briscoe. (1991). Underlying and proximate determinants of child health; Guldan, G. S., Zeitlin, M. F., Beiser, A. S., Super, C. M., Gershoff, S. N., & Datta, S. (1993). Maternal education and child feeding practices in rural Bangladesh. *Social Science & Medicine, 36*(7), 925–935.

84. Agha. (2000). The determinants of infant mortality in Pakistan; Bondy, Thind, Koval, & Speechley. (2009). Identifying the determinants of childhood immunization in the Philippines; Fedorov & Sahn. (2005). Socioeconomic determinants of children's health in Russia.

85. Dee, T. (2004). Are there civic returns to education? *Journal of Public Economics, 88*(9), 1697–720.

86. Chu, Y. H., & Huang, M. H. (2007). Partisanship and citizen politics in east Asia. *Journal of East Asian Studies, 7*(2), 295–321.

87. Ibid.

88. Blais, A., Gidengil, E., & Nevitte, N. (2004). Where does turnout decline come from? *European Journal of Political Research, 43*(2), 221–236.

89. Sondheimer, R. M., & Green, D. P. (2010). Using experiments to estimate the effects of education on voter turnout. *American Journal of Political Science, 54*(1), 174–189.

90. Klesner, J. L. (2007). Social capital and political participation in Latin America: Evidence from Argentina, Chile, Mexico and Peru. *Latin American Research Review, 42*(2), 1–32; Klesner, J. L. (2009). Who participates? Determinants of political action in Mexico. *Latin American Politics and Society, 51*(2), 59–90.

91. Gleason, S. (2001). Female political participation and health in India. *Annals of the American Academy of Political and Social Science, 573*, 105–126; Krishna, A. (2006). Poverty and democratic participation reconsidered–Evidence from the local level in India. *Comparative Politics, 38*(4), 439.

92. Marien, S., Hooghe, M., & Quintelier, E. (2010). Inequalities in non-institutionalised forms of political participation: A multi level analysis of 25 countries. *Political Studies, 58*(1), 187–213.

Part 1

TERTIARY EDUCATION AND TRANSITIONS

2

The Quest for Equity in Higher Education Across Racial, Ethnic, and Gender Groups

MOKUBUNG NKOMO

In a world that is increasingly intertwined and interdependent; a world in which knowledge and high-level skills define a society's well-being and prosperity, the need to provide educational opportunities to all citizens, regardless of ascribed attributes, has become more urgent than ever before. Knowledge and skills deprivation to any segment of a society becomes an albatross with dire socioeconomic consequences. Thus, educational equity, among other social justice issues, has assumed a compelling presence in most policy formulation processes and practices globally.

Providing greater access to educational opportunities is not merely a moral issue, but more critically a matter of vital national interest in virtually all modern states. A few examples follow. In noting the progress that the Australian higher education system is making, Van Vught observed that "economically successful countries must have a diverse higher education system as these tend to foster greater social mobility, the ability to better meet diverse labor market demands and increased institutional effectiveness."[1] The 2009 Leuven/Louvain-la-Neuve Communiqué, which is part of the Bologna Process (1999), emphasizes "social dimension" issues such as equity and, consequently, the provision of expansive education opportunities.[2] Equity in education is also viewed as a key to social progress and high on the list of priorities in the IBSA Declaration.[3] The United Nations Development Program 2004 report *Cultural Liberty in Today's Diverse World* provides a more explicit statement about the merits of equity.[4] Underlying all these developments and insights are both moral and material imperatives.

Yet, despite this swelling realization of the virtues of equity in education, staggering numbers in many societies still are trapped in vicious cycles of poverty, illiteracy, and innumeracy, and remain on the periphery of taken-for-granted social goods, including education. Such exclusion undermines their potential for development. The marginalized are invariably ethnic minorities, women, immigrants, and the disabled. In the Foreword to the 2010 Education for All Global Monitoring Report *Reaching the Marginalized*, Bokova acknowledges the achievements made in the school sector in the last 20 years but laments the large numbers "who are missing out on their right to education because of the simple fact of where they are born or who their family is."[5]

It is common knowledge that the top end of the education hierarchy is much narrower than the base. The inequality that exists in the lower rungs of the education pyramid is multiplied several fold at the tertiary level, where marginalization is quite acute. The development of societies, as well as that of the global community, depends on the universities' capacity to produce knowledge, develop high-level skills, engender scientific and social innovation, and adapt to inexorable change. To rise up to the challenges of both local and global development it is critical that equity be deeply embedded in admissions policies and institutional cultures to ensure a greater pool of human talent.

This chapter focuses on the challenges, vagaries, and achievements that South Africa has experienced in its efforts to promote equity in tertiary education, as well as explores the lessons that South Africa can offer to and learn from other countries. In this chapter, "equity" is understood to mean the application of the fairness principle, which in the South African case is premised on the acknowledgement of the effects of past discrimination and the need for redress in order to achieve equality for all.

From the Global to the Local

There is a broader global context within which the fundamental education rights documented below should be seated. Since the end of World War II, there has been a burgeoning of consciousness about human rights across the globe, with provision for their application in education. The Universal Declaration of Human Rights marked the beginning of a concerted effort to instill a human rights sensibility amongst UN member states and in Article 26 it enjoins them as follows: (1) "Technical and professional education shall be made generally available and higher education shall be equally accessible to all on the basis of merit;" (2) "Education shall be directed to the *full development of the human personality and to the strengthening of respect for human rights and fundamental freedoms. It shall promote understanding, tolerance and friendship among all nations, racial or religious groups*, and shall further the activities of the United Nations for the maintenance of peace [emphasis added]."[6]

On March 2–4, 1995, the Management of Social Transformations Program (MOST), an affiliate of UNESCO, convened a symposium in Roskilde, Denmark, with the following purpose: "[To] explore courses of action in order to go from a world characterized by the rise of social exclusion to one in which societies can regain social cohesion."[7] The symposium was immediately followed by the United Nations World Summit on Social Development in Copenhagen on March 5–12, 1995. The Social Summit, as it was called, brought together 120 heads of state and government to approve a plan of action aimed at addressing critical social questions such as unemployment, poverty, and social exclusion. The panel who addressed the topic, "From Social Exclusion to Social Justice," observed that: "Achieving social justice lies at the base of all changes that need to be made in the world. A more just society, social equality, equity and human rights need to be accepted as important societal goals."[8] A decade later, *Cultural Liberty in Today's Diverse World*, underscored the need for "unity within diversity."[9] Drawing from empirical studies, reflections, and examples from a wide range of countries, it provides a powerful guide for appropriate policies, especially in multicultural societies.

Clearly then, over time there has been a growing consciousness of, and commitment to human rights, social justice, democratic practice, and inclusivity in the governance of states. This consciousness and commitment are also applicable to higher education. Scores of studies worldwide highlight the need to entrench social justice and equity in educational environments and curricula. One such example is the publication by Banks et al., entitled *Democracy and Diversity*,[10] which distils a vast body of knowledge and skills on how to forge a common citizenship while, at the same time, acknowledging differences—what Nieto calls "diversity education."[11]

In most parts of the globe, the contagion of the human rights discourse could not be escaped. A whole host of factors influenced the slow but inexorable march toward, albeit contested, improved social relations in many countries, including educational environments. Examples of these historic events are: the defeat of the Herrenvolk and fascist ideologies at the end of World War II, the adoption of the United Nations Charter, the civil rights movement in the United States and elsewhere, and the international women's conferences (in Mexico City, 1975; Copenhagen, 1980; Nairobi, 1985; and Beijing, 1995). Commenting on the developments regarding gender equity, the Organisation for Economic Co-operation and Development (OECD) observes: "Given the favourable trend in women's participation in under-graduate tertiary education, it can be hoped that female representation, both in post-graduate programmes and, in due course, in leadership positions in academia and in society at large, will also improve satisfactorily over time."[12] It is reasonable and logical to draw a similar conclusion with regard to other marginalized or under-represented groups in many countries.

A Glance at Trends in Europe, the United States, and Other Countries

A study conducted by Breen, Luijkx, Müller, and Pollack analyzed trends in seven European countries, focusing on class differences in educational achievement over the first 60 years of the 20th century. They found that "inequalities between men and women in their educational attainment declined markedly." Their data indicate that there has been "a decline in class inequality in educational attainment for both men and women," thus challenging the prevailing notion of "persistent inequality" made by some scholars[13] and suggesting that progress on the road toward equity is possible.

In many ways, the above-mentioned developments constitute the backdrop to what has been unfolding in many tertiary institutions in countries of varying levels of development for approximately the past 40 years. In the United States, several studies show a significant increase in female participation in tertiary institutions. In their study on women in American colleges, Goldin, Katz, and Kuziemko indicate that parity was achieved in male–female undergraduate enrollment in the United States during the period from 1900 to 1930. However, in the 1930s, male enrollment began to increase, peaking in the late 1940s, prompted by the GI Bill that extended support to veterans of World War II. A reversal of this trend began in the 1960s, gained momentum in the 1980s, and reached a ratio of 1.3 female students for each male student at the undergraduate level in 2003.[14]

It is estimated that about 56% of students currently enrolled in tertiary institutions in the United States are women.[15] They tend to be enrolled in female-majority fields, such as social sciences and history (52%), biology and life sciences (60%), accounting (61%), education (77%), psychology (78%), and health and related services (84%). Males, on the other hand, tend to dominate in fields such as engineering, physical science, and science technologies,[16] which typically yield higher-paying, more prestigious jobs, reflecting the discriminatory gender segmentation of the labor market. However, upon a closer examination of the data in some of the fields not traditionally associated with women, it becomes clear that the glass ceiling is slowly but surely cracking. For instance, in 1969–1970, 9.3% of master's degrees were conferred on women, compared to 33.9% in 2000–2001. In engineering, 1.1% of women obtained degrees in 1969–1970, compared to 21.2% in 2000–2001. In physical sciences, 14.2% of women obtained degrees in 1969–1970, compared to 36% in 2000–2001. At the doctoral level, 0.7% of women received doctorates in engineering in 1969–1970, compared to 16.5% in 2000–2001. In 1969–1970, 5.4% of women received their doctorates in physical sciences, compared to 26.8% in 2000–2001.[17]

Although women in academia in the United States have made substantial strides with regard to undergraduate enrollments, their representation at faculty and senior management levels is less striking. Women with full-time, tenured appointments comprise 52% of female faculty, in contrast to 70% among male faculty.[18] Women presidents of colleges and universities constitute 22% of the presidents of the 2,000 colleges and universities reviewed.[19]

Similar changes have occurred in the racial composition of tertiary education in the United States. Enrollment of African Americans in United States tertiary institutions increased from 943,400 in 1976[20] to 2,383,400 in 2007[21]—a 40%

increase over a 31-year period. At present, however, African American faculty in all tertiary institutions roughly constitute 6.1% (61,183), the majority of whom are in historically African American tertiary institutions, including 2-year community colleges.[22]

The United States Constitution and relevant legislation were the motivating forces which, by and large, lay behind changes in social attitudes and institutional practices. The Supreme Court's 1954 decision on *Brown v. Board of Education*[23] declared the "separate but equal" doctrine unconstitutional and prohibited educational segregation. The court case spawned a spate of legislation, dubbed the "Brown progeny," and, together with a broader civil rights movement, led to the Civil Rights Act (1964), IDEA (1967), Title IX of the Education Amendments Act (1972), and the Americans with Disabilities Act (1990).

Encouraged by, and seeking to be compliant with federal legislation (and to avoid litigation), many U.S. tertiary institutions devised plans to improve the demographic profiles of their institutions. Perhaps the most poignant illustration of institutional will to diversify the demographic profile of student enrollment is that undertaken by the elite Amherst College when Anthony Marx became its president in 2003. He set aside 25% of the admissions for low-income students, established a $500 million endowment fund, dispatched admissions officers to low-income schools to recruit students, and periodically held fireside chats with students to discuss inequality.[24] The U.S. Military Academy (West Point), in a similar effort to integrate its army officer corps, has a Prep School designed to provide a 9-month remedial training for those who need it. It is reported that many of those who have gone through the Prep School have found it to help in their transition and instilled confidence in their adjustment to the Academy's rigorous academic program.[25] Many similar strategies are being used by other institutions, but there are still many universities and colleges that are at best lukewarm to the need for greater equity.

During the period from 2004 to 2008, the OECD conducted a review of tertiary education in 24 countries and produced a report entitled "OECD Thematic Review of Tertiary Education." It notes that: "A general equity objective in tertiary education is to achieve a student population that closely reflects the composition of society as a whole."[26] The report found that, over a 40-year period, enrollments in tertiary institutions had become "increasingly heterogeneous in terms of socioeconomic background, ethnicity, and previous education." Furthermore, it found that "the rise of female participation has been the most noteworthy trend. . . ."[27] However, it also noted that, although the expansion of women in postgraduate studies increased from "18% in 1990 to 40% in 2005,"[28] it is less striking when compared to undergraduate enrollment.[29] As is the case in the United States, women remained under-represented in technology and engineering and over-represented in the teaching and nursing professions.[30]

In 2003, India, Brazil, and South Africa committed themselves to the establishment of a Trilateral Joint Commission in what came to be called the Brasilia

Declaration. The Declaration is comprehensive and, among the strategic development issues it identifies, is the achievement of social equity.[31] All three countries developed policy instruments designed to increase the enrollment of targeted groups at tertiary institutions, and all have experienced significant enrollment of groups that were historically excluded. The key operative concepts used in promoting increased enrollments include: in South Africa "transformation," which in particular aims to increase participation of blacks and females in tertiary institutions; "targeting," which in Brazil is a strategy to identify and recruit greater numbers of underrepresented groups including Afro-Brazilians; and "affirmation," which in India is designed to end discrimination on the basis of gender, caste, and social class.[32]

Underlying these global advances is a common understanding that universities should seek to enroll as many capable or potentially capable students as possible in order to enhance their institutional achievements and contributions to society. Reliance on a small pool from a particular race, class, religion, or culture will severely restrict such chances, whereas a more diverse student body offers a higher probability for promoting individual and societal success.[33] For example, in *Grutter v. Bollinger*,[34] the United States Supreme Court (2003) ruled in favor of the University of Michigan's Law School policy to diversify its students, on grounds that such a policy would benefit the students, the university, and society at large. Interestingly, the United States Department of Defense supported the University of Michigan's Law School's appeal to maintain an affirmative action policy.

One of the most important books to argue in favor of race-sensitive admissions policies, *The Shape of the River,* by Bowen and Bok, presents a strong argument and massive data as to why such policies not only improve individual efficacy, but have long-term benefits for society at large.[35] However, a few arguments are made opposing this perspective. First, that affirmative policies are a form of "reverse racism" (to the extent that gender is also high on the equity agenda, the companion of this argument ought to be "reverse sexism") and should therefore be opposed. Second, that in countries like the United States, the reforms of recent years have nullified the necessity for affirmative action. Third, the arguments contend that affirmative action is ill-advised because many of the minority beneficiaries are from middle-class backgrounds. It is not the intention of the chapter to debate these perspectives here, except to concede that refinements have to be made to erase the quirks in such policies when they needlessly disadvantage other groups and when they only open doors to the middle-class and affluent. But that these policies have made a huge difference in the lives of many minorities, women, and the disabled and thus contributed to general social welfare is indisputable.

The South African Case

After the momentous political changes following the release of Nelson Mandela and other political prisoners and detainees, the unbanning of political movements in 1990, and the first democratic elections in 1994, South Africa was dubbed the "miracle nation." It also became anointed as the "rainbow nation," suggesting a prospective antithesis to the divisions wrought by the apartheid project. There were great expectations that the ghastly past would be transformed into a lustrous future. But questions remain: Are these epochal changes ephemeral and episodic? Or, will the changes be sustained? This chapter considers these questions as they pertain to the tertiary education sector in South Africa and beyond.

It is important to acknowledge that, since 1994, significant achievements have been made in transforming the broad structure and some substantive aspects of education in South Africa.[36] Examples are the creation of a single nonracial and nonsexist system, the various alterations in search of a realistic curriculum model suitable for South Africa's extreme conditions of inequality, the establishment of a national qualifications framework, the introduction of a more equitable funding formula and governance of education institutions, new forms of education management development, the incorporation of teacher colleges into universities, and the rationalization of universities.

Despite these changes, daunting challenges still remain. These are too numerous to be captured in a single chapter, so the focus will be on initiatives related to the quest to achieve race and gender equity within the higher education sector. In many ways, the South African experience reflects developments in countries such as the United States, some European countries, India, and Brazil as referred to above. However, it is worth noting that South Africa's experience is dictated by its own particular circumstances and history, as is the case with other countries.

Brief Historical Background

Under both the colonial and apartheid regimes, vast segments of South Africa's population were systematically denied the fundamental right to equal education opportunities, among many other basic human rights. Over a period of three-and-a-half centuries, this neglect resulted in a massive, racialized educational gap that one renowned educator,[37] writing in the 1960s and referring to blacks in particular, predicted it would take at least two generations to bridge if corrective measures were initiated at the time. Alas, 40 years later, it seems that the deficit or knowledge gap still gapes irreparably. The two generations mentioned in the 1960s could become three or four generations in the face of further delays. The critical skills shortage, an albatross that weighs down heavily on South Africa's prospects for a robust development trajectory is, to a large extent, the result of this gross neglect.

Under apartheid, access to higher education was racially segregated and severely restricted for blacks. Universities designated for blacks had restricted academic programs. For example, engineering and science were generally not offered and, even more insidiously, the development of a research culture at black universities was not encouraged. Behind this restrictive education policy was the ideology of white supremacy that found its most powerful expression in the then Prime Minister Hendrik Verwoerd's statement that "the Bantu must be guided to serve his own community in all respects. There is no place for him in the European community above the level of certain forms of labor. . . . For that reason it is of no avail for him to receive training which has as its aim absorption into the European community while he cannot and will not be absorbed there."[38] This pronouncement laid the disastrous foundation for the structure and content of inferior black education, which lasted for almost half-a-century, with dire consequences that are currently still palpable and threatening to linger on for the foreseeable future. The material and psychological costs of education deprivation are borne by the entire society—including whites.

ENROLLMENT PROFILE IN EARLY YEARS OF APARTHEID

South Africa's current educational challenges were hatched three-and-half centuries ago. However, for brevity and illustrative purposes, it will suffice to concentrate on the last 75 years or so (1930–2007). Table 2.1 indicates that, in 1930, university enrollment for blacks, who constituted roughly 88% of the population, was estimated to be 662.[39] In the same year, the enrollment of whites, who constituted 22% of the population, in higher learning institutions was 7,118. In 1950, 2 years after the whites-only National Party won the general election, black enrollment stood at 1,117, and for whites it stood at 18,438. By 1974, black enrollment had increased to 16,219 and white enrollment to 95,589.[40] The comparatively

Table 2.1 **White and Black Student University Enrollment: 1930–1975**[41]

Year	Total White Students Including UNISA	Total Black Students Including UNISA	Total
1930	7,118	662	7,740
1935	8,045	645	8,690
1940	11,411	667	12,078
1945	14,190	765	14,995
1950	18,438	1,117	19,555
1955	25,896	2,869	28,765
1960	39,662	4,419	44,081
1965	53,576	6,437	60,013
1974	95,589	16,219	111,808

larger increase in black enrollment was due to the establishment of segregated black universities.

It should be borne in mind that the ideology of white supremacy was only one dimension of apartheid, albeit it a primary one. Another was patriarchy, which manifested itself in higher education by the low enrollment of females and their confinement, as in the case in other countries mentioned above, to particular academic programs that were deemed appropriate for females.

At the core of the struggle for democracy in South Africa was a desire for freedom, equality, and social justice. Equity was, and still remains, a deeply embedded concept in these values and principles. Subsumed in the concept of equity is the notion of access to education as prescribed by the South African Constitution. To shed light and to give context to the issue Sayed, Kanjee, and Nkomo state that: "The apartheid system of education resulted in entrenched gross educational disparities and inequities between different racial groups. The need for rectification and parity in all aspects of education was thus a necessary imperative in a new democratic education system. The demand for rectification was captured in the commitment to equity and redress as cornerstone principles of all educational policies."[42] In the context of historical inequality, equity implies a commitment to compensate for the contrived disadvantage of particular groups as it seeks to achieve social justice.[43] Equity is therefore viewed as being at the center of the post-apartheid transformation project.

ENROLLMENT PROFILE IN THE POST-1994 PERIOD

With the advent of democracy in 1994 and the passage of the Higher Education Act in 1997, the demographics of higher education changed dramatically, as indicated in Table 2.2. Over the 8 years between 2000 and 2007, the total enrollment of blacks was 69% (including Africans,[44] Coloreds, and Indians). For whites, the enrollment declined from 35% in 2000 to 31% in 2007. Female enrollment during the same period was 55%—a level of participation higher than that during the apartheid era. Therefore, comparatively, the participation of blacks and females after the introduction of democracy was substantial.[45]

This trend, as indicated in Table 2.3, is similar at the master's degree level where, by 2007, black enrollment had increased to 60%, with the "African" segment showing the greatest increase from 36% in 2000 to 45% in 2007. White enrollment declined from 49% to 38% during the same period. Unfortunately, data for females at this level are unavailable.

A similar trend of increased enrollments at the doctoral level is indicated in Table 2.4, with aggregate black enrollment increasing from 37% in 2000 to 53% in 2007. Again, African representation increased from 25% to 39% during the same period. At doctoral level, white enrollment declined from 62% to 47%. It is important to note that overall enrollment for all groups rose over this period, suggesting that they actually all benefited.

Table 2.2 **Equity Profile of Undergraduate Degree Enrollments: 2000–2007**[46]

Race & Gender	2000	%	2001	%	2002	%	2003	%	2004	%	2005	%	2006	%	2007	%
African	144,776	51	162,424	52	175,194	52	178,615	51	169,742	49	170,772	49	181,265	50	194,144	52
Colored	14,137	5	16,090	5	18,730	6	21,527	6	23,086	7	24,042	7	25,438	7	26,405	7
Indian	26,102	9	28,279	9	31,332	9	34,457	10	36,500	11	37,358	11	36,960	10	35,177	10
White	97,846	35	106,259	34	113,224	33	117,669	33	115,409	33	115,654	33	116,208	32	113,690	31
Female	151,067	53	166,165	53	181,016	53	188,989	54	188,246	55	190,791	55	198,983	55	204,321	55
Male	131,933	47	146,959	47	157,551	47	163,450	46	157,108	45	157,645	45	161,589	45	165,879	45

Reproduced under Government Printer's Copyright Authority No. 11514 dated 04 November 2010.

Table 2.3 **Equity Profile of Master's Degree Enrollments: 2000–2007**[47]

Race	2000	%	2001	%	2002	%	2003	%	2004	%	2005	%	2006	%	2007	%
African	11,552	36	13,652	39	16,259	41	19,397	44	21,004	46	20,317	46	19,645	46	19,100	45
Colored	1,892	6	2,106	6	2,394	6	2,546	6	2,641	6	2,560	6	2,601	6	2,496	6
Indian	2,609	8	3,061	9	3,518	9	3,918	9	4,036	9	3,844	9	4,039	9	3,803	9
White	15,741	49	16,478	47	17,278	44	17,789	41	17,601	39	17,504	39	16,455	38	15,593	38

Reproduced under Government Printer's Copyright Authority No. 11514 dated 04 November 2010.

Although increasing equity for students is evident, the demographic picture for full-time instruction and research is the opposite of student enrollment, as indicated in Tables 2.2 to 2.4. The total black representation stood at 39% in 2007, as opposed to 59% for whites. At this level, the growth rate of black staff is insubstantial, with negative growth for Indians. During the period from 2003 to 2007, the numbers of white teaching/research staff remained more or less steady at about two-thirds of the total, with a slight average decline of 1.7%. A similar downward trend is indicated for Indians, at the average rate of 4%. On the other hand, with regard to Africans and Coloreds, the proportions increased on average by 2% and 3.6%, respectively over the same period. Table 2.5 indicates a slight increase in the numbers of women from 42% in 2003 to 43% in 2007, whereas the proportion of men declined slightly from 58% to 57% during the same period.

Table 2.6 indicates that during the period from 1995 to 2007, the concentration of women in academic positions was at the junior lecturer and lecturer rank, with a noticeable decline in 2007. The number of women at the professorial and associate professorial levels registered a steady increase from 13% in 1995 to 24% in 2007. Significantly, the decline in numbers at the lower ranks is translated into an increase at the professorial level, although it can be anticipated that the increase will be at a slower rate in the future because of the considerable time it takes to accumulate the requisite entry requirements into the professoriate and the limited openings at this level.

DEMOGRAPHIC PROFILE OF HEADS OF UNIVERSITIES

Out of the current total of 23 universities and universities of technology in South Africa, only five (UL, UV, UZ, UFH, and UWC)[48] remain largely black with regard to student enrollment, and their vice chancellors also remain black, as was the case before 1994. Three of the four universities that were exclusively designed for English-speaking students have black vice chancellors (the exception is the University of Cape Town, which, in the post-1994 period, had two black vice chancellors, including one female, before the current white vice chancellor was appointed). Four of the six universities (SU, UP, NMMU, UFS, UNW, and UJ)[49] that were set aside for Afrikaans-speaking students under apartheid currently have black vice chancellors, including, for the first time in history, a black female vice chancellor at the University of Pretoria. The remaining eight universities (CPUT, CUT, DUT, TUT, UNISA, VUT, WSUT, and UJ)[50] have new identities as a result of the mergers and incorporation processes that took place after 2004. Three out of the 23 vice chancellors are white males; four are black females and the rest are black males. Although female representation (17%) and white male representation (13%) are relatively low, it is quite clear that a major demographic change has taken place at the highest level of these institutions of higher learning.

Table 2.4 **Equity Profile of Doctoral Enrollments: 2000–2007**[51]

Race	2000	%	2001	%	2002	%	2003	%	2004	%	2005	%	2006	%	2007	%
African	1,610	25	1,869	27	2,236	29	2,531	30	2,932	32	3,275	35	3,583	36	3,889	39
Colored	327	5	367	5	419	5	450	5	529	6	572	6	565	6	565	6
Indian	464	7	533	8	619	8	696	8	768	8	754	8	813	8	797	8
White	3,993	62	4,202	60	4,486	58	4,685	56	4,861	53	4,811	51	4,819	49	4,750	47

Reproduced under Government Printer's Copyright Authority No. 11514 dated 04 November 2010.

Table 2.5 Head Count of Full-Time (Permanent and Temporary) Instruction/Research Staff by Race and Gender: 2003–2007[52]

Race and Gender	2003		2004		2005		2006		2007		Average actual increase
African	4,476	23%	4,378	23%	4,188	24%	4,832	24%	4,854	25%	2.00%
Colored	1,011	5%	1,018	5%	1,003	6%	1,077	5%	1,163	6%	3.60%
Indian	1,642	8%	1,658	9%	1,355	8%	1,790	9%	1,614	8%	-0.40%
White	12,371	62%	12,047	63%	10,911	62%	11,999	60%	11,535	59%	-1.70%
Unknown	343	2%	145	1%	105	1%	161	1%	318	2%	-1.90%
TOTAL	**19,843**	**100%**	**19,247**	**100%**	**17,562**	**100%**	**19,859**	**100%**	**19,484**	**100%**	**-0.50%**
Female	8,261	42%	8,000	42%	7,376	42%	8,540	43%	8,392	43%	0.40%
Male	11,581	58%	11,245	58%	10,186	58%	11,319	57%	11,092	57%	-1.10%

Note: Percentages may not always add up to 100, due to rounding off, and/or race/gender being unknown. Reproduced under Government Printer's Copyright Authority No. 11514 dated 04 November 2010.

Table 2.6 **Changes in the Proportion of Women Academics by Rank: 1995–2002**[53]

Year	Professors and Assoc Professors	Senior Lecturers	Lecturers	Junior Lecturers
1995	13	28	46	53
2002	18	38	53	55
2005	18.5	39.5	51	56.3
2006	19.1	40.6	50.9	54.7
2007*	24	40	48	47

*The 2007 figures are drawn from http://www.southafricaweb.co.za/page/higher-education-south-africa. Accessed February 25, 2010.

Forces Behind the Change

Prior to 1994, South Africa had endured almost three centuries of colonial rule culminating in half a century of extreme racial hegemony known as apartheid. The consequences of this history of total (political, social, economic, educational) disenfranchisement are deep and will be felt for a long time to come. However, as would be expected, such circumstances inevitably spawned resistance. Apart from the political protests over the years, efforts were also made to articulate a vision for a post-apartheid fair and equal society. The emergence of resistance organizations such as the African National Congress, the Congress Movement, the Pan Africanist Congress, the Black Consciousness Movement, and many other political formations provided space for the articulation of an alternative. Arguably the most powerful expression of the alternative to apartheid was the Freedom Charter that envisioned a South Africa that "belongs to all" with provisions for a democratic dispensation.

This history laid the foundation for a very progressive Constitution. Shortly before 1994, and in the immediate aftermath of the first democratic election, a number of crucial preparatory activities took place. In education, there was the National Education Crisis Committee (later becoming the National Education Coordinating Committee, 1990–1992), which dominated the education protest movement from the mid-1970s to the late 1990s. The NECC, as it was popularly known, then established the National Education Policy Initiative project, designed to investigate "policy options in all areas of education within a value framework derived from the ideals of the broad democratic movement."[54] The value framework was driven by five cross-cutting principles namely, *nonsexism, nonracism, redress, democracy,* and a *unitary education system.* In the higher education sector, an extensive consultative process managed by the National Commission on

Higher Education (1995–1996) looked into broadening the provision of higher education in a democratic South Africa and was informed by the above-mentioned value framework. As this process was unfolding, pressure continued to mount from the student and labor movements, among others.

EQUITY IN EDUCATION: THE EVOLUTION OF THE IDEA IN SOUTH AFRICA

The quest for an inclusive democracy in South Africa was long and tortured. Not only was it a call for political enfranchisement, it was also a struggle for economic empowerment, as well as for the social, cultural, and educational emancipation of the black majority and, by extension, women. Before reviewing programs that promote educational equity, it is useful to briefly examine the documented history of the struggle for the democratization of education.

Consciousness or sensibility about the unjust nature of the colonial and apartheid systems, which were based on racial oppression, dates back to the 17th century. Various competing political formations were united over the pernicious effects of segregated education, as was the case with regard to the remainder of the system of oppression, and only differed in the "how" to achieve democracy, including equality in education. At the beginning of the 20th century, those opposing discrimination in educational provision on the basis of race and gender employed a different vocabulary, as will be demonstrated below.

The African National Congress (ANC) is the oldest liberation movement in modern South African history, and currently governs the country. Therefore, it is useful, as an example, to consider ANC writings on the question of educational opportunities for the majority of the population, expressed over almost a century. In its earliest documented pronouncement on education (1919), the ANC stated the following as one of its goals: "To originate and expound the right system of education in all schools and colleges and to advocate for its adoption by State and Churches and by all other independent bodies in respect thereto."[55] Almost a quarter of a century later, in its Africans' Claims in South Africa (1943), a document designed to rebut the Atlantic Charter, it elaborated on the goal and insisted on "the right of every child to free and compulsory education and of admission to technical schools, universities and other institutions of higher education."[56]

Six years later (1949), in its Program of Action, the ANC further articulated its desire for equitable education opportunities via: (a) raising the standard of Africans in the commercial, industrial, and other enterprises and workers in their workers' organizations by means of providing a common educational forum wherein intellectuals, peasants, and workers can participate for the common good; and (b) the establishment of national centers of education for the purpose of training and educating African youth, as well as the provision of large-scale scholarships, tenable in various overseas countries.[57] The education clause of the

1955 Freedom Charter provides a more expansive conception of an equitable educational provision under the now famous slogan, "The doors of learning and culture shall be opened," stating the following:

> All the cultural treasures of mankind shall be open to all, by free exchange of books, ideas, and contact with other lands; the aim of education shall be to teach the youth to love their people and their culture, to honour human brotherhood liberty and peace; education shall be free, compulsory, universal, and equal for all children; higher education and technical training shall be opened to all by means of state allowances and scholarships awarded on the basis of merit.[58]

It is clear from the ANC's documented history between 1919 and 1955 that the lack of an equitable education was of great concern—to the extent that, as an expression of exasperation, the Program of Action and the Freedom Charter strongly advocated initiatives to study abroad to advance the education level of the majority of the citizenry. Although the "equity" concept was not used explicitly throughout the 1919 to 1955 period, there can be no doubt that these remonstrations were, in essence, equity-driven, as they deal with the lack of fairness in the provision of education.

PROMULGATING THE NEW ORDER: THE CONSTITUTION AND THE BILL OF RIGHTS

For the first time in South African constitutional history, the concepts of equity and inclusivity have become critical tenets in the country's constitutional democracy. The South African Constitution is quite explicit and comprehensive in its identification of areas that cannot serve as bases for discrimination. These include "race, gender, sex, pregnancy, marital status, ethnic or social origin, color, sexual orientation, age, disability, religion, conscience, belief, culture, language, and birth."[59]

The Equality Clause of the Bill of Rights begins by declaring: "Everyone is equal before the law and has the right to equal protection and the benefit of the law" 9(1), and continues in section 9(3): "The state may not unfairly discriminate directly or indirectly against anyone on one or more grounds, including race, gender, sex, pregnancy, marital status, ethnic or social origin, color, sexual orientation, age, disability, religion, conscience, belief, culture, language and birth."[60] More specifically, section 29(1), declares: "Everyone has the right: (a) to a basic education, including adult basic education; (b) to further education, which the state, through reasonable measures, must make progressively available and accessible."[61] Section 29(2)(a) of the Bill of Rights specifically refers to "equity," thus introducing a concept that has since gained widespread currency in the education discourse.

Casting the Lens on Initiatives to Achieve Equity in South Africa's Tertiary Sector: Post-1994

THE NATIONAL COMMISSION ON HIGHER EDUCATION

In recognition of the large-scale knowledge and skills deficits resulting from the apartheid education system, one of the immediate tasks of the new democratic government was the establishment of the National Commission on Higher Education (NCHE), whose directive was to review and make appropriate recommendations for the transformation of higher education. The NCHE report was released in 1996. Not surprisingly, the preamble to the report declares that "[T]he system is fundamentally flawed by inequities, imbalances and distortions deriving from its history and present structure." It further optimistically states that "higher education can play a pivotal role in the political, economic and cultural reconstruction and development of South Africa."[62] Among the five deficiencies that the report highlights, is the following: "Discriminatory practices have limited the access of black students and women students into fields such as science, engineering, technology, and commerce and this has been detrimental to economic and social development."[63] Transformation was therefore deemed imperative, and all of the legislative and policy pronouncements were informed by this logic.

A year later, in 1997, Parliament passed the Higher Education Act. The preamble to the Act declares its aim to "redress past discrimination and ensure representivity and equal access . . . [and] promote the values which underlie an open and democratic society based on human dignity, equality and freedom."[64] It echoed the same antipathy to discriminatory practices as articulated in the Constitution. A short time after the passage of the Higher Education Act, as a result of a growing dissatisfaction with the slow pace of transformation, another review of the higher education landscape was instituted. The National Plan for Higher Education (2001) is replete with equity imperatives regarding black and female student access to higher education opportunities (including, importantly, "equity in outcomes"), staff employment, program mix or differentiation, and the like.[65]

In the aftermath of the passage of the Higher Education Act in 1997 and policy proclamations at national and institutional levels there has been a flurry of assorted evaluations, reviews, criticism, and research activities. The common purpose of these studies has been to determine the extent to which transformation has succeeded or failed.

SYSTEM-WIDE REVIEWS

The first ambitious attempt at a systemic review of the South African higher education landscape was the comprehensive volume edited by Cloete et al., entitled *Transformation in Higher Education* (2002), of which the declared purpose was to "examine the extent to which the changes were in line with policy intentions, particularly with regard to equity, democratization, responsivity and efficiency. . . . "[66] The impact of global reforms on higher education institutions is featured in this volume and serves as a valuable comparison. Although the time frame was extremely limited, barely 5 years after the passage of the Higher Education Act of 1997, one of the general conclusions was that, "in some important respects the institutional landscape has changed considerably since 1994."[67] But caution is advised, especially with reference to research and curriculum, as "the more things change, the more they remain the same."[68]

INSTITUTIONAL CULTURE

Universities, like all other institutions, have their individual cultures that have been nurtured for decades, if not for centuries. Due to entrenched values, such as academic freedom and institutional autonomy, there is a belief that universities are immune to external pressure for change. Most have an almost instinctual tendency to shield themselves from any perceived or real external threat. Political change does not necessarily imply that equitable educational changes will follow. So, although there is evidence that, for example, there was noticeable growth in black and female student enrollments over the past 15 years or so, and that substantial institutional mergers were effected, the institutional cultures have not changed fundamentally.[69] And, in these circumstances, equity issues are central— not so much in terms of numerical representation, but crucially, in terms of the content or substance of what is being experienced culturally, pedagogically, and epistemologically. As a result of perceived discrepancies, there has been an increase in studies that focus on the institution-wide application of democratic practice in South African universities. In this regard, Higgins concluded in his critical analysis of the "institutional culture" concept that "universities need to develop a more self-conscious pedagogy if the real problems of institutional culture are to be addressed."[70]

EXAMPLES OF EMPIRICAL STUDIES

Since the late 1990s, a growing body of empirical research has probed into the nature of some universities after the implementation of the new Constitution, the 1994 democratic election, and the promulgation of the Higher Education Act in 1997. Two studies are cited here as examples of this body of research. Mabokela's study[71] considered the issue of black students on white campuses (i.e., the University of Cape Town and the University of Stellenbosch) and came to the general conclusion that black students were "alienated," due mainly to the dominant language and culture practiced in the previously all-white institutions. The study was conducted in the late 1990s and, since then, attempts have been made at both institutions to address the adverse impact of teaching in languages in which black students have insufficient proficiency (especially Afrikaans at Stellenbosch

University, which now has a parallel track—that is, providing separate classes in Afrikaans and English). Although some black students are fluent in these languages, they tend to be from middle class backgrounds, while those from poor backgrounds still suffer language discrimination.

Thaver's[72] study looked at diversity practices among academics in five South African universities, with the *equity* imperative placed at the center of her analysis, and found that the challenge to dislodge "the traditional and conservative social relations that are so characteristic of the academy," has been eclipsed by the "market logic."[73]

A BROADER INVESTIGATION: THE MINISTERIAL COMMITTEE ON HIGHER EDUCATION TRANSFORMATION REPORT (MCHET)

In early 2008, then minister of education Naledi Pandor established a committee whose purpose was "to investigate discrimination in public higher education institutions, with a particular focus on racism and to make appropriate recommendations to combat discrimination and to promote social cohesion."[74] It took the Committee roughly 6 months to study legislative and policy documents, review written submissions from universities, analyze questionnaires from universities, and visit the country's 23 public higher education institutions to conduct interviews with members of statutory, labor, and student representative bodies. Although in the public's mind the investigation was triggered by the Reitz incident at the University of the Free State,[75] it was in fact prompted by a series of reports that suggested that academia was not as equitable as it appeared on the surface. Rather, like the twists and turns that the rest of South African society was experiencing during this transition phase, the academic world was deeply troubled. As the MCHET Report concluded, "discrimination, in particular with regard to racism and sexism, is pervasive in our institutions."[76]

A fair assessment of the degree of transformation in South African higher education would entail two important features. The first relates to the significant quantitative improvement in black and female student enrollments—to a lesser extent in the composition of black and female academic staff—and in the often-overlooked racial and female profile of the vice chancellors. These changes constitute a quantum leap compared to the status quo during the apartheid era, although there is still substantial room for improvement in some areas, such as black and female representation in the science, engineering, and technology fields. The second feature is to be found in the core substantive domains of pedagogy, epistemology, and curriculum. Here, the record seems to be at best sporadic rather than routine. Reform efforts were undertaken at various higher education institutions, such as the "Grounding Program" at the University of Fort Hare and "Africanizing the curriculum" at the University of South Africa, both discussed briefly later in this chapter. These and other examples are indications that the imperative for broader reforms is inexorable, albeit uneven.

What Remains to Be Done?

It is widely accepted now that significant achievements have been made with black and female student enrollment at tertiary institutions, and that programmatic shifts have been effected, as evidenced by enrollment profiles in the various disciplines. Although enrollments have indeed increased, however, the high rates of attrition, failures, and longer periods of degree completion, especially with regard to black students, are cause for great concern. Although such problems are experienced worldwide, South Africa can draw lessons from institutions in countries such as Brazil, India, Malaysia, the United States, and Australia.

Although the demographic profile of black and female academic staff has improved, it lags significantly behind the student demographic profile. Black academic staff largely occupy the lower ranks within the professoriate, publish less, and migrate frequently from institution to institution.[77] Similarly, female academic staff are concentrated in the lower ranks and, like their black counterparts, predominate in the social sciences and humanities. Almost two decades after *de jure* apartheid was ended, there still exist attitudes and practices at many previously white higher education institutions (HEIs) that suggest the persistence of attitudes and discrimination based on race and gender. One example of this is captured in a study by Duncan at the liberal University of the Witwatersrand, which gives an account of the hurdles and humiliations suffered by black staff members at the hands of white administrators and even students.[78] Such accounts were common in interviews conducted by the MCHET team.

Institutional cultures remain largely racialized or Eurocentric, as evidenced by the slow pace of transformation in substantive curriculum reform. One example of the racialized nature of institutional culture is documented in Mabokela's study, in which an administrator at Stellenbosch University kept referring to white students as "our" students, and not using the same reference when talking about black students.[79] The sense of "home" or "belonging" for many students, as described by Thaver and others, is minimal, if not nonexistent.[80] The MCHET report also chronicles accounts of alienation among black students in particular.

EQUITY IN LANGUAGE

According to the UNDP's *Cultural Liberty in Today's Diverse World* report, "language is often the most contested issue in multicultural states."[81] Indeed, in South Africa, language has historically been one of the most contentious issues, especially as a medium of instruction. Although the political environment has changed substantially, respect and space for other languages (i.e., multilingualism) is promoted by the Constitution and by the Language Policy for Higher Education (2002).

A growing body of research offers compelling evidence that students achieve better results when taught in their own language.[82] Although some universities are indeed moving away from unilingualism, in principle, it is generally the case that unilinguism still remains in practice. Some universities, especially histori-cally white universities, offer options along the following lines: They provide English language foundation courses or extra language tutorials; they provide an African language for communication, administrative, and marketing purposes; or they provide an African language course to enable staff and students to communi-cate with one another.[83]

Despite these support mechanisms, enormous challenges still confront black students in particular at all the South African universities, since neither English nor Afrikaans is their home language. This has dire consequences for successful academic performance at the tertiary level. The following sample responses from interviews conducted with black and white students at the University of the Witwatersrand are indicative of existing problems. The question asked was : "Does language impact on your academic experience and in what way?"

> *Respondent 1:* "I come from an English background. Coming to univer-sity where you learn so much information and so many new words and terms, even for me it's a bit challenging. Coming from a background where language is an issue, when English is not your first language, it's tough."
>
> *Respondent 2:* "I think so because all lectures are taught in English, and if you have a strong background in that language, then you have a good understanding, whereas other people might take twice as long to understand statements."
>
> *Respondent 3:* "Obviously English is my home language, and I think it makes such a big difference because even if I have no clue where I want an essay to go or what I'm really writing, I can sit and put down ideas that sound eloquent and sometimes you can get away with it. If an essay sounds eloquent enough, people won't look under the surface to see whether it is solid or not. So language helps in bringing your ideas together and making your essay flow, so I think it helps to be coherent."
>
> *Respondent 4:* "It definitely does, because like in terms of say structur-ing and how you express yourself, sometimes I feel sorry for students who come from Bantu education schools,[84] because they may have an argument which has substance but because they don't have the right words with which to articulate themselves, they end up getting lower marks. So at the end of the day the school you come from really matters."[85]

It is clear from these responses that many students see learning in a second or third language as a serious barrier to successful academic performance. It is rea-sonable to deduce that the high failure or attrition rates[86] among black students are largely attributable to the language problem. There are, to be sure, a sizeable number of black students who perform remarkably well, which is good. But what should be cause for concern is the vast wastage in human resources due to the generally rigid system of language that still exists in practice at many universities—appropriate language policies notwithstanding.[87]

Equity in Epistemology

One of the most obstinate and change-resistant areas in the academic environment is found in notions of racial superiority and patriarchal ideologies. Since it is no longer respectable to overtly subscribe to such ideologies, they assume rather subtle expressions and are conveyed via a powerful hidden curriculum, where proof of evidence is difficult to come by. During the interviews conducted by the Ministerial Committee, several black students referred to examples of discouragement by their white instructors/professors regarding their prospects of passing accounting courses, for example, or by defending the absence of black philosophy writers in their syllabi by stating that there were none.

In 1998, the University of Cape Town was embroiled in what came to be known as the Mamdani Debate, the core of which was a contestation over curriculum reform and where the authority to do so is vested.[88] In short, the debate became a struggle of "old" versus "new" knowledge. In a broad reflection on autonomy and accountability, Van Vught[89] ironically suggested that universities may use these otherwise cherished values as shields against knowledge change. Cloete et al. further observed that new knowledge "is rarely welcomed by the higher education institutions that have, through their many incarnations, jealously guarded the right to control what they may teach and research."[90] Reviewing the stance of South African universities in general, Higgs and van Wyk noted that: "Academic knowledge has had a special, almost untouchable place in the universities that resisted outside attempts to interfere."[91] Lamenting this state of affairs, Jansen, in his inaugural speech as the first black vice chancellor of the University of the Free State, a historically white university, declared:

> The most important challenge is the problem of knowledge. The often troubled knowledge the student comes to university with—the knowledge of the past, the knowledge of black and white and, especially, the knowledge of the future. The university curriculum, here and elsewhere, has not yet confronted the crucial question of what a student needs to know in a dangerous and divided world.[92]

He continued by indicating that, in pursuit of this mission, he would seek the support of the University Senate to effect "a fundamental curriculum overhaul [so] that no student graduates from this university without engaging basic human questions, such as who we are and where we come from; without learning how to live and learn together in ways that prepare our youth for leadership in the workplace."[93] This is a tall order indeed. One must wonder whether these fundamental and necessary changes could be achieved without those who are in charge of knowledge production undergoing a fundamental epistemological and pedagogical transformation themselves. This actually amounts to phenomenal adjustments in personal worldviews.

ETHNOCENTRISM: THE HIDDEN TROJAN HORSE?

It is crucial to note that most of the research conducted on diversity and social cohesion in South African educational environments has largely been through a black–white lens. This is, to a large extent, due to a political strategy adopted during the anti-apartheid struggle to focus on the primary task, which was to topple minority white rule or racial hegemony. Thus, race was accorded primacy and other issues, such as social class, gender, and ethnicity, took a back seat. After the demise of apartheid, the terrain and dynamics of the struggle for democracy changed dramatically. Gender, social class, and other prejudices have progressively moved up the ladder of public concern. But ethnicity seems to be lagging far behind. It is important to recognize that ethnicity should be among the issues and concerns that deserve inclusion in the equity basket.

The above account touches on some of the critical *democratization of knowledge* issues that still face South Africa today: from "belonging and feeling at home," institutional culture and language, to epistemology and ethnicity. These critical issues also fall within the ambit of social justice, human rights, and equity, and therefore deserve focused attention.

GLIMPSES OF CHANGE: THE UNFOLDING LANDSCAPE AT SOME SOUTH AFRICAN TERTIARY INSTITUTIONS

As we look back over the past one-and-a-half decades, we can see a massive disruption of the old order that came in the wake of the Higher Education Act (1997), which laid the foundation for the dismantling of the legal architecture of racially segregated higher education in South Africa. Although the dismantling process is slow and contentious, nuggets of evidence suggest that some inexorable strides have been made toward the achievement of educational equity. The MCHET Report noted the following as indicative of such movement:

- The University of South Africa declared its intention to "Africanize" 50% of its curriculum; the University of Fort Hare is developing a first-year compulsory "Grounding Program," which is broadly intended to promote critical thinking skills, deepen understanding of the principles of "ubuntu" and democracy, and boost self-confidence, as well as support an appreciation of diversity and humanizing pedagogies and a culture of reading and writing—all these are to be nurtured under a decolonizing framework.

- The Cape Peninsula University of Technology developed community service programs that are aimed at advancing social development and social transformation.
- The University of Cape Town runs the Respect Project, which promotes the "right of individual dignity, concern for others, and appreciation of diversity," through the promotion of dialogue around, for example, issues of race and gender. It also sponsors the Khuluma and Mamela Projects, designed to address the fears of white staff on the one hand, and the alienation of black staff on the other.
- The University of the Western Cape has a program of open seminars, workshops, and lectures dealing with issues such as racism, homophobia, harassment, and xenophobia. These interventions are, however, not integrated into the curriculum, attendance is optional, and events are not always well attended.
- The University of Stellenbosch has a "multicultural week" and an "interfaith dialogues" program, and plans to host a "courageous conversations" program to facilitate the discussion of complex social issues.
- The Durban University of Technology offers the "University Forum," which is a 1-hour slot in the time-table, aimed at facilitating conversation on critical social issues in the university community.[94]

Apart from the University of Fort Hare's "Grounding Program" and the expressed desire of the University of South Africa to "Africanize" its curriculum, most of these examples are not integrated into the university curricula. It cannot be expected that the largely fragmented programs at the other universities would constitute a fundamental transformation of the apartheid epistemology. They do, however, constitute embryos of possibilities for the construction of knowledge based on equity, diversity, and social justice.

Several HEIs in South Africa have units like those enumerated above, which suggests a growing recognition of the importance of social justice. The Grounding Program at the University of Fort Hare seems by far the most advanced and comprehensive initiative, deserving emulation from the other institutions. There is also growing evidence of the establishment of an Office of Transformation at several institutions (e.g., University of Cape Town, University of the Witwatersrand, University of KwaZulu Natal), and the recently beleaguered University of the Free State is in the process of establishing an Institute of Race and Reconciliation. These are examples of programs that warrant replication at other tertiary institutions.

In the context of the history of South Africa, these are important achievements that need further impetus and expansion. Given the growing global equity consciousness mentioned above, it seems highly likely that South Africa will, all other things being equal, increase its efforts in the same direction and exceed its already commendable achievements in this regard. These achievements suggest that certain enabling instruments play an essential role in producing a growing and durable democratic culture that nurtures equity: a progressive constitution and a legislative and legal framework that is congruent with the fundamental values embedded in the Constitution, complemented by a vigilant civil society and a transformative leadership committed to democratic values and governance.

Conclusion

The overview in this chapter gave a detailed analysis of South Africa's success and limitations, as well as examples of a growing awareness of the equity imperative and strides made in selected countries such as the United States, Australia, and countries within the European Union. Most countries that have made reasonable progress in achieving equity in higher education have been able to do so mainly by force of their democratic constitutions, with their enshrined concepts of human rights and social justice values. South Africa has a progressive constitution and policy landscape that has become the backbone of its achievements. But the real drama and onus is within the universities themselves. Here, South Africa and other states can learn from specific and effective institutional strategies, such as those implemented at Amherst College. The assertive outreach program to low-income schools and the establishment of a substantial endowment to support students from such schools once they are admitted to the College should inspire emulation in South Africa and elsewhere, where there are still huge numbers of marginalized and under-represented populations. Brazil's "targeting" and India's "affirmation" strategies are also deserving of attention, as they are proving to enhance diversity. Even more important is to ensure that effective programs are in place that will ensure success once students from under-represented and low-income backgrounds are admitted to institutions of higher education.

The daunting developmental challenges facing South Africa require new ways of ensuring policy implementation and effective capacity-building initiatives for management, academic, and support staff. Apart from gaining the knowledge and skills to promote teaching and learning, there is a critical need to raise the concept of equity consciousness across all disciplines. Without a deep grounding of this consciousness in the national psyche, the South African social fabric will remain dangerously fragile and prone to disintegration at the slightest provocation. For the sake of posterity, prosperity, and social stability, the entrenchment of a democratic culture or mindset—more than mere deracialization—is most compelling. South Africa's cherished democracy is still very fragile, and a multiplicity of contradicting tendencies could undermine further work in sustaining its democracy project. Achieving the required level of equity consciousness, rooted in an entrenched democratic culture, is like reaching for a receding mirage: Only a holistic, determined, and sustained intervention program has the prospect of upholding an otherwise resilient tradition of democratic development. But it must not be ephemeral or episodic. It warrants remembering that South Africa's democracy is barely two decades old and therefore inchoate; it will take a generation or so to become mature and sustainable. If the invocation of the OECD's optimism regarding the inexorable logic of change is appropriate, as exemplified by the distance journeyed by South Africa since the apartheid days, then there is reason for hope.

NOTES

1. Higher education: World's most effective? (2010, March 14). *World Higher Education News*, no. 115.
2. Zgaga, P. (2010). *The making of Bologna 1999–2010: Achievements, challenges and perspectives.* Retrieved from http://www.duz.de/docs/downloads/duz_spec_Bologna.pdf
3. See Akoojee, S., & Nkomo, M. (in press). Widening equity and retaining efficiency: Considerations from the IBSA southern coalface. *International Journal of Education Development.*
4. United Nations Development Programme (UNDP). (2004). *Human development report 2004: Cultural liberty in today's diverse world.* New York: UNDP. Retrieved from http://hdr.undp.org/en/media/hdr04_complete.pdf
5. UNESCO. (2010). *Education for all: Global monitoring report 2010: Reaching the marginalized.* Paris: Oxford University Press.
6. United Nations. (1948). *Universal declaration of human rights.* Retrieved December 15, 2009, http://www.un.org/en/documents/undhr
7. Bessis, S. (March 1995). *From social exclusion to social cohesion: Towards a policy agenda.* UNESCO Management of Social Transformations, International Symposium, Roskilde University, Denmark. Retrieved January 12, 2010, http://www.unesco.org/most/besseng.htm#overview
8. UNESCO. (1995). *From social exclusion to social cohesion: Towards a policy agenda.* UNESCO, Management of Social Transformations, Policy Paper no. 2. Retrieved January 12, 2010, http://www.unesco.org/most/roskilde.htm
9. UNDP. (2004). *Human development report 2004.*
10. Banks, J., et al. (2005, April). *Democracy and diversity: Principles and concepts for educating citizens in a global world.* Invitational conference, Center for Multicultural Education, College of Education, University of Washington, Seattle.
11. Nieto, S. (2009). Diversity education: Lessons for a just world. In M. Nkomo, & S. Vandeyar (Eds.), *Thinking diversity while building cohesion: A transnational dialogue on education* (pp. 17–40). Amsterdam/Pretoria: Rozenberg/UNISA Press.
12. OECD. (2008). *Tertiary education for the Knowledge Society Vol. 2: Special features: Equity, innovation, labour market, internationalisation* (p. 88). Paris: OECD.
13. Breen, R., Luijkx, R., Müller, W., & Pollack, R. (2010). Long-term trends in educational inequality in Europe: Class inequalities and gender differences. *European Sociological Review, 26*(1), 31–48. For arguments of persistent inequality see, for example, Miriam, D. (2009, March). Social diversity and democracy in higher education in the 21st century: Towards a feminist critique. *Higher Education Policy, 22*(1), 61–79; and Mickelson, R. A. (2009). Race, ethnicity, and education. In D. Plank, B. Schneider, & G. Sykes (Eds.), *Handbook of education policy research* (pp. 240–257). Washington, DC: American Educational Research Association.
14. Goldin, C., Katz, L. F., & Kuziemko, I. (2006). The homecoming of American college women: The reversal of the college gender gap. *Journal of Economic Perspectives, 20*(4), 134.
15. Marable, M. (2002). *Blacks in higher education: An endangered species.* Retrieved February 14, 2010, http://nathanielturner.com/blacksinhighereducation.htm

16. Freeman, C. E. (2004). *Trends in educational equity of girls and women: 2004* (p. 82). Washington, DC: US Department of Education, National Center for Education Statistics.

17. Freeman. (2004). *Trends in educational equity*, p. 82.

18. Marable. (2002). *Blacks in higher education*, p. 1.

19. Ibid.

20. Kaba, A. J. (2005). Progress of African Americans in higher education attainment: The widening gender gap and its current and future implications. *Education Policy Analysis Archives, 13*(25), 2.

21. Vital Statistics: Statistics that Measure the State of Racial Inequality (2009). *Journal of Blacks in Higher Education, 63*. Retrieved from http://www.jbhe.com/vital/63_index.html

22. Marable. (2002). *Blacks in higher education*, p. 2.

23. *Brown v. Board of Education.* (1954). 374 U.S. 483.

24. Griffin, R. W. (2008). *Management* (9th ed., p. 167). New York: Houghton Mifflin Company.

25. Ibid.

26. OECD. (2008). *Tertiary education for the knowledge society*, p. 74.

27. Ibid., p. 3.

28. Ibid., p. 88.

29. Ibid., p. 87.

30. Ibid., p. 89.

31. For an analysis of initiatives in India, Brazil and South Africa in addressing racial, gender, caste and social class inequalities, see Akoojee, S., & Nkomo, M. (2011, forthcoming). Widening equity and retaining efficiency, 118–125.

32. Akoojee & Nkomo. (2011). Widening equity and retaining efficiency.

33. KPMG Econtech. (March 2009). *Economic modeling of improved funding and reform arrangements for Australian universities.* A commissioned study by Universities Australia.

34. Bollinger, G. V. (2003). *Certiorari to the United States Court of Appeals for the Sixth Circuit, No. 02-241. Argued April 1, 2003—Decided June 23, 2003.* Retrieved January 10, 2010, http://www.law.cornell.edu/supct/html/02-241.ZS.html

35. Bowen, W. G., & Bok, D. (1998). *The shape of the river.* Princeton, NJ: Princeton University Press. For some reviews that disagree with Bowen's & Bok's analysis, see http://www.ceousa.org/content/view/290/99/

36. See Cloete, N., Fehnel, R., Maasen, P., Moja, T., Perold, H., & Gibbon, T. (Eds.). (2002). *Transformation in higher education: Global pressures and local realities* (p. 268). Cape Town: Juta and Company; OECD. (2008). *Reviews of national policies for education: South Africa* (p. 21). Paris: OECD Publications; Council on Higher Education. (2009). *Higher Education Monitor: Postgraduate Studies in South Africa.* HE Monitor No. 7. Center for Research on Science and Technology.

37. Malherbe, E. G. (1977). *Education in South Africa, Vol. II: 1923–1975* (p. 617). Cape Town: Juta & Company.

38. Pelzer, A. N. (Ed.). (1966). *Verwoerd speaks: Speeches 1948–1966* (p. 83). Johannesburg: APB Publishers.

39. Malherbe. (1977). *Education in South Africa*, p. 700; *Official year book of the Union and of Basutoland, Bechuanaland Protectorate, and Swaziland,* No. 12, 1929–1930 (p. 861). Pretoria: The Government Printing and Stationery Office. (Note that the 88% black population comprises what the government referred to as "Bantu, Asiatic and Mixed and Other").

40. Malherbe. (1977). *Education in South Africa*, p. 731.

41. Ibid.

42. Sayed, Y., Kanjee, A., & Nkomo, M. (2010). *Educational quality in South Africa* (p. 6). Cape Town: HSRC.

43. Akoojee & Nkomo. (Forthcoming). Widening equity and retaining efficiency.

44. The designation "African" is fraught with misunderstandings and distortions. It is appropriated, for example, by narrow nationalists in an essentialist sense to exclude others, even when they are entitled to be regarded as African under international law with reference to birth right and citizenship. It was adopted by the Afrikaners in South Africa in an act of

self-legitimization and, at the same time, stripping the majority of the black population of the right to call themselves "African." As used currently, it also suggests total disregard for current archeological, paleontological, and biological findings about the origins of homo sapiens in Africa, which would entitle all humanity to be called "African." For a more insightful critique of the concept "African," see Zeleza, P. T. (2006). The invention of African identities and languages: The discursive and developmental implications. In O. F. Arasanyin, & M. Pemberton (Eds.), *Selected proceedings of the 36th annual conference on African linguistics: Shifting the center of Africanism in language politics and economic globalization*. Somerville, MA: Cascadilla Proceedings Project.

45. Department of Education (MCHET). (2008, November 30). *Report of the ministerial committee on transformation and social cohesion and the elimination of discrimination in public higher education institutions* (p. 124). Pretoria: Government Press.
46. Ibid. Reproduced under Government Printer's Copyright Authority No. 11514 dated 04 November 2010
47. Ibid., p. 125. Reproduced under Government Printer's Copyright Authority No. 11514 dated 04 November 2010.
48. UL, University of Limpopo; UV, University of Venda; UZ, University of Zululand; UFH, University of Fort Hare; UWC, University of the Western Cape.
49. SU, Stellenbosch University; UP, University of Pretoria; NMMU, Nelson Mandela Metropolitan University; UFS, University of Free State; UNW, University of the North West; UJ, University of Johannesburg.
50. CPUT, Cape Peninsula University of Technology; DUT, Durban University of Technology; TUT, Tshwane University of Technology; UNISA, University of South Africa; VUT, Vaal University of Technology; WSUT, Walter Sisulu University of Technology; UJ, University of Johannesburg.
51. MCHET. (2008). *Report of the ministerial committee*, p. 125. Reproduced under Government Printer's Copyright Authority No. 11514 dated 04 November 2010.
52. Ibid., p. 126. Reproduced under Government Printer's Copyright Authority No. 11514 dated 04 November 2010.
53. OECD. (2008). *Reviews of national policies for education: South Africa*. Paris: OECD.
54. National Education Policy Investigation. (1993). *The framework report and final report summaries* (p. vii). Cape Town: Oxford University Press.
55. African National Congress (ANC). (2007) *Constitution of the South African Native Congress*. Retrieved December 15, 2009, http://www.anc.org.za/show.php?id=207.
56. ANC. (1943). *Bill of rights: Full citizenship rights and demands*. Retrieved from http://www.anc.org.za/ancdocs/history/claims.html
57. ANC. (December 1949). *Programme of action: Statement of policy adopted at the ANC annual conference 17 December 1949*. Retrieved January 2, 2010, http://www.anc.org.za/ancdocs/history/progact.htm
58. ANC. (1955). *The freedom charter*. Retrieved November 15, 2010, http://www.anc.org.za/show.php?include=docs/misc/1955/charter.html
59. Constitution of the Republic of South Africa. (1996). *Bill of rights*.
60. Constitution of the Republic of South Africa. (1996). *Bill of rights*.
61. Ibid.
62. National Commission on Higher Education, 1996.
63. Ibid.
64. Higher Education Act, 1997.
65. The National Plan for Higher Education, 2001.
66. Cloete et al. (2002). *Transformation in higher education,* p. 1.
67. Ibid.
68. Ibid., p. 268.
69. See, for example, Cross, M., Jansen, J., Ravjee, N., Shalem, Y., Backhouse, J., & Adam, F. (Forthcoming). *Higher education monitor: Access and retention in South African higher education – three case studies*. Pretori: Council on Higher Education.

70. Higgins, J. (2007). Institutional cultures as keyword. In *CHE review of higher education in South Africa: Selected themes* (p. 116). Pretoria: CHE. The MCHET report also dwells extensively on the alienation endured by black students at historically advantaged higher education institutions.

71. Mabokela, R. (1998). Black students on white campuses: Responses to increasing black enrollments at two South African universities. Ph.D. dissertation, University of Illinois at Urbana-Champaign.

72. Thaver, B. (2009). Diversity and research practices among academics in South African universities. *Perspectives in Education, 27*(27), 406–414.

73. Ibid., p. 406.

74. MCHET. (2008). *Report of the ministerial committee on transformation and social cohesion.*

75. For the Free State University Reitz incident, see http://toomuchcoffee.co.za/2008/02/27/free-state-university-racist-video/ (Retrieved 13 January 2010); also see Northwest University acts on Facebook racists. (2008, October 13). *Daily Higher Education News*; Thompson, C. (2008, October 9). University identifies 13 students in racist group. *Daily Higher Education News.*

76. MCHET. (2008). *Report of the ministerial committee*, p. 42.

77. Potgieter, C. (2002). *Academics on the move.* Pretoria: Centre for Higher Education Transformation.

78. Duncan, N. (2005, October 18). *"Race," racism and the university.* Inaugural lecture delivered at the University of the Witwatersrand, Johannesburg.

79. Mabokela. (1998). Black students on white campuses.

80. Thaver, L. (2006). "At home," institutional culture in higher education: Methodological considerations. *Perspectives in Education, 24*(1) 15–26; also see Tabane, R. (2010). *African and Indian learners' understandings of "at home" in a desegregated former house of delegates school: A case study.* Ph.D. dissertation, University of Pretoria.

81. UNDP. (2004). *Human development report 2004.*

82. See, for example, Galabawa, J. C. J., & Lwaitama, A. F. (2005). A comparative analysis of performance in Kiswahili and English as language of instruction at the secondary level in selected Tanzania schools. In B. Brock-Utne, Z. Desai, & M. Qorro (eds.), *LOITASSA research in progress* (pp. 139–159). Dar-es-Salaam: KAD Associates; Langehoven, K. R. (2005). Can mother tongue instruction contribute to enhancing scientific literacy? A look at grade 4 natural science classrooms in two projects schools in the Western Cape. In B. Brock-Utne, Z. Desai, & M. Qorro (Eds.), *LOITASSA research in progress* (pp. 282–292). Dare-es-Salaam, TZ: KAD Associates; Senkoro, F. E. (2005). Teaching in Kiswahili at university level: The case of Kiswahili Department at the University of Dar es Salaam. In B. Brock-Utne, Z. Desai, & M. Qorro (Eds.), *LOITASSA research in progress* (pp. 212–223). Dare-es-Salaam, TZ: KAD Associates; Brock-Utne, B. (2006). Learning through a familiar language versus learning through a foreign language: A look at some secondary school classrooms in Tanzania. In B. Brock-Utne, Z. Zubeida, & M. Qorro (Eds.), *Focus on fresh data on the language of instruction debate in Tanzania and South Africa* (pp. 19–40). Cape Town: African Minds; UNDP. (2004). *Human development report 2004.* Retrieved from http://hdr.undp.org/reports/global/2004/

83. MCHET. (2008). *Report of the ministerial committee*, p. 96.

84. Bantu Education is the inferior form of education that designed for blacks from 1953 to 1994. Many believe that nearly six decades later, changes in black education, even after the demise of apartheid, have not improved sufficiently.

85. Council on Higher Education. (2006). *Student access, successes and institutional cultures.* Interviews with students at the University of the Witwatersrand, Johannesburg.

86. A recent study by the Human Sciences Research Council found that in 2004 the failure rate in South African tertiary institutions was 30% among first-year students, the majority of whom are black and the first generation to attend university. See Letseka, M., & Maile, S. (2008). *High university drop-out rates: A threat to South Africa's future.* HSRC Policy Brief. The study attributes the high attrition rate mainly to poverty. However, the data from the University of

the Witwatersrand's curriculum study suggest that language is a significant variable that should be taken into account.

87. For a comprehensive treatment of the significance and complexity of language in multicultural societies, see UNDP. (2004). *Human development report 2004.*

88. A whole issue of *Social Dynamics* (Vol. 24, No. 2, 1998) was devoted to the debate.

89. Vught, V. (1991). *Autonomy and accountability in government/university relationships.* Washington, DC: World Bank.

90. Cloete et al. (2002). *Transformation in higher education,* p. 266.

91. Higgs P., van Wyk, B. (2008). The curriculum in an African context. Paper presented at 52nd annual conference of the Comparative and International Education Society, Teachers College, Colombia University, March 17–21, p. 5.

92. J. Jansen. (2009, October 16). *Inaugural speech of the 13th rector and vice-chancellor of the University of the Free State.* Bloemfontein, South Africa.

93. Ibid.

94. MCHET. (2008). *Report of the ministerial committee,* p. 51.

3

Increasing Gender Equity in Tertiary Science and Engineering Programs

LAURA PILOZZI-EDMONDS

Increasing gender equity in education has been a great concern in the international development community. Goal 3 of the United Nations' Millennium Development Goals is to "promote gender equity and empower women" with its associated target 3a aiming to "eliminate gender disparity in primary and secondary education preferably by 2005, and at all levels by 2015."[1] The efforts associated with this goal have been greatly successful and, as of 2006, gender equity in terms of girls' enrollment in relation to boys' enrollment is at 100% in developed regions and at 94% for developing regions for both primary and secondary education.[2]

Gender equity in tertiary education, either university education or postsecondary vocational training, shows a much more variable distribution however. Whereas some developed countries such as Canada, Denmark, France, and others have more women than men enrolled in tertiary education, this is far from being the case everywhere. In fact, only 60% of developed countries have achieved gender parity in higher education and, of the 38 developing countries for which UNESCO has data, only four had gender parity in higher education.[3]

Many studies have shown that encouraging young women to stay in school as long as possible has both private benefits, such as higher wages and higher household income, and public benefits, such as improvements to health, quality of life, and society.[4] Studies have found that higher education levels among women are associated with delayed age of marriage, lower fertility, greater use of contraception, delayed age of first childbirth, lower mortality rate of their offspring in early childhood, greater desire for smaller families, and increased use of health services, in comparison with less educated women.[5-7]

Increasing gender parity in tertiary education specifically has important benefits for improving women's empowerment. Research shows that increasing the number of female teachers is strongly correlated with the number of women high achievers in a classroom.[8] Increasing women's access to tertiary education can have the benefit of raising the status of women in society, forming women role models for younger generations, and creating women's rights advocates, thus improving gender equity in the wider society.[9]

Women's access to tertiary education is particularly problematic in the sciences, in which women are under-represented, even in high-income countries that have more women than men accessing university overall. In Canada, for example, the total percentage of female graduates from tertiary education was 60% in 2004, but only 30% of students who graduated from mathematics, computer, and information sciences programs, and 25% of those who graduated from architecture, engineering, and related technology programs that year were female.[10]

Many reasons have been brought forward to explain why women are below parity in the fields of science and engineering in tertiary education in the developing world. These include differences in preparation between males and females in science and mathematics at the secondary level, different career orientation choices, greater attrition of females in secondary education, parental influences, lack of social and financial support, and psychological obstacles to achievement such as sex-stereotyped occupational expectations and sex-stereotyped abilities in sciences and mathematics.[11-13]

The following section takes a closer look at the factors preventing women from accessing tertiary science education in the United Republic of Tanzania and is followed by the description of a program intended to improved women's enrollment, as well as achievement, in a university engineering program.

The Tanzanian Context

Education in Tanzania has improved significantly over the last decade, especially in terms of enrollment in primary and secondary schools. In 2002, the Ministry of Education and Vocational Training implemented the Primary Education Development Plan (PEDP) aimed at increasing enrollment rates in primary school (Standard I to VII), which brought the number of students from 4,875,764 students in 2001 to 8,316,925 in 2007.[14] It was then followed by the Secondary Education Development Plan (SEDP) in 2004, which brought secondary school (form I to VI) enrollment from 289,699 students in 2001 to 1,020,510 in 2007.[15] Interestingly, Table 3.1 shows that, throughout this dramatic increase in enrollment rates, gender equity seems to have been preserved, particularly at the primary education level.

Although girls and boys are enrolling to the same extent in primary school and early secondary school, the discrepancy in enrollment between boys and girls becomes more important during secondary school. The gender equity gap widens

Table 3.1 **Primary School Net Enrollment Rate in Percentage Points for Tanzania**[16]

| | *Year* | | |
	1999	*2002*	*2006*
F	50	73	97
M	49	75	98
Total	50	74	98

between form II and form III, and between form IV and form V (the end of O-level and the beginning of A-level).[17] The national examinations at the end of form II and form IV need to be passed for a student to access the next level of education. As shown in Table 3.2, which compares the enrollment numbers between the different grades of secondary school for the entire country at the passage between the 2006 and 2007 academic years, the percentage of students, both male and female, passing from form II to form III and from form IV to form V is lower than in other years.

A greater difference is seen between the percentage of girls passing and the percentage of boys passing during those critical periods. Indeed, only 68% of girls passed from form II to form III in 2007, whereas 79% of boys passed, and only 45% of girls passed from form IV to form V in 2007, whereas 47% of boys passed. The last column to the right in Table 3.2 shows how this difference in passage decreases the gender equity in enrollment over the different grades.

Even those girls who finish their secondary education have difficulty in accessing tertiary education, thus widening the gender disparity. Indeed, access to tertiary education is exam-based, and girls perform less well than boys in national exams. For example, in 2006, 68% and 70% of division I and II students[18] in form VI national examinations were male.[19] Therefore, when it comes to admission into the university, girls are below the ultimate admission cutoff more often than boys. In the academic year of 2002–2003, 24% of students enrolled at the University of Dar es Salaam were female. This situation is more dramatic in the science-oriented programs, such as those given by the College of Engineering and Technology (CoET) where, in 2002–2003, only 7.3% of students were female (see Table 3.5).

Profile of the Program

This case study focuses on a program addressing the inequity affecting young women in Tanzania in accessing quality science education at the tertiary level described above. The University of Dar es Salaam (UDSM)'s Special Pre-Entry

Table 3.2 **Enrollment in All Secondary Schools (Governmental and Non-governmental) in Tanzania[20]**

		# Students		
	Form	Male	Female	% Female
	I (2006)	126,650	116,709	48%
	II (2007)	137,921	127,066	48%
A-level	% Passing	>100%	>100%	
	II (2006)	101,745	97,716	49%
	III (2007)	80,403	66,707	45%
	% Passing	79%	68%	
	III (2006)	60,846	54,199	47%
	IV (2007)	57,553	48,989	46%
	% Passing	95%	90%	
	IV (2006)	41,651	30,729	42%
O-level	V (2007)	19,778	13,778	41%
	% Passing	47%	45%	
	V (2006)	16,288	11,492	41%
	VI (2007)	12,002	8,333	41%
	% Passing	74%	73%	

Program (SPEP) for the College of Engineering and Technology (CoET) has been running since 2004 and helps young women with poor science grades in secondary national exams to be admitted into the University's College of Engineering.

DESCRIPTION OF THE SPECIAL PRE-ENTRY PROGRAM

The SPEP at the UDSM, currently under funding from the Tanzania Education Authority but previously funded by the Carnegie Foundation, has been running since 2004; it is intended for female candidates wishing to join an undergraduate program in the CoET, but who do not have the necessary grades to be admitted. Students coming out of A-level national examinations at the end of form VI must have accumulated 5.5 points to be eligible for application into the University's many faculties and colleges.[21] As could be expected, the number of students who are eligible for application into the University is much greater than the number of places available in each degree program and, since admission is exam-based, a higher cutoff, usually of 10 and above, is artificially created.

To improve gender equity at the CoET, the UDSM Gender Center began the SPEP in 2004. The program led to an immediate increase in the percentage of female students to 15.5% in the academic year 2004–2005. The program achieved this increase in enrollment by allowing girls with low cumulative points coming out of form VI to have a chance to be admitted into the CoET by giving them 8 weeks of intensive, targeted training in engineering science, mathematics, chemistry, and communication skills. The CoET then reserves a certain number of places for admission in its different degree programs,[22] ranging from 59 to 95 depending on the year, for those girls who pass an examination at the end of the training (see Table 3.3).[23]

The underlying assumption of the program is that some girls may underperform in form VI because of the limited educational opportunities at the secondary level. The program therefore aims to allow the girls to benefit from targeted, quality education in the subjects most important for success in an engineering degree program. Beneficiaries describe that, in essence, this program gives a chance to girls who performed poorly for a variety of reasons in form VI national exams to show that they can perform well in the appropriate environment.

To be eligible to apply for the SPEP, girls must have accumulated at least 4.5 points coming out of form VI and have done their A-levels in specific combinations: physics, chemistry, and mathematics (PCM); physics, geography, and mathematics (PGM); or physics, chemistry, and biology (PCB). In this way, the program not only gives a second chance to girls who were below the admission cutoff of the CoET, ranging from 6 to 13 depending on the degree program and the year, and who were also below the University cutoff for application (5.5), but also to girls from other A-level combinations, since CoET normally accepts applicants from PCM only. The program is also open to girls who did not go to A-level after form IV, but opted for a Technical College in an engineering field and got an average of C or higher in their Full Technician Certificate (FTC). Upon application, these girls must submit by a specified date in June a short letter of introduction indicating

Table 3.3 **Application Data for the Special Pre-Entry Program in the College of Engineering and Technology (CoET)**[24]

Academic Year	# Applicants	# Admitted into Pre-Entry training	# Admitted into CoET after Pre-Entry training
2004–2005	217	59	59
2005–2006	214	73	70
2006–2007	210	98	98
2007–2008	207	108	95
2008–2009	223	67	UK

their degree of choice, their form VI final grades (or FTC grades), and their birth certificate.

The selection of girls for admission in the pre-entry program is done by the Gender Center and is based on exam scores within the pool of applicants. The girls who have cumulative points higher than 7.5 or 8 are usually considered overqualified for the pre-entry program, and their application is sent to the CoET and recommended for direct admission. The Gender Center receives the applications and makes a preliminary selection, which it then sends to the University Senate for approval. The number of applications has varied from 207 to 223, and the number of admissions from 59 to 108 depending on the year (see Table 3.3).

Once girls are admitted into the pre-entry program, all training costs, including tuition and accommodation expenses, as well as 50% of their meal expenses are covered by the Gender Center with funds from the Carnegie Foundation. Also, to ensure that the girls receive supplementary academic support, the Gender Center provides extra tutorial classes at the end of each semester to review the more difficult subjects.

A HOLISTIC APPROACH

The SPEP is exceptional because of the comprehensiveness of its efforts to create the right environment for the pre-entry girls to perform once in CoET. Dr. Mukangara, the director of the Gender Center, described some of the important obstacles keeping girls from achieving in university as the "perseverance of sexual harassment in the university, the gender insensitivity of the staff, the glaring imbalances in terms of men and women around the campus especially in the academics."[25] In addition to giving the girls pre-entry training and admission into CoET, the Gender Center has given these girls the tools to perform well in CoET, such as textbooks and supplementary classes. It has also endeavored to develop integrated programs and initiatives that support the pre-entry girls both in a direct way and indirectly by creating a gender sensitive environment at the University. Figure 3.1 provides a schematic representation of the different activities and programs conducted by the Gender Center, and the direction of their impact on the SPEP.

The SPEP program is part of the Gender Center's affirmative action programs to increase gender equity in the University. Another component is their university-wide Female Undergraduate Scholarship Program (FUSP), started in 2001 and funded by the Carnegie Foundation. This program helps from 46 to 70 girls, depending on the year (see Table 3.4 below), to be admitted into their program of choice by lobbying university departments to reserve places for girls with lower grades from lower socioeconomic backgrounds, and it provides them with a full scholarship and up to three books a semester.

Since the onset of the SPEP in 2004, a yearly average of 62% of FUSP scholarships were given to SPEP students.[26] This derives from the fact that government

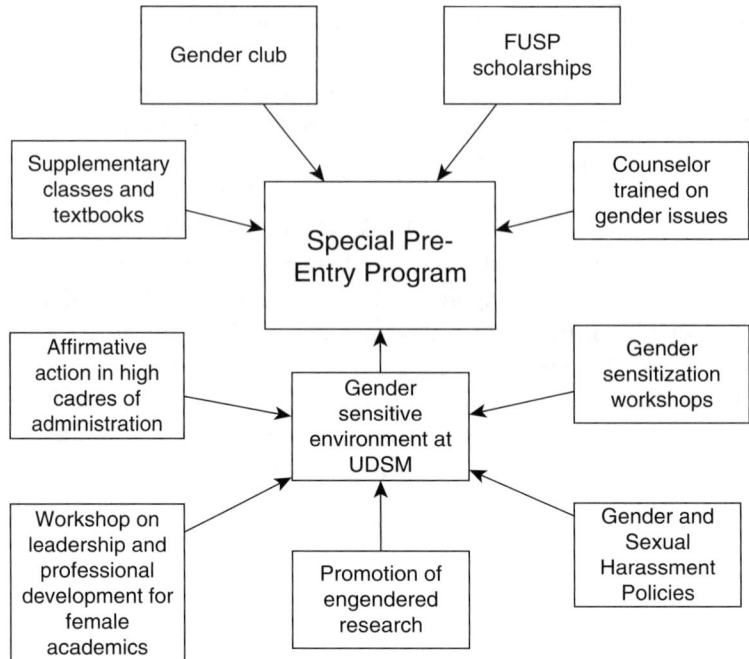

Figure 3.1 Gender Center activities and programs and their relation to the Special Pre-Entry Program.

loans for higher education are distributed based on exam scores, and most of the girls in SPEP would not qualify to receive support. Statistics from the Tanzanian Higher Education Students Loans Board indicate that 71% of loans for tertiary education were given to males and only 29% to females for the academic year 2006–2007.[27] The greater use of the FUSP initiative to help SPEP girls stems from

Table 3.4 **Number of Students Admitted to the University of Dar es Salaam (UDSM) Under a Female Undergraduate Scholarship Program (FUSP) Scholarship**[28]

Academic Year	# Admitted into UDSM under FUSP
2001–2002	50
2002–2003	46
2003–2004	56
2004–2005	65
2005–2006	70
2006–2007	56

an understanding that those who enter through SPEP are often disadvantaged socioeconomically, and it is crucial to secure their tuition and board to ensure that they perform to their full potential once in CoET.

Another affirmative action measure at the University, which could eventually affect the SPEP girls, is aimed at increasing the number of women in high administrative positions. This measure, started in 2006, dictates that when a dean of a faculty or a director of an institute must be replaced, if there is a woman in the top three choices for hire, she will be given the position. In an interview, the director of the Gender Center indicated that the current directors of the Faculties of Commerce, Science, and Education were hired through this measure. This measure potentially has the benefit of encouraging young women to stay in academia since the director believes that "the gender issues that have been established at this university are first and foremost about the lack of upward mobility in the academic staff."[29] The Gender Center also developed a workshop on leadership personnel and professional development of female academics that was given last year and in which 25 staff participated.

The Gender Center has put in place a number of other initiatives aimed at providing support for girls under FUSP and SPEP and at creating gender awareness on campus among all students. These include training professional counselors on gender issues and creating a gender club, now with 2,600 members, both male and female, in which students support each other and design gender equity–promoting activities. One example of the activities of the Gender Club aimed at promoting gender equity on campus is the creation of two plays by the students that portray the reality of the challenges that female students can face on campus. Another of the main activities of the gender club is to travel to rural secondary schools to inform girls about the availability of FUSP and SPEP at the university.

Overall, the main task of the Gender Center is seen as mainstreaming gender into UDSM governance and administration, including its policies, programs and procedures, and organizational culture. Ultimately, gender mainstreaming would provide a favorable environment for females to participate as much as males do in the University. To achieve gender mainstreaming, the Gender Center is involved in reviewing major current UDSM policies and programs with a gender perspective. In 2005, they helped develop an anti-sexual harassment policy for the University, and did the same for a gender policy in 2006. The Gender Center is also involved in promoting gendered research at the University, which means both increasing the number of women in research projects by helping them access grants, and ensuring that research conducted is designed to benefit both men and women equally. Finally, the Gender Center is heavily involved in the gender sensitization of members of the governing council, top administrators, college principals, deans and directors, and heads of departments at the University. In the words of the acting director of the Gender Center, "as you are bringing affirmative action into play simultaneously you have to empower those who are going to oppose, particularly men, by sensitizing them and making them appreciate it."[30]

Evidence of Success

In this analysis, the success of SPEP is measured in terms of how it increases gender equity and decreases discrimination within CoET from both qualitative and quantitative data. Qualitative results are based on semi-structured interviews and examine the perception of different actors on how the pre-entry girls are performing compared to direct-entry students within the college, on how discrimination toward women in the program has decreased, and on how the program has impacted its beneficiaries. The quantitative results are derived from raw data on attendance and performance of students of CoET from the 2007–2008 academic year, and their analysis is conducted in terms of enrollment and performance.

QUALITATIVE RESULTS

Performance

All the beneficiaries interviewed were either currently undergoing their 8-week pre-entry training or were currently pursuing a degree in CoET. They stated that they had performed well in the sciences in secondary school, but finished form VI with poor exam results. Consequently, before applying to the pre-entry program, most had applied to a university program and had been refused admission. Some of the girls explained that they performed poorly on the form IV national exams because their professors did not finish the A-level syllabus. All the interviewed beneficiaries of the SPEP also said that the 8-week pre-entry training helped them perform better once in CoET by giving them the necessary background academic knowledge, and that it may have acted as an adjustment period to a new environment.

All the beneficiaries interviewed who were in their third or fourth year in a CoET degree program, and most of the faculty members interviewed, agreed that they could not distinguish between pre-entry and direct-entry students in terms of performance in the classroom. As one student stated, "most were opposed to us. But they found out that we are good and better than the boys. So they said oh this can work."[31] In fact, the majority of faculty members interviewed declared that some of their best students entered through SPEP. The acting CoET principal pointed out that some girls from the program performed so well that they are currently working as teaching assistants or laboratory assistants in the college. According to a chemical engineering professor who teaches during the pre-entry training and in the degree program, and who has worked as a secondary school teacher in the past, most pre-entry girls work very hard once in the CoET degree programs because they take this second chance at a tertiary education very seriously. In an interview, he commented that "We see a group of girls who are highly ambitious."[32]

Overall, however, college administrators, faculty members, and Gender Center staff admitted that they did not know for certain that pre-entry girls as a group were performing as well as direct-entry students because no analysis of the performance has been made. The Gender Center admitted that they often faced doubts from university administrators as to whether the girls entering the College through the SPEP were keeping up with their male and female classmates who were admitted through the normal merit-based process.

Most of the beneficiaries interviewed who are currently studying at the CoET came from the chemical and process engineering program, which has a high number of female students, many of whom gained admission through the pre-entry program. These girls believed that they were doing well in this program in part because of female peer support; a third-year female student said: "We had reading groups and helped each other a lot . . . each of us has a solution, and then we combine the solution and give each other help. So it's like give yourselves hope."[33] They added that some of the girls who had entered the college with them through pre-entry and had been admitted to programs in which they were greatly outnumbered by male students tended to perform less well, which may indicate that a critical mass of female students is needed to create a conducive environment to achieve gender equity in terms of performance.

Discrimination

One of the most striking results of the SPEP program is the change in cultural attitudes that has occurred at the college, as indicated by interviewees. Understandably, SPEP girls in the first cohort faced the greatest challenges. Because the academic environment strongly values merit, they admitted that, in their first year, some of their male classmates and teachers had negative reactions to their presence. There was an overall feeling that the girls had gotten into the College by a "back door" and that they would lower the standard of the engineering education. Some of the girls were even called names in Swahili meaning they were of "low quality" by their male classmates. However, by the second year, after the beneficiaries had performed as well as their male counterparts, interviewees agreed that most of the negative reactions stopped.

The faculty members and administrators of the college also describe a similar change, and interviews indicated that the program is accepted and well regarded now by all members of CoET. Indeed, few have anything critical to say about it. One of the key elements in the successful integration of the SPEP into this historically male-dominated college is the fact that the program was valued early on by CoET administrators. Gender Center Director Dr. Mukangara stated that the principal of the college was very receptive to the program, and in fact, the running of the program has been completely taken up by the college in the last few years. In describing why they began SPEP at the college, Acting Principal Dr. Katima, explained: "Our belief is that engineering is supposed to solve societal problems, and, in Tanzania, we have almost 50% females, and you cannot pretend that men will always understand female problems, and so we saw that there was a need to increase the ratio of female students in our programs."[34]

Interviews with administrators, faculty members, and male students left the impression that CoET was a place that was very sensitive to the obstacles girls face in performing well in secondary education and accessing tertiary education, and that it was also sensitive to the importance of the SPEP in increasing gender equity and decreasing discrimination. As one interviewee suggested, the increase in female enrollment in the college through SPEP and the decreasing discrimination toward women may be responsible for the rise in the number of girls who enter the college based on exam score without SPEP, thus further contributing to the improvement of gender equity in enrollment.

Impact on Beneficiaries

Another subtler impact of SPEP is that "it empowers girls and gives them opportunities,"[35] as mentioned by a third-year CoET student who entered through pre-entry. Some of the girls interviewed who were currently undergoing the pre-entry training believed that they would probably not be able to access university were it not for this program. Although engineering was not the first choice of study for all the girls interviewed who had entered the college through pre-entry, all of them expressed pride in their degree. Many acknowledged a higher level of self-confidence, and many of the beneficiaries interviewed in their last year of study showed an ambition to further their studies at the master's degree level.

QUANTITATIVE RESULTS

Enrollment

As mentioned above, SPEP has significantly increased the enrollment of girls in CoET since it began in 2004. As we can see in Table 3.5, the program increased the female presence in the college from 7.7% to 24.5% in the 4 years since its

Table 3.5 **Student Admission into the College of Engineering and Technology (CoET)**[36]

	# Students		
Academic Year	Female	Male	% Female
2002–2003	86	1099	7.3
2003–2004	95	1142	7.7
2004–2005	198	1172	15.5
2005–2006	276	1165	19.1
2006–2007	383	1316	22.5
2007–2008	386	1187	24.5

Table 3.6 **Percent of Enrolled Students for the Academic Year 2007–2008 who are female, who entered through pre-entry (both coming from A-Level and from a technical college), and who entered through direct-entry for each of the four grades in the College of Engineering and Technology (CoET) degree**

Grade	% Pre-Entry	% Direct-Entry	% Female
Y1	19	8	27
Y2	13	12	25
Y3	11	10	21
Y4	11	15	26

inception, which is undeniably an improvement in gender equity in a college known for its traditionally very low female student population.

Table 3.6 was derived from the list of enrolled students for the academic year 2007–2008, and shows the percent of female students and the percent of pre-entry females (both coming from A-Level and from a technical college) for each of the 4 years in the CoET degree. The advantage of looking at each of the 4 years in the CoET degree for the past academic year is that, since there have only been 4 years in the program, this provides a good overview of what the program has accomplished as a whole so far.

The results from this table are consistent with those in Table 3.5 (although Table 3.6 gives the percentages of female students in all 4 years of CoET per academic year) in that the percentage of female students has been increasing steadily since the start of the program in 2004 (note that Y4 corresponds to the class that began in the 2004–2005 academic year). Table 3.6 also shows that most of the increase in the percentage of female students has been due to an increase in the enrollment of students from the pre-entry program. In fact, the percent of female students entering directly in the CoET who have qualified on their own merits has decreased. This decrease, however, is due to the increase in students in the college and not due to a drop in the absolute number of girls who have been admitted directly.

Indeed, if we look at Table 3.5, in the academic year 2003–2004, 1,142 males and 95 females (all direct-entry since there was no SPEP then) were enrolled in the College, whereas in the academic year 2007–2008 there were 1,264 males and 187 females who entered directly. This draws attention to the fact to which some of the interviewees alluded, which is that SPEP may be responsible for increasing the number of girls who enter the college based on exam score without SPEP, further contributing to the increase in gender equity in enrollment. Presumably, SPEP may accomplish this by increasing the awareness of the engineering degree through its advertisement of SPEP for CoET in the newspapers and through the outreach program conducted by the Gender Club. SPEP also increases the number of girls who apply directly to CoET by recommending for direct-entry all the girls who have applied to the SPEP program but have been deemed overqualified. Most importantly, in increasing the number of girls in engineering, the SPEP program may be raising the number of girls who enroll directly by changing the perception of potential applicants that engineering is a discipline for men.

The increase in female enrollment over the past 4 years has not been consistent throughout the different degree programs of the CoET, however. Certain programs, such as chemical and process engineering and industrial engineering and management, have almost reached gender equity with female admissions of 44% in the 2007 academic year, and 45% in 2008 (with 28% and 36% coming from SPEP, respectively). One degree program, food and biochemical engineering, had 59% female students enrolled in the 2007–2008 academic year (with 50% coming from SPEP). On the other hand, civil and structural engineering, mining engineering, mechanical engineering, and electrical engineering had the lowest female enrollment in the college with 11%, 11%, 13%, and 13%, respectively. Mining engineering only had 5% female enrollment among its first-year students.

Performance

As discussed in the qualitative section, there are some doubts among university administration as to whether the girls entering the college through the SPEP are keeping up with those of their male and female classmates who were admitted through the merit-based process. Figure 3.2 addresses this issue by comparing the performance (in terms of grade point average [GPA]) between girls admitted through the pre-entry program (further broken down into pre-entry girls coming from A-levels and pre-entry girls coming from a technical college in a related field) and boys and girls in the same program and year who were directly admitted for all 4 years (1 to 4) of the engineering program in 2007–2008.

The figure shows that, in their first year at CoET, females who entered through the SPEP (F A-Level and F FTC) have lower performances in terms of GPA than do females (F DE) and males (M) who have entered directly, with females coming from a technical college (FTC) entering through the pre-entry faring the least well, as has also been suggested by some of the interviewed faculty members of CoET. Interestingly, the disparity in performance decreases with years in the program. My assumption is that this figure, which shows the distribution of the results of all 1,683 students enrolled in the 2007–2008 academic year in the 4 years of the engineering degree, can be used to represent the evolution within CoET of those girls who entered through the SPEP.

The decrease in difference of the mean over the 4 years of the program between the pre-entry girls and the other students becomes no significant difference at all by the fourth year (the standard deviation for all the means is similar and averages 0.6) demonstrates that the pre-entry girls had the potential to perform just

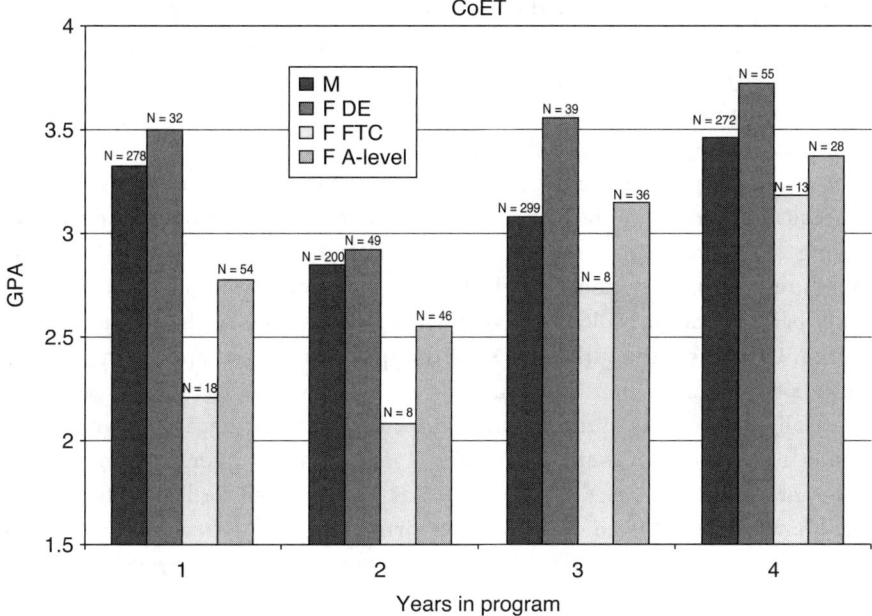

Figure 3.2 Grade point averages (GPAs) as a function of year in any degree program of the College of Engineering and Technology (CoET) in the academic year 2007–2008. M, male students; F DE, female students admitted through direct entry; F FTC, female students admitted from a technical college in to the pre-entry program; F A-Level, female students admitted from A-level into the pre-entry program.

as well as the males and females who had entered the college based on initial exam scores. Thus, the low performance of these girls upon application is due to the non-conducive context they faced in their earlier education. If provided the right environment, they can perform just as well as their peers.

Importantly, this demonstrates that the program managed to not only increase gender equity in terms of enrollment in the CoET, but also in terms of academic performance. The girls admitted through the "back door" of the SPEP are therefore not lowering the standards of the college.

Of course, the situation at the level of each degree program does not necessarily reflect the trend of the college as a whole. It is interesting to note that in those programs showing consistently higher percentages of female pre-entry students enrolled—such as food and biochemical engineering, chemical and process engineering, civil and water resources engineering, and industrial engineering management—the pre-entry students are doing as well as the boys throughout the degree, and end up surpassing them in terms of performance in the final year. This may be due to the fact that a critical mass of pre-entry girls is necessary for them to perform within a program because it may increase their acceptance within that program as well as their mutual cooperation in studying. This tendency might also result from the fact that there are too few pre-entry girls in the other programs for a clear trend to be detected at the individual program level.

Figure 3.3 compares the performance in terms of GPA of pre-entry girls coming from A-levels between those who were sponsored through FUSP and those who were not. The figure seems to indicate that being or not being supported by a FUSP scholarship may not have a great impact on the girls' performance. This may be because, according to the FUSP scholarship eligibility requirements, only those coming from poor socioeconomic backgrounds received a FUSP scholarship. Therefore, presumably, the non-FUSP recipients came from stronger socioeconomic backgrounds and did not have to struggle with financial issues during their studies. Of course, the girls who have dropped out do not appear in this data because their grades were not available, so it is possible that those struggling financially had serious difficulty with performance.[37] Another important consideration is that fact that there were no FUSP scholarship recipients among the year 1 pre-entry students since this program was discontinued for lack of funds. This could have contributed to the poorer performance of pre-entry girls in year 1 as seen in Figure 3.2, compared to their *consoeurs* in later years. However, this could

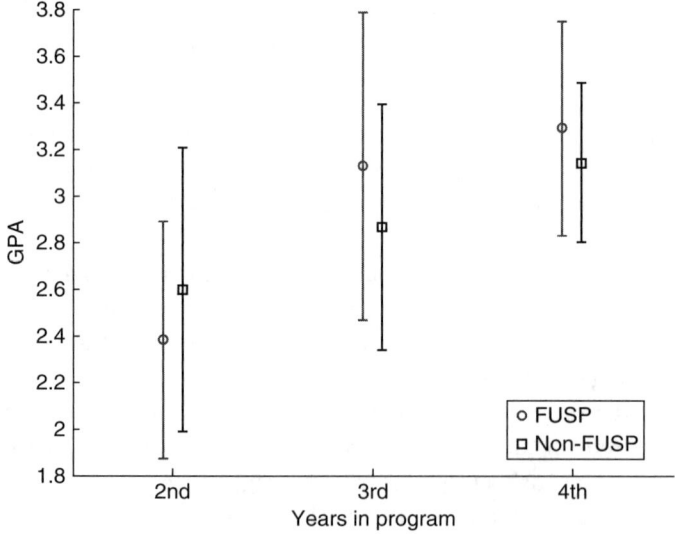

Figure 3.3 Grade point averages (GPAs) as a function of year in any degree program of the College of Engineering and Technology (CoET) in the academic year 2007–2008 with standard deviation error bars. FUSP, female students who entered through pre-entry and who are sponsored through a FUSP scholarship; Non-FUSP, female students who entered through pre-entry and who are not sponsored through a FUSP scholarship.

also be simply attributable to the fact that the benefits of the program take time to work their effects on beneficiaries' grades, as we have seen earlier.

Remaining Challenges

The SPEP did not increase enrollment for girls in the college of engineering equally in all of its degree programs. In the previous section, we saw that, since the beginning of SPEP, certain degree programs, such as chemical and process engineering, and industrial engineering and management, have almost reached gender equity, whereas others, such as civil and structural engineering, mining engineering, mechanical engineering, and electrical engineering, have particularly low female enrollment and take very few SPEP girls each year. We also saw that girls tend to perform as well as boys in those programs in which the enrollment nears equity, and that they do not perform nearly as well in those degree programs in which they are not well represented. This may indicate that a program needs a critical mass of female students to create a conducive environment for gender equity in terms of performance. The CoET still needs to expand that conducive environment from a subgroup of its degree programs to the entire college.

Moreover, some of the pre-entry girls currently enrolled in CoET believed that one of the main weaknesses of the program is that it is the only one of its kind currently being conducted at UDSM. Thus, a certain number of girls applied to the SPEP at CoET because they had no other options. The field of engineering might not have been their first choice of study. Perhaps because of this, or for other reasons, not all the girls do well once admitted into their CoET degree programs, and some of them drop out along the way.

Indeed, another challenge facing the SPEP is the greater discontinuation rate for those girls entering into engineering through this program than for male and female students who have entered directly (8%, 3%, and 4%, respectively). Some of the CoET professors believed that there were some girls who had come through the pre-entry program for whom the 8-week training was not enough to reach the level of basic sciences needed to perform in engineering, and these girls consequently dropped out by the second year of the program. Similarly, all the girls interviewed who were in their third or fourth year in a CoET degree program and who had gone through the pre-entry declared that they had worked very hard to stay in the program and knew of other pre-entry girls who failed along the way because of their inability to keep up with the material.

Finally, an important challenge facing the SPEP program is the termination of the FUSP in 2007 because of the end of the Carnegie Foundation grant covering this program. The CoET and Gender Center were not able to find a new sponsor for this program at the time this study was completed and, although the data in the previous section do not support that SPEP girls with FUSP funding perform significantly better than those without, it is still considered an important element for the success of the program since many girls from low socioeconomic backgrounds could not participate in the program otherwise.

Conclusion

The central finding from this case study is that poor grades at the end of secondary school national exams don't reflect young women's potential to perform well in tertiary education. By their last year of study in engineering, girls coming from the pre-entry program, and therefore with a far worse performance in A-level than their peers who entered on merit, are on par with the rest of the class in terms of performance. Therefore, policies should ensure that girls receive quality education at the secondary school level and are given the gender-sensitive environment necessary for them to develop to their full potential.

PROVIDING QUALITY SECONDARY EDUCATION

The Millennium Development Goal number 3 to "Promote gender equality and empower women" recommends the development of policies aimed at reducing girls' domestic responsibilities, reducing early pregnancy and marriages, increasing the number of female teachers to act as role models for young girls, providing curricula that are gender-sensitive, instituting gender sensitization programs for teachers and school administrators, ensuring safe transportation to school for girls, and providing separate school sanitation facilities for girls and boys.[38]

In their Education For All global monitoring report, UNESCO recommends that policies to promote quality education should concentrate on: "establishing appropriate goals for the curriculum, developing relevant content, using time well, ensuring that teaching styles are effective, carefully considering the language of instruction and developing a sound assessment policy . . . and enabling inputs that indirectly support quality teaching and learning: the supply, distribution and use of learning materials and a secure, accessible physical environment with appropriate facilities."[39]

These recommendations clearly address the problems in accessing quality secondary education that might be responsible for girls' underperformance in A-level national examinations. To these policy recommendations, one should also add that public awareness should be raised in the schools and in the community to encourage young women to engage and perform well in the sciences.

CREATING A CONDUCIVE ENVIRONMENT FOR PERFORMANCE IN TERTIARY EDUCATION

Policies that aim to increase women's enrollment in university, particularly in science-oriented programs, should include provisions to ensure that these women will have the conducive environment needed to perform to their full potential once enrolled, such as those in the program presented in this case study. Some of the key measures from the SPEP program are the pre-entry training that enables female applicants to catch up on material they might have missed in secondary school, as well as tutorial courses at the end of each semester; scholarships for those coming from low socioeconomic backgrounds; and efforts to provide a gender-sensitive environment at the university through gender mainstreaming initiatives.

Findings from this case study also indicate that creating a conducive environment for performance in tertiary education includes enrolling a critical mass of female students. We saw that those engineering programs with the most female students were also those where they performed best. Moreover, the program should be extended to other faculties to avoid having girls apply to the SPEP at CoET because they have no other options for accessing university.

ACKNOWLEDGMENTS

I would like to thank Dr. Jody Heymann, Katharine Markham Piper, and Magdalena Barrera from the McGill Institute of Health and Social Policy for the opportunity for doing this case study. You have shown incredible dedication and flexibility, and I greatly appreciate it. I would also like to thank Dr. Fanella Mukangara and Ave-Maria Semakafu from the Gender Center at UDSM for their time; I strongly admire your commitment. I would also like to extend my gratitude to Drs. Katima and Nalitolela, from the College of Engineering and Technology, for their time and their invaluable assistance. Finally, I would like to thank my mother, Hélène, my father, Frank, and my partner, Martin, for their unremitting support in all my endeavors.

NOTES

1. UN. (2008). *The millennium development goals report*. New York: UN. Retrieved July 2008, http://www.un.org/millenniumgoals/pdf/The%20Millennium%20Development%20Goals%20Report%202008.pdf
2. UN. (2008). *Millennium development goals*.
3. UNESCO. (2005). *Education for all global monitoring report 2005*. Paris: UNESCO. Retrieved July 2008, http://unesdoc.unesco.org/images/0013/001373/137333e.pdf
4. Jacobs, J. A. (1996). Gender inequality and higher education. *Annual Review of Sociology, 22*, 153–185.
5. Jacobs. (1996). Gender inequality.
6. Cleland, J., & van Ginneken, J. (1998). Maternal education and child survival in developing countries: The search for pathways of influence. *Social Science and Medicine, 27*, 1357–1368.
7. Schultz, T. P. (1993). Returns to women's education. In E. M. King, & M. A. Hill (Eds.), *Women's education in developing countries: Barriers, benefits and policies* (p. 352). Baltimore: Johns Hopkins University Press.
8. Tidball, M. E. (1986). Baccalaureate origins of recent natural science doctorates. *Journal of Higher Education, 57*(6), 606–620.

9. Jacobs. (1996). Gender inequality.
10. Council of Ministers of Education, Canada & Statistics Canada. (2007). *Education indicators in Canada: Report of the Pan-Canadian education indicators program 2007*. Ottawa: Canadian Education Statistics Council.
11. Jacobs. (1996). Gender inequality.
12. Ethington, C. A., & Wolfle, L. M. (1998). Women's selection of quantitative undergraduate fields of study: Direct and indirect influences. *American Educational Research Journal, 25*, 157–175.
13. Ware, N. C., & Lee, V. E. (1988). Sex differences in choice of college science majors. *American Educational Research Journal, 25*(4), 593–614.
14. The Ministry of Education and Vocational Training. (2007). *Basic education statistics in Tanzania (2006–2007)* (p. 93). Dar es Salaam, TZ: Ministry of Education and Vocational Training.
15. Ministry of Education. (2007). *Basic education*.
16. UNESCO Institute for Statistics. (n.d.). *Education in United Republic of Tanzania*. Paris: UNESCO. Retrieved July 2008, http://stats.uis.unesco.org/unesco/TableViewer/document.aspx?ReportId=121&IF_Language=eng&BR_Country=7620&BR_Region=40540
17. The structure of the Tanzanian education system is based on the British model. Primary education is a compulsory 7-year cycle that runs from Standard I to Standard VII and begins at age 7. At the end of Standard VII there is a national exam, the results of which are used for selection of students into secondary education. Secondary education consists of two consecutive cycles, the Ordinary level (O-level) consisting of Form I to IV and the Advanced level (A-level) consisting of Form V and VI. At the end of Form IV and Form VI there are national examinations, the results of which are used to select students to advance to the next educational level. Some of the A-level institutions are segregated by sex, others are not. Out of 24,813 students taking the form VI exam in 2007, 7,127 were from boys-only schools, 4,382 were from girls-only schools and 13,304 were from co-ed schools. Among these, the male students had a failure rate of 4.14% failure from boys-only schools and 3.87% from co-ed schools. On the other hand, the female students had a failure rate of 1.29% in girl-only schools and 2.47% in co-ed schools. The data for Form IV national examinations follow the same trend. From The Ministry of Education and Vocational Training. (2007). *Basic education statistics in Tanzania (2003–2007)* (p. 63). Dar-es-Salaam, TZ: Ministry of Education.
18. In Tanzania, the scores obtained by students in national examinations are divided into five categories, divisions I, II, III, IV and failed, in decreasing order of performance. As a general rule, students must aim to be in division I or II in order to be competitive when applying to a tertiary education program.
19. The Ministry of Education and Vocational Training. (2007). *Basic education statistics in Tanzania (2002–2006)*.
20. Ibid.
21. The score is calculated by adding the grades the student got in each principal subject, usually three, taken during A-levels. An A in a subject contributes 5 points to the total score, a B contributes 4 points, a C contributes 3 points, a D contributes 2 points, an E contributes 1 point, an F contributes no points, and supplementary subjects, which are pass or fail, contribute 0.5 point. For example, a girl who took a PCB (Physics, Chemistry, and Biology) combination in A-level with a general studies course as a supplemental who got a D in each of her subjects would end up with a grade of 6.5.
22. The 15 degree programs of the CoET are Computer Engineering and Information Technology (CI), Telecommunication Engineering, Electrical Engineering (TE), Electrical Power Engineering (EP), Civil and Structural Engineering (ST), Civil and Transportation Engineering (CT), Civil and Water Resource Engineering (CW), Mechanical Engineering (ME), Electromechanical Engineering (EM), Industrial Engineering and Management (IM), Production Engineering (PD), Food and Biochemical Engineering (FB), Mining Engineering (MN), Mineral Processing (MP), Electrical Engineering (EE), and Chemical and Process Engineering (CP).

23. Actually, the Gender Center submits the results of all of the girls at the end of the training and the top three program choices of the girls. This is technically a recommendation for admission, and the CoET is free to choose whom it admits, but it usually admits all girls who pass. The likelihood that a girl will get her first choice of degree program depends on her grades since admission is merit-based. The number of places in each degree program allocated to pre-entry girls varies widely since it depends on the number of vacant places it has in each degree program following the normal admission process.

24. University of Dar-es-Salaam Gender Center. (n.d.). *Details of special pre-entry programme for female students in faculty of Science and College of Engineering and Technology (CoET), from 1997/1998–2005/2006 academic years* (p. 6). Dar-es-Salaam, TZ: University of Dar-es-Salaam Gender Center.

25. Fanella Mukangara (Director of Gender Center of the University of Dar-es-Salaam, TZ). Interview, August 1, 2008.

26. For 2007/2008, no FUSP scholarships were distributed and there were none in the year in which this report was written either, because of lack of funding.

27. Higher Education Student Loans Board. (2008). *Table of number of students given loans and amount loaned from 2005/06 to 2006/2007* (p. 1). Dar-es-Salaam, TZ: Higher Education Student Loans Board.

28. University of Dar-es-Salaam Gender Center. (n.d.). *Details of special pre-entry programme for female students,* p. 6.

29. Mukangara, Interview, August 1, 2008.

30. Dr. Katima (acting Director of the CoET). Interview, July 17, 2008.

31. Female pre-entry student in her fourth year. Interview, July 31, 2008.

32. Dr. Akwilapo (Professor of chemical engineering, CoET). Interview, July 23, 2008.

33. Female pre-entry student in her fourth year. Interview, July 28, 2008.

34. Katima, Interview July 17, 2008.

35. Female pre-entry student in her third year. Interview, August 5, 2008.

36. University of Dar-es-Salaam Gender Center. (n.d.). *Details of special pre-entry programme for female students,* p. 6.

37. It is important to note that pre-entry girls have a higher dropout percentage over all four levels of the 2007/2008 academic year than the male and female students who have entered directly into the College. In this analysis, a dropout student is a student who in the final grading sheet for the academic year 2007/2008 had the mention of discontinued studies or postponed studies, either due to insufficient grades, sickness, or other. However, as indicated in the description of the research methodology, there are no grades or remarks due to unpaid fees for 16.5% of the males and 8% of the females.

38. UN. *Millennium development goals: Goal 3 fact sheet: Promote gender equity and empower women.* New York: United Nations. Retrieved July 2008, http://www.un.org/millenniumgoals/2008highlevel/pdf/newsroom/Goal%203%20FINAL.pdf

39. UNESCO. (2005). *Education for all global monitoring report.*

Appendix 1: Methodology
Case Study Approach

This case study was selected in the context of the McGill Institute for Health and Social Policy's Fellowship Program, which aims to conduct case studies on policies or programs whose goal is to increase equity or decrease discrimination. The United Republic of Tanzania was chosen as the site for a case study on successful gender equity policies because the country underwent a sharp increase in enrollment in the last 10 years (see Table 3.1) while maintaining gender equity in the classroom. After in-country groundwork, the case study focused on a specific program that showed success in increasing gender equity and decreasing discrimination in access to quality science education at the tertiary level.

Data Collection
QUALITATIVE DATA

Qualitative data on the education system in Tanzania and on SPEP at UDSM was collected in the form of semi-structured interviews over a period of 8 weeks in the city of Dar es Salaam, Tanzania. Semi-structured interviews were used with open-ended questions to provide flexibility to explore different issues with the participants. The interviews ranged from 5 minutes to 1 hour and 30 minutes, with the average interview lasting about 40 minutes.

A total of 58 individuals were interviewed, 19 males and 39 females, who were selected to cover diverse interactions with the program. For the background on education and gender in Tanzania, the following were interviewed: a cross-section of individuals working in national and international non-governmental organizations (NGOs) in the field of education and/or gender equity, individuals working in the gender and/or education departments of national and international governmental organizations, and academics in the field of education and in the field of gender at UDSM. For information on the SPEP, a cross-section of faculty members, females benefiting from the program, males students, program coordinators, administrative staff, and academics in the field of education and in the field of gender were interviewed. None of the beneficiaries who dropped out of the pre-entry training program or from the CoET were interviewed because they could not be reached.

All participants were above the age of 18, were interviewed alone, and were told that the content of their interview would be used for the purpose of writing a case study. All interviews were conducted in English, without the need for a translator. Most interviews were recorded on a digital recorder, and these were recorded with the consent of the participants obtained beforehand. All recordings of interviews were transcribed and notes were taken by the investigator during all interviews.

QUANTITATIVE DATA

The information collected from the semi-structured interviews was complemented with quantitative data in the form of statistics on educational gender
equity in Tanzania and on enrollment at the UDSM. In addition, raw data were
collected in the form of lists of girls in SPEP for 2004–2005, 2005–2006, 2006–
2007, and 2007–2008; the list of girls under FUSP; the list of application grades
for pre-entry girls and average of application grades for girls and boys admitted
directly for 2004–2005, 2005–2006, 2006–2007, and 2007–2008; and grades for
all 1,683 students in CoET for the academic year 2007–2008. Confidentiality of
individuals' grades was guaranteed.

Data Analysis

QUALITATIVE DATA ANALYSIS

The information contained in the notes from the semi-structured interviews was
extracted based on a thematic analysis. The transcripts of the interviews were
used to verify the information before its incorporation in the case study report
and were used to extract relevant quotes.

QUANTITATIVE DATA ANALYSIS

MATLAB programming software was used to generate graphs from the raw data
on grades for all 1,683 students in CoET for the academic year 2007–2008. These
data were used to compare, at the level of the different degree programs and at the
level of the college, males, direct-entry females, and pre-entry females in terms of
enrollment, application grades, performance, and dropout ratio.

It is important to note that, for 16.5% of the male students and 8% of the female
students, no grade was assigned because of unpaid school fees. This affects the
validity of the performance results since this population of students may not have
paid their fees because they knew they had failed, because they had dropped out, or
because they were suffering from financial difficulties. Also important to note is
that dropout students were considered those for whom there was a grade available
that was accompanied by the comment *discontinued studies* or *postponed studies*.

Appendix 2: List of Interviewees

Tanzanian Ministry of Education (Department of Policy and Planning)

- Acting Director of Policy and Planning
- One Gender Representative

University of Dar-es-Salaam (UDSM)

UDSM Gender Center

- Director of Gender Center
- Acting Director of Gender Center
- Two Gender Center Coordinators

UDSM College of Engineering and Technology (CoET)

- Acting principal of CoET
- One Senior Administrative Officer of CoET
- One Undergraduate Studies Coordinator for CoET
- One Coordinator of Pre-Entry Program for CoET
- Head of Department for Mechanical Engineering
- One Senior Lecturer in Chemical Engineering
- One Professor of Mathematics
- One Professor not involved in pre-entry training

Other UDSM Faculty and Administration Members

- One Former University Vice Chancellor
- Director of Policy and Planning
- Director of Development Studies
- One Former Coordinator of the Science Pre-entry Program

UDSM Students

- Three graduated students who benefited from Gender Center scholarships (not pre-entry students)
- Eleven students currently enrolled in pre-entry training
- Five students who have gone through pre-entry training and are now studying in the CoET (some with Gender Center scholarships and some without)
- Two male students of CoET

- One Gender Club leader and one Gender Club member (both not benefiting from FUSP or pre-entry, both male)
- Two alumni of CoET who have gone through pre-entry training (the first cohort graduated in 2008)
- Two alumni of the science pre-entry program

Sokoine University Pre-Entry Program

- Coordinator of Pre-entry Program

Non-governmental Organizations

Volunteer Service Organization–Tanzania

- One volunteer teacher
- One senior program manager for education

HakiElimu

- Two researchers

TEN/MET

- One coordinator

Aga Khan Foundation

- One education Coordinator

SESS project/affiliated with Ministry of Education

- One coordinator

Canadian International Development Agency and Canadian Cooperation Office

- One Education Advisor
- One Gender Equality Advisor
- One Senior Development Officer

4

Achieving Equity in Secondary and Tertiary Education for Students with Disabilities and Learning Difficulties

PETER EVANS AND SERGE EBERSOLD

This chapter discusses equity in secondary and tertiary education with a focus on children with disabilities and learning and behavior difficulties, using an international database developed by the member countries of the Organisation for Economic Co-operation and Development (OECD).[1] Outside of this work, there are no other internationally comparable datasets in this area with adequate coverage of the relevant levels of education.[2]

Most discussions of equity in education do not concern themselves with issues relating to students with disabilities and learning difficulties. Rather, their main goal has been to identify factors that would lead to the modification of educational provision to help students from economically disadvantaged groups to achieve at a similar level to students from economically advantaged groups. In doing this, they have focused mainly on issues of affordability and quality.[3]

Including students with all kinds of disabilities and learning difficulties into the discussion raises additional issues. The first issue, achieving equality of access to the curriculum, is likely to require adaptation since many disabilities affect the way the curriculum is accessed. For instance, students with visual impairments will learn many curriculum subjects in a different way from students with relatively unimpaired vision. Currently, many students with disabilities are not given the opportunity to learn alongside their peers and, as a result, they experience a different formal and hidden curriculum. Thus, the extent to which students with disabilities have full access to mainstream educational facilities at all levels is of great importance and a key indicator of equity.

Second, some students, such as those with profound intellectual disabilities, may be unlikely to achieve academically at the same level as their peers without this type of disability. Thus, educational equity for this group should not be viewed in terms of how to modify the system in order to achieve *equality* of outcome, but instead, how to develop a system that can maximize the potential of all students, regardless of the nature of disability.

In improving access and outcomes, it is important to recognize that one of the main policy tools for achieving equity is through differential resource distribution. Therefore, governments in all OECD countries spend more money per capita on students with disabilities and learning difficulties than on other students. This practice is consonant with Rawls' theory of social justice,[4] which stresses the importance of structuring institutions in favor of the most disadvantaged through the "difference principle," a logic that has been extended to students with disabilities.[5,6] In this way, the additional resources that countries provide for all students who are in need of extra support to help them access the curriculum promotes "corrective justice."[7] This is a key principle for achieving equity in education with the intention of increasing access and improving outcomes.

Further necessary elements to achieve equity for students with disabilities include considerations of the impact of gender, improving the processes that facilitate movement between the various levels of education, and coordinating education and other services, including health and family services.

As this short introduction details, it is clear that a consideration of equity in education must be substantially revised when students with disabilities and learning difficulties are included in the analysis. As a result, this chapter addresses, from an international policy perspective, five important areas involved in achieving equity in education for *all* students. They are: resource distribution, gender, access, outcomes, and process. However, before doing this, it is necessary first to describe the means used in this chapter to make international comparisons in the field of special educational needs.

Operational Definitions of Disability and Difficulty

Any discussion linking disability and learning difficulties with education in a comparative context must be concerned with current usages of the terms "disability" and "learning difficulty" since there are no internationally agreed upon definitions of these terms. In addition, in an educational context they become confounded with the commonly used concept of "special educational need" (SEN). In an attempt to overcome these difficulties, and in order to make international comparisons, OECD countries agreed to reinterpret the many national definitions of categories pertaining to SEN students that are in use in OECD countries in terms of a simple framework.[8] Since there is much more variability across countries in terms of the characteristics of students identified as having difficulties than there is for those identified as having disabilities, this chapter examines the two groups separately and will use the OECD's distinction between the two broad categories of "disabilities" and "difficulties." The former group includes students with difficulties that are often visible in all settings, such as those with physical and severe cognitive impairments, while the latter includes students whose diffi-culties may often be invisible, including those with learning disabilities as well as students with behavioral or emotional disorders.[9]

Discussing secondary and tertiary education introduces additional challenges. For example, students in tertiary education no longer fall under the same legal frameworks as do those in the formal and usually obligatory secondary level. They are subject to definitions used, for instance, by Ministries of Health as opposed to Ministries of Education.

Resource Distribution

LOWER AND UPPER SECONDARY EDUCATION

From a public policy perspective, how resources are distributed is a key issue to achieve equitable provision. In education, students with a SEN should receive sup-plementary resources in the form of improved teacher-to-pupil ratios and material resources, for example, to help them to access the curriculum and learn as far as possible on an equal basis to their peers. In OECD countries this rule is generally applied. However, the proportion of students receiving additional resources varies greatly from country to country, as revealed in Figures 4.1, 4.2, 4.3 and 4.4, which

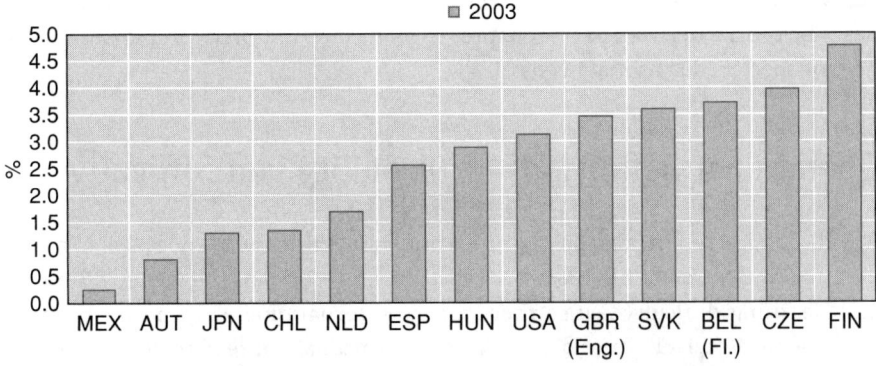

Figure 4.1 Resources for lower secondary students with disabilities. Proportion of students in lower secondary education receiving additional resources for disabilities as a proportion of all students in lower secondary education. AUT, Austria; BEL(Fl.), Belgium (Flemish Community); CHL, Chile; CZE, the Czech Republic; ESP, Spain; FIN, Finland; GBR(Eng.), Great Britain (England); HUN, Hungary; JPN, Japan; MEX, Mexico; NLD, the Netherlands; SVK, Slovakia; USA, United States of America. OECD. (2008). Students with Disabilities, Learning Difficulties and Disadvantages: Policies, Statistics and Indicators - 2007 Edition (p. 101). OECD Publishing, http://dx.doi. org/10.1787/9789264027619-en.

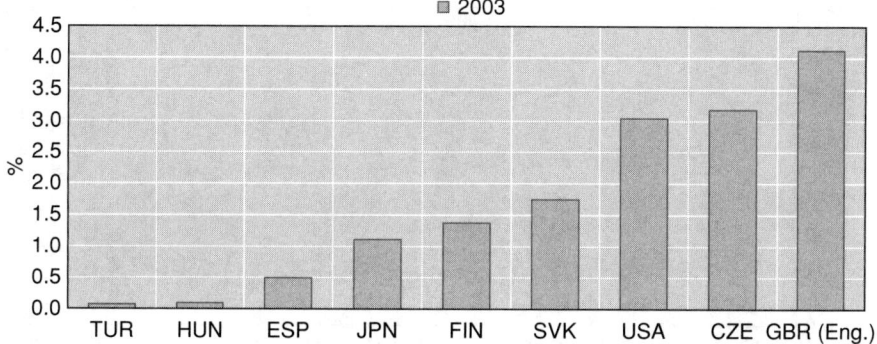

Figure 4.2 Resources for upper secondary students with disabilities. Proportion of students in upper secondary education receiving additional resources for disabilities as a proportion of all students in upper secondary education. CZE, the Czech Republic; ESP, Spain; FIN, Finland; GBR(Eng.), Great Britain (England); HUN, Hungary; JPN, Japan; SVK, Slovakia; TUR, Turkey; USA, United States of America. OECD. (2008). Students with Disabilities, Learning Difficulties and Disadvantages: Policies, Statistics and Indicators - 2007 Edition (p. 102). OECD Publishing, http://dx.doi.org/10.1787/9789264027619-en.

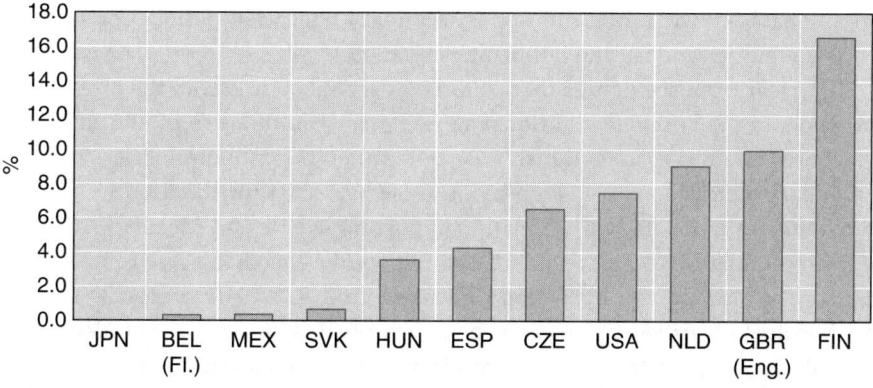

Figure 4.3 Resources for lower secondary students with difficulties. Proportion of students in lower secondary education receiving additional resources for difficulties as a proportion of all students in lower secondary education. BEL(Fl.), Belgium (Flemish Community); CZE, the Czech Republic; ESP, Spain; FIN, Finland; GBR(Eng.), Great Britain (England); HUN, Hungary; JPN, Japan; MEX, Mexico; NLD, the Netherlands; SVK, Slovakia; USA, United States of America. OECD. (2008). Students with Disabilities, Learning Difficulties and Disadvantages: Policies, Statistics and Indicators - 2007 Edition (p. 110). OECD Publishing, http://dx.doi.org/10.1787/9789264027619-en.

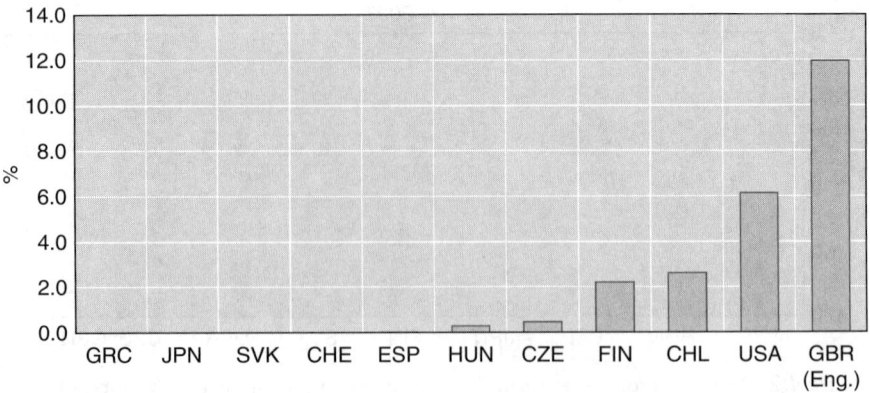

Figure 4.4 Resources for upper secondary students with difficulties. Proportion of students in upper secondary education receiving additional resources for difficulties as a proportion of all students in upper secondary education. CHE, Switzerland; CHL, Chile; CZE, the Czech Republic; ESP, Spain; FIN, Finland; GBR(Eng.), Great Britain (England); GRC, Greece; HUN, Hungary; JPN, Japan; SVK, Slovakia; USA, United States of America. OECD. (2008). Students with Disabilities, Learning Difficulties and Disadvantages: Policies, Statistics and Indicators - 2007 Edition (p. 111). OECD Publishing, http://dx.doi.org/10.1787/9789264027619-en

supply data for the lower and upper secondary education periods for students with disabilities and learning difficulties in 2003.[10]

It is clear from the figures that countries vary substantially in the proportions of students they provide additional support for at both levels of education and for both disabilities and difficulties. For students with disabilities at lower secondary education (see Figure 4.1), the median score for the countries able to provide data is 2.87%, with Finland supporting 4.76% and Mexico 0.26%. For upper secondary (see Figure 4.2), the corresponding median score is 1.37%. The proportions supported by Finland decrease to 1.37%, but there are no data for Mexico for this level. Thus, in general, countries support fewer students with disabilities at upper than lower secondary education, although there are exceptions. In the United Kingdom, for instance, the proportion increases from 3.45% to 4.12%.

For students with difficulties (see Figure 4.3), a parallel picture exists. A greater proportion of students are supported at lower than upper secondary levels (median lower secondary = 4.24%; median upper secondary = 0.37%). In lower secondary, there is a large range of scores, between 0% in Japan to 16.58% in Finland. In upper secondary, the proportion for Finland decreases to 2.21%, but, as with students with disabilities, the proportions increase in the United Kingdom, from 9.96% to 11.95%.

It is not altogether clear what underlies these differences between countries, but a number of explanations offer themselves. The differences in the proportions of students with disabilities and difficulties receiving resources may lie in:

- The extent to which school systems can cope with individual differences between students
- The assessment culture that has developed in the health and education services
- The value countries place on educating these students, which can lead some to offer very limited support and early tracking into vocational training
- The fact that many of these students will leave school at the end of lower secondary education, or drop out, thus reducing the numbers remaining in upper secondary

Whatever the explanation—and more work is needed to provide a fuller account—it is clear that by this indicator of equity substantial variation exists in the proportions of students supported and also in continuity of support across lower and upper secondary levels of education. If similar proportions of students across countries are in need of support, then this suggests that some systems are more equitable than others in their treatment of these two distinct groups of students.

TERTIARY EDUCATION

Additional financial support may be provided for students with disabilities and difficulties at the tertiary level, sometimes with beneficial terms such as no requirement to repay a loan.[11,12] However, research highlights the limitations to funding procedures that take insufficient account of the additional time required by some disabled students to complete their studies or the possibility that they may have to change direction during their study as a result of disability or illness.[13] For instance, in the United States, the average amount of financial support obtained by these students is less than for those in good health ($7,200 in contrast to $7,400 per annum). Although this difference may appear marginal, it must be remembered that students with disabilities have higher living costs on average than do those without disabilities and, moreover, the basic financial resources of many of these students is often less than for nondisabled students. In the United States, 46.7% of students with disabilities had financial resources of less than $20,000 per annum, in contrast to a figure of 39.8% for nondisabled students.[14] In Germany, in 2006, the resources received by disabled students were the same as those for their nondisabled peers, despite the extra costs that disability or illness might entail. In these funding arrangements, there appears to be little evidence of corrective justice through the provision of additional resources.

Few data are available concerning students with disabilities and difficulties in tertiary education, and the data that are available reveal, as with the data for lower and upper secondary, substantial variation between countries. Based on work carried out by the OECD,[15] it is clear that some students with disabilities do receive additional resources, but these are dependent on whether the student decides to disclose the nature of the disability or difficulty. With this caveat, the proportion of students in tertiary education with disabilities and difficulties receiving support was 6.5% in the United Kingdom (2007); 18.9% in Germany (2006); 0.4% in France (2006); and 11.3% in the United States (2003).

Gender

In OECD countries, in the way in which education is currently delivered, many more boys than girls receive support for disabilities and difficulties in the compulsory period.[16] Figure 4.5 reveals that, for those with disabilities receiving support, some 60% are boys—a figure that holds across most countries. Figure 4.6 shows the data for those with difficulties. Here, the proportion of boys is even greater, reaching 70% and more in some countries. The figures also show that the proportions have remained stable between 1999 and 2003.

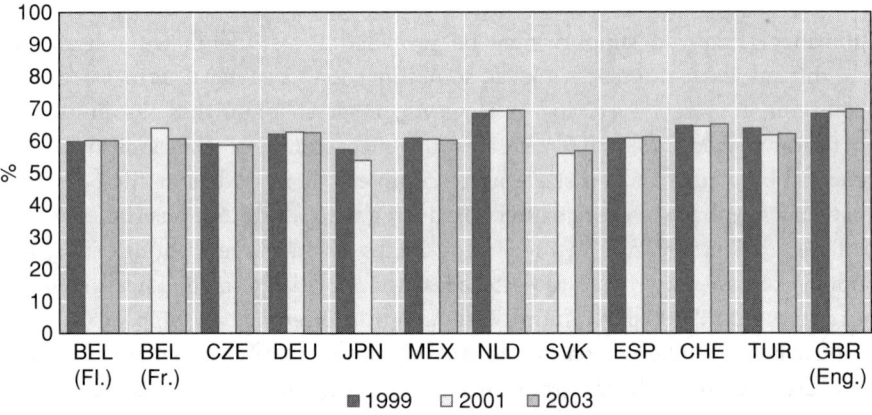

Figure 4.5 Gender of students receiving support for disabilities in compulsory education. Proportion of students with disabilities receiving support who are male (compulsory education): 1999, 2001, 2003. BEL(Fl.), Belgium (Flemish Community); BEL(Fr.), Belgium (French Community); CHE, Switzerland; CZE, the Czech Republic; DEU, Germany; ESP, Spain; GBR(Eng.), Great Britain (England); JPN, Japan; MEX, Mexico; NLD, the Netherlands; SVK, Slovakia; TUR, Turkey. OECD. (2008). Students with Disabilities, Learning Difficulties and Disadvantages: Policies, Statistics and Indicators - 2007 Edition (p. 175). OECD Publishing, http://dx.doi.org/10.1787/9789264027619-en.

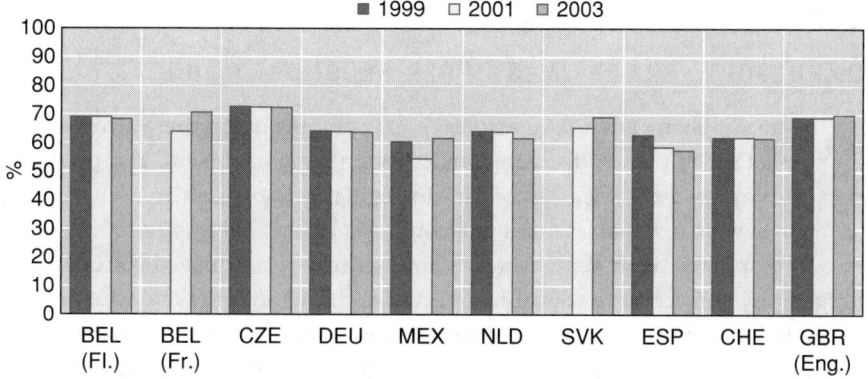

Figure 4.6 Gender of students receiving support for difficulties in compulsory education. Proportion of students with difficulties receiving support who are male (compulsory education): 1999, 2001, 2003. BEL(Fl.), Belgium (Flemish Community); BEL(Fr.), Belgium (French Community); CHE, Switzerland; CZE, the Czech Republic; DEU, Germany; ESP, Spain; GBR(Eng.), Great Britain (England); JPN, Japan; MEX, Mexico; NLD, the Netherlands; SVK, Slovakia; TUR, Turkey. OECD. (2008). Students with Disabilities, Learning Difficulties and Disadvantages: Policies, Statistics and Indicators - 2007 Edition (p. 175). OECD Publishing, http://dx.doi.org/10.1787/9789264027619-en.

It is clear that boys are receiving a greater proportion of available resources than girls. Is this situation equitable? One possible interpretation is that boys are genuinely more in need of extra support than girls. In the context of current education systems, more resources by this token would be equitable. For students with disabilities, there is good evidence that boys are more fragile than girls and that the greater prevalence of disabilities may well have a biological origin.[17,18] The same explanation is much less compelling for students with difficulties,[19] but more research is needed.[20]

Another interpretation is that the education of boys is viewed as more important than that of girls. In this case, preferring to support boys who are doing less well in comparison to the equivalent girls would be inequitable. However, identifying more boys may also lead to stigmatization associated with various forms of special interventions, such as special schools, which may lead to worse outcomes and fewer subsequent opportunities in life. Such a result would also be inequitable.

These data supply some facts about gender differences, but they are silent on the question of whether the disproportionate distribution of resources is equitable for males and females. Again, more data are needed. Furthermore, data on gender differences for these populations of students in tertiary education are not available.

Access

COMPULSORY, LOWER, AND UPPER SECONDARY EDUCATION

Apart from supplying additional resources to promote equity, there also needs to be a parallel set of policies focusing on achieving social inclusion. Yet, providing education for students with disabilities in regular schools has been an ongoing challenge over many years, with some countries being able to offer an inclusive location more effectively than others.[21] Equity cannot be achieved if students do not have physical access to educational facilities throughout the obligatory education period. In countries with fully developed education systems, almost all countries use special schools, special classes, and regular school provision for educating varying proportions of students with disabilities and difficulties. However, they vary substantially in the extent to which these three different forms of provision are used.[22]

The OECD has reported regularly on the status of inclusion over the past decade in terms of the location of education—in special schools, special classes, or regular schools. Figures 4.7, 4.8, 4.9, and 4.10 show where students with disabilities and difficulties are educated at lower and upper secondary levels.[23]

It is clear that large variations exist between countries in terms of where these students are educated. Figure 4.7 shows that, for students with disabilities at the lower secondary level, all countries that can supply data use some special school provision. One country, Chile, has all of these students in special schools. On the other hand, Spain has nearly all these students in regular schools. Other countries, such as Japan and the United States, make considerable use of special classes. Figure 4.8 reveals that, at the upper secondary level, there is slightly less use of special schools in some countries such as Hungary and Spain, whereas Japan uses only special schools.

Figure 4.9 shows the position for students with difficulties in lower secondary where, again, all three types of provision are used, with a tendency for more of these students to remain in regular schools. Figure 4.10 reveals that, at the upper secondary level, there is greater use of regular schools.

These figures show the variation that exists between countries in the location of education for these students and the inherent potential for inequity that may exist. There is widespread debate over the value of special schools in providing a high-quality education for students with disabilities and difficulties. At the international level, no data are available to help to shed further light on this question, and further research is required if the debate is to move forward based on quantitative evidence.

Outcomes

The data presented in the previous sections represent only a necessary beginning for understanding equity more fully. What is needed—and is currently almost

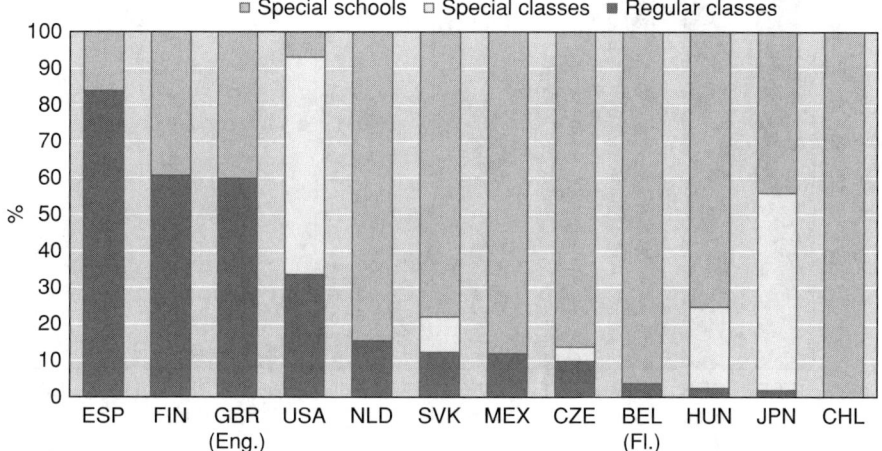

Figure 4.7 Schooling for lower secondary students with disabilities. Proportion of students with disabilities in lower secondary education by location 2003: special schools, special classes, and regular classes. BEL(Fl.), Belgium (Flemish Community); CHL, Chile; CZE, the Czech Republic; ESP, Spain; FIN, Finland; GBR(Eng.), Great Britain (England); HUN, Hungary; JPN, Japan; MEX, Mexico; NLD, the Netherlands; SVK, Slovakia; USA, United States of America. OECD. (2008). Students with Disabilities, Learning Difficulties and Disadvantages: Policies, Statistics and Indicators - 2007 Edition (p. 102). OECD Publishing, http://dx.doi.org/10.1787/9789264027619-en

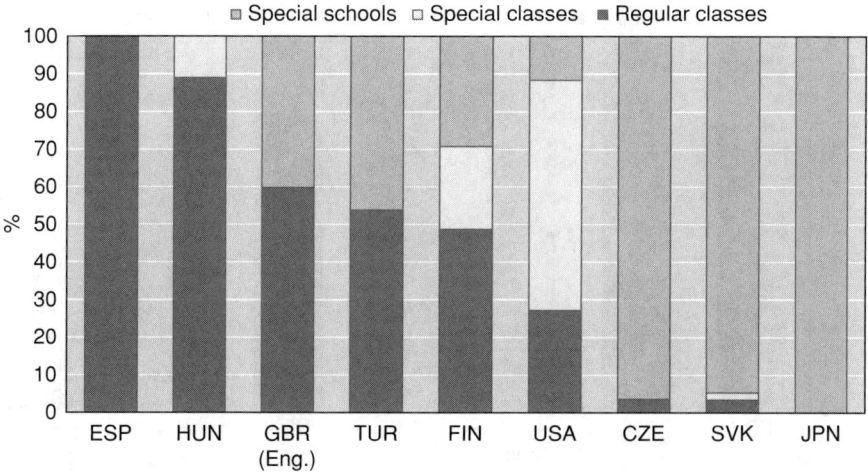

Figure 4.8 Schooling for upper secondary students with disabilities. Proportion of students with disabilities in upper secondary education by location 2003: special schools, special classes, and regular classes. CZE, the Czech Republic; ESP, Spain; FIN, Finland; GBR(Eng.), Great Britain (England); HUN, Hungary; JPN, Japan; SVK, Slovakia; TUR, Turkey; USA, United States of America. OECD. (2008). Students with Disabilities, Learning Difficulties and Disadvantages: Policies, Statistics and Indicators - 2007 Edition (p. 103). OECD Publishing, http://dx.doi.org/10.1787/9789264027619-en.

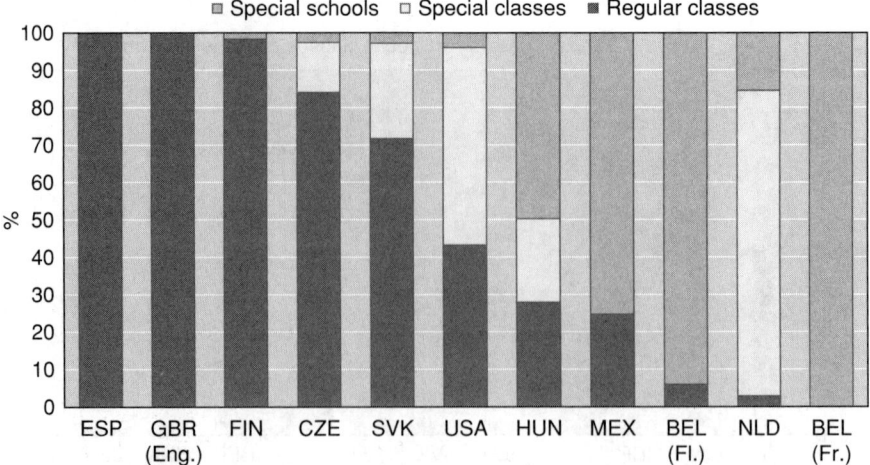

Figure 4.9 Schooling for lower secondary students with difficulties. Proportion of students with difficulties in lower secondary education by location 2003: special schools, special classes, and regular classes. BEL(Fl.), Belgium (Flemish Community); BEL(Fr.), Belgium (French Community); CZE, the Czech Republic; ESP, Spain; FIN, Finland; GBR(Eng.), Great Britain (England); HUN, Hungary; MEX, Mexico; NLD, the Netherlands; SVK, Slovakia; USA, United States of America. OECD. (2008). Students with Disabilities, Learning Difficulties and Disadvantages: Policies, Statistics and Indicators - 2007 Edition (p. 110). OECD Publishing, http://dx.doi.org/10.1787/ 9789264027619-en.

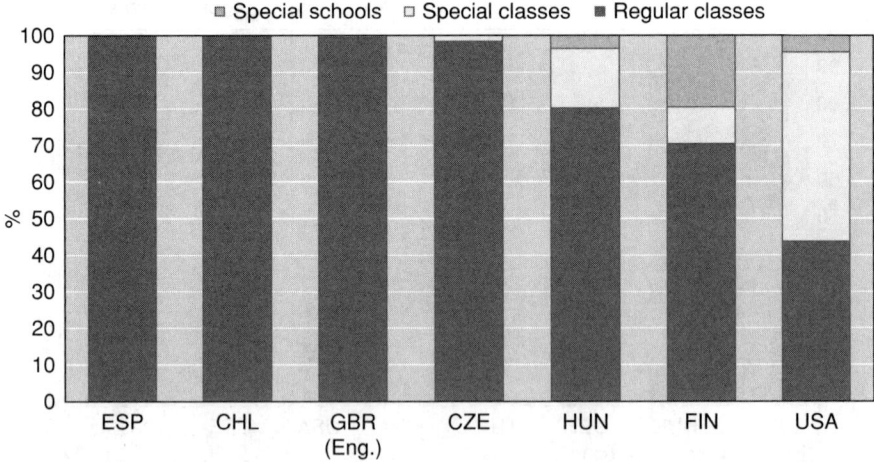

Figure 4.10 Schooling for upper secondary students with difficulties. Proportion of students with difficulties in upper secondary education by location 2003: special schools, special classes, and regular classes. CHL, Chile; CZE, the Czech Republic; ESP, Spain; FIN, Finland; GBR(Eng.), Great Britain (England); HUN, Hungary; USA, United States of America. OECD. (2008). Students with Disabilities, Learning Difficulties and Disadvantages: Policies, Statistics and Indicators - 2007 Edition (p. 111). OECD Publishing, http://dx.doi.org/10.1787/9789264027619-en.

totally lacking—are data on outcomes for students with disabilities and difficulties, which would allow for expenditure and the place of education to be linked with a range of outcome variables such as academic success and social integration. This would shed light on the question of whether and to what extent additional resources provide for "corrective justice."

In addition, many students with disabilities are educated in some form of special provision. There is a great deal of discussion on the question of inclusion and whether special schools should be closed since they may provide a marginalized education with different socializing and curriculum experiences for particular groups of students. Since these educational experiences are fundamentally different from those in regular schools, this in itself can lead to social isolation and limited access to both tertiary education and the labor market, and would be inequitable on the grounds that the education system is not providing equal opportunities. At the same time, when designed and resourced well, they may provide access to better services for some disabilities that are difficult to address, as well with small numbers of affected students in nonspecialized schools. Again, without information on outcomes, policy-making on whether or not to close special schools rests on limited sets of information often presented by pressure groups of one form or another.

The outcomes of education systems, mainly in the form of scholastic test results, are having an enormous impact on policy-making, as can be seen in the OECD's Programme for International Student Assessment (PISA).[24] However, outcome scores are simply not available for special needs students, either because they are not included in the testing arrangements or the data are not disaggregated. This appears to be true not only at the international level but also at the national level, although exceptions are beginning to emerge in countries such as the United Kingdom, through national curriculum assessment procedures, and the United States.

A fundamental premise of this chapter is that equity should be understood in terms of maximizing outcomes for all students, including those with disabilities and learning difficulties, by finding the most effective balance in resource distribution and access.

ACCESSING TERTIARY EDUCATION

One outcome measure that could, in principle, be helpful is the number of students who pass through the various levels of education and enter the tertiary level. Because of the importance of tertiary education to the economies of OECD countries, increasingly these countries are evaluating education systems in this way.[25] For instance, in the United Kingdom, the Higher Education Statistics Agency (HESA) keeps records of the number of students with disabilities who enter higher education, their background, the courses they follow, the type of disability, and so on. The available data reveal substantial variations between

countries, with evident changes over time. In the United Kingdom, the proportions have increased from 4.6% to 6.5% between 2002 and 2007. In Germany,
between 2003 and 2006, there was an increase from 12.5% to 18.9%. In France,
the increase was from 0.3% to 0.4% between 2001 and 2006, and in the United
States, from 5.6% to 11.3% between 1987 and 2003.

However, further analyses of these data show that the types of students accessing tertiary education are not the same across these countries. In the United
Kingdom, there is a large increase in the numbers with dyslexia (learning difficulties). In Germany, health problems are an important contributor to the numbers
identified, whereas in France the students have mainly physical and sensory disabilities—hence the low numbers that are reported. In addition, in most countries, many students with disabilities experience difficulty in gaining access to
tertiary education. For example, in the United States, just 14% of upper secondary school leavers with disabilities took an entrance examination for tertiary education in 2001–2002, although 47% wanted to enroll.[26] Despite the considerable
methodological issues identified above, these data also indicate large differences
between countries in the proportions of SEN students gaining access to tertiary
education. Again, this implies substantial inequities in the use of public resources,
in particular with regard to the flow of students from lower to upper secondary
education (see Figures 4.1–4.4) and onward to the tertiary level.

An important issue for data reliability and for the students themselves relates
to whether students with disabilities are prepared to disclose their disability.
This is especially problematic if, by disclosing, they become stigmatized or marginalized in some way. In the United Kingdom, the large increase in the numbers
of disabled people pursuing higher education is linked to improvements in identification of those requiring additional resources to complete their studies. There,
the proportion of students thought to have a disability without it being clearly
identified fell from 33.9% of those enrolled in 1995 to 2.2% in 2004.[27]

However, as we have seen, the numbers of students with disabilities and difficulties passing from lower to upper secondary are already diminished, and this
trend appears to be continued vis-à-vis the transition to tertiary education. The
statistics are, however, confounded since when students with disabilities pass
from childhood to adulthood, their service providers tend to change from ministries of education to ministries of health, with attendant changes in definitions of
disability. In the United Kingdom, for example, the definitions relating to the concept of SEN that operates in secondary education is different from that in the
further education sector,[28] which is based on disability and learning difficulty.[29]

Achieving equity in terms of outcomes can only be achieved if SEN students
can access tertiary education. This is especially important since postsecondary
education is strongly related to earnings.[30] Tertiary education also provides access
to a broader range of the cultural and scientific developments and creates more
favorable conditions for social inclusion.

All young people have to learn to cope with new expectations of them and to become increasingly autonomous, a process that is an even greater challenge for special needs students. Access to tertiary education offers persons with disabilities the same opportunities in professional terms as those who are nondisabled. For example, in the United Kingdom, the proportion of students with disabilities who had obtained their first degree in 2004 and who were actively employed on completion of their education was close to the corresponding figure for nondisabled students—57.4% in contrast to 61.2%.

It is crucial that students with disabilities have a chance not only to enter post-secondary education but to succeed there. Physical access to the pedagogy and buildings during tertiary education are problematic for students with disabilities. In Austria, for instance, 40% of these students feel disabled by the examination procedures, 34% by the coursework, and 43% by the study of written documents. They also attribute their difficulties to the conditions underlying their participation in courses and meetings, 25% to lack of access to internships and 10% to inaccessibility of buildings and transport.[31,32] In the Netherlands, the majority of these students are unaware of the support and facilities available to them, and almost half consider that the lack of suitable teaching materials and special arrangements for examinations put them at a disadvantage.[33]

On average, students with disabilities also achieve less well than their peers in tertiary education, and those with learning, behavioral or emotional difficulties may not complete their courses.[34,35] In France, the relative proportion of students with disabilities on master's degree-level courses is much lower than the proportion for students as a whole (19.6% compared to 32.4%).[36] In the Netherlands, it is estimated that 50% of students with disabilities fall behind in their studies, that they are more likely to drop out, and are twice as prone as their nondisabled peers to discontinue their undergraduate studies when enrolled in professional higher education.[37]

Policy Coherence: Coordination of Services Across Sectors

The effective education of students with disabilities depends not only on resource availability and curriculum and pedagogical issues but also on the availability of other support structures, such as health and social services. This need for coordination across sectors is often referred to as *policy coherence*. This need applies at all levels of education. Students with disabilities may need access to regular medication, physiotherapy, or speech therapy, for example, and at older ages to other specialized supports. In higher education, students may need similar supports, as well as funding—for instance, for sign language interpreters. The funding for these services and their delivery usually comes from outside the education budget and service. As a result, from the students' point of view, their provision may not always be timely and, as a consequence, may impact on the quality of student outcomes. In terms of judging the equity of provision, policy coherence therefore becomes a key factor. It is unclear to what extent countries have comprehensively addressed these issues with regard to the effective education of students with disabilities and difficulties or across the education system as a whole—for instance, for children at risk[38]—and for evaluating inclusive education.[39] These are other areas in need of further research and development.

ISSUES IN THE PROCESS OF TRANSITION FROM UPPER SECONDARY TO TERTIARY EDUCATION

The reviews of transition from upper secondary to tertiary education carried out by the OECD in Austria, England, France, Germany, the Netherlands, Norway, Switzerland, and the United States identified a number of important areas that can prevent students with disabilities and difficulties from benefiting as fully as they might from tertiary education. It is important to note that this period also corresponds to the transition from childhood to adulthood and, as noted above, this coincides with changes in the ways in which they are viewed by governments. In the United Kingdom, for instance, young people aged 16 and over become eligible for assistance in their own right instead of via their parents and are entitled to forms of support intended for adults.

The implications of changes in administrative categories for the young people involved need to be recognized. Earlier supports for students with disabilities may be suspended because of a lack of cooperation between child and adult welfare services, so that young people with disabilities may face unclear or unstructured pathways.[40] In Germany, "educational need" is no longer a formal administrative category once secondary education ends, so young people with learning difficulties, behavioral disorders, or language problems are not able to access support provided for in legislation concerned specifically with disabled people unless they have enrolled in education or training programs for those leaving special schools.

Moreover, tertiary institutions have different formal responsibilities towards students than do secondary institutions. In the United States, for instance, tertiary education institutions—unlike schools—are legally obliged to ensure access only in the case of men and women who have declared their particular disability and/or the specific nature of their requirements.[41-43] Those students with unseen disabilities, such as a learning difficulty or an illness, and who do not wish to disclose it because they fear the possible consequences of doing so are thus denied the requisite support and effectively deprived of their rights.[44]

These arrangements may lead to young adults having uneven experiences as they transition from secondary to tertiary education, with the result that they do not improve their employability. Issues of policy coherence and the coordination of services and the support they provide may then be central to the successful educational experience of young people with disabilities and learning difficulties.

If students with disabilities are to be successful in tertiary education, it is clear that, as in compulsory education, they will need additional support and resourcing.[45]

Data Limitations

Although the data provided by countries for lower and upper secondary education are probably reliable, too many countries are unable to provide comprehensive data for these levels of education. Furthermore, it is simply not known in statistical terms what happens to students with disabilities and learning difficulties when they leave school.

It is also difficult for existing datasets to provide a thorough picture of the situation experienced by students with disabilities. Data collection methods vary widely depending on particular administrative authorities or areas, as well as by the principles underlying the various components of education systems, and these offer a fragmented or even contradictory view of the conditions governing access and effective performance in education and employment. In Norway, for example, the counties responsible for gathering and analyzing information about students and adolescents with disabilities have no common approach to this activity, so that any comparison between them is impossible and no meaningful picture of the national situation can emerge.[46] In the United Kingdom, data on students with disabilities relate to those enrolled in higher education and generally fail to take account of people with disabilities in further education that is administered separately. The twenty-fifth annual report to the American Congress[47] notes that the data provided by the U.S. Census Bureau covers only households and excludes students living in university halls of residence, thus overlooking an estimated half-a-million students with disabilities. In France, special education and mainstream education are the responsibility of different ministries, with the result that the data are not readily comparable.

The data may also preclude any accurate analysis of the impact of policies, as the evaluation criteria adopted are not always consistent with the aims pursued. The twenty-fifth annual report to the American Congress[48] also points out that the criteria used to calculate the success rate of disabled students in lower and upper secondary education and how it changes over time are dissimilar to those used for nondisabled students. In France, there is little detailed information on the schooling and subsequent career paths of students with disabilities. This stands in contrast to available information for the school population as a whole.

The data that are gathered also provide little understanding of the changes in situations experienced by persons with disabilities and learning difficulties over time. In Germany, for example, key indicators concerning the transition into secondary education and toward tertiary education are scarce in national datasets on either the participation rate of people with disabilities in education or on vocational training and are also lacking in reports on the circumstances and participation rate of persons with disabilities and on their position in the vocational training market. Time series analyses may also be impeded by differences in the definition used to describe people with disabilities in successive surveys, thereby precluding any truly reliable comparison over time.

Conclusion

This chapter has discussed five policy-related themes relevant to achieving equity in secondary and tertiary education for students with disabilities and learning and behavioral difficulties, based mainly on internationally comparable quantitative and qualitative data gathered by the OECD. The themes discussed include additional resources, gender differences, access, outcomes, and process. All of these areas need to be addressed in terms of both policy and practice in order to provide the most effective primary, secondary, and tertiary education for these students.

Additional resources are made available for students with disabilities and learning difficulties in the countries reviewed at lower and upper secondary levels, and in tertiary education in recognition of additional difficulties they experience in accessing the curriculum. However, countries vary considerably in the extent of the provisions made. This raises the question of the equitable nature of the education provided in terms of social justice, especially in those countries offering fewer additional resources.

With regard to *gender,* substantial differences in the amount of support provided for boys and girls raise a particular conundrum. Boys seem to have more challenges than girls in adapting to schooling and are more often identified and awarded extra resources. This may be equitable if the problems are real and not, for example, because boys' education is seen as more important socially than girls' education. However, identification and extra resources may lead to inequitable outcomes if they result, for example, in special school placement and subsequent degraded educational and social experiences. A high-quality education for all in regular schools may be a solution.

The data presented above show the extent to which students with disabilities and difficulties have differential *access* to a country's education system (and hence its curriculum)—through special schools, special classes, or regular schools. Substantial variation exists between countries in the use of special settings, and this factor further supports the conclusion that there appear to be substantial inequities in some countries in the educational provision made available for students with disabilities and learning difficulties. The very minimal data that exist for the tertiary level suggests the same conclusion.

As far as *outcomes* are concerned, it is abundantly clear from the evidence presented in this chapter that serious data shortages prevent any assessment of whether the additional resources that countries spend on students with disabilities and learning and behavior difficulties are impacting positively or negatively on the access to, or outcomes of, national education systems. It is simply the case that data quality and the extent of coverage need to be substantially improved for any further analytical progress to be made. Furthermore, there are also real difficulties in making data-based comparisons between secondary and tertiary levels, for datasets are at best incomplete and at worst compounded by changing definitions across ministries. If coherent reforms could be made to data-gathering frameworks and on measuring outcomes, then evidence would become available that could lead to great progress being made in creating equitable provision for students with disabilities and learning difficulties.

The *processes* involved in supporting students with disabilities and learning difficulties throughout their education are also extremely important, and a lack of policy coherence across education, health, and social sectors can prove a barrier to achieving their full potential. It is clear that countries have been concerned to offer young people with disabilities who leave upper secondary education a broad range of educational and training opportunities. Some countries have put pressure on tertiary institutions to make the necessary changes to ensure reasonable accessibility and equality of opportunity. However, some have not applied the same pressure to their educational systems to give enough consideration to the transition from secondary to tertiary levels, with the result that the measures taken have not been as effective as they might have been.

Although this chapter has focused on high-income countries that are members of the OECD, the policy areas identified and the conclusions drawn are relevant to all countries. If "Education for All" is to be achieved, the needs of those children and students with disabilities and learning and behavior difficulties must be taken into account and given the necessary support. Achieving equity in education globally is thus clearly a work in progress.

NOTES

1. The Organisation for Economic Co-operation and Development (OECD) is an independent government funded organization with 32 member countries. It works on all levels of government policy and, based on international comparisons, makes recommendations to its member countries. It also has a substantial commitment to improving policy-making in and strengthening the economies of developing countries. The OECD member countries are: Australia, Austria, Belgium, Canada, Chile, the Czech Republic, Denmark, Finland, France, Germany, Greece, Hungary, Iceland, Ireland, Italy, Japan, Korea, Luxembourg, Mexico, the Netherlands, New Zealand, Norway, Poland, Portugal, the Slovak Republic, Slovenia, Spain, Sweden, Switzerland, Turkey, the United Kingdom and the United States. The Commission of the European Communities takes part in the work of the OECD.
2. OECD. (2007). *Students with disabilities, learning difficulties and disadvantages—Statistics and indicators of OAS countries.* Paris/Mexico City: OECD/Edebé.

3. Hutmacher, W., Cochrane, D., & Bottani, N. (Eds.). (2001). *In pursuit of equity in education–Using international indicators to compare equity policies*. Dordrecht/Boston/London: Kluwer Academic Publishers.
4. Rawls, J. (1971). *A theory of justice*. Cambridge, MA: Harvard University Press.
5. Brighouse, M. H. (2000). *School choice and social justice*. Oxford, UK: Oxford University Press.
6. Evans, P. (2002). Equity indicators based on the provision of supplementary resources for disabled and disadvantaged students. In W. Hutmacher, D. Cochrane, & N. Bottani (Eds.), *In pursuit of equity in education–Using international indicators to compare equity policies*. Dordrecht/Boston/London: Kluwer Academic Publishers.
7. Crahay, M. (2000). *L'école peut-elle être juste et efficace?* Bruxelles: De Boeck.
8. OECD. (2000). *Special needs education–Statistics and indicators*. Paris: OECD.
9. OECD. (2007). *Students with disabilities*.
10. The most recent data validated by the countries and available from the OECD are presented.
11. Department of Health (DH) and Department for Education and Skills (DfES). (2007). *A transition guide for all services. Key information for professionals about the transition process for disabled young people*. London: Council for Disabled Children, Department for Children, Schools and Families, Department of Health, and National Children's Bureau.
12. OECD. (2003). *Disability in higher education*. Paris: OECD.
13. Sociaal Economische Raad. (2007). *Meedoen zonder beperkingen. Meer participatiemogelijkheden voor jonggehandicapten*. Sociaal Economische Raad, Advies raport nr.6. Den Haag: Sociaal Economische Raad.
14. OECD. (2011). Inclusion of Students with Disabilities in Tertiary Education and Employment. Paris: OECD.
15. Ibid.
16. Data on the compulsory period is provided since the data on lower secondary and upper secondary are available separately for only a very few countries.
17. Skårbrevik, K. L. (2002). Gender differences among students found eligible for special education. *European Journal of Special Needs Education, 17*(2), 97–107.
18. Yeargin-Allsop, M. (2003). Prevalence of autism in a US metropolitan area. *Journal of the American Medical Association, 289*, 49–55.
19. Reschly, S. J. (1996). Identification and assessment of students with disabilities. *The Future of Children, Special Education for Students with Disabilities, 6*(1).
20. OECD. (2007). *Students with disabilities*.
21. The factors that lead countries to create inclusive education are not well known but any explanation will inevitably be complex and depend on the particular country's culture, history, political persuasion, and extant educational philosophy and practices.
22. Whether it is inequitable for students to be educated outside of mainstream schools is an important question but, in the absence of data on outcomes, the question cannot be satisfactorily addressed.
23. OECD. (2007). *Students with disabilities*.
24. OECD/Programme for International Student Assessment (PISA). (2009). *Assessment framework–Key competencies in reading, mathematics and science*. Paris: OECD/PISA.
25. OECD. (2008). *Pathways for People with Disabilities—Towards Tertiary Education and Employment: Preliminary Findings from a Literature Review Covering Selected OECD Countries*. Paris: OECD.
26. Ibid.
27. Higher Education Statistics Agency (HESA). Retrieved from http://www.hesa.ac.uk/index.php/component/option.com_datatables/Itemid,121/
28. In the United Kingdom, higher education refers to the University sector, whereas further education offers courses in vocational education and academic subjects necessary for university entrance.
29. Pricewaterhouse Coopers. (2007). *Review of further education provision for learners (16–25 year olds) with learning difficulties and/or disabilities in the NorthWest*. Retrieved from http://readingroom.lsc.gov.uk/lsc/NorthWest/LLDD_Report_Finalweb_1.pdf

30. OECD. (2008). *Education at a glance 2009–OECD indicators.* Paris: OECD.
31. OECD. (2008). *Pathways for people with disabilities.*
32. Wroblewski, A., & Unger, M. (2003). *Studierenden-Sozialerhebung 2002. Bericht zur sozialen Lage der Studierenden.* Vienna: Bundesministerium für Bildung, Wissenschaft und Kultur.
33. Sociaal Economische Raad. (2007). *Meedoen zonder beperkingen.*
34. Berthoud, R. (2006). *The employment rates of disabled people.* HMSO Research report no. 298. London: Her Majesty's Stationery Office (HMSO).
35. OECD. (2003). *Disability in higher education.*
36. Ebersold, S. (2007). Être étudiant et présenter une déficience, Ministère de la santé et des solidarités, Ministère de l'emploi, de la cohésion sociale et du logement, *Quelles trajectoires d'insertion pour les personnes handicapées?* Rennes: Échanges sociales et santé, ENSP.
37. Sociaal Economische Raad. (2007). *Meedoen zonder beperkingen.*
38. OECD. (1998). *Coordinating services for children and youth at risk. A world view.* Paris: OECD.
39. OECD. (1999). *Inclusive education at work: Including children with disabilities into mainstream schools.* Paris: OECD.
40. Prime Minister's Strategy Unit. (2005). *Improving the life chances of disabled people. Final report.* London: Prime Minister's Strategy Unit.
41. Izzo, M., & Lamb, M. (2006). *Self-determination and career development: Skills for successful transitions to postsecondary education and employment.* A white paper written in collaboration with Ohio State University, the Center on Disability Studies at the University of Hawaii at Manoa, and the Ministry of Education (France). Circular No. 2006–126, August 17, 2006, Official Bulletin, September 7, 2006.
42. Lamb, M. (2002). *Preliminary findings on a college success class for students with disabilities.* National Center for the Study of Postsecondary Educational Supports (NCSPES), University of Hawaii at Manoa, Honolulu.
43. Stodden, R., Jones, M. A., & Chang, K. B. T. (2002). *Services, supports and accommodations for individuals with disabilities: An analysis across secondary education, postsecondary education and employment.* Unpublished manuscript, Honolulu.
44. Wagner, M., Newman, L. Cameto, R., Levine, P., & Garza, N. (2006). *An overview of findings from wave 2 of the National Longitudinal Transition Study-2, (NLTS2).* Menlo Park, CA: SRI International. Retrieved from www.nlts2.org/reports/2006_08/nlts2_report_2006_08_complete.pdf
45. OECD. (2008). *Pathways for people with disabilities.*
46. Hvinden, B., Borg, E., Lindblad, S., & Grue, L. (2008). *Thematic review of the transition of people with disabilities beyond secondary education.* Background paper for the OECD. Oslo: *Nova/OECD.*
47. U.S. Department of Education. (2003). *Twenty-fifth annual report to Congress on the implementation of the Individuals with Disabilities Education Act.* Washington, DC: U.S. Department of Education.
48. Ibid.

Part 2

SECONDARY EDUCATION
AND TRANSITIONS

5

Leveling the Learning Bar in Secondary School Across Social Class

MARIE DURU-BELLAT

Globally, improving access to education is considered to be a priority. Different countries are extremely unequal in this respect, however, with primary enrollment rates currently varying from about 100% in the highest-income countries to less than 50% in the lowest-income ones.[1] The disparity is still larger at the secondary level, with nearly 100% enrollment in high-income countries such as Sweden and France, but less than 25% in several African countries—and as low as 14% in Burkina Faso and 9% in Niger.[2] Moreover, numbers on access tell only part of the story, as significant disparities exist in educational quality and outcomes. This chapter focuses on educational equity in the world's most affluent countries, where access to primary schooling is now universal and what is at stake is developing equitable secondary and tertiary schooling.

Education to Promote Competitiveness and Social Cohesion

More equitable education is the key for both economic growth and social cohesion. Recognizing this, European Union (EU) leaders put forward what is now called the *Lisbon strategy* in 2000, which aimed to make Europe "the most competitive and dynamic knowledge-based economy in the world." The Lisbon strategy was followed by the concrete *Lisbon goals*, which looked to education as a source of "sustainable economic growth with more and better jobs and greater social cohesion." Along with the EU, the Organisation for Economic Co-operation and Development (OECD) also emphasizes the social and economic benefits of addressing educational exclusion.

Particularly in regards to social cohesion, recent studies provide evidence that the distribution of education at the national level may be more important than the mean level of education.[3] As a result, both increasing the average level of education and improving educational equality are now considered priorities in the EU, and a set of corresponding objectives with precise quantitative benchmarks has been adopted.[4] Those objectives include lowering the number of early school leavers, reducing the percentage of low-achieving 15-year-olds in reading literacy, increasing access to tertiary education, developing participation of adults in life-long learning, and improving the level of educational attainment of the whole population.

Secondary education plays a particularly strategic role in achieving equity. Although the primary level is supposed to develop the foundations of learning and the tertiary level aims to develop higher and more specialized skills, the core of the schooling outcomes that need to be achieved are taught at the secondary level. Although students enter this level very unequal in terms of academic achievement, secondary schools are charged with the dual role of enabling all students to master the common core curriculum and preparing some of them to succeed in tertiary education. This is made more difficult by the fact that preparing students for tertiary education may require, for example, making the learning process denser and quicker, so that the best pupils' achievement may be maximized, at the risk of leaving the weakest ones far behind.

Several policies and programs aim to reduce the disparities of academic achievement between pupils at the secondary level and alleviate corresponding social inequalities. This chapter will first describe the main factors affecting whether students complete secondary school with equitable outcomes if they begin at different levels. Recognizing the strong, cumulative impact of inequities in the early years upon achievement at the secondary level, the chapter will go on to briefly consider interventions that affect equity at the beginning of secondary school. Third, the chapter will examine likely obstacles to implementing policies which promote equity. Finally, the chapter explores lessons that have emerged from the European experience.

The Impact of Separation and Segregation

The Programme for International Student Assessment (PISA) surveys[5] provide reliable information about what pupils really know at the end of their lower-secondary schooling. The PISA results thus allow some estimation of the effects of different school structures on pupils' secondary achievement across countries.[6] The PISA data show that both mean performance and disparities among pupils vary across countries of similar level of development. This demonstrates that countries' successes or failures at ensuring that all students succeed in secondary education is not inevitably tied to their level of economic development, but rather may be influenced by policy choices.

The PISA results have also demonstrated that a high degree of equality in student performance within countries (i.e., a small variance around the mean) can be achieved without lowering the overall level of achievement.[7] Contrary to common arguments that quality will necessarily suffer if school systems become more egalitarian, no trade-off seems to exist between efficiency and equity: Countries where pupils achieve a high mean level of performance are typically those in which the disparities between pupils are the smallest. Indeed, PISA data show that most countries with a high mean level of achievement, such as the European Nordic countries, Korea, and Hong Kong, are also more egalitarian, whereas very few countries have both above average mean student performance and a large between-student variation.

Countries with low disparities between students also register little variation in students' performance across schools. The guarantee of a certain level of quality to every pupil, whatever his or her school, is an important element of educational equity and social cohesion. In contexts in which schools do not provide a level playing field, the unequal social advantages that students possess when they arrive in the classroom will have a greater impact on their performance.

Comparative studies, and PISA data in particular, show that how pupils are grouped within and across schools influences the degree of dispersion of performance.[8,9] Two factors are well-documented in this respect.

The first factor concerns segregation between schools, which can be estimated by the proportion of student score variance explained by the school attended or the social composition of the student's environment. Research shows that, at the country level, social sorting between schools is associated both with a lower mean national level of performance and with larger academic and social disparities between pupils, as is the case in Germany and Belgium, among others.[10]

Besides the impact of the amount of segregation in the neighborhood, school segregation may occur whenever schools select pupils. Selection typically occurs on the basis of students' achievement, but this is actually closely related to their social background, considering the disadvantaged pupils' early difficulties. Such selection is implemented wherever the system is differentiated from the outset of secondary level. Systems with distinct schools, segregation, or early tracking channel students into specific learning environments according to their academic level and often to their correlated social background. The prevalence of selection by school explains why social segregation is so high in German-speaking countries.

Early tracking is associated with disparities of performance. On the other hand, the longer all students follow the same curriculum, the smaller the degree of inequality.[11] Both academic disparities and social inequality, as assessed by PISA at age 15, are the weakest among pupils attending homogeneous schools and classes, with a common core curriculum, postponed selection or subject specialization, and a socially mixed student body. The fact that social inequalities in achievement among students tend to be larger in countries with strong segregation shows that a part of the total influence of pupils' background on their level of achievement is explained by the school attended and not by specific sociocultural disadvantages. Importantly, the former source of disadvantage may be easier to influence through policy interventions than the latter ones.

The mechanisms underlying the detrimental impact of school segregation on educational equity are diverse. A first mechanism relates to what is now labelled as the *peer effect*, which maintains that the composition of the student body influences the quality of the learning environment through the resources the classmates represent for each other, the climate it generates in the daily life of the class, and the teaching practices that it allows or inhibits. Many studies show that pupils from working-class backgrounds attending a school with a mixed intake are less prone to developing anti-school attitudes and more likely to develop more ambitious educational aspirations.[12] A balanced social mix improves pupils' academic progress and attitudes without being detrimental to the mean level of achievement, as it strongly boosts the performance of the weakest pupils while putting only a slight brake on that of the highest-achieving ones.

Convergent trends concern the impact of the diffusion of immigrant students in schools. In countries where a large share of immigrant students attend schools with a high density of immigrant students, which is often the case in differentiated systems like the German or the Dutch ones, the gap in performance between immigrants and others is much larger than when they attend mixed settings. Integrating these pupils is therefore an important element of achieving equity.

A second group of mechanisms through which segregation affects achievement relates to the unequal quality of the teaching resources provided in segregated contexts. Often, the most privileged tracks or schools attract more financial resources and more qualified and experienced—and therefore more effective—teachers. Moreover, teachers in general develop higher expectations when confronted with more promising pupils, and the content coverage generally proves better, so that all across the board, the pupils' opportunities to learn are larger.

Reducing Socioeconomic and Academic Segregation

Social sorting between schools raises a problem of efficiency and fairness. A common sense of belonging to the same culture and citizenship, as well as more equitable chances of achieving academic success, would be better promoted if diverse pupils were educated together in the same schools.

The comprehensive model is designed to minimize segregation and its detrimental effects on efficiency and equity. Its purest form, which can be found in the Nordic European countries, includes a system of unstreamed neighborhood comprehensive schools from the primary to the lower secondary levels, with no repeating, no ability grouping, and without any choice during the transition between the two levels of schooling since primary and secondary education schools are integrated into one school.

However, even in countries where comprehensive schooling prevails, segregation may be generated by the way pupils are allocated to schools. Residential segregation is particularly significant in this respect since, in most countries, pupils generally attend their neighborhood school. Some countries have implemented strict zoning to reduce educational segregation, such as the *carte scolaire* or "school mapping" in France, but whenever spatial segregation exists, zoning cannot guarantee and may actually reduce social mixing in schools.

Even in contexts in which school zoning is in force, some parents strive to get exemptions for their children, so that they attend a school with a better reputation. Giving parents the choice of which school their child attends is becoming more popular and more widespread in Europe. This trend is due to the conviction that choice boosts efficiency, since efficient schools should attract a lot of pupils, whereas most would avoid inefficient ones. However, at least in Europe, the existence of choice within an education system is not correlated with better mean performance.[13] In fact, when the choice of school is completely free, as it is in Belgium, it can result in more hierarchical ranking of schools and more segregated learning environments.

This does not preclude the possibility that some forms of regulated choice may be associated with lower social inequalities. Oversubscribed schools could be required to accept certain proportions of disadvantaged or minority pupils, by implementing selection methods such as the lottery system used in some American school districts, or by balancing school choice by parental educational background. In countries where distances permit, "bussing" may also be implemented to allow pupils from poor neighborhoods to attend schools in more affluent neighborhoods. One example is a French experiment in which the pupils living in a very segregated area were bussed to schools in other neighborhoods. Although assessments are incomplete, the effects seem to be balanced.[14] Although academic achievement improved, the targeted pupils still suffered from a certain stigma vis-à-vis their more advantaged peers and may have developed lower self-esteem.

Efforts to reduce educational segregation along socioeconomic lines may encounter obstacles in the form of competing private interests. Research shows[15] that this is the case concerning parents' attitudes toward ability grouping. For parents whose children are achieving well, and who are often the most influential in schools, it is better if the school their children attend has ability classes (with distinct classes according to student academic level) because it has been demonstrated that academic progression is greater in high-level classes. For parents whose children are weaker, it would be better if the school had mixed heterogeneous classes, since these are more profitable for weak students, whereas the low-level classes in which they would be otherwise allocated are quite inefficient. The same tension arises where the possibility of school choice exists. When schools are not strongly differentiated, the most advantaged parents may avoid them and send their children to more selective (often private) schools. On the other hand, undifferentiated contexts prove more stimulating for the least advantaged pupils.

It must be stressed that families are directly involved in the creation of their children's school context, notably through participation in parents' associations or by exerting direct pressures. However, they will be very unequally efficient in so doing, precisely because they are unequal in status and resources. Inequality of resources may also affect the possibility of any choice, since to choose requires both information and financial capacity. Clearly, equality of opportunities can never be fully implemented as long as unequally advantaged families strive to allocate their children in unequal positions.

Although it may run counter to the most advantaged parents' preferences and strategies, organizing school admission with an aim of diversified school mix, at least until the end of compulsory schooling, is clearly important for advancing educational equality and social cohesion. To equalize the quality of what schools offer to every pupil, it is now widely admitted that some "positive discrimination" must be implemented. Potential approaches to achieving this include a focus on individuals, on schools, and/or on specific areas.

Providing Individualized Help

There exists a growing trend toward a more individualized form of help for pupils with difficulties, especially in the Scandinavian countries. Although originally designed to reduce repeating at the primary levels, this kind of individualized help concerns all levels of schooling, including secondary.

In Finland, the European country where the percentage of very weak pupils is the lowest in the PISA data (only 1.1% of students at the lowest level of achievement, compared with the OECD mean value of 6.7%), pupils' learning difficulties are tackled as soon as they appear and at different levels. First, a teacher works one-on-one (or sometimes in small groups) with pupils who are experiencing difficulty. He or she may also refer such pupils to an assistant working under his or her direction. This person will work with the pupils in need, again one-on-one, according to the teacher's directives and on the specific points that the pupils need help with. At a third level, the assistance of a qualified special needs teacher may be requested. The latter usually concentrates on basic subjects such as language or mathematics. The weakest pupils, such as those with serious disabilities, may be separated to attend special schools, but this occurs for less than 2% of students, whereas about 20% of a cohort benefit from this additional help.

In some cases, a fourth level of intervention is implemented for pupils with additional home or social problems. In this case, several partners outside the school, including psychologists, social workers, and representatives of the health sector and of the public housing sector if necessary, are invited to work with the school professionals representing the concerned pupils. Across the board, the approach is made more intensive and more diversified depending on the extent of the pupil's difficulties. However, the pupil's regular teacher is always involved, and every effort is made not to separate the pupil from his or her class and classmates. These two rules prove to be very important in ensuring the efficiency of this extra help.

In some countries, including France, extra help may be provided within small groups after the regular school day or even during the holidays. Research does not show dramatic effects, but this extra help proves more efficient when it is provided by qualified teachers rather than by volunteers from diverse associations. Other experimental devices, such as the British "study support" initiatives, which include a set of learning activities organized outside school hours, seem to lead to improved results and greater motivation.[16] If this extra help often proves inefficient, it is because enough attention is not always paid to identifying those pupils who would most benefit from this help. Without a rule of selection, some pupils doing rather well at school will request extra help, whereas weaker pupils will not, making the margin of progress brought by this extra assistance less important.

Another and much more efficient way to tackle failure in the early and later grades is to monitor what goes on in classes in a stricter manner. This has been done in the United Kingdom, with the national literacy and numeracy strategies implemented from 1998 onward to improve standards of English and mathematics, first at the primary level and currently at the lower secondary level as well. Very precise pedagogical frames were defined for literature and numeracy, recommending phases of different duration (e.g., for the literacy hour, x minutes for class reading, x minutes for group reading, etc.). The government defined precise targets for different key stages, and the assessment was conducted by the Office for Standards in Education (OFSTED). This managerial strategy was criticized by teachers from the outset, but pupils' significant progress demonstrated that it was efficient as well as very cost-effective. Moreover, this measure reduced disparities between boys and girls and between low- versus high-achievers.[17]

In summary, a first group of policies aimed at reducing the achievement gap and the correlated inequalities focuses on what is going on within classes, especially concerning the pedagogical interaction between teachers and pupils. However, more and more programs aimed at closing the achievement gap now focus upon the broader school environment.

Equalizing School Resources

Research increasingly demonstrates[18] that success and failure at school do vary according to the school (or the class) attended, everything else being equal, including the pupils' characteristics and country of residence. One path to equity involves achieving a fairer distribution of resources in different educational contexts by funding schools in disadvantaged areas more generously. This is the case in the Netherlands,[19] where diverse categories of disadvantaged children are distinguished and assigned a weighting factor for the allocation of school resources. For example, an ethnic minority pupil counts as 1.9, a Dutch working-class child counts as 1.25, and a nondisadvantaged pupil counts as 1.00. Schools are free to use the allocated resources according to their priorities, either to implement extra instruction programs or remedial teaching, to improve contacts between teachers and parents, or more often, to arrange smaller classes that enable more individualized attention from teachers. Schools are also given additional teachers depending on the socioeconomic and ethnic composition of their student body. It is worth noting that this both benefits the disadvantaged students and provides incentives to the advantaged schools to accept a mix of students.

Creating Geographic Priority Areas

In some countries, the focus has shifted from schools to larger geographical areas. This strategy is implemented in France, with the *zones d'education prioritaire* (ZEP), inspired by the earlier British Education Priority Action. Educational zones are defined on the basis of the socioeconomic characteristics of the population. The rationale here is that since children from the most disadvantaged or immigrant backgrounds face multiple problems, a variety of partners or institutions must be called upon to address these problems, including street educators, social workers, and sometimes policemen. Objective evaluations of the effects of initiatives focused on whole areas have been disappointing: Even if some positive impacts on achievement or attitudes have been produced, they have been cancelled out by the negative impact of the stigma attached to the schools and areas concerned. However, some argue that the evolution may have been even worse without this kind of action, because of the increased social segregation often observed in those areas as a result of middle-class flight. Others suggest that public funds may sometimes be targeted too loosely, since in France, for instance, as many as one out of four schools at the lower secondary level were included in the priority zoning. To address these concerns, in 2006, a new program called *ambition réussite* was launched in France. It is more strictly targeted and assessed, and attempts to attract more experienced teachers to these areas, as well as provide more individualized help. Moreover, it aims to help students with good results to have access to the best upper-secondary or tertiary schools, with special admission regulations and extra subsidies. This is aimed at boosting pupils' motivation during lower secondary schooling itself.

In the Netherlands, Educational Priority Areas have been designated, since 1985, in areas with an accumulation of disadvantageous factors. In these areas, primary and secondary schools, and other educational institutions such as libraries and daycare centers, are invited to work together to alleviate the disadvantages of the pupils concerned. They implement a variety of projects, such as preschool activities, reading promotion designs, homework help, and special guidance for early school leavers. Assessing the specific impact of each project is very difficult, and when evaluations are conducted, the impact of individual programs is often disappointing.[20] However, combining a variety of actions may be more successful.

The broad idea underlying the designation of priority areas is that school policies to reduce educational handicap should be nested in a wider package of measures to improve the well-being of families in disadvantaged communities. Importantly, when used alone, there is less evidence of their success than of the success of ensuring schools are not segregated.

Limiting the Impact of Preexisting Inequalities

Although the programs discussed above can play an important role in addressing the achievement gap at the secondary level, it is important to recognize the impact of the early years on equity at later stages. It is well-established that social inequalities matter for educational outcomes from the start and that the primary and secondary levels intervene too late to level the playing field.[21] In the absence of intervention, early difficulties accumulate during the schooling career, and it is much more costly to try to reduce them much later on. This section will therefore briefly discuss the equalizing role of three types of programs focused on reducing educational disadvantage before the start of formal schooling.

Early childhood care and education (ECCE) programs are often considered to bring the highest returns, not only for better success at school, but also for better life chances more broadly. They have been found to improve achievement at school, as well as employment rates and earnings, crime prevention, satisfying family relationships, and improved health. A Nobel laureate in economics, Heckman,[22] has recently supported this view by maintaining that high-quality early childhood programs can improve lifelong outcomes.

Some argue that the results of ECCE programs are often inconclusive and that it would be more cost efficient to reduce poverty and improve skills among the targeted children's families.[23] In a second approach to addressing early disadvantages, countries such as Belgium,[24] the United Kingdom,[25] and the United States[26] have consequently launched programs devoted to parental education around child-rearing during the early years. These aim to develop specific skills, such as linguistic interactions, learning incentives, or reading books.

In the later years of early childhood, pre-primary education offers a third approach to reducing inequities from the outset. Although in most countries the academic effects of preschooling are not dramatic, recent evidence from international surveys shows that attending preschool is positively related to later academic achievements and thus provides a better start. The pre-primary level is not compulsory in most countries; thus, to be effective in reducing social inequalities, this form of schooling must not be monopolized by the best-informed and highest-income parents, as is often the case.[27]

Remaining Gaps and Tensions in the Quest for Equity

Strategies implemented at the secondary level face a number of tensions in addition to the challenge of intervening at a late stage in the school life course. This discussion will set aside the inescapable tension between striving to allocate pupils to school environments that are as mixed as possible on the one hand, and focusing on the most disadvantages students on the other, which is easier to implement in segregated environments.

FINDING A BALANCE BETWEEN AUTONOMY AND ACCOUNTABILITY

When geographic areas are defined as a basis for educational intervention, municipal authorities (rather than national and central ones) are on the front line. This may unintentionally result in greater discrepancies between pupils, depending on the city they live in. Whether the latter is rich or less rich, and whether it is more or less committed to schooling problems, can make a significant difference in schooling outcomes. Moreover, focusing on specific schools may generate some flight on the part of the less disadvantaged pupils, whose parents may be put off by such a labelling. This was observed in France when the ZEP program was launched.

This inequality between municipalities leads to another difficulty, which concerns the monitoring of the changes and—even more broadly—the management of the education system. Today, in most European countries, some decentralization has been implemented. Decentralization is supposed to increase efficiency by limiting bureaucracy and allowing for better financial control and raise the responsiveness of schools to local communities, which would have more incentives to improve their own practices. However, the relationship between the various aspects of school autonomy and mean student performance proves to be weak,[28] and the widespread positive expectations that exist in regard to school autonomy and decentralization of decision-making are not supported. Moreover, and most importantly here, other studies[29] suggest that, like choice policy, decentralization proves detrimental to the homogeneity of performance across schools (or regions), thus fostering larger inequalities.

It is widely admitted[30] that without a centrally geared monitoring system and control of standards, decentralization and the correlative adaptation of schools to their student body are bound to bring an increase of the disparities of achievement and the different forms of social inequalities, which would in turn be detrimental to educational equity and social cohesion. The best way to boost efficiency without damaging equity and social cohesion, therefore, seems to involve articulating some national control, notably, for fixing standards and managing evaluation. For instance, in England, a country where schools and local authorities have long been granted a large degree of autonomy, a new equilibrium has been promoted since the 1990s. Schools are always accountable for the pedagogical services they offer, while the central authorities are responsible for setting the standards of a national curriculum, including detailed targets to be achieved, and which are to be assessed by regular testing. The Office for Standards in Education visits schools every 6 years, assessing pupils' achievements according to the list of given criteria, and then writes two reports, one of which is public and another one devoted to the school itself. The latter explains the strategies to be implemented to find solutions to the problems the inspection has disclosed.[31] Reaching such equilibrium between national management and local autonomy is difficult, however, and decentralization remains a risky path.

ADDRESSING CONTRADICTORY PRIVATE INTERESTS

Making a school fit more closely to its "customers" and adapting it to their needs also gives more leeway to private interests to manifest themselves. In other words, the stimulation of responsiveness to local requirements may sometimes induce mechanisms for choices or pressures favoring groups that are already advantaged.

In a given school setting, the families' private interests and those of teachers interact, since centralization may impact on the latter's autonomy and gives more weight to higher administrative levels. Moreover, even if most teachers are committed to educational equity, they are professionals whose working conditions matter, and there may be tension between these two issues. For instance, in France, although it is widely admitted that the weakest pupils need more time in school than their better-performing peers, the French Ministry of Education has recently shortened the school week to eliminate classes on Saturday mornings, with the teachers' unsurprising complicity.

It is a recurrent dilemma that, to be successful, any reform should be supported by teachers' and parents' genuine consensus. This is not always possible, given divergent interests concerning education, as unequal groups compete to make the most of always scarce educational resources for their children, in an environment in which the level of education achieved is the most efficient tool for social and economic mobility and as professionals struggle to preserve their working conditions. This results in, for instance, teachers defending homogeneous classes because they are characterized as easier to manage. Even if the weakest classes are more challenging to teach and less beneficial to the students, it seems easier to tailor teaching to students who are at the same level rather than manage classes with pupils at diverse levels of ability and learning. In this competition, private interests come first and a global objective, such as levelling the pupils' mean level or social cohesion, may seem an abstract one.

Like teachers, parents are far from being passive observers in the new distribution of resources implemented through policies at the local level. Whenever some actions or programs are open to all or are not precisely targeted, the most privileged parents tend to monopolize them for their own children. This is especially the case whenever tracking decisions have to be made. The best informed and most privileged families typically seek to place their children in the most demanding (but also the most rewarding) track, even if their son or daughter has only an average academic level of achievement. With the same academic level, working-class parents implement for their children a stronger self-selection.[32]

At the same time, it is often difficult to intervene with families to convince parents to use one or another program for their children. This is why, in some countries, programs are chosen to cover the larger environment, including neighborhood associations and resources. This leads to the concept of "learning communities." For instance, in Barcelona, a "City Educational Project" aims at promoting an integrated education network that brings together public institutions and civil society representatives. The latter offer a variety of activities, such as music or arts, while the former are in charge of developing public transport and renovating school equipment.[33]

Even though these programs are efficient in some respects, the main difficulty with promoting educational equality is that parents strive, with unequal resources, to lead their children to the highest degrees they can get, so that they may obtain the best position later on in life. Families closest to the school system in social and cultural terms are most aware of subtle inequalities between schools, between subjects, and between tracks.

LESSONS FROM THE FRENCH EXPERIENCE

In an attempt to balance the competing interests of students, parents, teachers, school authorities, and diverse levels of government, educational priorities and the correlated policies are tailored by policy-makers in a democratic process. These policy-makers must discard the temptation for simplistic directions for educational policies, despite their popularity. The most common course taken, because of its popularity, is to rely on the openness of the education system to reduce social inequalities. This has been the case in France, which has faced a dramatic expansion of education since the 1960s. The baccalauréat exam is taken at the end of secondary education to gain access to tertiary education. After a smooth increase in the percentage of students in a generation obtaining their baccalauréat from about 5% in 1950 to 28% at the beginning of the 1980s, the political objective set in 1981 of "80% of a generation with the baccalauréat level" saw figures rise rapidly to 55% in 1993 and 63% in 2005. It has remained between 63% and 66% since about 2000. This expansion of the education system was one of the main targets of the socialist government that took office in 1981 in France. It was reiterated by subsequent governments, whatever their political orientation, and met a consensus seldom observed in France on political matters, since it was supposed to result in an increased mean level of achievement but also reduce disparities among French pupils. Expanding education began to be promoted as an end in itself.

Increasing access may appear to be a less overtly class-biased policy than others, such as school choice. However, simply increasing access to education is not an efficient strategy. In France, a focus on pure quantitative targets led to the neglect of the question of educational quality; that is, what kind of education, for whom, and for what purpose. Research shows[34] that more education did not result in more social mobility, that it has been followed by some deterioration of degree holders' opportunities in the job market, and last but not least, that social inequalities have been shifting to a higher level rather than decreasing. The French example demonstrates that we need educational policy-makers to go beyond defining precise objectives and assessing their degree of realization in purely quantitative terms. Although even debatable objectives can generate important mobilization on educational goals, being able to evaluate such objectives and to react to what figures show remains another story. Although some researchers maintain that accountability is the key for improving the education system,[35] others fear that a strict reliance on accountability and evidence-based practices may come at the expense of democratic debates among parents, teachers, and all the persons concerned by education issues.[36]

Conclusion

At the national level, where education is an important and politically sensitive matter, the general interest is supposed to prevail. However, as this chapter has shown, defining the general interest can be challenging, and tradeoffs must be made in the pursuit of equity and social cohesion. Choices like whether to promote preschooling or life-long learning versus tertiary education, for instance, involve prioritizing either the currently least advantaged group or the most advantaged one, with the latter typically being the most influential.

National priorities matter too: A country will develop different educational policies if social cohesion rather than economic innovation is the overarching goal. In the first case, preschool or common core curriculum for every member of the community would take priority, whereas in the second, tertiary and competitive education for the highest achieving would prevail. Moreover, in the perspective of social cohesion, education should not be focused only on academic success; the development of social skills and the promotion of well-being may be judged as equally important. Thus, the content, quality, and distribution of education matters more than the quantity, although "more of the same thing" is often an easy and consensual objective.

Such tradeoffs are inevitable since no country has unlimited resources to allocate to education. If social cohesion is really the goal, priority should be given to high-quality pre-primary, primary, and secondary education, even if that must be at the expense of some more limited development of tertiary education. The choices to be made will induce some debates, since education, like other fields, is not ruled only by scientific research. Rather, social conflicts, political priorities, and tradeoffs between alternative policies also matter.

Schooling is not a panacea: Education is nested in the whole society. Research shows that disparities between children emerge before they enter school, due to the unequal environments outside of school. Attention to the local context in which pupils live and learn, which is now widespread in most European countries, results in more concern for housing conditions, urban renewal, income support for families, and local employment, among others. In this perspective, adult training becomes a crucial issue. It delivers a double benefit: Investing in adults can transform the way one works, as well as the way one brings up his or her child. Providing adult training, life-long learning, and offering second chances are important for economic, equity and social benefits.

In conclusion, it is impossible to have true equality of opportunity in an unfair society, and consequently, to achieve a satisfying level of social cohesion solely through educational solutions. Nevertheless, education remains one important piece of the puzzle in promoting a fair society.

NOTES

1. UNESCO. (2010). *Education for all global monitoring report 2010: Reaching the marginalized.* Oxford/Paris: Oxford University Press and UNESCO.
2. Ibid.
3. Green, A., Preston, J., & Janmaat, G. (2006). *Education, equality and social cohesion.* London: Palgrave.
4. European Commission. (2007). *Progress towards the Lisbon Objectives in education and training,* (SEC 2007, 1284). Brussels: European Commission.
5. PISA (Programme for International Student Achievement) assesses 15 year olds' skills in literacy, numeracy and basic science, relying on comparable exercises. See OECD. (2001). *Knowledge and skills for life. First results from PISA 2000.* Paris: OECD; OECD. (2003). *Literacy skills for the world of tomorrow. Further results from PISA 2000.* Paris: OECD.
6. OECD. (2003). *Literacy skills for the world of tomorrow.*
7. Danish Technological Institute. (2005). *Explaining student performance. Evidence from the international PISA, TIMSS and PIRLS surveys.* Paris: OECD.
8. OECD. (2004). *What makes school systems perform?* Paris: OECD.
9. Duru-Bellat, M., & Suchaut, B. (2005). Organization and context, efficiency and equity of Educational system. *European Educational Research Journal, 4*(3), 181–194.
10. Danish Technological Institute. (2005). *Explaining student performance.*
11. Hanushek, E. A., & Wössmann, L. (2006). Does educational tracking affect performance and inequality? Differences-in-differences evidence across countries. *The Economic Journal, 11,* 63–76.
12. Duru-Bellat, M. (2007). Social inequality in French education. In R. Tesse, S. Lamb, & M. Duru-Bellat (Eds.), *International studies in educational inequality, theory and policy 2* (pp. 1–20). Dordrecht, DR: Springer.
13. Mons, N. (2007). *Les nouvelles politiques éducatives.* Paris: PUF.

14. Duru-Bellat, M. (2007). Quelle marge de manœuvre pour l'école, dans un environnement d'inégalités ? In S. Paugam (Ed.), *Repenser la solidarité* (pp. 669–685). Paris: PUF.

15. Duru-Bellat. (2007). Social inequality in French education.

16. MacBeath, J., et al. (2001). *The impact of study support*. DfEE, Research Brief No 273, Londres.

17. Machin, S., & Mac Nelly, S. (2004). *The literacy hour*. Discussion paper. Bonn: Institute for the Study of Labor (IZA).

18. For a synthesis of research on teacher and school effectiveness, see Scheerens, J. (2000). *Improving school effectiveness*. Paris: UNESCO, Fundamentals of Educational Planning; for a discussion, see Lupton, R., & Thrupp, M. (2007). Taking local contexts more seriously. In Tesse, Lamb, & Duru-Bellat (Eds.), *International studies in educational inequality, theory and policy*.

19. Driessen, G., & Dekkers, H. (2007). Educational inequality in the Netherlands: Policy, practice and effects. In Tesse, Lamb, & Duru-Bellat (Eds.), *International studies in educational inequality, theory and policy*.

20. Ibid.

21. Feinstein, L., & Duckworth, K. (2006). *Development in the early years: Its importance for school performance and adult outcomes*. London: Centre for Research on the Wider Benefits of Learning.

22. Heckman, J. (2006). Skill formation and the economics of investing in disadvantaged children. *Science, 312*, 1900–1902.

23. Glass, N. (1999). Sure start: The development of an early intervention program for young children in the United Kingdom. *Children and Society, 13*, 257–264.

24. Pourtois, J. P., & Desmet, H. (1991). L'éducation parentale. *Revue Française de pédagogie, 96*, 87–112.

25. Glass. (1999). Sure start.

26. Rumberger, R., & Arellano, B. (2007). Understanding and addressing achievement gaps during the first four years of school in the United States. In Tesse, Lamb, & Duru-Bellat (Eds.), *International studies in educational inequality, theory and policy*.

27. Danish Technological Institute. (2005). *Explaining student performance*.

28. OECD. (2005). *School factors related to quality and equity. Results from PISA 2000*. Paris: OECD.

29. Mons. (2007). *Les nouvelles politiques éducatives*.

30. At least among American researchers. See Harris, D., & Herrington, C. (2006). Accountability, standards and the growing achievement gap: Lessons from the past half century. *American Journal of Education, 112*(2), 209–238. Even if this issue is less dealt with in Europe, some comparisons between countries support this thesis. See Duru-Bellat, M., & Meuret, D. (2003). English and French modes of regulation of the education system: A comparison. *Comparative Education, 39*(4), 463–477.

31. It is difficult to assess the specific impact of this mode of regulation; however, a comparison between England and France (with no regulation of this kind in the latter country) suggests that it may be partly responsible for the reinforcement of equity observed in the former country. See Duru-Bellat, M., & Meuret, D. (2003). English and French modes of regulation of the education system.

32. Duru-Bellat. (2007). Social inequality in French education.

33. Institut d'Educacio Ayuntament de Barcelona. (2005). *Schools and civic entities: Networking schools*. (PEC 2004–2007). Barcelona: Barcelona Educational Coordination Board.

34. Duru-Bellat, M. (2008). Recent trends in social reproduction in France: Should the political promises of education be revisited? *Journal of Education Policy, 23*(1), 81–95.

35. Wossman, L. International evidence on school competition, autonomy and accountability. *Peabody Journal of Education, 82*(2–3), 473–497.

36. Hammersley, M. (2005). Is the evidence-based practice movement doing more good than harm? *Evidence and Policy, 1*(1), 85–100.

6

Addressing Primary and Secondary Education for Socially Excluded Girls[1]

MARLAINE LOCKHEED AND MAUREEN LEWIS

Challenges: Girls from Socially Excluded Groups

Girls' education is a human right, provides economic and social benefits, and gender equality in education is an international goal.[2] These imperatives and benefits have inspired countries and donors worldwide, with positive results. Since 1960, primary school enrollment rates in the developing world have risen steeply for both boys and girls, with girls' participation generally converging with that of boys.[3] A similar improvement in secondary education has occurred in most regions. Yet, recent estimates find that about 64 million children of primary school age and 71 million adolescents of lower secondary school age are still out of school in developing countries.[4] A plurality of those who are out of school are girls–74 million in 2008, of which about 70% come from "socially excluded groups."[5] This chapter addresses the specific issues of these doubly disadvantaged girls.[6]

Socially excluded groups are population subgroups that are sidelined in their own countries, prevented by discrimination and indifference from receiving the social rights and protection meant to be extended to all citizens.[7] They include ethnic minorities, isolated clans, and groups in which a language other than the majority or dominant language is spoken. Such population subgroups are not simply different, however; their difference is accorded lower esteem by the majority population. Loury explains that they are marginalized due to one or more of the following phenomena:

- Stigmatization by recent historical trauma at the hands of a majority or dominant population. Examples include a history of slavery (as experienced by peoples of African descent in Brazil, Cuba, and the United States) or dispossession of a homeland (as experienced by Indigenous peoples of Canada or the United States)

- Ethnicity that differs from that of a dominant group, including differences in ethnic group, language, and religion—for example, non-Lao-Tai ethnic groups in Laos, Indigenous groups in Latin America, or people from nondominant tribal groups in sub-Saharan Africa
- Low status, whereby excluded groups are "ranked" or subordinated in the social hierarchy below a majority or dominant population, such as the Roma in Europe or lower-caste groups in India or Nepal
- Involuntary minority status (in contrast to immigrant groups that are voluntary minorities), such as groups that have been forcibly moved across borders

Socially excluded groups differ across regions. Countries that are highly ethnically and linguistically heterogeneous are particularly at risk. The educational consequences of social exclusion range from the merely disagreeable, such as teachers ignoring students in class, to the dire: destruction of schools and violence against teachers and communities. Discrimination by a dominant population effectively prevents all children from socially excluded groups from participating in education. But, compounding the problem for girls, certain socially excluded groups are *less likely* to send their daughters to school and *more likely* to allow them to drop out early, as compared to sons.

Although the largest number of school-aged girls who are out of school live in Africa, as compared with other regions, the double disadvantage of girls is most pronounced in Latin America, Asia, and Eastern Europe.[8] That is, in countries in these regions, the girls who are out of school are typically those from socially excluded groups. They are less likely to enroll in and complete primary school or to continue to secondary school than are boys from their own groups or girls from majority groups, and are therefore doubly disadvantaged, with gender gaps within these socially excluded groups being greater than gender gaps within the dominant group. For example:

- *Latin America*: In Guatemala, 26% of Indigenous, non–Spanish-speaking girls complete primary school, compared with 45% of Indigenous, non–Spanish-speaking boys and 62% of Spanish-speaking girls.[9] In Ecuador, 20% of Indigenous girls aged 15–17 are enrolled in school, compared with 40% of Indigenous boys and 54% of non-Indigenous girls of the same age.[10]
- *Asia*: In Laos, non–Lao-Tai girls living in rural communities complete fewer than 2 years of school, whereas non–Lao-Tai boys complete 4 years of school, and majority Lao-Tai girls living in urban communities complete 8 years of school.[11] In India, about 35% of tribal girls aged 15 are in school, compared with about 60% of tribal boys and nontribal girls of the same age.[12] In Vietnam, 31% of primary school-age Hmong girls are enrolled in school, as compared with 51% of Hmong boys and about 65% of majority Kinh girls and boys the same age.[13]

- *Eastern Europe*: In the Slovak Republic, 9% of minority girls are enrolled in secondary school, compared with 54% of Slovak girls.[14] In Romania, 25% of the female Roma population over 10 years of age has completed secondary school as compared with 34% of Roma males and 62% of non-Roma girls.[15] In Turkey, 48% of Kurdish girls aged 8–15 are enrolled in school, compared with 71% of Kurdish boys and 75% of Turkish girls of the same age.[16]

These examples provide an idea about the extent and degree of the problem of the double disadvantage, but a comprehensive search of the literature finds concrete evidence for fewer than 15 such countries (see Table 6.1 for details on the double disadvantage in school participation). In these countries, "double disadvantages" are found with respect to:

- *Having ever enrolled in school* in Bolivia,[17] Guatemala,[18] and China[19]
- *Current participation in schooling* in Ecuador,[20] Guatemala,[21] India,[22] Nigeria,[23] Turkey[24] and Vietnam[25]
- *Number of years or level of schooling completed* in Bolivia,[26] Ecuador,[27] Guatemala,[28] India,[29] Laos PDR,[30] Mexico,[31] Peru,[32] and Romania[33]
- *Achievement as measured by tests* in Ecuador,[34] Ethiopia,[35] India,[36] Laos PDR,[37] and Peru[38]

What Keeps Doubly Disadvantaged Girls Out of School?

Four main lines of evidence emerge from the literature on the factors that keep socially excluded girls out of school: legal or administrative barriers, poor quality and limited supply of schools, within-school discrimination, and low household demand for girls' education, including discrimination.

LAWS AND REGULATIONS

First, the most important legal and administrative barriers are the absence of compulsory education laws applying to all children. The number of countries lacking these laws, however, has declined substantially over the past decade, and in general, the lack of such laws on the books does not constitute a major barrier in most countries.[39] But some Ministry of Education policies and administrative rules have an unintended discriminatory impact on socially excluded girls. Particularly important barriers are policies and rules related to language of instruction, gender-segregated schools, and curriculum and ability tracking.

Rules imposing a national language of instruction for primary schools are detrimental for girls who speak a home language that is different from the language of instruction. This is particularly problematic in countries where the practice of

Table 6.1 **Gender-Within-Ethnicity Differences in School Participation in Low- and Middle-Income Countries**

Country	Study[40]	Finding
Bolivia	Jimenez, 2004	• Quechua- and Aymara-speaking Indigenous girls were less likely to enroll in school than were non-Indigenous children. • Quechua- and Aymara-speaking Indigenous girls were more likely than non-Indigenous children to discontinue their schooling prematurely.
Bolivia	Jimenez Pozo, Landa Casazola, & Yanez Aguilar, 2006	• 26% of Indigenous women aged 15 and above had no schooling, compared with 8% of Indigenous men the same age. • Indigenous girls aged 7–14 had a 39% probability of being in school; Indigenous boys the same age had a 64% probability of being in school.
China	Hannum & Adams, 2007	• In rural counties where minorities accounted for roughly one-third of the population, minority participation rates were substantially lower than those of Han children. • Girls' participation was inconsistent across these minority groups. Among ten minority ethnic groups, five were more likely to enroll girls in school, whereas four were less likely to do so. Among Han children and children from one minority group, no gender differences in enrollment were observed.
Ecuador	Larrea & Montenegro Torres, 2006	• 33% of Indigenous women aged 15 and above had no schooling, compared with 14% of Indigenous men of the same age.
Ecuador	Garcia Aracil & Winkler, 2004	• The school completion rate for Indigenous girls in Ecuador was half that of non-Indigenous girls and only one-third that of all boys (controlling for residence and socioeconomic status). • The probability of primary school dropout was higher for girls in rural than in urban areas, and ethnicity was a factor explaining dropout from rural but not urban schools. Girls living in urban areas, whether Indigenous or not, were 34% more likely to stay in school than males, but 35% less likely to be in school than males in rural areas.

(continued)

Table 6.1 (**continued**)

Country	Study[40]	Finding
Ecuador	Garcia Aracil & Winter, 2006	• 62% of Indigenous girls aged 12–14 were enrolled in school, compared with 73% of Indigenous boys the same age and 83% of non-Indigenous girls. • 20% of Indigenous girls aged 15–17 were enrolled in school, compared with 40% of Indigenous boys and 65% of non-Indigenous girls.
Guatemala	Hallman & Peracca, 2007	• 25% of Indigenous girls aged 15–19 have completed primary school, compared with 45% of Indigenous boys aged 15–19. • A higher share of Indigenous boys than Indigenous girls have ever been in school. • Being Indigenous raises the probability of rural dropout by almost 30%.
India	Wu, Goldschmidt, Boscardin, & Azamm, 2007	• About 35% of girls aged 15 from scheduled tribes were enrolled in school, compared with about 60% of boys the same age from scheduled tribes.
India	Census of India, 2001	• 63% of girls aged 7–14 from scheduled castes or scheduled tribes were enrolled in school, compared with 74% of boys aged 7–14 from the same groups.
India	Asadullah, Khambampati, & Boo, 2009	• 52% of girls aged 6–18 from scheduled tribes were enrolled in school, compared with 60% of boys from scheduled tribes and 58% of Hindu girls.
India	Bhalotra, 2009	• 66% of rural girls ages 12–14 from scheduled castes reported attending school, compared with 82% of rural boys of the same age from scheduled castes and 76% of rural girls from high Hindu castes. • 57% of rural girls ages 12–14 from scheduled tribes reported attending school, compared with 73% of rural boys of the same age from scheduled castes and 76% of rural girls from high Hindu castes.
India	UNESCO Institute for Statistics, 2005	• Controlling for home background (parental education, household size, wealth, religion and caste), community factors (region, urban vs. rural), girls aged 6–10 had 5.9% lower probability of attending school, compared with boys the same age, and tribal children had a 3.5% lower probability of attending school than nontribal children. • Thus, tribal girls had a 9.4% lower probability of attending school compared with nontribal boys.

Table 6.1 (*continued*)

Country	Study[40]	Finding
Laos	King & van de Walle, 2007	• 48% of rural Hmong-lu Mien girls aged 6–12 were enrolled in school, compared with 66% of rural Hmong-lu Mien boys and 81% of rural Lao-Tai girls the same age. • 33% of rural Chine-Tibetan girls aged 6–12 were enrolled in school, compared with 39% of Chine-Tibetan boys the same age. • 6.5% of rural non-Lao Tai girls aged 12–15 were enrolled in school, compared with 12% of rural non–Lao-Tai boys and 32% of rural Lao-Tai girls the same age.
Mexico	Ramirez, 2006	• 27% of Indigenous women aged 15 and above had no schooling, compared with 17% of Indigenous men. • Indigenous women aged 15–21 completed on average 6.5 years of school, compared with 7 years completed by Indigenous men.
Nepal	Stash & Hannum, 2001	• Boys were 7 times more likely to enter school than girls (controlling for caste and socioeconomic status [SES]). • High-caste children and elite Newar children were 4–5 times more likely to enter school than low-caste children (controlling for gender and SES). • High-caste boys were 1.5 times more likely to enroll in school compared with high-caste girls (controlling for caste, gender, and SES). • Newar boys were half as likely as Newar girls to enroll in school (controlling for caste, gender, and SES).
Nigeria	UNESCO Institute for Statistics, 2005	• Girls aged 6–10 had a 12% lower probability of attending school compared with boys the same age, and Hausa-speaking children had a 24% lower probability of attending school compared with Yoruba-speaking children (controlling for residence and SES). • Thus, Hausa-speaking girls aged 6–10 had a 36% lower probability of attending school than Yoruba-speaking boys.

(*continued*)

Table 6.1 (**continued**)

Country	Study[40]	Finding
Pakistan	Lloyd, Mete, & Grant, 2007	• In rural communities, girls' school attendance rates were 45 percentage points below those of boys for the lowest income group but only 15 points below boys for the highest income group.
Peru	Trivelli, 2006	• Indigenous women aged 15 and above completed 5.6 years of school, compared with 7.6 years for Indigenous men of the same age. • Indigenous girls aged 7–14 completed 3.5 years of school, compared with 3.6 years of school for Indigenous boys of the same age.
Romania	Open Society Institute, 2007	• 25% of rural Roma girls reached secondary education, as compared with 34% of rural Roma boys and 62% of rural girls in general.
South Africa	Lam, Ardington, & Leibbrandt, 2007	• Controlling for SES and past school performance, African girls were more likely to be enrolled in school than African boys. • There were no gender differences among Colored children.
Sri Lanka	Arunatilake, 2006	• Girls aged 9–11 were 3% less likely to be in school compared with boys the same age, and Tamil children were 7% less likely to be in school than Sinhalese children (controlling for SES and location). • Thus, Tamil girls aged 9–11 were 10% less likely to be in school than Sinhalese boys the same age.
Turkey	Kirdar, 2007	• Turkish-speaking girls aged 6–15 were 1.98 as likely to be *not* enrolled in school as compared with Turkish-speaking boys (controlling for region and family characteristics). • Kurdish-speaking girls were 3.21 as likely to be *not* enrolled in school as compared with Kurdish-speaking boys (controlling for region and family characteristics). • Arabic-speaking girls were 2.29 as likely to be *not* enrolled in school as compared with Arabic-speaking boys (controlling for region and family characteristics).

Table 6.1 **(continued)**

Country	Study[40]	Finding
Vietnam	Chi, 2009	• In Phu Yen province, 57% of H'Roi girls age 12 were enrolled in school, compared with 82% of H'Roi boys, and in Lao Cai province, 72% of Hmong girls age 12 were enrolled in school, compared with 81% of Hmong boys; 98% of Kinh girls the same age were enrolled in school.
Vietnam	DeJaeghere & Miske, 2009	• 31% of primary school-aged Hmong girls were in school, compared with 51% of Hmong boys and 93% Kinh majority girls and boys the same age. • At the secondary level, 2% of secondary school-aged Hmong girls and 7% of Hmong boys were in school, compared with about 65% of Kinh majority girls and boys the same age.
Vietnam	Nguyen, 2006	• Controlling for SES and region, girls aged 6–18 were 55% as likely to be enrolled in school as boys, and non-Kinh (minority) children were 33% *more* likely to be enrolled in school than Kinh (majority) children. • Thus, non-Kinh girls were 22% *less* likely to be enrolled in school as compared with Kinh boys the same age, controlling for region and other variables.

sequestering girls and women may deprive them of any opportunity to learn a second, national language prior to starting school.[41] For example, Berber-language–speaking girls in Morocco and Kurdish-speaking girls in Turkey have few opportunities to learn Arabic or Turkish, respectively, before starting school. Berber or Kurdish boys, by comparison, have the opportunity to learn a national language from the "street" or from their fathers, who may use the language for their work.[42]

Some countries require that boys and girls attend gender-segregated schools, as in Pakistan.[43] If a village can afford to build only one school, this often means that girls have fewer opportunities for learning than do boys. Since many socially excluded groups live in small, remote villages that actually have only one school, mandated gender segregation is likely to have a larger impact on socially excluded girls. Interestingly, in Pakistan, which provides single-sex education in government schools, parents in rural villages were willing to send their sons and daughters to private coeducational schools and to send their small sons to their daughters' girls schools, which suggests that parents may be less concerned about coeducation than are education authorities.[44]

Some countries have "selection" or "guidance" examinations following primary or lower secondary school that stream girls and socially excluded children into different schooling opportunities at the secondary level.[45] Many countries have separate vocational tracks for girls and boys at the secondary level; often, the girls' track prepares them for lower-paying occupations than does the boys' track. Since socially excluded children are more likely to be enrolled in vocational programs than in academic programs, this practice again places girls from these groups at a disadvantage. But this is not always the case. In India, lower-caste boys pursued traditional "caste-appropriate" occupations in Marathi-language schools while lower-caste girls were not able to do so. Instead, the girls enrolled in English-language schools and benefitted in both labor and marriage markets, with better employment options, higher wages, and upward mobility through marriage into a higher caste.[46] Administrative rules governing the rights of girls to remain in school during—or to return to school following—a pregnancy have been found in many countries. Often, these rules require expulsion from school, meaning that the girls are deprived of any opportunity for further education, a penalty that is not imposed on the boys who are involved. Since girls from socially excluded groups often marry at younger ages than do girls from mainstream groups, this policy may disproportionately affect them.

SUPPLY AND QUALITY OF SCHOOLS

Second, socially excluded children are more likely to live in rural areas, farther from schools. For example, in Vietnam, majority children live, on average, only 0.2 km from the nearest lower secondary schools, whereas minority children live over ten times farther from a lower secondary school: 2.4 km on average.[47] In Laos, rural majority Lao-Tai children live on average 7 km from a lower secondary school, whereas rural minority non-Lao-Tai children live 20 km from the nearest lower secondary school.[48] In some rural communities in Ethiopia, the average distance to the nearest school was over 8 km.[49]

Rural children also attend schools with poorer *physical* quality compared with schools attended by urban children. Across 14 countries in sub-Saharan Africa, rural schools had less well-constructed buildings, less electricity and water, fewer toilets, and fewer other facilities and equipment as compared with urban schools.[50] Moreover, schools attended by socially excluded children also often suffer from poorer *instructional* quality: lack of materials, teacher absenteeism, instruction in a national or regional language that is incomprehensible to the child, and teacher-centered pedagogy. In 14 countries in Africa, for example, rural schools had fewer instructional materials for reading, and their teachers scored less well on a test of reading, as compared with urban schools.[51] In Laos, rural schools serving language minority groups were less well provisioned than were rural schools serving the dominant Lao-Tai ethnic group.[52] Rural schools also suffer from higher rates of teacher absenteeism than do urban schools; across six countries, 20%–50% of teachers were absent at the time of an initial first visit by researchers.[53] These disadvantages affect both boys and girls, but some research suggests that girls are more sensitive than boys to greater distances to school and poorer education quality, which, therefore, affects socially excluded girls more than socially excluded boys.[54]

DISCRIMINATION

Third, parents may keep their children out of school because of perceived discrimination and mistreatment by schools and teachers.[55] Girls from socially excluded groups may be seated far from the teacher, provided with fewer textbooks and other learning materials, and not encouraged to participate in classroom discussions.

Teachers may evaluate the performance of girls from socially excluded groups less favorably than they evaluate the performance of boys or children from dominant groups. A recent experiment conducted in India found that lower-caste teachers discriminated against lower-caste girls when grading their tests, although higher-caste teachers did not do so.[56] There is limited research on this type of double disadvantage inside classrooms, and a paucity of classroom observations studies in developing countries, but a few studies of *either* gender *or* ethnic discrimination in classrooms suggest that this may be a problem. For example, in Yemen, primary school girls were typically seated at the rear of the classroom, far from the blackboard and the teacher,[57] and in India, low-caste Dalit children were ignored or even mistreated in class by their teachers and by their non-Dalit classmates.[58]

Another type of discrimination comes from the content of school textbooks, which often ignore the contributions of women and minority groups or may reinforce stereotyped images of them. Girls and women are depicted less frequently than boys and men in textbooks from "countries at all levels of economic development and at all levels of gender equality."[59] For example, only one-quarter of the illustrations of people in textbooks from countries as diverse as Kuwait, Peru, Singapore, and Zambia portrayed girls and women, the remaining three-quarters were images of boys and men. While newly revised textbooks in Turkey portray girls and boys about equally, illustrations of men outnumber those of women two to one.[60] Often, when girls and women appear in textbooks, they are portrayed in traditional, domestic, or submissive roles relative to boys and men. For example, in West African secondary textbooks, men were three times as likely to appear in modern occupations as were women.[61] In Kenya, women were represented entirely in domestic activities, and in Tanzania, occupational stereotypes were observed in textbooks for primary school students, with twice as many men illustrated as women, working in twice as many occupations.[62] In China, occupational and personality gender stereotypes were found in elementary-level textbooks for all grades and subjects.[63] In some cases, ethnic minority groups are stigmatized in textbooks, leading to greater social exclusion.[64] Rural children may find textbooks foreign to them, as in Bangladesh, where national textbooks "mostly illustrate urban settings, characters, and examples, marginalizing the rural population [and] reinforcing gender stereotypes."[65] Ethnic minorities also may be under-represented in textbooks in an attempt to promote social cohesion and national unity, as in the case of Turkey.[66]

DIRECT AND OPPORTUNITY COSTS OF SCHOOLING

Fourth, parents may keep children out of school because of the direct and opportunity costs of education, and the perception that the returns to investment in girls' education will be low.[67] The economic need for child labor has been identified as one of the most important reasons for not sending rural children to school.[68] Most socially excluded groups are poor, and the direct costs of schooling can amount to significant shares of household income. These costs include those for school uniforms, textbooks, and transportation, even when school fees are eliminated or subsidized, and can prevent families from enrolling children in school.[69] Since the economic returns to education are lower for socially excluded women in many countries, as compared with the economic returns to education for men and majority women, due in part to discrimination in the labor market, parents may be unwilling to invest in girls' education.[70] Finally, concerns for girls' safety are also important, as adolescent girls in particular are targets for abuse, rape, and abduction, some of which occurs at or in transit to school.[71] To avoid these risks, parents may keep girls at home. Distance from school is a significant constraint on girls' school participation in many countries because longer distances expose them to greater danger. As noted above, doubly disadvantaged girls often live in habitations that are relatively far from the nearest school.

Programs That Promote Equity for Socially Excluded Girls

In countries with many socially excluded groups and high levels of ethnic, linguistic, economic, and social diversity, girls from socially excluded groups are doubly disadvantaged educationally. Raising the availability and quality of schools for all socially disadvantaged children in such countries will reduce much of this gender gap, but compensatory programs designed for and targeted at socially excluded girls will also be required.

Yet, most of the available evidence regarding the effectiveness of interventions to boost schooling for girls and socially excluded groups focuses on either one or the other—gender or social exclusion—rather than both; few studies actually examine the program impacts on educational outcomes of socially excluded girls specifically.[72] What we can infer, however, is that getting and keeping socially excluded girls in school entails both different approaches and higher costs. Cultural variations, linguistic differences, and the special needs of girls drive up costs, because they require new methods tailored to each group. Investment on two fronts—improving the supply of school opportunities and boosting the demand for education—is essential for enrolling and retaining socially excluded children in general, and girls in particular. But hard evidence about the effects of programs specifically targeted to socially excluded girls is limited, and the work of multilateral agencies and non-governmental organizations (NGOs) is rarely empirically evaluated.[73] Although many questions remain, several types of programs hold promise—and some evidence of effectiveness—for doubly disadvantaged girls.

PREPARING CHILDREN FOR SCHOOL AND ADAPTING SCHOOLS TO CHILDREN

Preschool programs that help new mothers and also provide health and nutrition interventions can improve their children's readiness for school. Since girls' undernourishment is often closely linked to gender discrimination in society,[74,75] such programs could be particularly effective for advancing the educational and life chances of socially excluded girls. Programs that offer early childhood enrichment and work closely with disadvantaged mothers are significantly more successful than are programs that offer only custodial care for the children. These programs can be held in either education centers or homes, and home-based programs that provide daycare, nutrition, and educational services have been found to boost disadvantaged children's school readiness. In India, early childhood education centers for poor girls helped raise their subsequent retention in primary school. In Brazil, Turkey, Bolivia, and India, preschool programs that involved both mothers and children from excluded groups have been effective in reducing children's subsequent primary school dropout and in boosting their achievement.[76]

Providing primary school education in a local language—as is the case in many Latin American countries with significant Indigenous populations, in India and Ethiopia where home language instruction is an educational policy and, more recently, in Morocco where children in Berber communities have only just obtained the right to study in their home language—may increase opportunities for girls. However, the evidence is slim. Benson's review of literature for UNESCO argues that introducing reading, writing, and thinking skills in the child's home language is particularly beneficial for excluded girls' school enrollment and retention.[77] But she also notes that, "using the mother tongue for teaching and learning does not in itself equalize opportunities for female learners, but there are clear indications that it improves conditions for all learners, and especially girls."[78] Another study notes, with respect to the double disadvantage of girls from linguistic minority groups in sub-Saharan Africa, "there appears to be no in-depth research available on which to establish a robust connection between the use of the mother tongue in primary education, or bilingual education involving the mother tongue, and girls' school participation and success."[79] Adapting schools to accommodate linguistic heterogeneity through bilingual or multilingual education can provide a bridge from home language instruction to instruction in a national language.[80] But experts caution that the success of these programs is largely dependent upon many different factors.

ENSURING THAT SCHOOLS HAVE THE BASICS FOR TEACHING AND LEARNING

Increasing the supply of schools is essential for reaching socially excluded girls, as distance to school is a significant barrier in many countries.[81] In Pakistan, having a school in the village increases the probability that girls aged 10–14 will enroll in school, and in rural areas of that country girls are less likely to drop out when the school is less than 2 km from their home.[82] In Laos, girls are much more likely to enroll in a school located in the community than in one that is farther away.[83] In Afghanistan, establishment of community-based schools in villages of two rural districts boosted the school enrollment of girls aged 6–11 years from 18% to 68% and significantly lowered their rates of early dropout.[84]

Ensuring that a school is located in a village often requires constructing new schools. Even though new school construction may not specifically target girls or communities of socially excluded groups, such construction may benefit them, as was the case in Indonesia, where a massive school construction program cut the gender gap in educational attainment by half and significantly reduced the rural–urban gap.[85] In India, 15 years of school construction and expansion (the District Primary Education Program followed by Sarva Shiksha Abhiyan), which was initially targeted at districts with below-average female literacy rates, had positive effects on the school enrollment of older girls; it also apparently helped boost the enrollment rates of tribal girls from 17% in 1983 to 52% in 2004.[86]

The quality of the school is also important, since school quality affects whether girls enroll in school and how long they stay in school. Both the quality of the school's physical facility and the quality of the instructional program matter. Poor-quality schools can include schools with leaking roofs, shattered walls, and dysfunctional sanitary facilities, as well as those where teachers are absent and where textbooks and teaching materials never arrive.

Girls are more sensitive than are boys to the quality of schools' physical facilities, and variations in quality affect the school enrollment and retention of girls from socially excluded groups. Studies by King and van de Walle in Laos, and by Lloyd and her colleagues in Egypt, found that girls were less likely to enroll in and more likely to drop out from poor-quality schools, compared with boys.[87] In Pakistan, girls were more likely to stay in mixed-sex private schools that had better physical facilities—water, toilet, electricity, furniture—than in single-sex government schools, which were more poorly resourced.[88] In Laos, girls were more likely to be in school if it was a school with all primary grades, had electricity, and did not have a leaky roof.[89] In Mozambique, girls but not boys were more likely to enroll in schools that had more cement classrooms.[90] In Indonesia, the presence of a toilet in the school was associated with higher math scores for girls, but not for boys, suggesting that girls might have come to school more regularly when toilets provided them necessary privacy.[91]

Weak student performance is also an indicator of poor school quality, and directing quality improvement programs at poorly performing schools benefits excluded children. An example comes from Chile. There, three educational programs in the 1990s provided additional support to improve the quality of the lowest performing schools. McEwan's analysis of the eighth-grade achievement of nearly 200,000 students in Chile found that these programs not only boosted learning, they substantially reduced the gaps in learning achievement between Indigenous and non-Indigenous students—by 30%.[92]

More time for instruction and better instructional quality may also advantage girls more than boys. In Pakistan, girls were less likely to drop out from schools in which the teacher was present and lived in the community and in which classes were smaller.[93] In Egypt, girls were less likely to drop out from schools having a longer school day and a regular teacher, as compared with schools with multiple shifts and temporary teachers.[94] Successful programs to improve teacher attendance in rural schools include direct incentives for showing up coupled with camera verification in India and community-based hiring and supervision of contract teachers in Kenya, but the impact of neither of these programs for rural students was greater for girls than for boys.[95] In Kenya, the effects of school quality on girls' dropout rates from mixed-sex schools were mixed; girls were less likely to drop out from schools with more instructional materials and with teachers who reported that they considered mathematics important for girls, but were more likely to drop out from schools having more credentialed teachers; these factors were not associated with higher rates of boy's dropping out.[96]

In some cases, single-sex schools and more female teachers provide safer and more secure options, particularly for girls in secondary school, although girls' schools may be less well resourced than schools for boys. For example, in rural Pakistan, girls' schools were less likely to have water, electricity, or furniture as compared with boys' schools, and teachers in girls' schools were less educated and more likely to be absent than were those in boys' schools.[97] The effects of single-sex schools vary across countries. In Kenya, for example, girls in single-sex schools are less likely to be harassed by male teachers and classmates and are therefore more likely to stay in school than are girls in coeducational schools; by comparison, in Pakistan, where single-sex schools are mandated by law, communities' preferences for establishing schools for boys means that girls often lack any accessible school.[98]

Efforts to eliminate discrimination in the classroom have been slow to take root in developing countries. Most such efforts have focused on eliminating bias and stereotypes in textbooks, but these have moved slowly and often only in response to external forces.[99] However, establishing criteria for identifying gender and ethnic bias in textbooks, and choosing representative committees to review textbook illustrations and content can raise awareness of the issues.

INVOLVING PARENTS AND COMMUNITY

Community-based schools, or schools located in a single village or community, have been successful in increasing girls' enrollments in Afghanistan,[100] Burkina Faso,[101] and India.[102] In Afghanistan, the PACE-A program supports community-based schools for rural villages in 17 provinces; the community provides the school place, while the program provides educational materials for students, teaching materials, and training for teachers, as well as ongoing teacher support. An impact evaluation of the program as implemented in two districts of Ghor Province found that it increased the enrollment rate for girls aged 6–11 by 50 percentage points, compared with an increase in the enrollment rate of boys the same age by 35 percentage points.[103] In Burkina Faso, the BRIGHT program constructed schools in rural villages in 10 provinces of the country in which girls' enrollment rates were lowest; it also provided complementary interventions, including daily school meals, food incentives for girls' regular school attendance, a mobilization campaign, and adult literacy training. An impact evaluation found that the enrollment rate for girls aged 6–12 years increased from 34% to 56%, compared with the enrollment rate for boys the same age, which increased from 36% to 54%.[104] In Rajasthan, India, community-based schools employed paraprofessional teachers, allowed the community to select and supervise teachers, and hired part-time workers to escort girls from excluded groups to school. A 1999 World Bank study found that children in these schools had higher enrollment, attendance, and test scores compared with students in public schools.[105]

Informal schools, often targeted at girls and children from rural communities and operated by NGOs, have been remarkably effective in providing education to socially excluded children. When these schools offer a high-quality education aimed at facilitating successful integration into the formal system, rather than a lower-quality alternative to formal schooling, they can have a positive impact on girls' education. A widely known example comes from Bangladesh, where schools operated by the Bangladesh Rural Advancement Committee (BRAC) have been operating for 30 years. BRAC schools provide a 2- to 3-year education in the child's home language that enables children to transfer into the formal system; over 70% of the students in BRAC schools are girls, and most of them successfully transfer.[106] Bangladesh is one of the few low-income countries to have reached gender parity at both primary and secondary education, but it is known for being relatively ethnically homogeneous.[107] Many other such programs exist, but they are rarely formally evaluated for the specific impact on doubly disadvantaged girls. For example, a review of "complementary education programs" across 39 countries in sub-Saharan Africa identified 152 such programs, serving several million children, but most were not formally evaluated for impact, and the data were not disaggregated by either gender or ethnicity.[108]

PROVIDING ALTERNATIVES TO SCHOOLS THROUGH DISTANCE EDUCATION AND EXTENSION COURSES

Distance education is another option to increase access for socially excluded girls. Interactive radio instruction, which provides structured lessons in math, national language, and science, has been applied effectively in primary schools in more than 20 countries. Because the instruction is delivered via radio, it can reach even remote rural communities of socially excluded children, and studies have shown that the children learn significantly more than do students in schools with regular teachers, even in taxing circumstances.[109] At the secondary level, a program in Mexico, Telesecundaria, established over 40 years ago, reaches over 1 million students in grades 7–9 annually through television and the Internet, providing access for children in rural communities that lack lower secondary schools. Three-quarters of the students who enter grade 7 complete grade 9.[110] The program has been expanded to other countries in the region, with substantial adaptation in Guatemala, where many Indigenous girls lack educational opportunities.[111] Addressing distance to secondary education is especially valuable for sparsely populated areas, where girls might need to travel many kilometers to reach a regular school and would be exposed to the risks that such travel entails. However, the availability of distance education programs for children in socially excluded communities could serve as a disincentive, both for parent to send girls to formal schools and for the government to provide formal schools in greater proximity to the communities.

PROVIDING COMPENSATORY PROGRAMS

Parental support for education contributes to better learning, and poorer households often are unable to provide the types of support needed: books in the home, educational study aids such as a study desk or table for the student's use, and early home literacy activities such as playing with alphabet toys or reading aloud to children. To compensate for the effects of poverty on home learning resources, many countries have established targeted, tailored programs for socially excluded children, focused on improving learning outcomes.

In-school tutoring programs for children who are falling behind have boosted their achievement, enabling them to catch up with their classmates. Brazil, India, and Spain all have offered targeted, compensatory in-school or after-school programs designed to bolster the performance of disadvantaged students. Evaluations find that these programs help children of excluded groups stay in school and raise their achievement. For example, in a randomized evaluation of a remedial education program in India, where female high school graduates were hired to tutor primary school-age children who were lagging behind, Banerjee and his colleagues found that the program raised the targeted children's test scores significantly, with the largest achievement gains recorded for the most economically disadvantaged children and showing no differences by gender.[112] Another randomized evaluation of a program in India—an in-school software-based education program to help students in grades 2 and 3 learn English—found that the program boosted the achievement of girls from scheduled tribes by 0.62 standard deviations, whereas it boosted the achievement of boys from scheduled tribes slightly more, by 0.67 standard deviations.[113] Although these programs have not been found to disproportionately advantage girls, the benefits for children of both genders within targeted populations suggest that remedial education programs targeting socially excluded girls could raise their achievement.

After-school tutoring for disadvantaged children has also raised school enrollments, lowered repetition and dropouts, and boosted test scores. However, after-school tutoring can be a problem when it provides incentives for teachers to teach less during normal school hours—teaching for fewer hours and covering less of the curriculum—or when it incurs heavy financial costs on lower-income families.[114] Girls' household responsibilities may also limit their ability to participate in after-school tutoring. After-school tutoring programs need to be implemented with caution to avoid these negative consequences.

FINANCING INCENTIVES FOR GIRLS' SCHOOLING

Socially excluded groups are typically among the poorest households in a country. These households also may not view an educated daughter as an asset, and the direct and indirect costs of her schooling may be an additional barrier.[115] Thus, incentives to send girls to school may be necessary. Research shows that conditional cash transfers, scholarships, and even the opportunity to win a scholarship have boosted girls' learning and kept girls from poor families in school.

Conditional cash transfers (CCTs) extend resources to households to defray some of the costs of sending their children to school, tying social assistance payments to desirable behaviors. Although challenging to administer in many settings, CCTs offer incentives for families to send children to school.[116] Programs in Bangladesh, Brazil, Ecuador, and Mexico, among others, have been successful in increasing school enrollment and attendance, but studies have not specifically looked at these programs' success for socially excluded girls. Brazil's *Bolsa Escola*, which provided transfers to the poorest families on the condition that children in the household regularly went to school, raised attendance and lowered dropout for these children. In Ecuador, a randomized evaluation of a CCT program based on Brazil's incentive boosted school enrollment overall by 3.7 percentage points, with greater benefits for girls.[117] In Bangladesh, a Food for Education program for poor households, contingent on school participation, boosted girls' enrollment and attendance. In one case, a program differentially benefitted Indigenous boys as compared with girls. In Mexico, the *Oportunidades/Progressa* program provided grants to families that continued to send their daughters to school. Although the program was successful in attracting female dropouts back to school, the effects on Indigenous girls was not as expected. Specifically, the program benefited Indigenous *boys* more than Indigenous *girls*.[118] Without better targeting, resources spent on CCTs may not have the desired impact. Moreover, in countries with relatively few socially excluded girls, such as Mexico, the incremental costs of incentive systems may be affordable, but in countries with large numbers of girls out of school, the use of CCTs may not be feasible.

Scholarships and stipends also offset the cost of schooling. Secondary school scholarship programs offer girls financing and encouragement to stay in school. They compensate families for the direct and indirect costs of education and are effective for families that view cost as an impediment to girls' schooling. They have been highly effective in several countries, notably Bangladesh, where scholarships increased girls' enrollment to twice that of the national average.[119] Stipend programs also compensate parents for the cost of schooling, but are tied to such school inputs as uniforms, books, materials, and transportation. Even the opportunity to earn a scholarship has been found to boost student achievement. In Kenya, Kremer and his colleagues carried out a randomized evaluation of the impact of girls' scholarship incentives (i.e., the opportunity to receive a scholarship) on girls' learning achievement. The experiment, involving 127 schools, found that both boys and girls in schools with girls' scholarship programs achieved higher scores than did those in control schools.[120] Studies of scholarship programs have not, however, separately examined their impact on socially excluded girls.

Remaining Gaps in the Evidence

To date, very few impact evaluations have provided empirical evidence regarding programs that are effective specifically for girls from socially excluded groups. Identifying and evaluating successful programs for socially excluded girls requires data on both social exclusion and gender, but on a country-by-country basis the incidence of double disadvantage is not well documented.

According to UNESCO, the 14 large countries at risk of not attaining education for all by 2015 contribute 80% of all children out of school; of these, all but four have high shares of socially excluded groups.[121] Yet, most international sources and national data from developing countries do not disaggregate education data by both gender and type of social group. By comparison, several OECD countries disaggregate educational attainment data for male and female majority and minority group members; for example, Australia, Canada, New Zealand, and the

United States report high school completion rates separately for male and female Indigenous peoples and non-Indigenous peoples. In some countries, household surveys and censuses have asked questions capable of providing this information, but the data remain unanalyzed; notable exceptions include studies summarized in Table 6.1.

Information on the success of programs targeted toward socially excluded girls (as opposed to girls in general) is even more limited. Some programs rely on geographical targeting, which is suitable when socially excluded groups live in their own, often isolated, communities and can be identified through language, as is the case in Cambodia, Guatemala, Laos, and Vietnam. Directing programs to girls in rural, poor ethnic enclaves could boost their school participation. However, directing programs toward socially excluded girls in urban areas may be more difficult, as sensitivity regarding ethnic identification may arise. Many questions remain, among them:

- Exactly how large is the problem? That is, how many out-of-school girls are members of excluded groups on a country-by-country basis?
- Under what conditions are various programs effective in bringing these socially excluded girls into school? Keeping them in school? Teaching them?
- What would it cost to implement these programs?

Conclusion

The largest challenge remaining to achieve universal primary and secondary education is that of socially excluded girls. Programs that have been found to be effective in attracting and retaining girls in school have remarkably similar characteristics: They establish schools within the village or community, provide good-quality instructional materials for students and teachers (often in local languages), support teachers through training and other regular professional development, and may include specific incentives for girls to attend school regularly. Of course, such programs also may be advantageous for socially excluded children in general.

Achieving good educational programs for socially excluded girls is not easy, for at least three reasons. Per-student expenditures for these community-based schools may be higher than national averages, national motivation for providing and improving education for socially excluded groups may be weak, and external resources may be limited. Moreover, the available empirical evidence regarding effective programs is based on research in only a handful of countries, making generalizations about program effectiveness difficult.

On a positive note, the continued expansion of education opportunities in developing countries will undoubtedly continue to raise the school participation of socially excluded girls, as it has done in the past, although gaps will remain.

RECOMMENDED ACTIONS

Accelerating education will require concerted efforts in three areas.

A first step is a better understanding of the nature of exclusions in countries and subregions within countries. This will ensure better targeting of efforts. Along this line, the UNESCO Institute for Statistics should request countries to report school participation and achievement data that are disaggregated by gender within social groups, wherever possible. Disaggregation of international data on school enrollment by gender was essential in monitoring progress toward gender equity, and the same will be the case for monitoring improvement in education for socially excluded girls.

Second, donors should support programs that have empirically demonstrated positive effects for socially excluded girls. This review has highlighted some such programs, but most research is relatively silent about what works for socially excluded girls, in particular. A trust fund could be established to provide the financial basis for expanding successful efforts to reach, retain, and teach socially excluded girls.

Third, given the paucity of rigorous, independent impact evaluations of programs focused on improving school participation of socially excluded girls, it is crucial that bilateral, multilateral, and private donors should help expand the knowledge base about what works, through support to research and evaluation. Two program approaches are needed. The first would focus on programs for countries that have relatively few children out of school, with the largest group of out-of-school children being socially excluded girls, as in Latin America. A wide range of interventions may be feasible in these countries, since the modest scale of exclusion renders most approaches affordable, and research and evaluation could help narrow the choices to the most cost-effective ones. A second approach would focus on programs in Africa and South Asia, where evidence is slim, the largest share of excluded girls reside, and cost constraints may render some approaches less feasible. Here, a narrower range of lower-cost alternatives might be evaluated.

In recent years, significant strides have been made in implementing program impact evaluations in developing countries, but as this review suggests, much remains to be done. Although knowledge regarding the impact of specific interventions is not sufficient to obtain broader donor support for such interventions, recent attention to evidence-based policy suggests that, without such evidence, few donors will be willing to step forward with their resources.[122] But with evidence in hand, it may be possible to accelerate progress toward closing the schooling gap that these girls from socially excluded groups experience.

NOTES

1. This chapter is based on Lewis, M. A., & Lockheed, M. E. (2006). *Inexcusable absence: Why 60 million girls still aren't in school and what to do about it.* Washington, DC: Center for Global

Development; and Lewis, M. A., & Lockheed, M. E. (Eds.). (2007). *Exclusion, gender and education: Case studies from the developing world*. Washington, DC: Center for Global Development.

2. Birdsall, N., Levine, R., & Ibrahim, A. (Eds.). (2005). *Towards universal primary education: Investments, incentives and institutions*. Sterling, VA: Stylus Publishing; Schultz, T. P. (2002). Why governments should invest more to educate girls. *World Development, 30*, 207–25; UNESCO. (2010). *EFA global monitoring report 2011: The hidden crisis*. Paris: UNESCO; Baker, D., & Wiseman, A. (Eds.). (2009). *Gender, equality and education from international and comparative perspectives*. Bingley: Emerald Group Publishing.

3. Baker, D., & LeTendre, G. (2005). *National differences, global similarities: World culture and the future of schooling*. Palo Alto, CA: Stanford University Press.

4. UNESCO. (2010). *EFA global monitoring report 2011*.

5. Lewis & Lockheed. (2006). *Inexcusable absence*; Lewis & Lockheed (Eds.) (2007). *Exclusion, gender and education*.

6. Much has been written on the general topic of girls' education in developing countries. See, for example: Birdsall, Levine, & Ibrahim (2005). *Towards universal primary education*; King, E., & Hill, A. M. (Eds.). (1993). *Women's education in developing countries: Barriers, benefits and policies*. Baltimore: Johns Hopkins University Press; Lloyd, C. (Ed.). (2004). *Growing up global: The changing transitions to adulthood in developing countries*. Washington, DC: National Academies Press.

7. Loury, G. C. Social exclusion and ethnic groups: The challenge to economics. In B. Pleskovic, & J. Stiglitz (Eds.), *Annual World Bank conference on development economics*. Washington, DC: The World Bank; Meerman, J. (2005). Oppressed people: Economic mobility of the socially excluded. *Journal of Socioeconomics, 34*, 543–567.

8. Lewis & Lockheed. (2006). *Inexcusable absence*.

9. Hallman, K., & Peracca, S. (2007). Indigenous girls in Guatemala: Poverty and location. In Lewis & Lockheed (Eds.), *Exclusion, gender and education*. Washington, DC: Center for Global Development.

10. Garcia-Aracil, A., & Winter, C. (2004). Gender and ethnicity differentials in school attainment and labor market earnings in Ecuador. *World Development, 34*, 289–307.

11. King, E., & van der Walle, D. (2007). Girls in Lao PDR: Ethnic affiliation, poverty and location. In Lewis & Lockheed (Eds.), *Exclusion, gender and education*. Washington, DC: Center for Global Development.

12. Wu, K. B., Goldschmidt, P., Boscardin, C. K., & Azam, M. (2007). Caste and tribal girls in India: Residuals of historic discrimination. In Lewis & Lockheed (Eds.), *Exclusion, gender and education*. Washington, DC: Center for Global Development.

13. DeJaeghere, J., & Miske, S. (2009). Limits of and possibilities for equality: An analysis of discourses and practices of gendered relations, ethnic traditions, and poverty among non-majority ethnic girls in Vietnam. In Baker & Wiseman (Eds.), *Gender, equality and education*. Bingley: Emerald Group Publishing.

14. Ringold, D., Orenstein, M., & Wilkens, E. (2005). *Roma in an expanding Europe: Breaking the poverty cycle*. Washington, DC: The World Bank.

15. Open Society Institute. (2007). *Equal access to quality education for Roma, Vol. 1*. Budapest: Open Society Institute.

16. Kirdar, M. (2007, November 7). *Explaining ethnic disparities in school enrollment in Turkey*. Middle East Technical University, Personal RePEc Archive Paper No. 2649, Munich.

17. Jimenez, W. (2004). Diferencias de acceso a la educación primarios según condición étnica en Bolivia. In D. Winkler, & S. Cueto (Eds.), *Etnicidad, raza, genero y educación en América Latina*. Washington, DC: Inter-American Dialogue, Partnership for Educational Revitalization in the Americas.

18. Hallman & Peracca. (2007). Indigenous girls in Guatemala.

19. Hannum, E. (2002). Educational stratification by ethnicity in China: Enrollment and attainment in the early reform years. *Demography, 39*, 95–117.

20. Garcia-Aracil & Winkler. (2004). Gender and ethnicity differentials.

21. Hallman & Peracca. (2007). Indigenous girls in Guatemala.

22. Census of India 2001; Asadullah, M. N., Kambhampati, U., & Lopez Boo, F. (2009). *Social divisions in school participation and attainment in India: 1983–2004,* Inter-American Development Bank Research Department Working Paper 4637. Washington, DC: Inter-American Development Bank.

23. UNESCO Institute for Statistics (UIS). (2005). *Children out of school: Measuring exclusion from primary education.* Montreal: UNESCO.

24. Kirdar. (2007). *Explaining ethnic disparities.*

25. Nguyen, P. (2006). Effects of social class and school conditions on educational enrollment and achievement of boys and girls in rural Viet Nam. *International Journal of Educational Research, 45,* 153–175; Chi, T. H. (2009). *Schooling as lived and told: Contrasting impacts of education policies for ethnic minority children in Vietnam seen from Young Lives Surveys.* Paper commissioned for the *Education for all global monitoring report 2010: Reaching the marginalized.* Paris: UNESCO.

26. Jimenez. (2004). Diferencias de acceso a la educación primarios.

27. Garcia-Aracil & Winkler. (2004). Gender and ethnicity differentials.

28. Hallman & Perraca. (2007). Indigenous girls in Guatemala

29. Asadullah and others. (2009). Social divisions in school participation and attainment in India.

30. King & van der Walle. (2007). Girls in Lao PDR.

31. Ramirez, A. (2006). Mexico. In G. Hall, & H. A. Patrinos (Eds.), *Indigenous peoples, poverty and human development in Latin America.* New York: Palgrave.

32. Trivelli, C. (2006). Peru. In Hall & Patrinos (Eds.), *Indigenous peoples, poverty and human development in Latin America.*

33. Open Society Institute. (2007). *Equal access to quality education for Roma.*

34. Garcia-Aracil & Winkler. (2004). Gender and ethnicity differentials.

35. Woldehanna, T., Jones, N., & Tefera, B. (2005 January 1). Children's educational completion rates and achievement: Implications for Ethiopia's second poverty reduction strategy, 2006–2010. (Young Lives Working Paper 18). London: Young Lives.

36. Wu, K., Goldschmidt, P., Boscardin, C. K., & Azam, M. (2007). Girls in India: Poverty, location and social disparities. In Lewis & Lockheed (Eds.), *Exclusion, gender and education.* Washington, DC: Center for Global Development.

37. Postlethwaite, N., personal communication to Marlaine Lockheed, 2006.

38. Cueto, S., & Secada, W. (2004). Oportunidades de aprendizaje y rendimiento en matemática de niños y niñas aymará, quechua y castellano hablantes en escuelas bilingües y monolingües en Puno, Perú. In Winkler, & Cueto (Eds.), *Etnicidad, raza, genero y educación en América Latina.* Washington, DC: Inter-American Dialogue, Partnership for Educational Revitalization in the Americas.

39. Tomaschevski, K. (2001). *Annual report to the UN Commission on Human Rights by the Special Rapporteur on Education.* Geneva: Commission on Human Rights.

40. All studies in this table have been cited in this chapter, with the exception of the following: Arunatilake, N. (2006). Education participation in Sri Lanka–Why all are not in school. *International Journal of Educational Research, 445,* 137–151; Jimenez Pozo, W., Landa Casazola, F., & Yanez Aguilar, E. (2006). Bolivia. In G. Hall, & H. A. Patrinos (Eds.), *Indigenous peoples, poverty and human development in Latin America.* New York: Palgrave; Hannum, E. and Adams, J. (2007). Girls in Gansu, China: Expectations and Aspirations for Secondary Schooling. In M. A. Lewis & M. E. Lockheed (Eds.). *Exclusion, Gender and Education: Case Studies from the Developing World.* Washington, D.C.: Center for Global Development; Larrea, C., & Montenegro Torres, F. (2006). Ecuador. In G. Hall, & H. A. Patrinos (Eds.), *Indigenous peoples, poverty and human development in Latin America.* New York: Palgrave; Stash, S., & Hannum, E. (2001). Who goes to school? Educational stratification by gender, caste and ethnicity in Nepal. *Comparative Education Review, 45,* 354–378; Lam, C., Ardington, C., & Leibbrandt, M. (2007, April). *Schooling as a lottery: Racial differences in school advancement in urban South Africa.* University of Michigan Department of Economics, Ann Arbor; Bhalotra, S. (2009). Educational deficits and social identity in India. Paper commissioned for the *EFA global monitoring report 2010: Reaching the marginalized.* Paris: UNESCO.

41. Benson, C. (2005). *Mother tongue-based teaching and education for girls*. Bangkok: UNESCO.
42. This would not affect girls from cultures where the seclusion of women is not practiced, as in the case of the relatively egalitarian Meitei of Bangladesh. A study of Meitei speakers found no gender differences in comprehension of Bangla, the national language. Kim, A., & Kim, S. (2008). *Meitei (Manipuri) speakers in Bangladesh: A sociolinguistic survey*. SIL Electronic Survey report 2008–002 (February), SIL International. Retrieved from http://www.sil.org/silesr/abstract.asp?ref=2008-002
43. Greg Mortenson has brought widespread attention to this issue in his books *Three Cups of Tea* and *Stones into Schools*, but it has also been well documented in the scholarly literature on girls' education in Arab and Arab-influenced countries; see, for example, Kirk, D., & Napier, D. (2009). Issues of gender, equality, education and national development in the United Arab Emirates. In Baker & Wiseman (Eds.), *Gender, equality and education*. Bingley: Emerald Group Publishing.
44. Lewis & Lockheed. (2007). *Exclusion, gender and education*.
45. Mete, C. (2004). The inequality implications of highly selective promotion practices. *Economics of Education Review, 23*, 301–314; Lockheed, M., & Mete, C. (2007). Tunisia: Strong central policies for gender equity. In Lewis & Lockheed (Eds.). (2007). *Exclusion, gender and education*. Washington, DC: Center for Global Development.
46. Munshi, K., & Rosenzweig, M. (2006). Traditional institutions meet the modern world: Caste, gender and schooling choice in a globalizing economy. *American Economic Review, 96*, 1225–1252.
47. van de Walle, D., & Gunewardena, D. (2001). Sources of ethnic inequality in Viet Nam. *Journal of Development Economics, 65*, 177–207.
48. King & van der Walle. (2007). Girls in Lao PDR.
49. Woldehanna, Jones, & Tefera. (2005). *Children's educational completion rates and achievement*.
50. Zhang, Y. (2006). Urban-rural literacy gaps in sub-Saharan Africa: The roles of socioeconomic status and school quality. *Comparative Education Review, 50*, 581–602.
51. Ibid.
52. King & van der Walle. (2007). Girls in Lao PDR.
53. Chaudhury, N., Hammer, J., Kremer, M., Muralidharan, K., & Rogers, F. (2005). Missing in action: Teacher and health worker absence in developing countries. *Journal of Economic Perspectives, 19*, 91–116.
54. Lewis & Lockheed. (2006). *Inexcusable absence*.
55. Ringold, Orenstein, & Wilkens. (2003). *Roma in an expanding Europe*; Narayan, D. (2000). *Voices of the poor*. New York: Oxford University Press.
56. Hanna, R., & Linden, L. (2009). *Measuring discrimination in education* (NBER working paper 15057). Cambridge, MA: National Bureau of Economic Research.
57. Worth, R. F. (2008, February 27). Despite caste-less society in Yemen, generations languish at bottom of ladder. *New York Times*, p. A14.
58. World Bank. (2003). *World development report 2004: Making services work for poor people*. Washington, DC: World Bank. (1996). *India: Primary education achievement and challenges*. South Asia Country Department Report No. 15756-IN. Washington, DC: World Bank.
59. Blumberg, R. (2007). *Gender bias in textbooks: A hidden obstacle on the road to gender equality in education*. Background paper for the 2008 Education for All Global Monitoring Report, *Education for all by 2015–Will we make it?* (p. 33). Paris: UNESCO.
60. Esen, Y. (2007). Sexism in school textbooks prepared under education reform in Turkey. *Journal for Critical Education Policy Studies, 5*(2); Mkuchu, S. (2004). *Gender roles in textbooks as a function of hidden curriculum in Tanzania primary schools*. Unpublished doctoral dissertation, University of South Africa.
61. Biraimah, K. *Gender division of labor in West African secondary school textbooks*. Unpublished doctoral dissertation. As cited in Mkuchu, 2004.
62. Mkuchu. (2004). *Gender roles in textbooks*.
63. Blumberg. (2007). *Gender bias in textbooks*.
64. Heyneman, S., & Todoric-Bebic, S. (2000). A renewed sense for the purposes of schooling: The challenges of education and social cohesion in Asia, Africa, Latin America, Europe and Central Asia. *Prospects, 30*, 145–166.

65. Banu, L. F. A. (2009). Problems and misconceptions facing the primary language education in Bangladesh: An analysis of curricular and pedagogic practices. *BRAC University Journal, 6*(1–10), 6.
66. Esen. (2007). Sexism in school textbooks.
67. Alderman, H., & King, E. (1998). Gender differences in parental investment in education. *Structural Changes and Economic Dynamics, 9*, 453–468.
68. Basu, K., & Tzannatos, Z. (2003). The global child labor problem: What do we know and what can we do? *World Bank Economic Review, 17*, 147–174.
69. Kattan, R., & Burnett, N. (2004). *User fees in primary education.* Washington, DC: World Bank, Human Development Network.
70. Nopo, H., Saavedera, J., & Torero, M. (2004). *Ethnicity and earnings in urban Peru.* Discussion paper 980, Institute for the Study of Labor, Bonn, Germany; Hall & Patrinos (Eds.). (2006). *Indigenous peoples, poverty and human development in Latin America*; Mario, E. G., & Wolcock, M. (2007). *Assessing social exclusion and mobility in Brazil.* Brasilia: Instituto de Pesquisa Economica Applicada and World Bank.
71. Kim, J. H., & Bailey, S. (2003). *Unsafe schools: A literature review of school-related gender-based violence in developing countries.* Arlington, VA: Development and Training Services, Inc.; Mbassa Menick, D. (2001, September 28). *Les abus sexuels en milieu scolaire au Cameroun.* Paper presented at the Committee on the Rights of the Child Day of General Discussion on Violence against Children within the Family and in Schools, Geneva; Ohsako, T. (Ed.). (1997). *Violence at school: Global issues and interventions.* Paris: UNESCO; Mgalla, Z., Boerma, J. T., & Schapink, D. (1998). Protecting school girls against sexual exploitation: A guardian program in Mwanza, Tanzania. *Reproductive Health Matters, 7*, 19.
72. For example, the Abdul Latif Jameel Poverty Action Lab (J-PAL) of MIT carries out regular impact evaluations of important education interventions for poor children, but to date the studies have not examined program impacts on socially excluded girls.
73. A recent scan of the *Best Evidence Encyclopedia* found only one review of effective education programs in developing countries, all of which focused on CCTs: Slavin, R. (2009 February). *Can financial incentives enhance educational outcomes? Evidence from international experiments.* Baltimore, MD: Johns Hopkins University School of Education Center for Data-Driven Reform in Education (CDDRE).
74. UNICEF. (2009). *State of the world's children 2009.* New York: UNICEF.
75. UNICEF. (2009). *Tracking progress on child and maternal health and nutrition: A survival and development priority.* New York: UNICEF.
76. Paes de Barros, R., & Mendonça, R. (1999). *Costs and benefits of pre-school education in Brazil.* Rio de Janeiro: Institute of Applied Economic Research; Kaul, V., Ramachandran, C., & Upadhyaya, G. C. (1993). *Import of early childhood education on retention in primary grades: A longitudinal study.* New Delhi: The National Council of Educational Research and Training, New Delhi; Kagitcibasi, C. (1996). *Family and human development across cultures: A view from the other side.* Mahwah, NJ: Lawrence Erlbaum; Behrman, J. R., Cheng, Y., & Todd, P. (2004). Evaluating preschool programs when length of exposure to the program varies: A nonparametric approach. *Review of Economics and Statistics, 86*, 108–132.
77. Benson. (2005). *Mother tongue-based teaching and education for girls.*
78. Ibid., p. 6.
79. Alidou, H., Boly, A., Brock-Utne, B., Diallo, Y. S., Heugh, K., & Wolff, H. E. (2006). *Optimizing learning and education in Africa–The language factor* (p. 45). Paper prepared for the Association for the Development of Education in Africa 2006 biennial meeting. Libreville, Gabon.
80. Kosonen, K., Young, C., & Malone, S. (2006). *Promoting literacy in multilingual settings.* Bangkok: UNESCO.
81. Filmer, D. (2004). *If you build it, will they come? School availability and school enrollment in 21 poor countries* (World Bank Policy Research Working Paper 3340). Washington, DC: World Bank.
82. Bilquees, F., & Saqib, N. (2004). *Dropout rates and inter-school movements: Evidence from panel data in Pakistan.* Islamabad: Pakistan Institute of Development Economics; Lloyd, C. B., Mete, C., & Grant, M. (2007). Rural girls in Pakistan: Constraints of policy and culture. In Lewis & Lockheed (Eds.), *Exclusion, gender and education.* Washington, DC: Center for Global Development.

83. King & van de Walle. (2007). Girls in Lao PDR.
84. Burde, D., & Linden, L. (2009). *The effect of proximity on school enrollment: Evidence from a controlled randomized trial in Afghanistan*. New York: Columbia University and New York University.
85. Duflo, E. (2000). Schooling and labor market consequences of school construction in Indonesia: Evidence from an unusual policy experiment. *American Economic Review, 91*(4), 795–813; Jayasundera, T. (2005, November). *Who benefits most from public investment in education: Evidence from Indonesia*. Paper presented at the 75th Annual Southern Economic Association Conference, Washington, DC.
86. Jalan, J., & Glinskaya, E. (2003). *Improving primary school education in India: An impact assessment of DPEP-Phase 1*. Washington, DC: World Bank; Asadullah, Kambhampati, & Boo. (2009) *Social divisions in school participation and attainment in India: 1983–2004*.
87. King & van de Walle (2007). Girls in Lao PDR; Lloyd, C. B., El Tawila, S., Clark, W., & Mensch, B. (2003). The impact of educational quality on school exit in Egypt. *Comparative Education Review, 47*(4), 444–467.
88. Lloyd, Mete, & Grant. (2007). Rural girls in Pakistan.
89. King & van de Walle. (2007). Girls in Lao PDR.
90. Handa, S. (2002). Raising primary school enrolment in developing countries: The relative importance of supply and demand. *Journal of Development Economics, 69*, 103–128.
91. Suryadarma, D., Suryahadi, A., Sumarto, S., & Rogers, F. H. (2004). *The determinants of student performance in Indonesian public primary schools: The role of teachers and schools* (Working Paper). Jakarta: Social Monitoring and Early Response Unit (SMERU) Research Institute.
92. McEwan, P. (2006). *The fortuitous decline of ethnic inequality in Chilean schools*. Wellesley, MA: Wellesley College.
93. Lloyd, Mete, & Grant. (2007). Rural girls in Pakistan.
94. Lloyd, El Tawila, Clark, & Mensch. (2003). The impact of educational quality on school exit in Egypt.
95. Banerjee, A., Banerji, R., Duflo, E., Glennerster, R., & Khemani, S. (2010). Pitfalls of participatory programs: Evidence from a randomized evaluation in education in India. *American Economic Journal: Economic Policy, 2*(1), 1–30; Duflo, E., Dupas, P., & Kremer, M. (2007). *Peer effects, pupil-teacher ratios and teacher incentives: Evidence from a randomized evaluation in Kenya* (Working Paper). Cambridge, MA: MIT/ Poverty Action Lab.
96. Lloyd, C. B., Mensch, B. S., & Clark, W. H. (2000). The effects of primary school quality on school dropout among Kenyan girls and boys. *Comparative Education Review, 44*(2), 113–147.
97. Lloyd, Mete, & Grant. (2007). Rural girls in Pakistan.
98. Ibid.
99. Blumberg. (2007). *Gender bias in textbooks*.
100. Burde & Linden. (2009). *The effect of proximity on school enrollment*.
101. Levy, D., Sloan, M., Linden, L., & Kazianga, H. (2009). *Impact evaluation of Burkina Faso's BRIGHT program*. Princeton, NJ: Mathematica Policy Research.
102. Sipahimalani-Rao, V., & Clarke, P. (2003). *A review of educational progress and reform in the District Primary Education Program (DPEP I and II)* (DPEP Evaluation Report 1). New Delhi: World Bank, Human Development Department of the South Asia Region.
103. Burde & Linden. (2009). *The effect of proximity on school enrollment*.
104. Levy, Sloan, Linden, & Kazianga. (2009). *Impact evaluation of Burkina Faso's BRIGHT program*.
105. World Bank. (1999). *PAD for Rajasthan district primary education program*. Washington, DC: World Bank.
106. Rugh, A., & Bossert, H. (1998). *Involving communities: Participation in the delivery of education programs*. Washington, DC: United States Agency for International Development.
107. UNESCO. (2010). *EFA global monitoring report 2011*.
108. Balwanz, D., Moore, A. S., & DeStefano, J. (2006). *Complementary education programs in Association for the Development of Education in Africa (ADEA) countries*. Paper prepared for the ADEA Biennial on Education in Africa, Libreville, Gabon.
109. Bosch, A. (1997). *Interactive radio instruction: Twenty-three years of improving educational quality*. Washington, DC: World Bank, Human Development Network; Ho, J., & Thrukal, H.

(2009). *Tuned in to student success: Assessing the impact of interactive radio instruction for the hardest-to-reach*. Washington, DC: Education Development Center, Inc.

110. Calderoni, J. (1998). *Telesecundaria: Using TV to bring education to rural Mexico*. In Education and Technology Technical Notes Series, 3(2). Washington, DC: World Bank.

111. Hall & Patrinos (Eds.). (2006). *Indigenous peoples, poverty and human development in Latin America*.

112. Banerjee, A., Cole, S., Duflo, E., & Linden, L. (2006). Remedying education: Evidence from two randomized experiments in India. *Quarterly Journal of Economics, 122*, 1235–1264; Banerjee, Banerji, Duflo, Glennerster, & Khemani. (2009). *Pitfalls of participatory programs*.

113. He, F., Linden, L., & MacLeod, M. (2007). *Teaching what teachers don't know: An assessment of the Pratham English language program* (draft). New York: Columbia University.

114. Bray, M. (1996). *Counting the full cost: Parental and community financing of education in East Asia*. Washington, DC: World Bank; Bray, M. (2007). Governance and free education: Directions, mechanisms and policy tensions. *Prospects, 37*, 23–36.

115. Much has been written on why parents may not view girls' education as an asset: a girl may be married out of the family and community, taking her "asset" to the new family; educated girls may have difficulty finding a comparably educated husband; the opportunity cost of girls' time in terms of household work may be higher than boys.

116. Morley, S., & Coady, D. (2003). *From social assistance to social development*. Washington, DC: Center for Global Development; Schady, N., & Araujo, M. C. (2006). *Cash transfers, conditions, school enrollment and child work: Evidence from a randomized experiment in Ecuador* (Policy Research Working Paper 3930). Washington, DC: World Bank.

117. Schady & Araujo. (2006). *Cash transfers, conditions, school enrolment and child work*.

118. De Janvry, A., & Sadoulet, E. (2006). Making conditional cash transfer programs more efficient: Designing for maximum effect of the conditionality. *The World Bank Economic Review, 20*, 1–30.

119. Khandker, S., Pitt M. M., & Fuwa, N. (2003, March). *Promoting girls' secondary education: An evaluation of the female secondary school stipend programs of Bangladesh*. Paper presented at the annual meetings of the Population Association of America, Minneapolis.

120. Kremer, M., Miguel, E., & Thornton, R. (2004). *Incentives to learn*. Cambridge, MA: MIT/Poverty Action Lab.

121. UNESCO. (2010). *EFA global monitoring report 2011.*; Lewis & Lockheed. (2006). *Inexcusable absence*.

122. See, for example, the International Institute for Impact Evaluation (3iE).

7

Effective Approaches to Making Inclusive Education a Part of Education for All

BOB PROUTY, KOLI BANIK, AND DEEPA SRIKANTAIAH

The Education for All (EFA) movement is a worldwide effort to ensure that all children have access to a good quality education.[1] EFA has made significant progress. In 2000, the number of children not in primary school decreased from 100 million to 72 million.[2] Despite this progress, children with physical and mental disabilities are the largest group of children excluded from education.[3] In addition, some countries have policies of official discrimination against children with disabilities, administered via labels such as "intellectual deficits" and/or "genetic factors."[4]

This chapter addresses the challenges associated with increasing access to education for children with disabilities and presents what is being done internationally to address these challenges. In particular, the chapter looks at programs to promote equity and the challenges that remain in implementing such programs. Examples are given from countries with disability programs that are receiving support through the Education for All–Fast Track Initiative (FTI).[5]

Challenges to Equitable Education for Children with Disabilities

THE EXTENT OF THE GAP IN ACCESS

Of the estimated 150 million children around the world with disabilities,[6] four out of five live in low-income countries, with very limited access to services. The highest percentage of people living with disabilities is in sub-Saharan Africa. Few children with disabilities in these countries have effective access to education, health, rehabilitation, or support services. The mortality rate for children with disabilities under the age of 5 can be as high as 80% in some poor countries and children with severe disabilities have a low probability of surviving childhood because of a lack of basic primary health care.[7] In addition, schooling is more likely to be denied for a child with a disability than for any other child, and access to real learning may well be denied even for those few who do go to school, because of ill-adapted teaching methods, assessment tools, and facilities.

The link between disability and marginalization in education is evident in the rates of primary school enrollment and completion in low-income countries. For example, the 2010 EFA Global Monitoring Report notes that, in Malawi and Tanzania, disability doubles the probability that children will not attend school; in Burkina Faso (Figure 7.1) this probability is even greater.[8,9]

National data often reveal different educational consequences depending on the nature of the disability. In Burkina Faso, the attendance rate for children with a physical impairment is 40%, only slightly below overall national attendance rates, but children reported as deaf, mute, blind, or living with a mental impairment are far less likely to be enrolled in school than those with other physical impairments not requiring adaptation in teaching.[10] Children who are deaf or who have limited hearing have historically faced major attitudinal problems, and it was only in 1984 that UNESCO recognized sign language as a valid medium of instruction for deaf and hard-of-hearing children. Only a handful of the more than 100 distinct sign languages in use around the world have actually been used in classrooms.

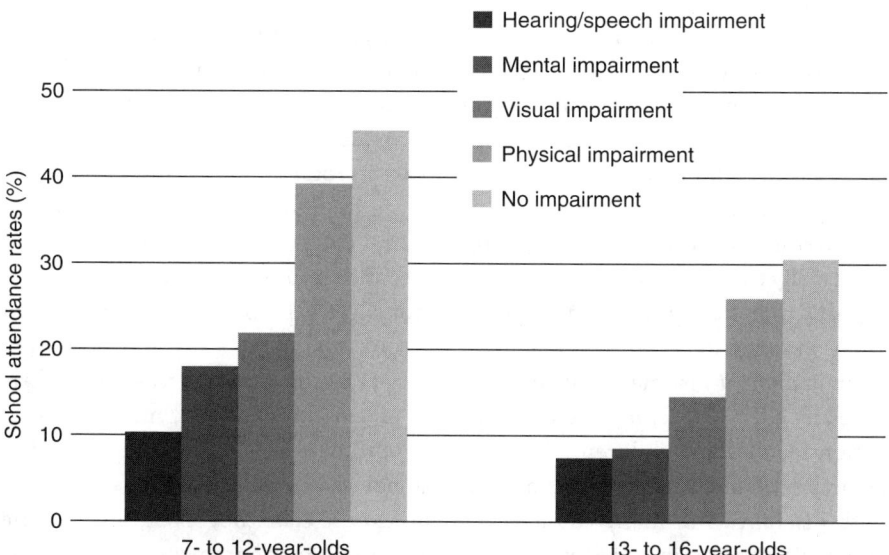

Figure 7.1 Burkina Faso's children with disabilities face deep but varied levels of disadvantage. From UNESCO. (2010). *EFA Global Monitoring Report, Reaching the Marginalized*. Paris: UNESCO.

BARRIERS TO ACCESS

Studies show that attitudes, fear, lack of knowledge, stigmatization, and isolation from the community are the primary reasons why educational systems and services do not currently respond to the needs of disabled children.[11] Particularly problematic are perspectives of education that portray disabled children as incapable of intellectual achievement. Furthermore, the high degree of stigmatization often associated with disability may mean that parents and other family members are reluctant to report that a child has a disability. In many cases, the births of disabled children are not even registered, and therefore, are not known to social services or schools.[12]

Another barrier to access involves a lack of capacity to provide specialized social and technological support. Many low-income countries with the highest number of out-of-school children lack technologies to aid children with disabilities or rely on inappropriate imported technology. Although Metts found that many countries are "beginning to augment and replace their imported programs and projects with approaches better suited to their social and economic environments," the harsh reality is that many more countries are providing very little by way of support.[13] Moreover, in rural areas in particular, the majority of children lack access to social services, but those with mobility impairments and/or multiple disabilities are even further marginalized. The physical distance to school, the layout and design of the facilities, and the shortages of qualified teachers are among the barriers children with disabilities in rural areas face in attending and completing school.[14]

Conflict-afflicted countries or those with humanitarian emergencies or natural disasters also face particular challenges in educating children with disabilities. These countries typically experience an increase in the number of children with disabilities, as well as a reduced capacity to provide them with schooling and other services. According to the UN Office of the Secretary-General for Children of Armed Conflict, around 6 million children are injured or permanently disabled due to conflict. These children are often the first to be abandoned by families and are usually the last to receive emergency relief and support.[15] In addition, UNICEF reports that humanitarian workers are not always prepared to help disabled children or victims.[16]

In many low-income countries, these barriers to educational access are exacerbated by a disconnect between teacher training and predominant models of education for disabled children.[17] This lack of coordination is often reflected in the structure of educational provision. Educational services for school-aged children with disabilities in many countries, to the extent that they exist, are not the responsibility of ministries of education, nor are there programs to integrate disabled children into the larger education system. Even for donors, the education of disabled children is rarely seen as central to the EFA challenge at national or international levels. This means that the way in which global education efforts are currently supported and delivered does little to address barriers to access for disabled children, because there are no consistent or aligned support systems for disability programs.

Providing schools with the tools required to enable disabled children to access a quality education is one of the biggest challenges the development community faces. It also presents an important opportunity, however, as improving accessibility actually reduces the cost of inclusion overall and provides many benefits to all children. Inflated estimates of the cost of accessibility typically reflect a lack of knowledge and experience.[18] The expense of making school buildings accessible to children with disabilities is generally less than 1% of total construction costs; however, the cost of retrofitting existing buildings is far greater.

CHALLENGES TO DEFINING DISABILITY AND INCLUSION

Improving access to education for disabled people ensures their right to participate in their community and is an important step in giving them the same rights and choices as nondisabled members. A lack of international agreement on the definitions, classifications, and characterization of disabilities, however, makes comparative research on what works to promote equity for this group difficult to validate.[19] Countries frequently use widely differing classifications, definitions, and thresholds to differentiate "disabled" and "nondisabled" persons.[20] The 2010 EFA Global Monitoring Report writes that "disability" is "a generic term covering a multitude of circumstances. Children with . . . autism [for example] are likely to face very different education-related challenges than children who are partially sighted, or who have lost a limb."[21]

There is also considerable debate about what constitutes "inclusion." Some question the practicality of total inclusiveness. Many in the deaf community, for instance, see the provision of support to deaf children among other deaf children and teachers as a matter of human rights. Inclusion in this context is understood as inclusion within an environment of understanding and shared communication and experience. This vision is held by some outside the deaf community as well, and can be at odds with the thrust of inclusive education. This presents a set of dilemmas. For instance, the establishment of short-term Special Needs Education classes or schools could function as a barrier to a long-term perspective of inclusion of students in regular classes. Developing more flexible and holistic strategies that encompass useful short- and long-term perspectives is crucial to resolving these dilemmas.

In recent years, the overall social perception of disability and inclusion has evolved from medical- and charity-based to social, human rights–based approaches, although this varies widely. The 2010 EFA Global Monitoring Report notes that:

[U]ntil recently, the "medical model" was dominant: those with disabilities were seen as having a condition that set them apart from the rest of society. It is now increasingly accepted that, while disabilities involve varying levels and types of impairment, it is social, institutional and attitudinal barriers that limit the full inclusion of people with disabilities. Understanding disability in this way highlights the importance of identifying and removing the barriers. Education has a key role to play in changing attitudes.[22]

UNESCO defines *inclusion* as "a process of addressing and responding to the diversity of needs of all learners through increasing participation in learning, cultures and communities, and reducing exclusion within and from education."[23] Inclusive education means that schools can and should provide good education to all irrespective of their varying abilities. This is a perspective that is broader than disability; it is an understanding of education that responds to each individual learner.[24] This chapter will adopt this concept of inclusion to assess strategies that work to improve equity in education for children with disabilities.

CHALLENGES TO POLICY DEVELOPMENT AND IMPLEMENTATION

The issue of how best to promote inclusive education remains unresolved despite decades of research, advocacy, and education efforts. Globally, mainstreaming of disabled students in classrooms with their nondisabled peers does not have a long institutional history of acceptance and implementation of the rights-based policies advocated by the United Nations Convention on the Rights of Persons with Disabilities (UNCRPD) has resulted in a mixture of partial accomplishments, partial failures, and outright legislative and policy setbacks.

Even in high- and middle-income countries with significant human and material resource bases, successfully increasing inclusion requires policy development, intense advocacy, and constant engagement with numerous stakeholders. For instance, the Americans with Disabilities Act of 1990 is the most comprehensive statement on inclusion policy in the United States. Despite the fact that around 19% of the U.S. population is affected by some type of disability, the passage of the act required a tremendous amount of legislative and policy parsing to the point that some of its provisions did not come into full force until 2008.[25] Similarly demonstrating the struggle even in high-resource countries, in 2007, Canadian parents and advocacy groups took the issue of lack of equal access to educational services for children with autism to the Supreme Court of Canada, which allowed previous judgments against them to stand without comment.[26]

Although substantial in all countries, deficiencies in both policy and implementation are particularly prevalent in lower-income countries. This may in part reflect the fact that inclusive education requires clear policy approaches in order to target efforts, but few low-income countries have national strategies to educate disabled children.[27]

Global Efforts to Promote Educational Inclusion

Despite the challenges outlined above, progress is being made globally to improve the social and educational inclusion of people with disabilities. This section will focus on what non-governmental organizations (NGOs), governments, and international actors in low-income countries are doing to increase access to quality education for this group.

NON-GOVERNMENTAL ORGANIZATIONS WORKING TO PROMOTE INCLUSION

There are a number of international and national NGOs working to promote the integration of persons with disabilities into society. These NGOs assist governments and other partners in formulating policies and implementing programs to ensure that inclusion and disability issues are discussed and addressed. NGOs are particularly important in supporting people with disabilities in communities that lack access to facilities. NGOs may also administer government-funded social safety net programs.

Non-governmental organizations are also involved in providing services that improve accessibility.[28] Among others, the International Council for Education of People with Visual Impairment (ICEVI) promotes equal access to appropriate education for children and youth with visual impairment. Their mission includes making sure educational services are available for the visually impaired, developing educational materials for the visually impaired, ensuring that teachers and others are properly trained to work with the visually impaired, and ultimately helping children live in environments where they are not discriminated against. Projects include a global campaign and program entitled Education for All Children with Visual Impairment (EFA-VI), which is in partnership with the World Blind Union (WBU) and seeks to ensure that all visually impaired girls and boys receive an education. In another project, ICEVI is helping to support blind students attending university in Indonesia. Handicap International similarly works to promote inclusion for persons with disabilities, primarily in post-conflict and low-income countries. Among many other programs, it supports the Kenya Media Network on Disability (KEMNOD), which strengthens reporting on issues related to disability and HIV/AIDS.

INCREASING GOVERNMENT ACTION ON INCLUSIVE EDUCATION

Governments around the world are also implementing initiatives to address inclusion. Many countries receiving support through the Fast Track Initiative (FTI) are showing increased awareness of the need for greater attention at the system level to the issue of education for all children with disabilities. In 2007, the FTI

Secretariat conducted a desk review of 28 FTI-endorsed country education sector plans (ESPs) and country appraisal and endorsement reports.

The number of ESPs covering learning outcomes, children with disabilities, girls' education, and HIV/AIDS increased from 2001 to 2004 and from to 2005 to 2006 (Figure 7.2). Between 2001 and 2004, only two of the 12 endorsed ESPs described a strategy for children with disabilities. By 2005–2006, eight out of the 16 ESPs included a discussion and/or strategy for disabled children. This increase could be attributed to the preparation and communication of updated appraisal guidelines, which put greater emphasis on increasing capacity for disabled children and requesting gross enrollment, net enrollment, and completion rates for disabled children. Unfortunately, too many plans continue to overlook disability or to provide only broad proposals lacking in operational specificity, and very few have provided systematic plans to address the needs of children with disabilities (Table 7.1). Currently, only 36% of ESPs include plans for children with disabilities (Figure 7.3).

Those countries that do have strategies for inclusion present varying descriptions and details for making schools accessible to children with special needs. Some plans are very specific while others provide no details about what the strategy will entail or when it will be developed. Guyana's education sector plan, for example, identifies the number of schools the country has for physically and mentally handicapped children and lists specific activities to be taken, such as conducting a national study to determine the number of students with special needs and creating special resource centers. On the other hand, Moldova's plan does not discuss children with disabilities in the body of the ESP, although it is mentioned in its action plan. The action plan has an objective to provide access and equal opportunities to children in particularly difficult situations. Specific activities listed include creating and developing a system of alternatives to institutionalization and adjusting education institutions and the physical condition of buildings to the needs of children in particularly difficult situations. More specifically, Moldova's ESP outlines activities for adjusting its national legislation to align

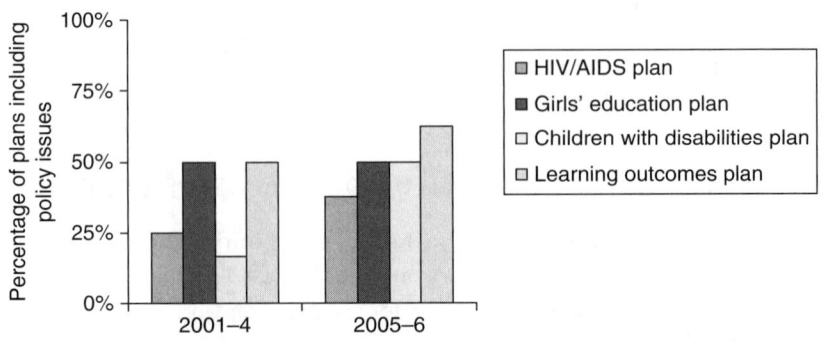

Figure 7.2 Inclusion of policy issues in education sector plans (ESPs).

Table 7.1 **Strategies for Children with Disabilities Described in Education Sector Plans (ESPs)**

Strategy for Children with Disabilities Described in ESPs	Developing a Strategy	Strategy Not Identified
Guyana	Albania	Burkina Faso
Ethiopia	Cambodia	Cameroon
Kenya	Guinea	Ghana
Lesotho	Niger	Honduras
Mali	Rwanda	Madagascar
Moldova		Mauritania
Mongolia		Mozambique
The Gambia		Nicaragua
Senegal		Niger
		Tajikistan
		Timor-Leste
		Vietnam
		Yemen

with existing international documents, including the Dakar Action Framework, the UN Convention on the Rights of the Child, and the World Program of Action Concerning Disabled People.

COUNTRY EXAMPLES

As was identified by the publication, *Education's Missing Millions*, policies on disability and inclusion should contain several critical components. These include commitments to and advocacy for equal rights; partnerships with people with

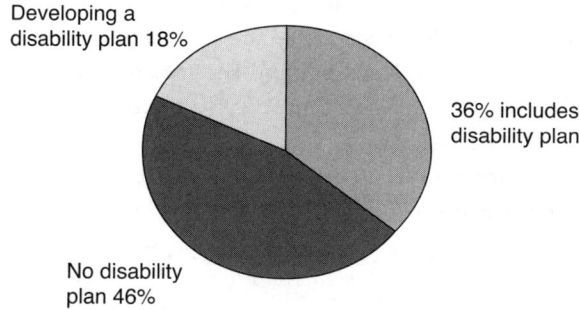

Figure 7.3 Rates of plans for children with disabilities in education sector plans (ESPs).

disabilities and those who represent them; establishment of standards for accessibility, as well as a commitment to coherence and flexibility in implementation; data collection and evaluation; preparation of a range of options for program delivery; identifying and supporting points of program delivery and fostering innovation; training key members of the educational and broader community; expanding successful initiatives; promoting coordination among different service providers and government sectors; analyzing and projecting costs of implementing policies on inclusion; and ensuring consistent and comprehensive monitoring and evaluation of programs.[29]

This section will look at countries in Asia and sub-Saharan Africa that are beginning to incorporate these critical components into their policies for children with disabilities. Although these programs are still at a very early stage and years from being fully operational on a national scale, they indicate that inclusion for children with disabilities is making gradual but important progress.

CAMBODIA

The government of Cambodia has made improving access for children with disabilities one of its main education policies, and the Cambodian plan is seen as a model for other FTI-endorsed and nonendorsed countries to follow. With a well-defined Policy on Inclusive Education for Children with Disabilities (ECWD), the ESP has strategies to enhance access to and quality of primary education in both academic disciplines and life skills among vulnerable and disadvantaged groups. The ESP places a special focus on disadvantaged children. The main beneficiaries will include children in remote areas, those from poor families, and those with disabilities, with careful attention to gender equality. Overall, Cambodia's program will strive to reach the most disadvantaged children by preferentially targeting girls, ethnic minority areas, children with disabilities, and communes with high levels of poverty.

Over the long term, this investment will benefit Cambodian primary school children nationwide by strengthening the institutional and technical capacity for education quality improvement planning and administration. The recent adoption of a policy on the disabled has enabled the allocation of an FTI grant to fund the government's policy to find, enroll, and service appropriately the needs of children with disabilities. The government will also sponsor a disability prevalence survey to estimate how physical and mental disabilities may affect school participation and performance in order to draw lessons to better target school services. This will enable an estimation of out-of-school prevalence rates for Cambodia.

LESOTHO

In the government of Lesotho's recently revised education sector plan, one of its main objectives is to create durable gender- and disability-friendly classrooms for primary and kindergarten classes. This is in line with the government policy of ensuring access to all children with disabilities. The government will construct at least 1,000 new classrooms and additional facilities, particularly latrines, where necessary. In particular, issues of gender and disability will be considered in the standard design. Benefits are intended to spread to over at least 300 schools. The government has also included in its program documentation the need for classroom furniture to reflect a focus on disability. These proposed efforts aim to increase enrollment and retention of students in primary school.

In addition to school construction, the Ministry of Education and Training in Lesotho provides grants and awards to the neediest students. In 2008, 19,200 monetary awards were distributed. Such awards were provided to abandoned children, single orphans with a sick remaining parent, children whose parents have disabilities that prevent the parent from earning a living, and children with parents who are over the age of 55. Support is also provided to children with disabilities. In order to receive a grant or award, the child must be of school age and attending a registered government, community, or church school.

OTHER SUB-SAHARAN AFRICAN COUNTRIES

Inclusive education is gaining momentum in sub-Saharan Africa through the development of four coinciding and complementary initiatives with the potential to shape education reform and provision. These initiatives are: the EFA Initiative, the New Partnership for Africa's Development (NEPAD), the Africa Decade for persons with disabilities (1999–2009), and a work program of the Association for the Development of Education in Africa (ADEA) that supports a regional movement for education by promoting policy dialogue, developing partnerships, and building national capacity to provide good quality education in Africa. All three initiatives require governments to make new investments in education to ensure that all children attend and complete primary school. There are also national commitments to inclusive education in Burkina Faso, South Africa, Uganda, and Mali.

International Action for Inclusion

The efforts of NGOs and governments to promote educational inclusion for children with disabilities have been bolstered by international action, including improved legal protections, policy coherence, and screening tools.

STRENGTHENING INTERNATIONAL COMMITMENTS

For 40 years, the United Nations and other international bodies have worked to strengthen international commitments for people with disabilities. These include the 1971 Declaration on the Rights of Persons with Mental Retardation, the International Decades of Disabled Persons, the 1993 Standard Rules on the equalization of opportunities for persons with disabilities, and the 1994 Salamanca Statement and Framework for Action. In Salamanca, 92 governments and 25 international organizations formed the World Conference on Special Needs Education. During this conference, a Framework for Action was developed under which regular schools were to accommodate all children, regardless of their physical, intellectual, social, emotional, linguistic, or other conditions.

These efforts were dramatically expanded with the 2006 signing of the United Nations Convention on the Rights of Persons with Disabilities (UNCRPD). The Convention is an attempt to increase the focus on persons with disabilities on the human rights agenda by detailing the actions that states and non-state actors must take to ensure that people with a comprehensive range of disabilities can enjoy their full scope of rights on an equal basis with all others. Three of the guiding principles of the Convention include: "Respect for inherent dignity and individual autonomy, including the freedom to make one's own choices, and independence of persons; full and effective participation and inclusion in society; and respect for difference and acceptance of persons with disabilities as part of human diversity and humanity."[30]

The Convention has now been ratified by more than a hundred countries. For the first time, the parties are required to review their policies on a regular basis to ensure compliance with the letter and the spirit of the Convention, with compliance to be evaluated based on reports or research produced by both government and non-governmental stakeholders.[31] Although the UNCRPD covers a range of rights, Article 24 requires that state parties ensure that:

> "(a) Persons with disabilities are not excluded from the general education system on the basis of disability, and that children with disabilities are not excluded from free and compulsory primary education, or from secondary education, on the basis of disability; (b) Persons with disabilities can access an inclusive, quality, and free primary education and secondary education on an equal basis with others in the communities in which they live; (c) Reasonable accommodation of the individual's requirements is provided; (d) Persons with disabilities receive the support required, within the general education system, to facilitate their effective education; (e) Effective individualized support measures are provided in environments that maximize academic and social development, consistent with the goal of full inclusion."[32]

Despite progress in the realization of rights, in 2006, the Office of the United Nations Special Rapporteur on Disability found that the increased recognition of the rights of persons with disabilities had not translated into improved services for children. Thirty countries reported taking no measures to enable children with disabilities to receive education in integrated settings.[33]

THE FTI PARTNERSHIP AS A POLICY CATALYST

Recognizing that international commitments are not enough to guarantee equity on the ground for children with disabilities, the FTI is working to influence policies that will make these commitments a reality. As the report *Education's Missing Millions* recommended, "the role of the FTI, not only in relation to endorsement and funding, but as a policy catalyst and hub for information exchange, makes it a critical contributor in relation to improving policies, provision, and practice for disabled children, and ensuring the millions of disabled children still out of school are seen as an integral part of the challenge to achieve universal primary completion (UPC) by 2015."[34] More specifically, the report recommended that the FTI Partnership play a greater role in catalyzing greater responsiveness to disability by:

- Promoting policy dialogue and good practices within the Partnership, with both partner countries and donors
- Acting as a policy "champion" for inclusion, advocating the critical importance of the participation of disabled children to the achievement of universal primary education, to increase both political and funding commitments to ensuring their inclusion[35]

The FTI Partnership continues to move forward with the recommendations from *Education's Missing Millions*. In 2009, the FTI Secretariat commissioned a study entitled, "Reaching Out to Out-of-School Children: Putting Inclusive Education on the Fast Track," to explore how the EFA FTI Partnership could develop a targeted outreach program. In targeting out-of-school populations, overall approaches need to: (a) tailor the approach to specific marginalized groups, (b) reduce obstacles for children to go to school, (c) use an inclusive lens, and (d) use multisectoral approaches. Representatives from a range of institutions reviewing the study recommended that EFA FTI focus on country-level and subnational regions, expand collaborative efforts at the global level, and ensure that inclusive education is integrated into overall EFA FTI structures and processes. As a result, in 2010, the FTI is requesting all FTI countries to develop a statement and regional action plans to improve the quality and access to schools for marginalized groups.

In addition, the FTI will encourage the widespread use of the Equity and Inclusion Toolkit by governments. The toolkit was developed by the UN Girls' Education Initiative (UNGEI), the UNAIDS Inter-Agency Task Team (IATT) on Education, the Global Task Force on Child Labor and Education, the EFA Flagship on the Right to Education for Persons with Disabilities (convened by UNESCO), the FTI Secretariat, and civil society partners including World Vision. The toolkit was designed primarily for ministries of education as they prepare and revise their education sector plans, for coordinating agencies and local education groups as they provide support to governments in preparing their education sector plans, and for donors as they review plans for FTI endorsement in conjunction with the FTI Indicative Framework and Appraisal Guidelines. The toolkit was piloted in Kyrgyzstan, Lesotho, and Malawi in 2009. Overall, it was found to be effective for members of the Local Education Group in assessing key issues of marginalized groups. The final tool aims to be an adjunct to other tools available in the context of the EFA FTI, with a special focus on the most disadvantaged children in society and their right to education.

Despite its important role as a policy catalyst, the FTI Partnership has not yet elaborated a clear policy on inclusion of children with disabilities. Development of such a policy should be an urgent priority for all member countries of the FTI Partnership. It would help to both demonstrate and crystallize support for the development of disability and inclusion strategies and could be a strong basis for advocacy. The Partnership should also consider developing systematic set-asides when it finances textbooks and trade books, reserving a portion of the funding for large-print and Braille materials.

GLOBAL EFFORTS TO SCALE UP THE USE OF DISABILITY SCREENING TOOLS

International organizations are also working to improve visibility and access to services for people with disabilities by improving identification tools. The Organisation for Economic Co-operation and Development (OECD)/World Bank Disability Screening of Children Initiative was developed to identify and screen children with disabilities in developing countries. The method is a two-stage process that first uses a Ten-Question Screening Instrument (TQSI) and then a professional assessment by medical doctors and psychologists.

Ongoing Challenges to Inclusion

Efforts to advance educational inclusion for children with disabilities must be sustained and accelerated in the years to come if equity for this group is to be achieved. This includes addressing remaining gaps in provision, including the shortage of trained teachers, locally adapted pedagogies, and essential data to monitor progress and gaps for children with disabilities.

SCARCITY OF TRAINED TEACHERS AND INCLUSIVE PEDAGOGIES

There is a shortage of trained teachers to teach children with disabilities. Although in a few countries, teachers are teaching inclusively without the benefit of specialized training, many lack confidence in their ability to meet the needs of students with disabilities.[36] Research shows that teachers can overcome this lack of confidence with easily provided support.[37]

Although widespread training is urgently needed, this training needs to be locally adapted. Education specialists have long advocated for more culturally sensitive instructional modes to be used in the classroom. Scribner and Cole wrote in 1973 of the risk of creating a "specialized set of educational experiences which are discontinuous from those encountered in everyday life [for children in relation to their culture and local environment] and [which] promotes ways of learning and thinking which often run counter to those nurtured in practical daily activities."[38] A study by Balshaw and Lucas in 2000, *"Effective Schools for All" in Macedonia and Harrow: An International Comparison*, found that the following questions are helpful when developing instructional strategies for inclusive education:

> How does our school turn perceived "difficulties" into opportunities?
> How do we learn to cope with change more effectively?
> Are these developments seen as central to more inclusive approaches?
> How do we use staff development with all the staff, not only the teachers, to aid the task?
> In what ways do we seek to "build capacity," i.e., not always assume more resources is the only answer?[39]

Others note that education should be locally embedded to prevent discontinuity between home and school life for children.[40]

The Salamanca Framework for Action also notes the importance of incorporating the community's perspective in education systems. Ogat discusses successful examples in Kenya, where communities ensure adequate resources for the disabled in the community.[41] For example, the use of local language in instruction in schools is important to help disabled children make connections between their local environments and what is taught in school. Furthermore, Ogat acknowledges the importance of oral cultures to help teachers enhance educational experiences for disabled students. Incorporating storytelling, puns, riddles, folklores, and other forms of traditional methods of learning into classroom instruction brings relevance and can involve the community in the schools.

THE DATA DISCONNECT

The lack of sufficient data collection and monitoring on disability in low-income countries is another significant obstacle to establishing programs that promote equity for this group. The data disconnect is a fundamental barrier to any initiatives that seek to reach out to out-of-school children and has contributed to the failure of many countries to develop appropriate policies and strategies to include children with disabilities within the EFA movement. Many global institutions lack data collection methods as well as databases to store the data on children with disabilities. Other data weaknesses include lack of subnational information by region, lack of cost data, and difficulties in collecting data on many out-of-school populations.

The UNESCO Institute for Statistics has assembled the best available information on the education of persons with disabilities, which it makes available in the 2009 EFA Global Monitoring Report. This information comes with several caveats, however. The report notes that data are simply not available for some countries with large populations. It also raises questions about the size of school-aged populations and the accuracy of administrative data on enrollment, and calls for targeted surveys focusing on specific out-of-school groups. There is a need for *longitudinal* datasets and *comparative* data based on shared definitions.

The need to understand and obtain costing parameters is also a consideration. The unrealized potential of disabled children—in both low- and high-income countries—can have an enormous effect on gross domestic product (GDP). Through an inclusive education lens, the question may also be reversed—policymakers could well be asked to consider the costs of *not* implementing inclusive education. Metts, an associate professor of economics at the University of Nevada and the chief executive officer of the Disability Policy and Planning Institute, has calculated the total annual value of GDP lost due to disability. He estimated that the total value of GDP lost globally each year was between US$1,365 billion and US$1,936 billion. This includes between US$900 billion and US$1,300 billion lost in high-income countries, between US$339 billion and US$480 billion in middle-income countries, and between US$135 billion and US$182 billion in low-income countries.[42] Over the last decade other researchers have relied on these findings to estimate costs in high-, middle-, and low-income countries.

Collecting, analyzing, synthesizing and, above all, using data on out-of-school children that are timely, up-to-date, and accurate is basic to understanding the reality of the challenge and to more fully understanding the needs of educational systems in terms of access and quality. Data on the types of impairments and the number of children affected can inform service delivery and the provision of appropriate aids.[43] An *Index for Inclusive Schooling* and an *Inclusion Checklist* are useful tools for identifying gaps and corresponding strategies to close data and monitoring gaps in moving towards inclusive education.[44]

The most useful statistics are those disaggregated by gender, age, ethnicity, and urban/rural residence. It is also important to have data on the extent of the impairment, the number of children living at home or placed in institutions, and the number enrolled in special schools or inclusive education.[45]

Recently, efforts have been made to systematize data collection. For example, in 2005, the United Nations Statistics Division initiated the systematic and regular collection of basic statistics on human functioning and disability by introducing a disability statistics questionnaire to the existing data collection system.[46]

These tools provide standardized definitions of disability for systematic use in data collection strategies.

Conclusion

In this chapter, we have outlined knowledge gaps, capacity development initiatives, and country-level experience with inclusive education. Although there have been some modest positive developments in both policy formulation and educational outcomes at the microlevel, it is clear that the overall lack of a framework in the education sector for inclusive education continues to create serious obstacles. There is a clear need for supporting the sector on several fronts. These include agreement on the standards of classification to enable policy-makers to engage in a meaningful dialogue or to develop comparative research; the development of a coherent strategy for the provision of services and appropriate access in schools, appropriate professional development of teachers and other services; and developing a knowledge base for scaling up lessons learned to the national level.

There are a number of areas where the education sector is well suited to play a leading role in changing attitudes and providing services to those with disabilities. These include training of a cadre of individuals able to promote realistic social models of inclusive education, the development of good data within the education sector, and the commitment to linking this data with service provision.

The EFA movement can act as a catalyst for change. An important step will be the understanding that a rights-based approach in education implies that education services must be made available for all children. Provision has too frequently followed a linear trajectory whereby the most easily reached children are given full services before more marginalized children are given any services. This must change if EFA is to be reached.

Education for All will fail as a movement unless it explicitly provides for all children with disabilities. All must mean all. The Fast Track Initiative must scale up its ability to provide incentives to national governments and other stakeholders to use an inclusive education lens at all stages from design to evaluation. As the FTI Partnership develops a new results-focused framework for monitoring progress, the development and implementation of policies in support of children and teachers with disabilities should be an integral part of how success is defined and measured.

NOTES

1. This goal is also reflected in the second and third Millennium Development Goals.
2. UNESCO. (2010). *EFA global monitoring report: Reaching the marginalized.* Paris: UNESCO.
3. Just over half of children out of school live in countries affected by conflict; one-third are children with disabilities. UNESCO.(2009). *EFA global monitoring report.* Paris: UNESCO.

4. Blue, A. W., Darou, W. G., & Ruano, C. (2002). Through silence we speak: Approaches to counseling and psychotherapy with Canadian First Nations clients. *Online Readings in Psychology and Culture,* unit 10, chapter 4. Retrieved December 13, 2009, http://orpc.iaccp.org/index.php?option=com_content&view=article&id=105&Itemid=15; Darou, W. G., Bernier, P., & Ruano, C. (2003). Sow's African personality and psychopathology model. *Cross-Cultural Psychology Bulletin, 37*(March–June), 29–34. Retrieved December 13, 2009, http://www.iaccp.org/bulletin/PDF/web03%281-2%29.pdf; Ruano, C. R. (1996). *From Cholo to terrorist: Ethnicity as illness in Peruvian society.* Student Papers from the Sociology of Knowledge Doctoral Seminar (pp. 56–58), University of Toronto.

5. The Education for All-Fast Track Initiative (FTI) is a global partnership between developing countries and donors to accelerate progress toward the goal of universal completion of quality primary education by 2015. Each government within the partnership defines its education policies in an education sector plan or strategy. Currently the FTI Partnership has endorsed 40 country education sector plans.

6. According to the United Nations Convention on the Rights of Persons with Disabilities (2007), persons living with disabilities are those who have long-term physical, mental, intellectual, or sensory impairments, which in interaction with various attitudinal and environmental barriers, hinder their full and effective participation in society on an equal basis with others. Also, UNESCO's website (2011) notes that "inclusive education is based on the right of all learners to a quality education that meets basic learning needs and enriches lives." Retrieved from http://www.unesco.org/new/en/education/themes/strengthening-education-systems/inclusive-education/

7. UNICEF. (2007). Promoting the rights of children with disabilities. *Innocenti Digest, 13,* 35–36.

8. Kobiané, J. F., & Bougma, M. (2009). *Rapport d'analyse du thème IV. Instruction, alphabétisation et scolarisation [Analytical report on theme IV: Teaching, literacy training and schooling]* (p. 182). Ouagadougou, Burkina Faso: Institut National de la Statistique et de la Démographie; Eide, A. H., & Loeb, M. (Eds.). (2006). *Living conditions among people with activity limitations in Zambia: A national representative study* (Report no. A262, 2006). Trondheim, NO: SINTEF Health Research. Retrieved from http://www.sintef.no/lc

9. UNESCO. (2010). *EFA global monitoring report: Reaching the marginalized.*

10. Ibid., p. 182.

11. Ibid., p. 181; Yeo, R., & Moore, K. (2003). Including disabled people in poverty reduction work: 'Nothing about us, without us.' *World Development, 31*(3), 571–590.

12. UNICEF. (2007). Promoting the rights of children, pp. 35–36.

13. Metts, R. (2000). *Disability issues, trends and recommendations for the World Bank* (Social Protection Discussion Paper no. 7, p. 30). Washington, DC: World Bank.

14. UNESCO. (2010). *EFA global monitoring report: Reaching the marginalized,* p. 183.

15. Jones, H. (2000). Disabled children's rights. *Disability Studies Quarterly, 20*(4).

16. UNICEF. (2007). Promoting the rights of children, pp. 35–36.

17. Peters, S. (2004). *Inclusive education: An EFA strategy for all children* (p. 20). Washington, DC: World Bank.

18. Steinfeld, E. (2005). *Education for all: The cost of accessibility* (p. 4). Washington, DC: World Bank.

19. International Disability Rights. (2007). *International disability rights monitor: Europe 2007 report card.* Retrieved from http://www.idrmnet.org/pdfs/IDRM_Europe_2007.pdf

20. UNICEF. (2007). Promoting the rights of children, pp. 35–36.

21. UNESCO. (2010). *EFA global monitoring report: Reaching the marginalized,* p. 182.

22. Ibid., p. 18.

23. UNESCO. (2005). *Guidelines for inclusion: Ensuring access to education for all* (p. 13). Paris: UNESCO.

24. Ibid.

25. Arizona State University. (2009, October 9). Disability center comes to Cronkite school. *ASU News.*

26. The Supreme Court of Canada. (2007). *Judgments of the supreme court of Canada 2007.* Retrieved January 2010, http://scc.lexum.umontreal.ca/en/news_release/2007/07-04-12.3a/07-04-12.3a.html

27. UNICEF. (2007). Promoting the rights of children, pp. 35–36.

28. Ogat, O. (2006). *Transforming education systems to respond to all learners: Experience from Oriang Chesire inclusive education project.* Enabling Education Network. Retrieved January 2010, http://www.eenet.org.uk/resources/eenet_newsletter/news8/transforming_education_systems.php

29. Bines, H. (2007). *Education's missing millions: Including disabled children in education through EFA FTI processes and national sector plans* (p. 11). Milton Keyes, UK: World Vision UK.

30. Office of the United Nations High Commissioner for Human Rights. (2007). *United Nations convention on the rights of persons with disabilities.* New York: United Nations. Retrieved December 13, 2010, http://www2.ohchr.org/english/law/disabilities-convention.htm

31. International Disability Rights. (2007). *International disability rights monitor*

32. Office of the United Nations High Commissioner for Human Rights. (2007). *United Nations convention on the rights of persons with disabilities.*

33. UNICEF. (2007). Promoting the rights of children, pp. 35–36.

34. Bines. (2007). *Education's missing millions,* p. 19.

35. Ibid., p. 5.

36. UNICEF. (2007). Promoting the rights of children, pp. 35–36.

37. Peters, S. (2004). *Inclusive education,* p. 12.

38. Scribner, S., & Cole, M. (1973). Cognitive consequences of formal and informal education. *Science, 182,* 553–559.

39. Balshaw, M, & Lucas, H. (2000, July). *Effective schools for all in Macedonia and Harrow: An international comparison.* Unpublished paper presented at ISEC 2000, Manchester, UK.

40. Armstrong, J. (2000). A holistic education, teachings from the Dance-House: "We cannot afford to lose one native child." In M. K. P. A. Nee-Benham, & J. E. Cooper (Eds.), *Indigenous educational models for contemporary practice in our mother's voice* (pp. 35–44). Mahwah, NJ: Lawrence Erlbaum Associates; Easton, P. (1998). *Senegalese women remake their culture* (Indigenous Knowledge Note no. 3). Washington, DC: World Bank; Jegede, O. (1994). African cultural perspectives and the teaching of science. In J. Solomon, & G. Aikenhead (Eds.), *STS education: International perspectives on reform* (pp. 3–17). New York: Teachers College Press; Kawakami, A. J. (1999). Sense of place, community, and identity: Bridging the gap between home and school for Hawaiian students. *Education and Urban Society, 32*(1), 35–61; Srikantaiah, D. (2005). *Education: Building on Indigenous knowledge* (Indigenous Knowledge Note no. 87). Washington, DC: World Bank.

41. Ogat. (2006). *Transforming education systems.*

42. Metts, R. (2000). *Disability issues, trends and recommendations for the World Bank.*

43. UNICEF. (2007). Promoting the rights of children, pp. 35–36.

44. These tools are available online from UNESCO at: http://unesdoc.unesco.org/images/0014/001402/140224e.pdf

45. UNICEF. (2007). Promoting the rights of children, pp. 35–36.

46. Ibid.

Part 3

PRIMARY EDUCATION AND TRANSITIONS

8

Achieving Quality Primary Education for the Poor Through State–NGO Partnerships

EBONY BERTORELLI AND ANEEL BRAR

Policy-makers and researchers around the world have come to recognize that, in the race to achieve universal primary education, improving *quality*[1]—in addition to *access*—is central to attaining any meaningful outcomes.[2] Beyond ensuring physical access to schools and working to increase enrollment rates—both fundamental steps toward achieving universal education—it has been demonstrated that achieving quality education plays a crucial role in increasing enrollment of the hardest to reach groups as well as raising retention rates and the opportunity to continue forward in the education system.[3] India, with among the world's largest elementary school-aged population (6–14 years) of 210 million, is one of the front lines in the battle for universalization and, although major progress has been made in aggregate enrollment, significant obstacles remain in terms of improving quality. As succinctly stated by a senior World Bank educationist, India "is where Education for All, globally, is going to be won or lost."[4]

The goal of universalizing primary education, which was based on the goals of the Education for All (EFA) framework first established at Jomtien in 1990, dovetails well with India's own stated aspirations of free education for all elementary school-aged children, which was first articulated in the country's original 1950 Constitution. Although India's rhetoric has not been matched by the reality of its educational outcomes for the remaining part of the 20th century, recent groundbreaking changes to policy and government priorities have positively affected primary enrollment and access.[5] Many of these recent achievements have occurred with the creation of India's first national primary education program, the *Sarva Shiksha Abhiyan* (SSA) in 2001.[6]

Created to ensure universal enrollment by 2010, and in part spurred by the commitment to the Millennium Development Goals (MDGs), the SSA's programs and policies focus on children who are marginalized from accessing primary education due to various socioeconomic inequalities.[7] Funded by a special national 2% tax levy as well as in small part by the World Bank and the United Kingdom's Department for International Development, the goals of the SSA are buoyed by the largest educational budget in Indian history and have resulted in the rebuilding of the country's primary education institutions and the unparalleled commitment of the federal government to inducing change.[8] Indeed, the goal of universal enrollment is within grasp for many Indian states and has already been effectively achieved in several. According to the most recent survey data, 95.7% of rural children aged 6–14 are enrolled in school, which is the highest enrollment rate that India has ever achieved.[9] (See Table 8.1).

Notwithstanding these successes, Indian education remains characterized by high levels of inequity that are inextricably linked to issues of education quality.[10] Enrollment figures often mask retention and dropout rates, which are key performance indicators of the education system. It has been estimated that India's retention rate—defined as the proportion of a cohort that entered the school system 5 years previously reaching grade 5—was 70.26% in 2006–2007, meaning that 30% of this cohort repeated a grade or dropped out of the system before finishing primary school.[11] Even more troubling is the claim by Kumar, the head of India's National Council of Education Research and Training (NCERT), that "these [types of] figures are in fact recognized as inaccurate and the ground reality is reported to be worse."[12] The overwhelming majority of children who are out-of-school, or who have dropped out of school, are from the most marginalized and poorest sections of society that are most in need of the benefits of education.[13]

Unfortunately, one of the major reasons why these children and their parents decide against attending school is the belief that the education available is of low quality and of little value compared to other activities such as working or taking care of the household.[14] In terms of learning outcomes, it appears as though these concerns are largely correct. A massive national-level survey conducted by the educational non-governmental organization (NGO) Pratham—known as the Annual Status of Education Report (ASER)—indicates that, in 2008, only 67% of children in grades 3–5 could read grades 1 level text or higher in their own language, and that that only 55% of children in grades 3–5 could do subtraction or more.[15]

Despite a rhetorical commitment to quality, the majority of efforts in India to achieve universal education have centered overwhelmingly on enrolling children and not on providing meaningful education that would keep enrolled students in school and ensure that they learn while they are there.[16] The retention rates and learning outcomes exhibited by the Indian system have made clear for the SSA and other stakeholders the need for a more substantial focus on quality in primary education planning.[17] Correspondingly, within key international commitments to EFA such as the Dakar Declaration and the MDGs, securing high-quality education is increasingly seen as a highly valued objective since reducing poverty

Table 8.1 **Enrollment for Himachal Pradesh, Uttar Pradesh, and India Based on Pratham's National Survey Data (ASER 2008) for Ages 6–14 Based on School Type**[18]

State		2008		
	Gov't	*Private*	*Other*	*Total enrollment*
Himachal Pradesh	75.1	24.3	0.1	99.5
Uttar Pradesh	56.4	35.9	2.1	94.4
India	**71.9**	**22.5**	**1.3**	**95.7**

"Other" schools include *madrassas* and other informal school programs targeting children with disabilities and difficult-to-reach children (i.e., migrants). All figures are percentages based on representative samples (Himachal Pradesh, n = 9,003; Uttar Pradesh, n = 78,269; India, n = 510,985).

and inequality, improving health and nutrition, and increasing social participation and empowerment, are all linked to the spread of quality education.[19]

As part of the international efforts addressing primary education there have increasingly been calls to expand governance and educational resources by fostering partnerships between governments and NGOs to address quality issues at the local level more effectively.[20] The following case study focuses on a state–NGO partnership between India's largest educational NGO, Pratham, and the governments of Uttar Pradesh (UP) and Himachal Pradesh (HP) in Northern India. Pratham has created and implemented state-specific quality improvement programs in an effort to improve quality and raise the learning achievements of marginalized students in government schools.

Understanding the challenges that Pratham faces and assessing whether their programs have been successful in overcoming obstacles to quality improvement in each state's particular context offers important insight not only for education planning in India but also for similar efforts around the world. The central question of the study is: How successful have Pratham's programs and collaborative efforts with state governments been at improving education quality and delivering meaningful education in India? The unit of analysis will be *Nai Disha* and *Adhaar*, two of Pratham's collaborative programs with the state. *Adhaar* aimed to eradicate illiteracy and innumeracy among children at the lowest learning levels in HP and to improve the math and reading skills of children in grades 2–5. *Nai Disha* focused on increasing the reading, comprehension, and arithmetic learning levels of children in grade 1 and 2 across the state of UP, with a strong focus on the weakest students. Both programs were implemented with an innovative focus on highly engaging and participatory activities and continuous monitoring and assessment.

We argue that the success of these initiatives is in affecting education policy through advocacy, changing state behavior, and raising the consciousness of people and governments regarding vital education issues rather than the direct influence of the program's inputs. Fundamentally, given India's context, we also argue that an effective NGO–state partnership needs to recognize that the bulk of the responsibility of public good delivery must ultimately come from the government.

Background

NGO–STATE PARTNERSHIPS AND QUALITY EDUCATION

The partnership between Pratham and the state governments of UP and HP is reflective of the global trend since the 1990s of increasing NGO involvement in the development strategies of low- and middle-income countries. This strategy often involves NGO–state collaboration for the delivery of public services. It is estimated that there are over 1 million active nonprofit organizations operating in India, earning the country the reputation of being "the NGO capital of the world."[21] The rise in the number of NGOs in India has been attributed to several factors, including the state's failure as a development agency, the tensions caused by fiscal irresponsibility and increasing public debt, the retreat of the state from economic development in favor of market forces, and international linkages created by globalization.[22]

In the education sector specifically, "the general public today," according to one well-respected Indian educationist, "are [sic] systematically losing faith that they will get any public service called education in this country."[23] Non-governmental organizations, along with private schools, have emerged to fill the perceived gap in provision. Interestingly, much of the impetus for NGO involvement in India has come from the government itself, possibly as a way to compete with private provision.[24] One prominent researcher noted that there have been contradictory pressures on governments to, on the one hand, privatize or "NGO-ize" public services and, on the other hand, improve their own capabilities in service provision.[25]

Non-governmental organization involvement in public service delivery is subject to much debate. In India, the level of insulation of public institutions and their bureaucratic "inertia" combined with the sheer magnitude of the country's development problems are often cited as factors that curtail the impact of even the most well-funded and far-reaching NGOs.[26] Additionally, the massive monetary investment made by the central government in SSA can make the influence of education NGOs seem negligible. However, NGOs have been noted for introducing innovations, providing external inputs, and otherwise informing the education system in ways that governments cannot. Non-governmental organizations are therefore seen as capable of filling gaps in service provision and strengthening moves toward reaching quality universal education.

PRATHAM'S PURPOSE AND ACTIVITY

Philosophy

The Indian educational NGO Pratham has made education quality and learning achievement central to its programming and partnerships with state governments. Pratham's philosophy is to be a supporter of the government rather than a critic, as it seeks to strengthen the capabilities of government schools and mobilize support for quality universal primary education.[27] In this vein, Pratham engages with existing structures and networks including the government, community members and organizations, and corporate and international donors. According to Pratham, "these partnerships intend to foster sustainability and ownership, inspire new ways of thinking about problems, and, most importantly, reach as many children with high-quality programs as possible."[28]

Pratham engages in a three-pronged strategy to influence how government schools operate. As shown in Figure 8.1, Pratham attempts to mobilize the state's SSA and the local community while itself directly engaging schools through training programs, monitoring, and material/pedagogical inputs.[29] This allows the government, through the SSA, and corporate and international donors through

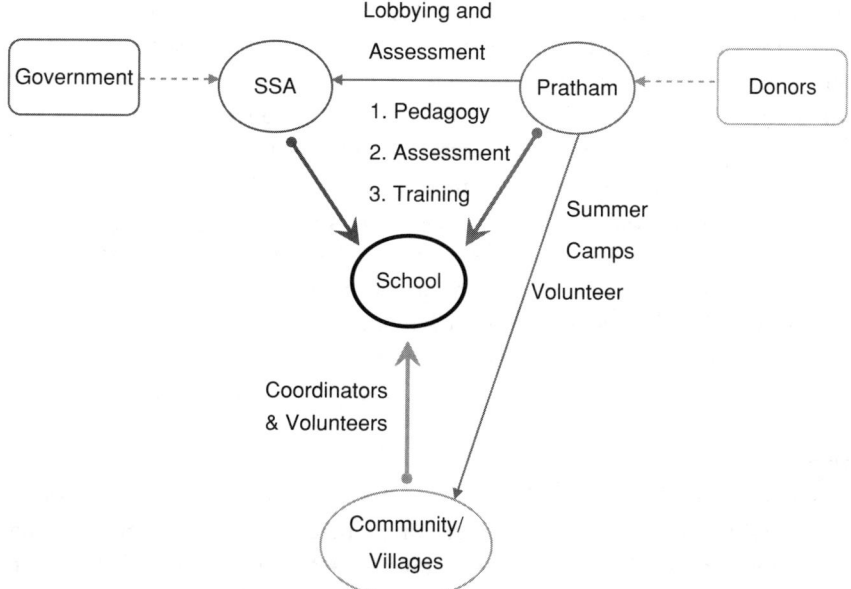

Figure 8.1 Pratham's three-pronged strategy to influence government schools.

Pratham, to have a top-down influence on the education system while community members, empowered by their involvement in Pratham's programs, can place pressure from the bottom-up. Every part of this overall strategy is meant to be flexible and adaptable to local contexts. Although this case study focuses on the NGO–state collaborative aspect of the Pratham's education initiative, much of its programming is effectively outside of the government system. For example, community programs such as summer camps, the recruiting of volunteer teachers, and the production of learning materials generally occur outside of state auspices even though they are meant to support the quality of government provision.

Pedagogy

The three pillars at the core of Pratham's strategy for improving education quality and outcomes are innovative pedagogy, training programs to implement this pedagogy, and vigorous evaluation programs to assess outcomes. Pratham believes that reducing dropouts is a function of improving learning levels. Pratham's pedagogy contains a strong ideological emphasis that places the child at the center of education and focuses on individual progression, especially among those children who exhibit the lowest levels of learning achievement.[30] This is done with accelerated reading and math learning techniques that, in theory, will enable students to move on to higher-level curriculum with greater ease and confidence.

This pedagogy was designed primarily to break down deeply entrenched barriers between the teacher and the student, pervasively found to be a principal determinant of poor instruction in government schools.[31] Thus, basic math and language learning units are based on highly energetic and participatory activities.[32] For language and literacy skills, Pratham developed a curriculum of game- and activity-based learning that utilized various inputs, such as flashcards with letters and words printed on them, *barakhadi*[33] posters, "story cards" containing both short and long texts, and colorful story books designed to engage children through questions, physical activity, and elaboration.[34] In addition, many activities require children to write answers on the chalkboard, wall, or ground. Arithmetic activities center on the use of simple yet engaging participatory tools such as straws and elastic bands and play money.[35] The inclusion of these participatory and "fun" activities has resulted in a unique pedagogy—dubbed "play-way"—that won Pratham the 2000 Global Development Network Award sponsored by the World Bank and the Government of Japan as one of the top three "most innovative development projects" for its ability to achieve quality enhancement.[36]

Training

Pratham's ability to operationalize its method and disseminate its vision of quality education was largely dependent on its teacher training sessions. Besides introducing Pratham's pedagogical innovations to the state's educators, the training sessions provided virtually the only opportunity for Pratham to convince teachers that the quality initiative was a worthwhile endeavor. This was vital for instilling belief in the system and ensuring wide-scale implementation. Other than the logistics of organizing the intensive training sessions, the biggest hurdle to overcome for Pratham was the cynicism of teachers, many of whom would have seen countless, well-intentioned government and non-governmental programs come and go without substantial changes.[37]

Initial training sessions—referred to as "Master Teacher Trainer" sessions—were carried out in 4-day blocks followed by monthly 1- or 2-day "refresher" sessions for feedback and problem-solving.[38] Much of the training was devoted to how to conduct learning-level testing. Trainees were able to apply the methods they learned during "field trips" to local government schools, which allowed unforeseen problems or issues that arose in the learning environment to be directly addressed.

Importantly, subsequent levels of training down the cascading organizational structure (see Figure 8.2A and B) always involved less time, less field work, and an increased focus on motivating fatigued volunteers and teachers. A major concern regarding Pratham's training is the loss of information, technique, and ideology from one teacher to the next as the cascading training process progresses. One senior-level Pratham official commented that, as important as the pedagogical innovations and learning materials were, the main point of every training session

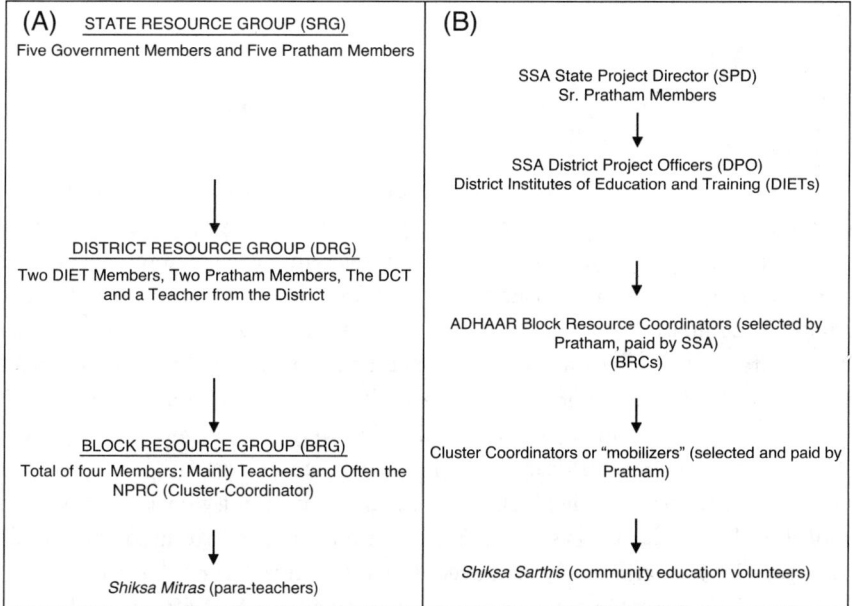

Figure 8.2 *(A)* Cascading resource group structure of *Nai Disha*. *(B)* Cascading organizational framework of *Adhaar*.

was to sensitize teachers and the community to the quality imperative and to make explicit the low learning achievement of their students. He asserted that if teachers are aware of the basics of Pratham's method and see how it corresponds to problem areas highlighted through testing, improvement will occur regardless of whether the full training regimen is passed on.

Evaluation and Assessment

A critical part of Pratham's training sessions involves teaching evaluation methods. Pratham's evaluation methods were designed as a means of assessing the program generally, but more importantly as a tool to situate each child in a specific learning level category.[39] These categories are meant to accurately reflect a child's stage of educational achievement, allowing the instructor to understand the educational needs of the child throughout the program.[40] Pratham's evaluation methods also serve a critical function in national assessments. Since 2005, Pratham has organized the yearly publication of the ASER, an ambitious national-level survey of India's primary education system that serves as a third-party check on data collected by the Indian government. The production of the ASER report has gained tremendous legitimacy and now garners considerable media coverage at its annual release.[41] Part of this legitimacy comes from its tacit acceptance by some government bureaucracies and support from large external donors such as Google.org, OxfamNovib, and UNICEF.[42]

Pratham has now implemented its quality education initiative in 21 out of 28 states in India, allowing it to work with and reach millions of children across the country.[43]

HIMACHAL PRADESH AND UTTAR PRADESH: GOVERNMENT INVOLVEMENT AND EDUCATION CHALLENGES

Although the educational systems in HP and UP experience similar difficulties that are typical of India, each is at the opposite end of the spectrum of relative success. For example, literacy rates in both states remain well below international standards. The most recent census data from 2001 indicates a male literacy rate of 70% in UP, compared to the national average of 76%, and an even lower female literacy rate of 43%, with a far more substantial gap from the national female average of 54%.[44] Male, female, and total adult literacy in HP stand at 86%, 68%, and 77%, respectively, which, although still objectively low and gender-inequitable, out-performs not only UP but the neighboring states of Punjab, Jammu and Kashmir, and Haryana. Indeed, HP's literacy has consistently been at or near the top of the all-India rankings since 1981.[45] Furthermore, according to government statistics, HP has effectively achieved universal enrollment.[46] Although UP's enrollment in both government and private schools is at 94.4% (see Table 8.1), only 67% of those children regularly attended class, which partially accounts for learning levels that are well below both HP and national averages. In 2006, the year that Pratham's programs were introduced in both states, only 51% of children in grades 3 to 5 in UP could read level 1 text or higher in their own language, compared to 74% in HP and 66% nationally. Furthermore, only 47% of children in these grades could perform subtraction or more in UP, compared to 72% for HP and 65% nationally.[47]

The two states also differ greatly on several indicators of educational quality. A 2005 survey of 3,700 schools in 20 major states indicated that, in UP, government school teachers were absent 26.3% of the time, above HP's absentee rate of 21.2% and the Indian average of 24.8%.[48] In terms of facilities, 16% of UP's schools do not have safe drinking water and 46.6% of schools do not have a useable washroom. Last, if all UP students enrolled in school were to be in attendance, pupil–teacher ratios would average 59.4:1.[49] HP, on the other hand, is frequently cited as an Indian success story and consistently does better than its counterparts not only in terms of education, but also in overall human development and economic growth, ranking among the top states in India in all three categories.[50] According to the 1999 PROBE survey, it is not uncommon to find perfectly functioning schools with single-grade classrooms, active teachers, sturdy infrastructure, and engaged students.[51]

In terms of socioeconomic environments, HP is largely a rural state that has a higher than average Scheduled Caste (SC) and, in a few districts, Scheduled Tribe (ST)[52] population, which are demographic characteristics that usually correlate with lower literacy and worse educational outcomes.[53] UP stands out as having one of the most unequal social, economic, and political environments in the country. Endemic levels of poverty, pervasive issues of caste, and some of the most extreme gender gaps in the world are all deeply ingrained within UP society.[54] Due to the enormity of its population—estimated at 186 million people as of 2007 and 30 times that of HP—changes in UP's education system can have a profound impact on the lives and futures of millions on a global scale.[55] If regarded as its own country, UP would be one of the world's most populated and underperforming; thus, in global efforts toward EFA, UP plays a significant role.

Results

In HP, Pratham piloted *Adhaar* in 2,104 schools in various locations between September and December 2006, before scaling up the following year to run in every government primary school (10,613 in total) across HP's 12 vastly different districts.[56] The average enrollment per school was 50, which meant that, in 2007, Pratham directly engaged over 500,000 students with its rapid learning techniques and materials.[57] This was the first time the state had directly partnered with an NGO on such a large scale.[58]

In UP, *Nai Disha* focused on increasing grade 1 and 2 students' learning levels in reading and comprehension as well as basic arithmetic skills. In its first year, *Nai Disha* ran from November 2006 to April 2007 in 20 of UP's 69 districts, directly engaging 45,000 schools, 55,000 instructors, and 1.17 million students from across the state.[59] In its second year (2007–2008), *Nai Disha* ran for 4 months in 20 additional districts, increasing the coverage of students by 865,000 for a total of over 2 million children in 40 diverse rural and urban districts.[60]

ORGANIZATIONAL FRAMEWORK

To cover such vast areas and numbers of children in both states, Pratham implemented its programs using a top-down organizational structure that mirrored that of each state's SSA. This would generally include, from top to bottom, education secretariats and SSA directors at the state-level, district project officers (DPOs) and district institutes of education and training (DIETs),[61] block resource coordinators (BRCs), and cluster resource coordinators (CRCs), village education committees (VECs), and *panchayats* (village councils) at the local level.[62] Generally, within SSA's framework everything from policy implementation to fiscal disbursement for salaries and infrastructure costs channels down the structure until it is in the hands of VECs and *panchayats*.[63] Pratham's framework involved a collaborative effort between its own parallel structure and the SSA from the state level down to the district level, in HP, and the higher cluster level (i.e., groups of villages/communities and nearby schools) in UP. It was a depth of teamwork and cooperation that had never before been attempted between an NGO and the SSA for a quality initiative in either state.

The prominent organizational feature of *Nai Disha* was resource groups comprised of a varying membership from the state and Pratham that were formed at all stages, save the cluster and village levels (see Figure 8.2A).[64] The responsibilities of each resource group were decided at the state level by a coordinator from the SSA and Pratham. For both the 2006–2007 year and the 2007–2008 year, the state resource group (SRG) was given the tasks of overall program design and implementation of *Nai Disha*, including goal setting, training, assessment, and analysis. The District Resource Group (DRG) was responsible for selecting and training the BRGs, ensuring timely and systematic evaluation, and facilitating academic support and guidance for all areas of the program.[65] Last, the BRGs were directly responsible for the training of the para-teachers *(shiksha mitras)* employed to teach grades 1 and 2, as well as for facilitating and leading monthly feedback meetings.[66] This organizational structure aimed to make *Nai Disha's* format easily replicable, efficient, and locally responsive.

In HP, the responsibility of implementation, goal-setting, and monitoring for *Adhaar* was bestowed directly on the SSA at the state and district levels, with constant interaction and support from Pratham members (see Figure 8.2B).

GOAL-SETTING, MONITORING, AND ASSESSMENT

The implementation of Pratham's in-school programs involved goal-setting, monitoring of the program, and learning-level assessment. For both *Adhaar* and *Nai Disha*, coordination and discussion at the state level established program objectives. Those at the state level believed that all goals set by the program needed to be easily understood by all persons involved.[67] Additionally, it was agreed that these goals should correspond to preexisting expectations of learning achievement for children in each state, based on the common curriculum, and, most importantly, that the goals would be realistic and motivating.[68] Therefore, *Adhaar* and *Nai Disha* did not seek to extend or expand the existing expectations and goals of basic education, but to support the learning levels and achievements of the earliest learners so that, as they progressed through the basic education system, they would have more of an opportunity to meet these expectations and goals.

Based on these understandings, it was mandated that, in the first year of *Adhaar*, teachers were to eradicate illiteracy and innumeracy among the weakest students and have all children in grades 2–5 functional, at the very least, at a grade 2 level in math and reading within a timeline of 3–4 months. These objectives were thought to be very achievable, given HP's relatively high performance in education. For UP, it was mandated that, by the end of *Nai Disha*, all children in grade 1 would be able to write simple words, read and write sentences, and complete basic addition and subtraction equations with numbers ranging from 1 to 20. For grade 2, it was mandated that all children would be able to read stories, write easy sentences, and perform basic addition and subtraction equations with numbers ranging from 1 to 100.[69] In *Nai Disha's* second year, these goals were narrowed slightly due to a decision to target the large numbers of children in the "nothing" levels.[70] To reflect these changes, the writing components for both standards were dropped.

A system of monitoring was implemented to ensure adherence, quality, and motivation throughout the program's duration. In both states, pedagogical and administrative personnel from the government and Pratham participated in monitoring. In the first year of *Nai Disha*, all Pratham members of the SRG conducted daily school visits for the duration of the campaign. They also met with DIET heads, district magistrates, and basic education officers within the visited districts.[71] Moreover, for the month of March during the program's first year, the entire SRG conducted school visits in every district and, based on these visits, formed district reports that were discussed and disseminated with district officials.[72] In both of *Nai Disha's* runs, the primary role of all members of each DRG was to conduct monitoring within the schools throughout the program's duration, to maintain and ensure the quality of operations.[73]

Another fundamental aspect of implementation centered on Pratham's system of evaluation and assessment. During all runs of *Adhaar* and *Nai Disha*, children's learning levels were systematically tested across all districts to assess the cognitive impact of the quality initiative. Para-teachers or volunteers conducted a standardized baseline test before the learning modules of the program began and reported the results to the block and district levels.[74] A mid-term test was conducted in the same manner to monitor progress and ensure that teachers were aware of and actively engaged in tracking children's learning levels. A final test was conducted at the conclusion of the programs' run to assess their overall impact on children's learning levels.

Successes

PRATHAM'S INPUTS AS EFFECTIVE TOOLS FOR QUALITY IMPROVEMENT

Evaluation

Pratham's rigorous standardized evaluation and monitoring system was a crucial input for basic education in the participating districts. The majority of instructors interviewed in UP stated that, before the introduction of *Nai Disha*, they did not utilize a standard form of testing to evaluate their students.[75] When asked how they ascertained their students' learning levels and academic progress, many teachers commented that they were able to intuitively evaluate their students through daily classroom interaction.[76] A small number of instructors administered evaluation tests, but these tests were most often written by the teachers themselves and not standardized across districts, making their results incomparable and uninformative from a policy perspective.[77] Additionally, for the many students in HP and UP who cannot read and write, written tests have little utility. When questioned about the evaluation component of Pratham's initiatives, all instructors who were knowledgeable about the programs underscored the particular success of this input and stated that they had seen significant improvement in their students from the results of the baseline test.[78] Learning level assessment, as described by one instructor from *Nai Disha,* worked because it allowed "level-appropriate teaching based on assessment."[79] Similar statements were echoed independently by several other instructors in both states.

Nai Disha and *Adhaar* represented most teachers' first opportunity to concretely place their students in a defined progression of cognitive achievement and use these data to prescribe the suitable method of teaching to boost each student's learning levels. Teachers also began to feel accountable for the changes in levels from the baseline to final tests. Additionally, for the first time at the state level, the SSA had relevant learning achievement data available to track and compare the progress of entire districts and identify where best to concentrate future efforts.[80] The implementation of a standardized assessment program that was operational on a massive scale demonstrated for teachers and policy-makers the importance and utility of individual student learning level assessment and program monitoring.

Pedagogy

A second success from the programs was the effect of their pedagogy and associated learning materials on children's learning enhancement. One teacher noted that "the [old] resources are here, but [teaching] by story, by playing and singing, these techniques were not there. But now trying them, [the children] are now interested to learn, so the learning standards [have] improved. . . . "[81] According to another instructor, "earlier the teachers were teaching only the front row children [who] were paying attention and progressing, but with these techniques the children in the last row are even learning because they are paying attention and they are participating."[82] The importance of Pratham's learning materials in stoking such engagement cannot be understated, especially in UP where textbooks, reading books, flashcards, and posters had been almost nonexistent until the provision of basic workbooks in 2006 with aid from UNICEF.[83] Therefore, the generation of these materials at the local level for hundreds of thousands of children across the state represented an educational milestone. The learning materials also contributed to teachers buying into Pratham's method at master training sessions. Asked about the materials at one such training session, all senior government school teachers remarked on how they represented a vast improvement over what was previously available and would be valuable tools in helping underachieving children progress.

Training

The hands-on training for imparting Pratham's pedagogy was a third instrumental factor in the program's success. Pratham's innovative focus on training all members within the program was completely innovative. This widespread training ensured that the experiences found within schools would directly inform and impact policy-makers, teachers, coordinators, and volunteers participating in the program and sensitize all those involved in education provision to issues of quality. This was crucial since many key individuals running the program at the state level had never before stepped inside a classroom. Therefore, Pratham's inputs served the dual purpose of raising consciousness and providing the tools to address the issues that came to light through training and testing.

Impact on the Community

Finally, Pratham's education initiatives were successful in fostering community involvement and providing a sense of local ownership. Specifically, the participation of the lower levels of the organizational structure in the creation and dispersion of learning materials and in the implementation of the program created a greater sense of community involvement and teacher engagement.

Pratham's encouragement of teachers at the school level and DIET officials at the district level to be involved in the creation of learning materials was generally viewed as a pioneering accomplishment. *Nai Disha* was the first initiative of its kind in UP to provide space for active participation of those working most closely with the program, and it led to the creation of reading materials for children in entire districts independent of the program's funding.[84,85]

For HP especially, it was evident from field visits that the responsibility for the success of the program was largely on the shoulders of locals. The point of interaction among volunteers, coordinators, and the children occurred at the lower levels of the organizational structure, and the efficacy of this interface was dependent on the commitment of those who filled these positions. This was apparent for both in-school programs and Pratham's summer camps, which were out-of-school programs run by volunteers.[86]

Young volunteers, most of whom were not formally trained to be educators, were the focal point of implementation in HP, and they used games, play money, field trips, and whatever else their imaginations could come up with to teach children math and reading skills. Of the visited sites, the attendance level, active engagement of students, use of Pratham's learning material, and resemblance of teaching activity to Pratham's "play-way" pedagogy tended to positively correlate with the skill, ingenuity, and level of engagement of the volunteer teacher. This in turn was highly dependent on the commitment of block coordinators and, especially, the mobilizers.[87] In the most successful district observed, the mobilizer spent at least 6 hours a day ensuring that things were running smoothly and traveling to as many sites as possible at great personal expense.

Partnering for Education: Opening the Door for NGO Collaboration

The innovative structure of the partnership upon which the programs were based was another central achievement, according to those who worked on the initiatives. The blending of the state's and Pratham's particular resources and areas of expertise, and the wider net of civic and government ownership cast through their partnership, created a relatively effective and efficient partnership that could serve as a model for other Indian states.[88] Moreover, the feasibility and success of the SSA's integration of Pratham's initiatives set the precedent for greater collaboration in the future.[89]

The division of labor and resources and the shared vision and goals for the program were continually noted as key features that appealed to the HP and UP governments.[90] Pratham's offer to share the program's costs was an especially important draw for the UP government.[91] When asked about how private collaborations like *Nai Disha* affected the SSA, one of the top SRG coordinators from the SSA commented, "Other NGOs and other partners always take interest in money, so we can't [collaborate with them]. But Pratham is different from other NGOs because they're funded from other sources . . . they have a lot of material to teach us, and they have given free-of-cost consultancy with us."[92] Another draw for both states was Pratham's educational expertise, its pedagogical inputs, and its human resources. As a top-level SSA official noted, "Pratham is a leading organization in the area of education, so it was easier to work with them because they had an expertise in education . . . and with them it was easier to carry out the studies and the development of the program or the modules, then the training of the teachers and then the monitoring and supervision also."[93]

Pratham members echoed these sentiments, as the benefits of working with the SSA were seen as equally attractive and integral to the programs' functioning. In particular, the cascading structure of the SSA's organizational, human, and financial resources was a massive incentive for the implementation of such comprehensive, large-scale programs, as was the support and interest of the leadership in the SSA at the time.[94]

Based on the strength of the initial partnership between Pratham and each state's SSA, the opportunities for further collaboration and the desire of the state to seek out innovative partnerships grew. Both states reinstated their partnership with Pratham for a follow-up year after the pilot year and implemented a series of additional projects. The mutual capacity-building, motivation, and collaboration undergirding the initial Pratham–state collaboration led to scaling-up of the program over time and, in HP, to the introduction of Pratham-led pilot projects in English language instruction, quality initiatives for higher-level children (called *Adhaar* plus), and the creation and testing of newer teaching games and learning materials.[95]

In sum, *Nai Disha* and *Adhaar* could not have been undertaken by either Pratham or the SSA exclusively. The structural, fiscal, and human resources and expertise provided by the Pratham–SSA partnership fundamentally enabled the acceptance and implementation of the programs and lent largely to their successes and expansion.

Challenges

TOP-HEAVY RELIANCE AND THE PARADOX OF STRONG LEADERSHIP

Although the Pratham–SSA collaboration is seen as a success in terms of inputs and innovations, changing perceptions, fostering community involvement, and opening the door for effective NGO partnerships, some aspects of the programs impeded success. Specifically, both *Adhaar* and *Nai Disha* exhibited signs of unsustainability and incomplete implementation. These and other failures were directly related to the mixed effects of strong, top-down leadership and the cascading implementation structure used in both states. Paradoxically, although strong leadership was essential for getting both programs up and running, the top-down structure of implementation led to a relationship in which the top levels relied on the often insufficiently prepared and ill-supported lower levels to carry out the program. At the same time, the lower levels required unsustainable pressure and support from top levels to remain effective.

Key individuals from Pratham and the SSA, motivated by a commitment and belief in their ability to change the fundamental tenets of primary education, worked tirelessly to push for the acceptance of the programs and to make sure that they ran as smoothly as possible. Interviews and observations with those involved in the initial implementation from both the government and Pratham revealed the depth of commitment and personal sacrifice. For example, to get the governments of UP and HP to buy into the initiatives, Pratham workers would often relocate from New Delhi to government centers in UP and HP, to maintain a constant dialogue with local offices.[96] Interviews with Pratham workers and government officials revealed that two senior SSA bureaucrats in UP and one in HP played a fundamental role in the initial acceptance and implementation of the programs due to their dedication to increasing education quality. It was universally acknowledged that the programs would not have been implemented without these individuals, and their transfers away from education posts to other offices in the government, as well as the relocation of Pratham staff to other projects and areas, contributed greatly to declines in the programs' efficiency.

Following these changes in leadership there would inevitably be a period during which commitment to implementation of policies, guidelines, and monitoring procedures relaxed as pressure and motivation waned. With changes in personnel during *Nai Disha's* second year, the role of the SRG was lessened as they no longer traveled across districts to ensure its proper implementation as they had in the first year.[97] This resulted in critical gaps in program implementation. Most notably, the external monitoring of *Nai Disha*, which was mandated to be carried out solely by the DRGs in 2007–2008, was not followed in many of the districts simply due to a lack of commitment.[98] Not surprisingly, Pratham's own evaluations found that the implementation of *Nai Disha* was not as thorough and successful as it was in its initial year.[99]

PIECEMEAL IMPLEMENTATION AND THE ABSENCE OF LASTING IMPACTS

The central and most striking limitations of *Nai Disha* were the inconsistent implementation of the program and the absence of lasting pedagogical and curricular impacts at the school level. The fact that any improvements in learning levels occurred with *Nai Disha* despite the incomplete implementation of the program is a testament to Pratham's emphasis on sensitizing teachers to the quality imperative, more so than implanting pedagogical techniques.

In almost all the schools visited in UP, very few instructors seemed to have understood and implemented the program wholly according to the main principles and framework outlined. In all but two of the schools visited, *Nai Disha* had been implemented in both 2006–2007 and 2007–2008. With the experience of running the program for 2 consecutive years, instructors should have had the opportunity to become familiar with the pedagogy and curriculum, assuming there was little teacher turnover. However, observations and interviews conducted with instructors during school visits clearly illustrated the inconsistent and often incorrect implementation of *Nai Disha*. In almost all of the schools visited, upon first entering the classroom no "teaching" was occurring at all. Teachers were usually seated at a desk merely managing children who were left to work independently in notebooks, which many children did not even have.

Although most *Shiksa Mitras* were able to speak about the program in detail, they were often failing to use the central aspects of Pratham's philosophy in their teaching.[100] In fact, none of the schools visited in UP was utilizing interactive game-based education techniques or a child-centered pedagogy in the classroom at the time of observation. In many schools, posters, flashcards, *tilis*, and bundles were kept in separate rooms not in use, or locked up in cupboards or closets.[101] One *Shiksa Mitra* commented that she kept the flashcards that she had made by hand at home because the children ripped them up and made them "messy" by using them.[102] In the vast majority of schools in which a demonstration of teaching activity was given, the extent of interaction between the child and the teacher consisted of the teacher pointing to a poster or a flashcard and asking the children to call out the number, letter, or word in unison.[103] In the exceptional instances of schools that encouraged physical movement of children, in accordance with Pratham's "play-way" methodology, only three or four children were participating in an activity—usually picking up a flashcard, or writing a correct answer on the chalk board—while the majority of the class sat and watched.[104] Consequently, many children were unable to see what was occurring and remained completely inactive in the learning process.

In several schools, instructors explained that when implementing the program only children of the lowest learning levels were engaged while children considered competent were left to work on their own in notebooks or utilized to monitor the other children.[105] In a school that gave a particularly good demonstration of a *Nai Disha* activity, instructors raced to put up posters and pull out implements that had been locked away and out of use before the classroom was entered for casual observation.[106] In another school, instructors proudly showed off an entire classroom that had been decorated with posters, streamers, paintings, and flashcards to be used strictly for *Nai Disha* activities for students of all ages throughout the school year. However, during the school visit, the model room remained empty, and traditional management style and instructor-based teaching continued in the other classrooms.[107] Therefore, even in schools that understood how to use the implements and techniques of *Nai Disha* and that claimed to value their benefit, the motivation to carry on these practices when not being watched or instructed was not apparent.

Importantly, in 14 of the 25 schools visited, grades 1 and 2 were taught in the same class using the same activities.[108] In many of these schools, and the overwhelming majority of schools visited in the urban districts, grades 1–5 were in the same classroom, meaning that learning environments contained children ranging from 6 to 12 years of age. Such situations were antithetical to Pratham's notion of grouping children according to abilities and focusing the intervention accordingly.

Instructors noted that these situations were not ideal or by choice, but necessary due to the incredibly high pupil–teacher ratios within the school and the dearth of facilities in which to conduct separate classes. A *Shiksa Mitra* instructing both grades 1 and 2 in the same class candidly acknowledged that the use of multigrade teaching negatively affected the children's learning rates, but was resigned to the notion that "nothing [could] be done."[109] The helplessness in the *Shiksa Mitra's* tone is reflective of the structural obstacles that exist in UP, which are a challenge to *Nai Disha* rather than an outcome of the program, and the inability of any input—government or NGO—to fully overcome them.

THE POLITICS OF NGO INVOLVEMENT

Another challenge that the programs faced was the contentious nature of Indian politics. The Indian political system creates little incentive for politicians to enact policies and programs that require long-term investment and planning since results occur too late for incumbents to benefit from them.[110] There is more incentive for newcomers to scrap those programs associated with previous office holders—regardless of their efficacy—in an attempt to gain recognition for their own initiatives. Short terms in bureaucratic posts can also cause discontinuity and inconsistency as programs and policies tend to end when individuals most concerned with their proper implementation are no longer involved.[111]

The vicissitudes that result from this dynamic were present in both HP and UP. Immediately after the pilot years of both programs, state-level elections installed new governments. In UP, two head SSA officials were relocated within the government at approximately the same time, and HP's SSA state director was transferred after only 9 months in office. These changes occurred even though the transferred officials were responsible for bringing in the respective programs and, in the case of HP, would have rather stayed to see the programs through.[112] Even though interviews with most state-level officials indicated a high level of regard for the partnership with Pratham, opposition politicians did not continue their predecessors' programs.

State-Level Politics

In HP, the debates regarding Pratham's presence revolved around three issues. First, it was questioned whether an NGO should be so heavily involved in the delivery of education; second, the use of public SSA funds to support Pratham's initiatives was strongly criticized; and third, state officials questioned whether Pratham was actually serving the needs of primary-level children.

The question of NGO involvement in the delivery of education has both normative and practical dimensions. Normatively, many state-level bureaucrats were concerned that education should be the sole responsibility of the state. Despite the state's undeniably poor performance in providing quality education and the successes that some NGOs have had, the belief that the role of NGOs should be minimal led many state officials interviewed to advocate for the devolution of the partnership with Pratham and the rapid absorption of the programs into state structures. According to one senior education official in HP, "you cannot go with NGOs for a long time. Naturally [the] state has to take responsibility somewhere today or tomorrow."[113] The official further emphasized that "there must be strength within the system to move on [from the partnership]."

Pratham's interventions were also becoming a political liability. The perception was different in UP, where the state benefited greatly from Pratham's resources, than in HP, where the state's education resources were used to fund a large portion of *Adhaar's* management structure. Whereas Pratham utilized the entire SSA education infrastructure to manage *Nai Disha*, *Adhaar* selected 118 of their own BRCs and paid them with SSA funds. Since HP already had employees at the block level serving a similar function for the SSA, questions arose among government critics regarding the necessity of paying Pratham's coordinators. Additionally, Pratham's motive for using public money was questioned since it was known that the organization was well-resourced. Current SSA officials expressed concern regarding the transparency and accountability of the organization's use of public funds.[114]

State officials also questioned the applicability of Pratham's pedagogical method to the needs of HP's primary-level students. There was concern that higher-level children's learning achievement would suffer from the program's focus on the lowest-level students. According to one senior teacher in the Shimla district of HP, the implementation of *Adhaar* resulted in the completion of only 80% of the curriculum for higher-level children compared to previous years. This was a problem for grade 5 students, who would have to write year-end exams to move on to secondary school. The teacher noted that this issue was reflected in the opinion of parents, who expressed great satisfaction with *Adhaar* if their children were in lower grades, but tended to be dissatisfied if their child was at a higher level. These concerns prompted state-level SSA officials to attempt to expand the scope of *Adhaar* to include quality improvement measures for higher-level children in a program known as "*Adhaar* Plus."[115] Although Pratham claimed to be developing measures to address these concerns, state officials consistently expressed the opinion that the development and implementation of *Adhaar* Plus should be a government-only endeavor. As one education official noted, "earlier we were taking the help of the NGO, this year we may or may not take [their help], because [the] NGO may not be involved, but *Adhaar* will go [on nonetheless]."

Local-Level Politics

According to the former SSA official most responsible for bringing in *Adhaar*, there was relatively little resistance to a partnership with Pratham at the policy level; rather, "the resistance came when we started going to the school."[116] Although the majority of opinions regarding *Adhaar* were positive, interviews revealed a critical number of teachers who perceived the program to be an indictment against their abilities and viewed the influx of enthusiastic volunteers as a threat to job security. These teachers perceived Pratham to be an organization that was "coming from outside, evaluating them and then presenting a bad picture about them."[117] According to the former SSA official, "there was some component of jealousy . . . some kind of a feeling that they [*Shiksha Sarthis*] are giving [better] results [while] these teachers are being paid so high [*sic*] and are not giving results."[118]

It is important to contextualize this tension. For government school teachers in HP, the privileges of being a public servant are excellent and include pension and health care benefits, decent monthly wages with regular pay increases, and the security of permanent employment that is not subject to performance assessments or attendance.[119] Public service employment is extremely difficult to achieve and thus highly coveted. As a consequence, HP has an abundance of qualified teachers, many of whom are unemployed and volunteered as *Shiksha Sarthis* in the hope that a permanent government school position would follow. Volunteers were consequently seen as trying to impinge on the territory of established teachers. However, the negative opinion of teachers typically waned upon seeing the successes of Pratham's inputs, and only a small number continued to hold an overall negative view of the program.

ACCURACY OF ASSESSMENTS

The final challenge to the programs came with the assessment procedure. As mentioned, interviews with instructors and other stakeholders suggest that quantifiable learning-level assessments were one of the most important achievements of the collaboration. However, the method in which the data were collected and the resulting assessments leave some of the purported achievements open to question.

Learning-level assessments were conducted by teachers, and the data were verified by the DRG or SRG. In such circumstances, teachers and administrators, threatened by the failure of the program, may feel motivated to produce data indicating success and may teach to the tests rather than to the needs of the child. This is a serious concern in terms of the reliability of the data, especially in UP, a state known for endemic corruption and falsification of official data.[120] Although steps were taken to mitigate falsification through selective blind testing verification and cross-verification, these concerns were still acknowledged by various participants at the top level of *Nai Disha's* framework. One DIET official in UP suggested that they felt assured that "seventy-five to eighty percent of the data is correct and perfect," yet acknowledged that it was likely that the remaining data could be flawed.[121] The standard belief of participants at all levels of the program seemed to be that, although falsification was a possibility, it could be controlled through the verification procedures. However, because the external random monitoring mandated to be conducted by all DRGs was not undertaken in the 20 new districts for the 2007–2008 run of the program, that year's data are further subject to questioning.

Table 8.2A **Pratham Baseline and Final Learning-Level Results for Grade 1 Children in the First and Second Years of *Nai Disha* (Reading)**[122]

	Grade 1					
	Original 20 districts Pilot year (2006–2007)		Original 20 districts Second year (2007–2008)		20 new districts Second year (2007–2008)	
Reading levels	Baseline	Final	Baseline	Final	Baseline	Final
Paragraph + stories	1.2	8.8	Incl. data	Incl. data	0.0	0.0
Sentences	1.9	13.7	Incl. data	Incl. data	1.4	13.5
Words (for second year words and above)	7.5	27.4	13.7	53.1	5.6	28.2
Letters	31.7	41.2	32.5	38.8	29.1	41.4
Nothing	57.8	8.8	53.8	8.1	63.9	16.9
Total %	100	100	100	100	100	100
Total tested (millions)	1.29	1.26	1.23	1.26	0.86	0.81

Table 8.2B **Pratham Baseline and final Learning-Level Results for Grade 1 Children in the First and Second Years of *Nai Disha* (Arithmetic)**[123]

	Grade I					
	Original 20 districts Pilot year (2006–2007)		Original 20 districts Second year (2007–2008)		20 new districts Second year (2007–2008)	
Arithmetic levels	Baseline	Final	Baseline	Final	Baseline	Final
Addition and subtraction	3.4	24.3	3.1	23.6	2.8	18.4
Number recognition (21–100)	12.4	30.4	12.4	31.8	1.9	14.6
Number recognition (1–20)	22.9	35.7	28.1	36.9	36.1	55.0
Nothing	61.3	9.1	56.4	7.7	59.2	12.0
Total %	100	100	100	100	100	100
Total tested (millions)	1.29	1.26	1.23	1.26	0.86	0.82

Some stakeholders also expressed concern about the validity of statistical results in measuring learning achievement. In both years that *Nai Disha* ran, the overwhelming majority of the gains in learning-level achievements involved the movement of children from the "nothing" levels to a level one or two categories higher (see Tables 8.2A and B). Children in grades 1 and 2 have received very little, if any, formal education. Therefore, a "nothing-level" child being able to recognize letters or numbers, or read simple words and perform basic calculations during his or her first year of school, may simply be due to his or her introduction into even the most basic of school environments.

After submersion in 4 months of regimented learning enhancement activities, combined with a strict focus on the improvement of learning levels, it is reasonable to expect quality initiatives like *Nai Disha* and *Adhaar* to produce results in early learners that exceed the recognition of letters or numbers. However, a state such as UP that consistently showcases abysmal learning achievements may well offer support for the programs' general success even when progress occurs at lower levels. Yet, available statistics from the program are not able to reliably illustrate that the increases in the lowest learning levels were actually due to the implementation of the initiatives, either through a control study or through a post-program assessment of children to see if the results had long-term effects.

Despite these concerns, the overwhelming feeling among the majority of stakeholders familiar with *Nai Disha* and UP's education system is one of optimism and success regarding the collaboration. One high-level Pratham member noted that "in a state like UP where there's no reading material, where a child in UP, millions of children, only gets one desk which they will use for the entire length of their primary education, where textbooks never reach [classrooms] on time . . . any progress is a huge."[124] Again, the reflections of a former high-ranking SSA bureaucrat deeply involved at the time of the inception of *Nai Disha* demonstrate an awareness of the assessment weaknesses, but also the sense of optimism brought in by Pratham:

> Whether it [the positive results] was showing up because this was a set of people [i.e., children] who had never had any input, [and] suddenly they got an input; whether it will sustain or whether the baselines were credible, these are some of the issues, which we did raise with Pratham and perhaps they looked into that as well. But, it seemed to be working and . . . there was excitement in the system at something new and worthwhile being done.[125]

Discussion

Pratham's collaborative initiatives have less to do with the efficacy of inputs and challenges of implementation than with affecting ideas on primary education

Table 8.3A **Pratham Baseline and Final Learning-Level Results for Grade 2 Children in the First and Second Years of *Nai Disha* (Reading)**[126]

	Grade II					
	Original 20 districts Pilot year (2006–2007)		*Original 20 districts Second year (2007–2008)*		*20 new districts Second year (2007–2008)*	
Reading levels	*Baseline*	*Final*	*Baseline*	*Final*	*Baseline*	*Final*
Paragraph + stories	6.5	25.2	Incl. data	Incl. data	6.8	32.4
Sentences	6.9	18.1	Incl. data	Incl. data	0.0	0.0
Words (for second year Words and Above)	13.8	25.6	42.3	75.5	13.5	30.3
Letters	34.5	26.5	36.9	22.0	36.1	28.8
Nothing	**38.3**	**4.6**	**20.9**	**2.6**	**43.6**	**8.6**
Total %	100	100	100	100	100	100
Total tested (millions)	1.19	1.26	1.27	1.30	0.89	0.84

Table 8.3B **Pratham Baseline and Final Learning-Level Results for Grade 2 Children in the First and Second Years of *Nai Disha* (Arithmetic)**[127]

	Grade II					
	Original 20 districts Pilot year (2006–2007)		*Original 20 districts Second year (2007–2008)*		*20 New Districts Second year (2007–2008)*	
Arithmetic levels	*Baseline*	*Final*	*Baseline*	*Final*	*Baseline*	*Final*
Addition and subtraction	13.5	42.1	19.2	44.4	13.0	35.8
Number recognition (21–100)	18.1	27.0	25.7	29.7	6.5	18.7
Number recognition (1–20)	26.7	25.7	34.0	23.3	44.2	39.2
Nothing	**41.6**	**4.8**	**21.0**	**2.6**	**36.3**	**6.3**
Total %	100	100	100	100	100	100
Total tested (millions)	1.19	1.17	1.27	1.29	0.89	0.85

among community members, educators, and government officials. In the case of India, and especially UP, the truest test of the collaboration's success is not whether the programs were implemented perfectly, but whether consciousness building and policy changes, including recognition of the importance of quality in education, are resilient against institutional inertia and politics over time. This case suggests that NGO–state collaboration can provide an important tool for creating awareness to achieve goals and may provide resources to fill gaps in policy-making and provision.

THE DEBATE REGARDING THE USE OF NGOS IN PUBLIC SERVICE DELIVERY IN INDIA

Pratham is an exceptionally well-funded and resourced NGO with tremendous experience operating over vast areas and serving millions of children in hundreds of thousands of schools. Despite this scale and reach, there are questions as to whether India's problems can be addressed, even remotely, by non-governmental collaboration. Reflecting on this point, a prominent educationist, who happened to be a member of Pratham's board of governors at the time of interview, noted that:

> You can create a parallel mechanism [of education provision], it will work differently for a few years, then . . . after two-three years [when] the novelty has gone [sic], then they [the NGO providers] will also start behaving the same way as the larger system. Because the inertia is so heavy you cannot really stay afloat. . . If we don't really change that I don't think the social sectors in general will change. . . . [On the other hand NGOs can] contribute in terms of new ideas [and] new thinking. Pratham has been able to really bring in some new vibrancy in the field, in making people do things and then show things and demonstrate the possibility that . . . if you work you can really make children learn.[128]

Several government officials in HP considered Pratham's programs successful because they brought in innovation and an infusion of energy and enthusiasm that would continue to inform future policy directions, whether the collaboration and programs persisted or not. Pratham's original philosophy, seeking short-term engagement until the government is capable of providing quality education on its own, is an implicit recognition that lasting change will occur only if the state is willing to make the necessary changes on its own accord. As pithily stated by one educationist, "transformation can come only when the state . . . realizes that they have to transform."[129] If NGO–state collaborations are founded on this premise, it is possible that a group like Pratham can increase accountability and impact policy directions as it did in UP, with the infusion of new pedagogical techniques, and in HP, where *Adhaar* led directly to the development of *Adhaar* Plus and the English pilot programs. According to a top-level SSA official in HP, "it was actually a result of this Pratham experiment . . . that we broadened this whole scope and started to focus on real quality issues."[130] Indeed, as a testament to such thinking, following the rise of quality initiatives across the state and largely under NGO auspices, as of 2008, a percentage of SSA funds are now earmarked solely for quality initiatives.[131]

Besides the government's philosophical openness to external input, it must also be emphasized that what was accomplished by Pratham's programs could only occur because of actual government enablement in monetary and infrastructural support. As much as private provision is increasing in India, the bulk of the responsibility of primary school provision rests with the state, which chooses the direction that primary education policy takes as well as who will have a seat at the table. Crucially, even if NGOs were to one day rival the state in fiscal strength and capacity in delivery of services, and this fiscal and resource base was to be sustainable on a long-term basis, it will still never be able to replace the state in one crucial function: accountability through democratic processes, and by extension, legitimacy. Even a massive NGO such as Pratham has no mechanism for direct accountability to the hundreds of millions of impoverished people it seeks to help. This normative side of the NGO equation is critical, and it must also be acknowledged when engaging in a dialogue concerning the future and impacts of NGO-based service provision in the realm of education.

CONSCIOUSNESS BUILDING AND CONTEXTUALIZING SUCCESS

Pratham brought profound changes in ideas and policy to the educational landscape through its collaborative programs. This is especially clear in UP, where *Nai Disha* brought unprecedented distribution of learning materials to millions of children, a committed focus from the top levels of the state to educational equity, and a standardized method of assessment to evaluate learning outcomes. Based on the wide range of interviews conducted with government officials and in schools, it is clear that Pratham's activities will likely influence policy and public demand well beyond the termination of these particular programs.

Changing fundamental perceptions about education and equity within a system of actors is tightly tied to consciousness-building, which involves sensitizing stakeholders to previously unconsidered problems or issues and giving them the tools to deal with these problems, thereby instilling a sense of empowerment among teachers and policy-makers. Such consciousness-building has been a central mandate within all of Pratham's programming. By situating the bulk of their programs outside of the government education system while being able to work within it, and by utilizing local youth as volunteers, Pratham was able to empower communities with the knowledge and tools to educate themselves and to create pressure for the government to prioritize educational equity and quality. In UP, where the education system has been characterized by extreme inertia and inequity for decades, creating this type of excitement, empowerment, and recognition is monumental for the shape and aims of future education initiatives. Fundamentally, Pratham has planted the seeds to effect changes in government policy. Even during field visits to HP when Pratham's MOU with the government had not been renewed and the NGO's presence was minimal, interviews with state SSA officials revealed that the focused and engaged pedagogy, constant monitoring and evaluation, and passion and enthusiasm for change that Pratham had brought to the table were still observable among those working on *Adhaar* Plus and the English pilot projects.

There are, perhaps, few places facing as many obstacles toward widespread educational equity as India. The observed problems of implementation, the questions regarding some learning-level assessments, and the variable commitment on behalf of the government may legitimately be deemed problems. However, in India, and especially in regions such as UP, despite these obstacles the successes of the program that were seen can be considered a large triumph in moving quality education forward. Importantly, although this case study illustrates that NGOs may not be panaceas for leading and implementing widespread policy change in education quality, they can and do play a large role in spurring, implementing, and building support for programs and can meaningfully influence long-term policy changes. This case study offers critical lessons for countries undergoing similar moves toward educational equity, and offers hope for those facing especially monumental obstacles.

NOTES

1. Some of the major indicators of quality include sufficient levels of teacher competence and training, adequate facilities within the school such as classrooms and usable washrooms, manageable teacher–pupil ratios, inclusive education creating an equitable environment for all children, an active and child-centered pedagogy, the achievement of a standard level of cognitive learning skills, and a curriculum that is locally meaningful and relevant. Ramachandran, V. (2003). Backward and forward linkages that strengthen primary education. In V. Ramachandran (Ed.), *Getting children back to school: Case studies in primary education* (pp. 1–16). New Delhi: Sage Publications.
2. UNESCO. (2008). *Education for all global monitoring report 2009: Overcoming inequality: Why governance matters.* Paris: Oxford University Press; Bruns, B., Mingat, A., & Rakotomalala, R. (2003). *Achieving universal primary education for every child by 2015: A chance for every child.* Washington, DC: World Bank; Ramachandran. (2003). Backward and forward linkages.
3. The majority of children who have never been to school or have dropped out of school are usually those who are marginalized due to various socioeconomic inequalities such as gender inequality, poverty, and ethnicity. Therefore, children marginalized by these inequalities from basic education are often termed as "hard to reach." UNESCO. (2008). *Education for all global monitoring report 2009*, p. 17; Yadav, M. S., Bharadwaj, M., Sedwal, M., & Gaur, N. (2002). Learning conditions and learner achievement in primary schools: A review. In R. Govinda (Ed.), *India education report: A profile of basic education* (pp. 167–188). New Delhi: Oxford University Press.
4. Carlson, S. (World Bank Educationist, 2008). Interview with Aneel Brar and Ebony Bertorelli, August 8, 2008.
5. Govinda, R. (2002). Providing education for all in India: An overview. In R. Govinda (Ed.), *India education report: A profile of basic education* (pp. 1–20). New Delhi: Oxford University

Press; Kingdon, G. (2007). The progress of school education in India. *Oxford Review of Economic Policy, 23*(2), 168–195.

6. Kingdon. (2007). The progress of school education, pp. 188–189.

7. Ibid.

8. Ibid. Also see: World Bank. (2008). *Implementation completion and results report on a credit in the amount of SDR 334.9 million to the Republic of India for an elementary education project (Sarva Shikha Abhiyan).* New Delhi: World Bank; World Bank. (2008). *Project appraisal document on a proposed credit in the amount of SDR 364.4 million to the Republic of India for a second elementary education project (SSA II).* New Delhi: World Bank.

9. According to the most recent data with complete national coverage, India's net enrollment ratio (NER) increased from 84.53 in 2005–2006 to 92.75% in 2006–2007. India's gross enrollment ratio (GER) for elementary grades (I to V) increased from 103.77% to 110.86%. Gross enrollment ratio (GER) is a nation's total enrollment in a specific level of education, regardless of age, expressed as a percentage of the population in the official age group corresponding to this level of education. Net enrollment ratio (NER) is the ratio of the number of children of official school age (as defined by the national education system) who are enrolled in school to the total population of children of official school age—in this case grades 1 to 5 and ages 6 to 11. Note: 2005–2006 and 2006–2007 are the first and latest years with complete data coverage. It is projected that India will have 7,208,000 out-of-school children in 2015. See Mehta, A. (2008). *Elementary education in India analytical report 2006–07: Progress towards UEE.* New Delhi: National University of Educational Planning and Administration (NUEPA); UNESCO. (2008). *Education for all global monitoring report 2009*, pp. 62–66.

10. Ramachandran. (2003). Backward and forward linkages; Kumar, K. (2004). Quality of education at the beginning of the 21st century: Lessons from India (Background Paper). *Education for all global monitoring report: The quality imperative.* New Delhi: UNESCO.

11. Mehta. (2004). *Elementary education in India*, pp. 107–111; World Bank. (2008). *Implementation completion and results (Sarva Shikha Abhiyan),* p. A-34.

12. Kumar, K. (2004). Educational quality and the new economic regime. In A. Vaugier-Chatterjee (Ed.), *Education and democracy in India* (pp. 113–127). New Delhi: Manohar.

13. Govinda. (2002). Providing education for all, pp. 1–20; Drèze, J., & Sen, A. (2002). *India: Development and participation.* New York: Oxford University Press.

14. Drèze & Sen. (2002). *India: Development and participation;* Drèze, J., & Gazdar, H. (1996). Uttar Pradesh: The burden of inertia. In J. Drèze, & A. Sen (Eds.), *Indian development: Selected regional perspectives* (pp. 33–108). New Delhi: Oxford University Press; Lieten, G. K. (2000). Children, work and education-I: General parameters. *Economic and Political Weekly, 35*(24), 2037–2043; UNESCO. (2008). *Education for all global monitoring report 2009.*

15. Pratham. (2009). *ASER 2008—Annual status of education report.* Mumbai: Pratham Resource Center.

16. Ibid.

17. World Bank. (2008). *Project appraisal document on a proposed credit (SSAII).*

18. Pratham. (2009). *ASER 2008.*

19. UNESCO. (2008). *Education for all global monitoring report 2009;* Drèze & Sen. (2002). *India: Development and participation.*

20. Draxler, A. (2008). *New partnerships for EFA: Building on experience.* Paris: UNESCO-IIEP; Ikekeonwu, C., Randell, S., & Touwen, A. (2007). *Civil society partnerships and development policies: Emerging trends.* Paris: UNESCO; UNESCO. (2008). *Education for all global monitoring report 2009.*

21. See Brown, L., et al. (2000). *Globalization, NGOs and multi-sectoral relations* (Working Paper no. 1). Cambridge, MA: The Hauser Center for Non-profit Organizations/The Kennedy School of Government; Kudva, N. (2005). Strong states, strong NGOs. In R. Ray, & M. F. Katzenstein (Eds.), *Social movements in India: Poverty, power, and politics.* Lanham, MD: Rowman & Littlefield; Ikekeonwu, C., et al. (2007). *Civil society partnerships and development.* Paris: UNESCO Forum.

22. Behar, A., & Prakash, A. (2004). India: Expanding and contracting democratic space. In M. Alagappa (Ed.), *Civil society and political change in Asia.* Stanford, CA: Stanford University

Press; Zaidi, S. A. (1999). NGO failure and the need to bring back the state. *Journal of International Development 11*, 259–271.

23. Senior educationist, National University of Educational Planning and Administration (NUEPA). Interview with Aneel Brar and Ebony Bertorelli, June 27, 2008.

24. For example, space for NGO activity has been included in India's recent 5-year economic plans and explicit endorsement of NGO-state collaboration has been integrated into the government's public service strategies, including that of the Sarva Shiksha Abhiyan (SSA). See Planning Commission. (1985). *The seventh five year plan 1985–90.* New Delhi: Planning Commission. Additionally, in 2005 Uttar Pradesh's (UP) SSA created a formal mechanism whereby NGOs could apply for funding or state collaboration for education projects in an effort to widen the avenues available to enhance primary education. With their proposal for *Nai Disha*, Pratham was one of the first NGOs to take advantage of this mechanism and to initiate an in-depth collaborative effort with the state. Similarly, in Himachal Pradesh (HP), Pratham represented that state's first major NGO collaboration for education and was the product of the government's own desire—or at least the desire of the state's top SSA officials at the time—to harness the potential benefit of involving an external actor.

25. Director (former), National Council for Education Research and Training (NCERT). Interview with Aneel Brar and Ebony Bertorelli, June 26, 2008.

26. This opinion was reflected in interviews with government officials involved in primary education as well as with local educationists during field work. Also see: Drèze & Gazdar. (1996). Uttar Pradesh: The burden of inertia; Kapur, D., & Mehta, P. B. (Eds.). (2005). *Public institutions in India: Performance and design.* New Delhi: Oxford University Press; Zaidi, S. A. (1999). NGO failure.

27. Pratham Delhi Education Initiative. (2008). *Annual report 2006–07.* New Delhi: Pratham Delhi Education Initiative; Pratham. (2009). *ASER 2008.*

28. Banerji, R., Chavan, M., & Rane, U. (2005). Learning to read. *Changing English, 12,* 186. (Note: the authors of the above article include Pratham's founders.)

29. Pratham employee in Punjab. Interview with Aneel Brar, August 10, 2008.

30. Pratham. (2007). *Nai Disha: A new direction.* Report submitted to the Government of Uttar Pradesh (GOUP), September, 2007.

31. Ibid.

32. Pratham, through their extensive field experience, surmised that many Indian children simply did not gain the basic foundations of reading and math in the early grades. According to Pratham, early grade instruction often leaves children unprepared and unable to handle higher-level curriculum thereby encouraging many to simply stop attending classes. In situations where children do complete grade IV or V it had been found that many were still unable to read or do simple arithmetic. Banerji et al. (2005). Learning to read.

33. The innovations of Pratham's pedagogy are based on extensive field experience, classroom "experiments" in which they would test new methods, and the work of Dr. A. K Jalaluddin, who studied the efficacy of using a traditional *barakhadi* chart of consonants and vowels to teach nonreaders how to read. Banerji et al. (2005). Learning to read.

34. Ibid.

35. Activities included "*Tili* Bundle" games, in which individual straws or *tilis* were used to represent units of one and ten *tilis* tied with an elastic band into a bundle were used to represent a single unit of ten. Using activities based around *tilis* and bundles, the curriculum required children to physically engage in counting, addition, subtraction, and place value exercises, as well as shouting out answers, counting out loud, and volunteering to answer questions. Additionally, like the reading comprehension units, arithmetic activities also involved the use of number flashcards, number charts and posters.

36. Pratham. (2009). *History.* Retrieved from http://www.pratham.org/M-13-2-History.aspx

37. The vast majority of teachers interviewed on their first day of "Master Teacher" training expressed doubt regarding Pratham's motivations and methods, and they would actively challenge the trainers, who were often younger, less experienced and, indeed, not formally trained as primary-level educators. A total of 20 of the 80 teachers were interviewed throughout the training session.

38. Pratham. (2007). *Nai Disha*; Pratham. (2008). *Nai Disha: Phase II*. Report submitted to the GOUP, September, 2008.
39. Ibid.
40. Ibid.
41. See Pratham. (2009). *ASER 2008*, for examples.
42. Ibid. ASER's legitimacy and strength as a lobbying tool is largely bolstered by the participation of Mr. Montek Singh Ahluwalia, the former Deputy Chairman of India's Planning Commission—the Government of India's institution that formulates its 5-year economic plans—in the annual ASER release event. According to Sam Carlson, "when you have the chairmen of the national Planning Commission launching the release of Pratham's Annual Survey of education, ASER, that's political acumen, but it's also credibility." (Personal communication).
43. Pratham. (2009). *History*.
44. Registrar General & Census Commissioner. (2001). *Census of India*. New Delhi: Government of India. Retrieved from http://www.censusindia.gov.in/
45. De, A., Noronha, C., & Samson, M. (2002). Primary education in Himachal Pradesh: Examining a success story. In R. Govinda (Ed.), *India education report* (pp. 297–311). New Delhi: Oxford University Press; Government of Himachal Pradesh. (2002). *Himachal Pradesh human development report 2002*. Shimla, Himachal Pradesh: Himachal Pradesh Government.
46. Only one of Himachal's 12 districts, the extremely remote and isolated Lahaul and Spiti, has a GER lower than 100% according to government data. NUEPA. (2008). *Elementary education in India: Where do we stand? District report cards 2006–07*. New Delhi: NUEPA; Pratham. (2008). *Annual Status of Education Report (Rural) 2007*. Mumbai: Pratham Resource Center; Pratham. (2009). *ASER 2008*.
47. Pratham. (2009). *History*; Pratham. (2009). *ASER 2008*.
48. For example, of all the schools visited in Jean Dreze and Haris Gazdar's 1997 study, not a single one was found to be actively engaged in teaching activities at the time of observation; Drèze & Gazdar. (1996). Uttar Pradesh: The burden of inertia.
49. Ibid. Additionally, most surveys and studies are conducted in rural areas, yet, in urban areas of UP teacher shortages are documented as being far more severe. As of 2008, research in major urban centers of UP indicate common pupil–teacher ratios of 100:1. Brid, Smitin, et al. (2008, March). *Challenges for schools and society: Pratham experiences in urban Uttar Pradesh* (Preliminary Draft). New Delhi: Pratham Resource Center.
50. De et al. (2007). Primary education in Himachal Pradesh; World Bank. (2007). *Himachal Pradesh: Accelerating development and sustaining success in a hill state*. New Delhi: World Bank.
51. PROBE Team, The (1999). *Public Report on Basic Education in India*. New Delhi: Oxford University Press.
52. The social groups that experience the most socioeconomic inequity in India are Scheduled Castes (SCs) or *Dalits*, traditionally known as "untouchables," and Scheduled Tribes (ST), otherwise known as *Adivasis* or "original inhabitants," who constitute 16% and 8% of the population, respectively; Deshpande, A. (2005). Affirmative Action in India and the United States. In *World development report 2006: Equity & development-Background papers*. New York: The World Bank and Oxford University Press.
53. De et al. (2007). Primary education in Himachal Pradesh.
54. Drèze & Gazdar. (1996). Uttar Pradesh: The burden of inertia; Rathor, A. (2004). *Slum dwellers: Curse on development*. New Delhi: Sarup and Sons; Lerche, J., & Jeffery, R. (2003). Uttar Pradesh: Into the twenty-first century. In J. Lerche, & R. Jeffery (Eds.), *Social and political change in Uttar Pradesh: European perspectives* (pp. 17–53). New Delhi: Manohar; McDougall, L. (2000). Gender gap in literacy in Uttar Pradesh: Questions for decentralized educational planning. *Economic and Political Weekly*, 35(19), 1649–1658.
55. Mehrotra, N. (2008). *Uttar Pradesh: Midterm assessment of EFA goals*. Working Paper for the Government of UP, Revised Draft, February, 2008.
56. McGinnis, L. (2008). *Himachal Pradesh–it can be done: Success with Adhaar*. Draft report for Pratham.

57. Ibid.
58. Ibid.
59. In its first year, the 20 districts slated for *Nai Disha's* implementation were chosen by the state government and Pratham solely based on the desire to achieve a geographical spread across the state. Out of the districts that were chosen, there was a clear representation of designated urban centers, including the districts of Varanasi, Lucknow, and Agra, which are home to three of the largest metropolises in UP, as well as a large representation of designated rural regions. Pratham. (2007). *Nai Disha.*
60. In the second year of the program, the expansion of *Nai Disha* to another 20 districts was conducted based on further criteria, such as the selection of districts that had exhibited poor learning levels as indicated by the previous year's ASER report, districts that would again ensure an even-handed geographical representation, and last, districts that were both large and small to ensure further balance.
61. DIETs are local, government-run teacher training institutes.
62. *Panchayats* are locally elected bodies designated with responsibilities for education in rural areas.
63. Notably, although the SSA utilizes this structure of decentralization across India, UP is even more decentralized in areas of fiscal disbursement. Distinctly within UP, the SSA at the state level channels funds directly to the village level through a body called the Village Education Committee (VEC), whereas, in other areas, funds move through the decentralizing system described above.
64. Pratham. (2007). *Nai Disha.*
65. Ibid.
66. Ibid.
67. Ibid.; McGinnis. (2008). *Himachal Pradesh.*
68. Pratham. (2007). *Nai Disha.*
69. Ibid.
70. Ibid.
71. Ibid.
72. Ibid.
73. Ibid.
74. Ibid.; Pratham. (2008). *Nai Disha: Phase II.*
75. School observation dates in UP ran from July 15 to August 5, 2008, and were conducted by Ebony Bertorelli.
76. Ibid.
77. Ibid.
78. In two cases instructors knew about the program but could not comment on the program's success because they stated they had nothing to compare *Nai Disha* to, as they had only been teaching as long as the program had been running. However, when asked their general thoughts on the program, they both commented that they enjoyed the pedagogy and curriculum of *Nai Disha* and found it very useful in the classroom. Shiksa Mitra (Rural district of Varnasi, Uttar Pradesh). Interview with Ebony Bertorelli, July 22, 2008; Shiksa Mitra (Urban district of Lucknow, Uttar Pradesh). Interview with Ebony Bertorelli, July 16, 2008.
79. Shiksa Mitra (Rural district of Lucknow, Uttar Pradesh). Interview with Ebony Bertorelli, July 19, 2008.
80. Senior professional, SSA (Lucknow, Uttar Pradesh). Interview with Ebony Bertorelli, July 18, 2008; Senior Professional, SSA (Lucknow, Uttar Pradesh). Interview with Ebony Bertorelli, August 1, 2008.
81. Shiksa Mitra (Rural district of Varanasi, Uttar Pradesh). Interview with Ebony Bertorelli, July 22, 2008.
82. Ibid.
83. Former SSA official (Lucknow, Uttar Pradesh). Interview with Ebony Bertorelli, July 15, 2008.
84. Pratham. (2007). *Nai Disha*; Anonymous, Former SSA (Lucknow, Uttar Pradesh). Interview with Ebony Bertorelli, July 15, 2008.

85. School observation dates in UP ran from July 15 to August 5, 2008, and were conducted by Ebony Bertorelli.

86. Summer camps are another modality used by Pratham to affect student learning. They are run by volunteers outside of schools in local communities. Because of the extreme variation in seasonal weather in HP, government schools operate according to two distinct school years. "Summer-closing" schools in low-lying districts run through the winter, when temperatures are mild, whereas "winter-closing" schools in mountainous, high-altitude regions run through the summer to avoid the extreme conditions of winter. Summer camps were, therefore, observed in the southern districts of Sirmaur and Solan, HP. The goals of the summer camps in HP were to either (a) continue the improvement of learning levels that began with the initial *Adhaar* year, or (b) serve as a bridge program to promote out-of-school children to enroll with confidence in the coming school year. In the same vein, the summer camps were meant to prevent laggard children from dropping out by instilling a sense of excitement about learning and mitigating any fear of returning to regular classes.

87. Mobilizers have responsibilities that range from recruiting and training volunteers to monitoring and acting as the medium through which the complaints and concerns of volunteers were voiced to higher-levels in the scheme. Observation of the summer camps revealed that logistics, such as recruiting and gaining local support for the camps, rather than pedagogy and training, was the greatest challenge for the mobilizers who were responsible for up to 20 dispersed villages in a given area.

88. Indeed, the state of Punjab agreed to partner with Pratham based on the successes of *Adhaar* in HP.

89. As stated in this chapter, the scale and character of the collaboration between Pratham and the SSA was unprecedented in the state, and to facilitate this collaboration a new policy was created in the SSA to create an application process for NGOs to collaborate with the state and even to appeal for funds for this collaboration. This transparent and easily accessible process is now used by NGOs across UP to initiate formal collaboration.

90. Senior Professional, SSA (Lucknow, Uttar Pradesh). Interview with Ebony Bertorelli, July 18, 2008; Senior Professional, SSA (Lucknow, Uttar Pradesh). Interview with Ebony Bertorelli, August 1, 2008; Former SSA official (Lucknow, Uttar Pradesh). Interview with Ebony Bertorelli, July 15, 2008; Former SSA official (Lucknow, Uttar Pradesh). Interview with Ebony Bertorelli, August 6, 2008; DIET member (Lucknow, Uttar Pradesh). Interview with Ebony Bertorelli, August 1, 2008.

91. Ibid.

92. Senior Professional, SSA (Lucknow, Uttar Pradesh). Interview with Ebony Bertorelli, August 1, 2008.

93. Senior Professional, SSA (Lucknow, Uttar Pradesh). Interview with Ebony Bertorelli, July 18, 2008.

94. Project Director, Pratham (Lucknow, Uttar Pradesh). Interview with Ebony Bertorelli, July 19, 2008; Volunteer Teacher, Pratham (Lucknow, Uttar Pradesh). Interview with Ebony Bertorelli, August 6, 2008; Volunteer Teacher, Pratham (Lucknow, Uttar Pradesh). Interview with Ebony Bertorelli, July 13, 2008.

95. English pilot projects were developed by Pratham and implemented in the district of Solan under the auspices of the SSA district project officer and the local DIET. Newer teaching methods and materials included the use of play money in transaction games and a number jumping game reminiscent of "hop-scotch."

96. Describing these initial stages of interaction, a prominent member of the leadership team of Pratham states, "We realized that it took a lot of advocacy to get the government to accept that something like [Nai Disha] is needed. You regularly visit people, you talk to them, we have to say, you know learning is important . . . Of course there were larger level influences that Rukmini and Madhav [executive members of Pratham], did at their own level but, yes, on our level we regularly kept in touch for them to realize this is serious organization, this is an organization which can carry off [a program like Nai Disha]." Volunteer Teacher, Pratham (Lucknow, Uttar Pradesh). Interview with Ebony Bertorelli, August 6, 2008.

97. Pratham. (2007). *Nai Disha*.

98. Ibid.

99. Pratham. (2008). *Nai Disha: Phase II.*

100. There were instances where instructors who were present during implementation simply did not remember the program or suggested that they had heard of it but that it was never brought into the school. There were also instances where instructors had knowledge of *Nai Disha* but their understanding of the program's philosophy was incomplete or incorrect. For example, during a school visit, when asked to explain the program of *Nai Disha*, an instructor initially described the program as purely math-based. It was only when questioned further concerning a literacy component that the instructor recalled that there were reading activities using flashcards and posters. These situations, however, were quite rare. Shiksa Mitra (Rural District of Lucknow, Uttar Pradesh). Interview with Ebony Bertorelli, July 19, 2008.

101. School observation dates in UP ran from July 15 to August 5, 2008, and were conducted by Ebony Bertorelli.

102. Ibid.

103. Ibid.

104. Ibid.

105. Ibid.

106. Observation A (Rural district of Varanasi, Uttar Pradesh). Observation conducted by Ebony Bertorelli, July 22, 2008.

107. Observation B (Rural district of Varanasi, Uttar Pradesh). Observation conducted by Ebony Bertorelli, July 22, 2008.

108. Barring the two schools visited in the district of Basti, one school in urban Lucknow in which no teachers arrived to run the school for the day, and a secondary school that was shared with a primary school in the same building.

109. Shiksa Mitra (Rural district of Lucknow, Uttar Pradesh). Interview with Ebony Bertorelli, July 18, 2008.

110. Mehta, P. B. (2003). *The burden of democracy*. New Delhi: Penguin.

111. World Bank. (2007). *Himachal Pradesh: Accelerating development*; World Bank. (2004). *Resuming Punjab's prosperity: The opportunities and challenges ahead*. New Delhi: World Bank.

112. Former SSA official (Lucknow, Uttar Pradesh). Interview with Ebony Bertorelli, July 15, 2008; Former SSA official (New Delhi). Interview with Ebony Bertorelli, August 6, 2008; Former SSA State Project Director (Himachal Pradesh). Interview with Aneel Brar, July 21, 2008.

113. Current SSA state-level officer (Himachal Pradesh). Interview with Aneel Brar, July 23, 2008.

114. Ibid.

115. Within "*Adhaar* plus," quality improvement measures brought in by Pratham were to be adapted to the needs of higher-level children, including the implementation of English-language instruction. Ibid.

116. Former SSA State Project Director (Himachal Pradesh). Interview with Aneel Brar, July 21, 2008.

117. Ibid.

118. Ibid.

119. World Bank. (2008). *Secondary education in India: Universalizing opportunity*. New Delhi: World Bank.

120. The issue of falsification of data within UP was a major concern of most SSA and Pratham officials interviewed.

121. DIET member (Lucknow, Uttar Pradesh). Interview with Ebony Bertorelli, August 1, 2008.

122. Pratham. (2007). *Nai Disha*; Pratham. (2008). *Nai Disha: Phase II.*

123. Ibid.

124. Rural Team member, Pratham (Lucknow, Uttar Pradesh). Interview with Ebony Bertorelli, August 6, 2008.

125. Former SSA official (New Delhi). Interview with Ebony Bertorelli, August 6, 2008.

126. Pratham. (2007). *Nai Disha*; Pratham. (2008). *Nai Disha: Phase II.*

127. Ibid.

128. Senior educationist, National University of Educational Planning and Administration (NUEPA). Interview with Aneel Brar and Ebony Bertorelli, June 27, 2008.

129. Ibid.
130. Former SSA State Project Director (Himachal Pradesh). Interview with Aneel Brar, July 21, 2008.
131. Senior Professional, SSA (Lucknow, Uttar Pradesh). Interview with Ebony Bertorelli, July 18, 2008; Senior Staff, Pratham (Lucknow, Uttar Pradesh). Interview with Ebony Bertorelli, July 12, 2008.

Appendix 1: Methodology

CASE SELECTION

This case study is a qualitative empirical inquiry based on 114 non–randomly selected interviews and field observations in 29 locations in the Himachal Pradesh (HP), Punjab, and New Delhi, and 29 school visits in Uttar Pradesh (UP). The field work was conducted over 8 weeks from June to August, 2008 (See Appendix 2 for a list of locations). Semi-structured informal and formal interviews were conducted with leading academics, policy-makers, government officials, World Bank officials, parents, teachers, volunteer teachers, and Pratham workers, and other NGO actors.

Our purpose with this case study was to look at the northern Indian experience with NGO–state collaboration in primary education and attempt to infer some lessons that can be generalized to a broader context. Pratham was targeted as an organization of interest for a case study on quality education because of its scale, its focus on quality education, and the unique public–private framework upon which many of its programs are based.

Documents and state-level statistics were obtained from the SSA and DIET. School-level statistics were collected from the teachers themselves, including attendance rates, enrollment rates, Scheduled Caste (SC), Scheduled Tribal (ST), and Other Backwards Caste (OBC) enrollment rates, female–male ratios, and learning achievement outcomes. Quantitative educational data evaluations and reports were also obtained from local NGOs.

Due to assurances of anonymity and confidentiality, and to prevent censure and penalization of those interviewed, the names of the respondents were not used throughout this case study, but they are referred to by the organization of which they are a part, as well as by their level of authority in that organization. Observations consisted of unannounced visits to schools and communities accompanied by a translator, and involved the observation of classes, teaching methods, and facilities of the school; conducting formal and informal conversations with teachers, parents, community members; and data collection from within the schools. Translators used in UP were volunteers of Pratham fluent in Hindi and English. To maintain transparency, objectivity, and accuracy in translation, several criteria were applied. In all but two cases, volunteers utilized were not part of the *Nai Disha* program, and no volunteer utilized was taken to an area in which he or she had any involvement or were known by any members of the community or school. Moreover, translators at no time signified they were part of Pratham and introduced themselves as independent researchers. Last, interviews were recorded, and thus verifiable records were created to ensure direct translation from Hindi or Punjabi. All but two school and village interviews in HP were conducted with a translator who was external to Pratham. The remaining school and village interviews were translated by a state-level Pratham official whose position was unknown to the interviewee. Interviews with government and SSA officials, as well as those in New Delhi and Punjab, were all done in English and did not require a translator.

SELECTING THE DISTRICTS

For UP, the schools and communities observed were located within the districts of Lucknow, Rae Barelli, Basti, Varanasi, and Agra. These districts were chosen against several selection criteria. The first was to ensure a geographic spread across the state, to prevent the influence of a regional bias. Moreover, districts visited and the schools visited within them were also selected to ensure a mix of large- and medium-sized metropolitan areas, as well as semi-rural and rural areas to avoid the influence of either an urban or a rural bias. Beyond these criteria, the districts and schools chosen were largely random. However, a small number of schools in two districts were specifically selected because data from *Nai Disha* indicated that they had performed extremely well, in terms of implementation as well as learning achievement outcomes. Last, the district of Basti was specifically selected due to outstanding circumstances, in which the district magistrate independently requested the implementation of *Nai Disha* throughout the district in an attempt to increase the quality of schools, based on the reputation of both Pratham and the program in particular.

Some of Pratham's activities in HP were observed while embedded with Pratham. These included visits to schools in Shimla, to summer camps in Sirmaur, and to training sessions in Kangra and Hamirpur. All other program observations in HP and Punjab were done independently and with an unattached local translator. Additionally, since not all of HP's 12 districts have the same school year, some southern regions were running Pratham's summer camps and were selected because of timing.

Appendix 2: List of Interviewees

One hundred fourteen interviews were conducted for this study. All interviews were anonymous and therefore, to conserve space, the interviewees are listed according to their geographic location and the role of the interviewee.

Himachal Pradesh

- One College Director, Hamirpur District
- One Pratham volunteer, Sirmaur District
- One Pratham coordinator, Kangra District
- One Government school teacher, Shimla District
- Four Government or SSA officials (current and former)
- Fourteen Volunteer teachers, Sirmaur District
- Three Volunteer teachers, Solan District

Punjab

- Seven Government School Teachers, Bathinda District

Delhi

- Six Academics, researchers and policy-makers
- One Former SSA official
- Three Pratham officials
- Two World Bank Officials

Uttar Pradesh

- One Academic, Lucknow District
- One DIET official, Basti District
- One DIET official, Lucknow District
- Six Government or SSA officials (current and former)
- Three Government school teachers, Agra District
- Four Government school teachers, Basti District
- Nine Government school teachers, Lucknow District
- Two Government school teachers, Rae Barelli District
- Five Government school teachers, Varanasi District
- Two Parents of students, Lucknow District

- Three Parents of students, Basti District
- Three Pratham workers, Lucknow District
- Two Volunteer teachers, Agra District
- Two Volunteer teachers, Basti District
- Two Volunteer teachers, Rae Barelli District
- Seventeen Volunteer teachers, Lucknow District
- Eight Volunteer teachers, Varanasi District

Appendix 3: Glossary of Terms

Adhaar. Pratham/State collaborative quality education program in Himachal Pradesh

Barakhadi. Chart of consonants and vowels

BRC. Block Resource Coordinators (BRCs)

CRC. Cluster Resource Coordinators (CRCs)

DIET. District Institutes of Education and Training

DPO. District Project Officers

HP. Himachal Pradesh

Nai Disha. Pratham–state collaborative quality education program in Uttar Pradesh

NGO. Non-governmental organization

Panchayats. Local, village-level governing council

Shiksha Mitras. Government-hired para-teacher (nonpermanent teacher status)

Shiksha Sarthis. Pratham-recruited volunteer

SRG. State Resource Group

SSA. *Sarva Shiksha Abhiyan*

UP. Uttar Pradesh

VEC. Village Education Committees (VECs)

9

The Role of Language of Instruction in Promoting Quality and Equity in Primary Education

CAROL BENSON

It is 10 December, Human Rights Day. I have received messages from a number of concerned colleagues and organizations, one of which reminds me that 75 million children around the world will not attend primary school today and another 225 million will never make it to secondary school. These children cannot fully participate in society "because they are blocked from classrooms by obstacles like high schooling fees, long and unsafe distances to the nearest school, and insufficient numbers of teachers."[1] These figures are disturbing, and the conditions difficult. Yet I am reminded once again that the fundamental role of language too often goes unspoken. What is the point of getting children into classrooms if they are not taught in a language they understand?

Introduction to Language Issues in Education

When the school fails to use a language that the learner speaks and understands well, the school fails the learner in virtually every way. Teaching through a foreign language has been called "submersion"[2] because it is comparable to holding learners under water without teaching them how to swim. It is obvious that teachers and students need to communicate with each other for effective learning to take place. Their relationship is only a step away from that of parent and child, who interact meaningfully in their home language or "mother tongue." So why do schools throughout the world continue to use languages that children do not understand, languages that teachers themselves may have difficulty speaking?

The reasons range from malign to benign, including benign neglect. In the worst cases, the aim of schooling is to erase learners' languages and cultures and assimilate them into dominant society, meanwhile depriving them of their civil, human, and linguistic rights. An example of this is the explicit *castellanización* or

"Spanishizing" of Indigenous language speakers in colonial and post-colonial education systems throughout Latin America, a historic process that has left persisting negative attitudes in countries like Bolivia and Guatemala, even as bilingual programs gain credibility.[3] In more benign cases, schools aim to provide maximum exposure to a second (foreign) language with the hope that it will improve learners' future opportunities, a hope that their parents share. This is true of countries like Vietnam, where constitutional guarantees of minority language rights have not yet been operationalized due to the widespread belief that ethnolinguistic minority learners require maximum exposure to Vietnamese.[4] In cases of benign neglect, the same type of education is offered to all, regardless of learners' linguistic and cultural backgrounds, resulting in inequitable access to learning. Until recently, this latter situation was true of many African countries like Mozambique, which continued post-independence to use the former colonizer's language, in this case Portuguese, for all levels of education, only recently introducing a bilingual option.[5]

Whether or not the reasons are well-meaning, the results are strikingly similar: limited access to schooling; high repetition, failure, and dropout rates; poor quality of education; and low learner self-esteem, all of which are well documented.[6] While acknowledging that the language factor does not stand alone, Walter[7] has used UNESCO and other development data to demonstrate a distributional relationship between learners' access to education in their first language (L1) and level of national development, highlighting the fact that countries that do not provide access to L1 education experience the lowest levels of literacy and educational attainment worldwide. Use of a single (dominant) language of instruction is problematic even in high-income countries because it exacerbates differences between people from dominant and nondominant social groups. In low-income countries, the effects are particularly devastating because they are compounded by health and safety issues, particularly for girls, as well as low levels of teacher education, content-heavy and inappropriate curricula, and lack of adequate school facilities.[8]

Teaching in the learner's home language may not address all of these problems, but it has the potential to make schools more inclusive and participatory, and to make basic literacy accessible and curricular content comprehensible. At the root of promoting Education for All (EFA) is the assumption that basic education offers people a way out of poverty, ill health, and social injustice. Focusing on appropriate early literacy, relevant content learning, and effective classroom communication is necessary for education to make a difference in marginalized children's lives, especially if other factors cause them to drop out after a few years. As pointed out in a 2000 assessment of EFA strategies, "To ignore the question of language choice means potentially not fully addressing the central concerns of basic education."[9]

The purpose of this chapter is to illustrate the essential role played by the language of instruction in improving educational access, quality, and equity. I begin with a discussion of the obstacles to access, quality, and equity caused by a foreign language of instruction.[10] Next, I review how and why learners' home languages should be used for literacy and learning, and how teaching additional languages should be part of a systematic approach to the school curriculum through bi- or multilingual education. Finally, I discuss policy-making with regard to languages in education, explore where the problems lie, and suggest strategies for moving forward.

Why a Foreign Medium of Instruction Does Not Work

Assuming the educational intentions are well-meaning, the underlying notion of using a foreign medium of instruction would be to expose learners to the new language through both literacy and content learning, resulting in successful language learning. This is the notion behind the Canadian French-English bilingual immersion programs that began in the 1960s, stimulating research in first and second language (L2) learning and growth of the field of bilingual education worldwide.[11] Immersion models and theories were developed in majority contexts, where learners are surrounded by competent speakers of the "target" language at school and in society, and where both languages have standard forms and high prestige—yet these models and theories have been adopted in low-income multilingual contexts, sometimes inaccurately and often without proper adaptation. For example, the most serious misunderstanding of immersion education is that it ignores literacy in the learner's home language, which it does not.[12] Recent research in developing countries[13] has demonstrated the challenges and contributed to refining theories, terminology, models, methods, and materials for contexts in which the so-called "second language" may be completely foreign to learners, teachers, and even society, but there is more to be done. Basic principles from the field as well as the latest thinking regarding their application in developing countries are discussed in the next section; this section continues by illustrating how programs intended to take an immersion approach become submersion in practice due to contextual factors, thus limiting learners' access to equitable quality education.

A recent study in Mozambique by Chimbutane[14] captures the difficulty of classroom interaction when learners who are speakers of Changana must learn through Portuguese, the official language of the country. This excerpt is from a grade 4 Portuguese lesson on parts of the human body (Chimbutane's translation):

> *Ms. C*: What can you see in this picture here? (with the textbook raised up, she shows a picture of a boy with the three main parts of the human body specified)
> *Students*: (silence)
> *Ms. C*: What can you see here?
> *Carla*: I can see a boy.

Ms. C: What?

Carla: I can see a boy. (Carla's answer is echoed by a few pupils)

Ms. C: There is a boy in here and. . . is it just a boy that you can see here?

Students: Yes (they answer timidly)

Ms. C: What?

Students: Yes/No (there are contradictory answers–some pupils say "yes," whereas others say "no")

Ms. C: What else can you see here?

Students: (silence)

Ms. C: What else can you see here?

Students: (silence)

Ms. C: This boy. . . was anything divided up?

Students: It was divided up.

Ms. C: Into how many parts did they divide it? [the picture of] This boy here. . .?

Students: They divided it into three parts.

Ms. C: WHAT? (she shouts very loudly)

Students: They divided it into three parts.

Ms. C: They divided it into three parts.

Chimbutane's study,[15] which contrasts classroom discourse in learners' L1 with Portuguese, confirms the findings of countless others with regard to the virtual absence of meaningful communication in the foreign language, making it impossible for students to understand basic instructions or answer questions that would be insultingly simple in their home language. Note that the teacher is not able to vary her language, and that the content of this grade 4 lesson—three body parts—could easily have been mastered in a single grade 1 or even preschool lesson had it been discussed in a language shared by teacher and students.

As in Mozambique, teachers worldwide who are charged with using a foreign language to teach curricular content lack strategies other than "talking at" students and eliciting rote responses. Comparing their observations in South African and Peruvian submersion classrooms, Hornberger and Chick used the term "safe-talk" to describe typical question-answer exchanges like "Do you understand?"/ "Yeeesss" which maintain the illusion that teaching and learning are taking place and allow teachers to "save face."[16] Based on observations of foreign language-medium classrooms in Southeast Asia, Latin America, and Africa, I have found that teachers sometimes save face at the expense of learners, for example, by chastising them for not following the lesson or for failing to respond appropriately. As Mbatha found in English-medium classrooms in Swaziland,[17] teachers may even switch to the L1 to make put-downs more deeply felt by the children whose personalities they share a responsibility for developing.

Another major problem caused by school use of a foreign language is what happens to initial literacy learning. Whether the teaching approach is based on phonemic understanding of language (sound–symbol correspondence), on whole language (word recognition in context), or on a combination of these, the essence of learning to read is making the connection between spoken and written meaning. Children learning to read in a language they understand can employ "psycholinguistic guessing strategies based on knowledge of that language,"[18] a process that is necessary for reading to become automatized and meaningful. Those learning to read in a foreign language are limited to decoding words letter by letter without recognizing their meaning. An illustration from my fieldwork in Guinea-Bissau[19] comes from the first grade 1 "reading" lesson based on a simple sentence in Portuguese—*O pato nada* [The duck swims]—which was "taught" daily for many weeks, in the following unchanging sequence:

1. Chorus of "*O pato nada o pato nada o pato nada o pato nada*" with no sense of beginning or end.
2. Call–response format with mechanical repetition of each word in order.
3. Call–response format with mechanical repetition of each word out of order.
4. Recitation of the sentence broken down into syllables: "*o-pa-to-na-da-o-pa-to-na-. . .*"

Systems like Guinea-Bissau's that submerge children in foreign languages are extremely inefficient for teaching initial literacy, since it is a matter of years before most children are able to discover meaning in what they are "reading"; in fact, my study found that even after 5 or more years of primary schooling, students had less than survival-level oral Portuguese and highly limited literacy skills.[20] Since many children drop out in the early years of submersion schooling, they are not likely to gain enough basic literacy to sustain them throughout their lives.

Thus the main obstacles to learning in submersion schooling are understanding curricular content and learning to communicate through reading and writing. Underlying these are other aspects related to the impossibility of communication, including the findings that:

- Only teacher-centered pedagogies can be used.
- Teachers have no means to draw on learners' prior knowledge, experience, or identity.
- Student self-confidence and self-esteem are compromised.
- Learning cannot be fairly assessed because it is impossible to determine whether students have difficulty understanding the concept itself, the language of instruction, or the language of the test.
- Parents are excluded from supporting learning or even communicating with teachers.

In sum, education through a foreign language creates insurmountable obstacles to access, quality, and equity. At the World Education Forum in Dakar in 2000, one of the main goals was "to ensure that by 2015 all children, especially girls, children in difficult circumstances, and children from ethnic minorities, have access to complete free and compulsory primary education of good quality."[21] Unfortunately, government education ministries, development agencies, and donors have been slow to link this goal to the language of instruction, focusing instead on increasing access to schools and teachers. Thus even as greater numbers of school-aged children enter the classroom, a foreign medium of instruction blocks their access to the curriculum. Educational quality is limited to shamefully low expectations and attainment in both literacy and content learning, as demonstrated above. As enrollment and throughput figures demonstrate, only the clever few manage to break the code and proceed through the system in spite of the obstacles,[22] and only a tiny minority of these are girls, since their home-based duties make them most likely to miss portions of the school year and least likely to gain exposure to the foreign language outside school.[23] We can thus conclude that it is impossible for any country to reach its EFA goals using a foreign medium of instruction.

How and Why L1-based Schooling Works

Bi- or multilingual education can be defined as teaching and learning in more than one language. In multilingual countries serving diverse language speakers, there is growing recognition that the best approaches involve using the "first language first"[24] and aiming not only for bi- or multilingualism but also bi- or multiliteracy, meaning reading and writing as well as speaking more than one language.[25] There are various types of languages involved:

- The learner's "mother tongue" or home language, known as the L1, which is used to teach beginning reading and writing skills along with academic content. In cases in which multiple languages are spoken in the home or locality, schooling may be provided in one of the learner's home languages, in another local language, or in a lingua franca.[26] Acknowledging the terminology issues in multilingual contexts, L1 continues to be used to identify a language that children speak and understand reasonably well by the time they enter school.
- An additional language, known as the L2, which is taught systematically beginning with oral communication skills, so that learners can gradually transfer literacy skills and knowledge from the known language (L1) into the new one. In North American and European contexts, languages are considered second (L2) or foreign (FL) depending on whether or not learners are exposed to them in the outer community. In multilingual contexts, the term L2 continues to be used even when the additional language is foreign to learners, teachers, and society, which may mislead people into thinking that immersion models are appropriate in foreign language situations, as mentioned above. Calling a country's official language "foreign" is often difficult for political reasons (since

it has been claimed as one of the country's languages) or linguistic ones (the elite may speak it as a first or second language, whereas others have limited but varying degrees of access). Thus, to be able to discuss educational language issues, scholars still use L2 to refer to the order in which the language is learned in bilingual schooling.

- In multilingual programs, another new language or L3 may be introduced. Multilingual models and practices vary, as do their results, and an L3 may be introduced as early as preschool or later in primary or secondary school. What effective multilingual schools[27] have in common is their focus on the L1 in the early years (so that students can acquire and develop literacy skills in addition to understanding and participating in content lessons) and throughout schooling (so that learners benefit from mulilingualism and multiliteracies).[28]

Bi- and multilingual approaches use languages systematically in the classroom, so that language and curricular content are learned. The three largest and most widely cited research studies supporting L1-based bilingual learning were longitudinal studies conducted in North America and reported by Ramirez et al.[29] in 1991 and Thomas and Collier[30] in 1997 and 2002, all showing that the longer and stronger the use of the L1, often in parallel with the L2, the better the school achievement in all subjects. Early studies done in low-income countries documented better literacy skills for bilingually educated learners than for children from the same language backgrounds taught only in the L2 (e.g., Modiano[31] in Mexico, and Williams[32] in Malawi and Zambia), as have many studies done since then, with mixed results due to the failure of most programs to develop L1 skills sufficiently for learners to benefit from transfer.[33] The 6-year Yoruba-medium experiment in Nigeria[34] provided the first quantitative evidence from a low-income context that long-term educational investment in the L1 had benefits for both languages as well as for content learning. Since then, similar quantitative effects have been documented in countries like South Africa[35] and Guatemala[36]; the latter has also been the subject of analyses that demonstrate bilingual programs to be cost-effective when balancing costs with savings in higher throughput and improved school success. Recent studies in Eritrea[37] and Ethiopia,[38] where learners' L1s are used for up to 8 years of schooling, reveal higher achievement for longer-term use of the L1. These latter studies confirm the North American findings and indicate that even though short-term transitional models provide some support for learning, they do not fully exploit the benefits of first language development.[39]

Schooling that continues to develop L1 language and cognitive skills provides learners with a strong foundation for educational achievement and offers significant pedagogical advantages that have been reported consistently in the academic literature:

- Use of the L1 to teach beginning literacy facilitates learners' understanding of sound–symbol or meaning–symbol correspondence and allows them to gain meaning from print. Children learn to read in the first year of school, and they can communicate their ideas through writing as soon as they understand the rules of the orthographic (written) system of their language. Numerous studies have demonstrated the effectiveness of the first language for initial literacy by comparing test results between bilingually taught cohorts and monolingually taught "control" groups.[40]

- Use of the L1 to teach curricular content allows children to learn new concepts from the beginning of their school careers. Teachers and learners can interact naturally and negotiate meanings together, creating the potential for participatory learning environments that are conducive to cognitive as well as linguistic development. Children can be observed asking questions and even pointing out teachers' mistakes, which has not been observed in classrooms with foreign languages of instruction.[41]
- Student learning can be accurately assessed in the L1. When students can express themselves, teachers can diagnose what has been learned, what remains to be taught, and which students need further assistance. This appears to be particularly beneficial for girls because any negative preconceptions on the part of teachers are challenged.[42]
- The affective domain, involving confidence, self-esteem, and identity, is strengthened by use of the L1, increasing motivation and initiative as well as creativity. L1 classrooms allow children to be themselves and develop their personalities, as well as their intellects. Enjoyment of school and experiencing success are factors that improve attendance, participation, and achievement, as documented by studies of classroom interaction and interviews with students, teachers, and families.[43]
- Use of the home language in school makes the school, teacher, and curriculum more accessible to all. This demystifies the school, which means that parents can and do approach the teacher to ask for information regarding their children's progress, to offer support, or even to question the teacher and hold her or him accountable. Parents can also help their children with schoolwork, and perhaps learn L1 literacy along the way.[44]

These characteristics of L1-based schooling stand in stark contrast with submersion conditions such as those illustrated by the grade 4 body parts lesson described above. During a recent visit to Mozambique, I had the opportunity to visit some newly bilingual schools, instituted since the 2002 curriculum reform, which offers a bilingual option. These schools continue to suffer from lack of materials and teacher training; in short, very little has changed except the medium of instruction. In Incaia, Gaza province, I observed a grade 2 class practicing literacy in Changana, their home language. It was a Monday, and about 50 children, all seated on the floor, had been asked to write what they had done over the weekend. The teacher had written two sentences about his own weekend on the board. As each child read her or his sentences, and my colleague translated for me, I was struck by the authenticity of their communication in Changana. Each had written his or her own thoughts and experiences, some in flowing sentences, some in short, less developed phrases. There were even some who scribbled instead of actually writing, not having fully learned their letters, but they "read" to us about their weekends just the same, clearly understanding that the point of reading and writing is to communicate meaning. Lessons like this demonstrate that, even under minimal conditions, effective pedagogy is made possible by use of the L1.

The experience of Ethiopia provides some of the most compelling evidence to date that educational success is directly proportional to the degree to which the L1 is used and developed. The national language-in-education policy adopted in 1994 calls for learners' home languages (known as nationality languages) to be used for the full 8 years of primary schooling. Because implementation has differed between Ethiopia's nine semi-autonomous regions and two city administrations, it is something of a microcosm of different approaches to bi- and multilingual education, with a range of practices and levels of success. By correlating the national grade 8 assessment results with the degree to which each region is using learners' L1, our research study[45] found that students with the maximum 8 years of L1, whose teachers are also trained in that language, achieve the highest scores across the curriculum—significantly higher than those with little or no L1 medium. Regions using the most L1 also have the highest percentage of students achieving at levels that will allow them to enter secondary school. We can thus conclude that in a low-income, resource-poor education system, the best results are likely to come from maximum use and development of L1 instruction.[46]

Multilingualism and Multiculturalism in Education for Development

Bi- or multilingual schooling is not only about the L1; learners must gain access to the additional language(s) that will be needed for full participation in society. As the field of bilingual education has grown internationally to incorporate multilingual societies in low-income countries, there is continued research support for certain principles of language and literacy learning. Building a foundation in the home language is the first, but the next is teaching the second/foreign L2 systematically. Usually this means teaching the L2 orally for the first few years of school, after which learners begin to transfer skills they have already learned in the L1. Some programs expose children simultaneously to literacy in both languages. Either way, the process of transfer[47] facilitates learning, as we only need to learn to read once in our lives. Transfer from L1 to L2 is the most efficient, since it is based on the most familiar language, but a range of studies have shown that transfer is bi- or multidirectional, meaning that whatever is learned in one language can be accessed in and/or applied to another language.[48] There is also evidence from multilingual classrooms in Europe and North America that transfer occurs whether or not the languages are linguistically related (for example, between English and Hindi as much as between Spanish and Portuguese)[49] and whether or not the languages have the same writing systems.[50] Transfer is a semi-automatic process in which learners begin to transfer knowledge and skills as they gain understanding of the L2, but the process can be facilitated by explicitly comparing and contrasting aspects of the two (or more) languages in age-appropriate ways.

Along with developing learners' languages, many programs recognize the cultures that they may represent, encouraging multiculturalism or understanding of diverse cultural values. Interculturalism, the ability to mediate between languages, cultures, and peoples, has long been a feature of Latin American bilingual programs. More recently, interculturalism has been operationalized to emphasize Indigenous knowledge and values while challenging traditional inequalities between groups.[51] This is considered essential if education is to have a transformative function in society—that is, to give traditionally marginalized groups equitable educational and life opportunities.

One common practice in bilingual education as developed in North American contexts is for the L2 to be used as a part-time medium of instruction, usually after 1 or 2 years of communicative skill development. This approach, known as language teaching "across the curriculum," is seen as effective because of the specialized vocabulary and cognitive demands of academic subjects.[52] Teachers taking this approach must be able to scaffold meaning by using bilingual methodologies (including the L1), employing body language or visual aids, and activating prior knowledge and other strategies, so that students do not miss important content while learning the new language.[53] These strategies require teachers to be highly proficient in both languages, which is the Achilles' heel in low-income contexts, since teachers rarely have opportunities for effective L2 learning themselves, much less adequate training to teach language. Thus, in low-income contexts, there is justification for longer periods of L1 medium learning (like Ethiopia's), specialized L2 teaching (L2 as a subject, possibly by specialist teachers), and materials that support use of bilingual methodologies for upper-level content instruction.

The following are what we now consider to be desirable characteristics of L1-based multilingual education programs, as contrasted with submersion in a foreign L2:[54]

- The L2 is taught explicitly and systematically, beginning with oral skills and familiar contexts that allow students to understand new words and phrases. In contrast, submersion teachers are often forced to translate or code-switch[55] to convey meaning, making concept learning inefficient and even impeding language learning.
- Transfer of linguistic and cognitive skills from L1 to L2 is facilitated. Once students have basic literacy skills in the L1 and communicative skills in the L2,

they can begin reading and writing in the L2, efficiently transferring the literacy skills they have acquired in the familiar language.[56] Although it is possible for students who learn only in the L2 to transfer their knowledge and skills later to the L1, the process is highly inefficient, as well as being unnecessarily difficult.

- Curricular content is taught through the L1 for at least 3 to 5 years, after which the L2 is phased in using bilingual methodologies. Bilingual methodologies like "alternate day" and "preview-review" use each language strategically to promote content and language learning simultaneously, and bilingual materials can support these processes.[57] In the absence of bilingual teachers, an effective approach is for classroom teachers to use the L1 for all instruction and for L2 specialist teachers to teach the second language as a subject, as mentioned above. Either approach is systematic, unlike submersion, which fails to make content comprehensible to learners or to teach the L2 systematically.

- Appropriate content assessment can be done intentionally in the L1, in the L2, or bilingually, so that learners can express their knowledge. For example, test questions can be presented in both/all languages, and students can choose the language of their response; alternatively, different questions can be presented in different languages depending on the level of language production required.[58] As noted above, because submersion education uses only the L2 to assess, it is impossible to know if student difficulties are content-related, language-related, or both.

- The education system aims to make students bi(multi)lingual and bi(multi)literate. Unlike submersion programs, which attempt to promote a new language by replacing a known one—thus limiting learner competence in both languages—bilingual programs encourage learners to understand, speak, read, and write more than one language. Bi- and multilingualism has been associated with higher cognitive and intellectual skills, better performance on tasks requiring understanding of language structure and thought processes, and higher overall educational achievement, even in lower-income countries like India.[59]

Not all of the features of bi- or multilingual education discussed here are present in programs that use learners' home languages, and herein lies the challenge. In her exhaustive review of African bilingual programs, Heugh[60] criticizes continued reliance on "subtractive" models in which the L1 is used only as a temporary measure and the L2 becomes the medium of instruction before learners are sufficiently proficient to understand lessons. Despite the fact that subtractive models provide at least short-term classroom understanding, they do not promote effective learning of either L1 or L2, hence they are not able to promote long-term school success. They may even dissuade stakeholders from investing in a bilingual approach; in the case of Niger, Nikiema[61] describes how insufficient development of L1 skills has led parents to lose confidence in bilingual schools. Systems like

Ethiopia's—allowing for long-term development of L1 literacy and learning across the curriculum—are few, and despite the pedagogical advances are still challenged in many ways. The next section discusses the difficulties of implementing bi- and multilingual programs.

Implementing Multilingual Schooling: The Challenges

Throughout this chapter, I have alluded to the special conditions of low-income, multilingual contexts and the need for Northern theories and practices to be tempered by practical, realistic, and appropriate decision-making in the South. The growing body of research on low-income multilingual contexts, more often by scholars who are from these contexts, is a sign that adaptations are being made, that Southern experiences may be most relevant to each other, and that they have a great deal to contribute to the field of multilingual education. Meanwhile, there are challenges to be acknowledged and struggles to be undertaken. Table 9.1 lists some of the challenges, along with approaches that have been taken to addressing them.

Table 9.1 could be longer and more developed, but these examples demonstrate that many of the challenges presented as justification for maintaining a foreign language of instruction have been acknowledged and dealt with in a variety of creative ways. A growing body of research and resources is available to stakeholders, and in a growing range of languages.

Policy-Making in Educational Development: Some Underlying Issues

Given the overwhelming research and pedagogical support for L1 medium schooling, it might seem surprising that stakeholders don't find the evidence conclusive, and that they allow their educational systems to continue using a foreign language of instruction despite evidence that it prohibits access to good quality, fair, and equitable schooling. There is clearly more going on than adopting straightforward pedagogical solutions to language issues in education, but what factors are involved?

Underlying decision-making on languages in education are unequal power relations within multilingual societies, as well as between the economically developed North and the low-income South. Historical relationships created by regional dominance or by colonization, combined with the concept that nation-states should be "unified" under single exogenous languages,[75] have done a great deal to convince the modern world that some languages are much more important than others. These relationships are reflected throughout societies and are reproduced

Table 9.1 **Challenges and Responses to Language of Instruction Issues**

Challenges	Responses/approaches
Linguistic concerns about the L1: Few literacy materials. No standard written form. Lack of vocabulary/ materials for content teaching (e.g., math, sciences). Need for reference materials like dictionaries.	Survey available literature; written materials exist in many languages due to ancient practices or past missionary/development efforts. Linguistic organizations like SIL International[62] help communities develop and standardize writing systems for their languages; see also UNESCO toolkit.[63] Reading materials can be self-made by learners dictating their experiences to teachers, interviewing family members, or writing/telling stories. Standard written forms develop over time and with use; Lalit in Mauritius published in three orthographies over 25 years until agreement was reached.[64] PRAESA has developed procedures for terminology development in math and sciences in South Africa.[65]
Linguistic diversity concerns: National unity is compromised. Too many languages to serve all. Not everyone wants/needs L1 education.	National unity is promoted when education offers equitable opportunities for all. Decentralized decision-making, as in Ethiopia, allows regions to determine which languages meet local needs.[66] In Bolivia, smaller language groups followed examples set by larger groups like Quechua and Aymara.[67] The Mozambican curriculum reform allows schools to choose monolingual, semi-bilingual, or bilingual modes.[68]
Limited school use of the L1: No official use of L1 in school. L1 used only for preschool, or only for early primary school.	Experience in Cambodia shows that L1 use in non-formal education can pave the way for formal education.[69] Foot-in-the-door strategies bring L1 closer to school: authorization of oral L1, teach L1 as a subject, organize L1 clubs, use local curriculum to promote L1 literacy.[70] Pilots/experiments demonstrate how longer-term use of L1 results in improved achievement and affective benefits.
Concerns regarding teacher skills: Non-literate in L1. Low proficiency in L2. Little formal training.	At least part of pre- or in-service teacher training needs to be given through L1.[71] It is faster and more efficient to improve teacher literacy in L1 than to improve teacher proficiency in L2.[72] Organizing L2 subject teaching by specialized L2 teachers is a way to maximize resources, minimize costs, and improve the quality of L2 teaching.[73] All teachers in multilingual countries need training in languages, bilingual methodologies, and interculturalism.

(continued)

*Table 9.1 (**continued**)*

Challenges	Responses/approaches
Costs of shifting from submersion to multilingual education: High start-up costs for teacher training and materials. Higher publishing costs for smaller print runs for each language.	Cost-benefit analyses balance start-up costs with savings to per-pupil expenditure due to higher throughput, with break-even point after about 2 years.[74] Local publishers often have L1 expertise and deserve investment. There is cost savings in collaboration between language teams and in two-sided bilingual materials, in which the L2 side remains constant and the L1 side is switched out. Desktop publishing and self-made materials may suffice for some needs.

in schools whose language use includes some while excluding others. Through benign neglect, governments fail to change education systems by continuing to rely on foreign languages of instruction, to which only the elite have access. Former colonial languages are not the only favored ones; regionally or politically dominant languages continue to be exclusive languages of education, such as Lao in Laos, even though it is the home language of a numerical minority.[76]

Perhaps more benign reasons for choosing a foreign medium of instruction have to do with parental response to what Bourdieu[77] calls the *linguistic market*, which is to aspire to proficiency in "official" dominant or so-called "global" languages. Speaking of the Indian context, Mohanty[78] calls this an "anti-predatory strategy" by disadvantaged communities to survive within existing unequal power structures. Even if few succeed, stakeholders (parents in particular) continue to invest in promises of access to linguistic capital, as in the case of Tanzania, where Rubagumya[79] finds that low-quality private schools are drawing children away from better-quality national schools by advertising English as a medium of instruction. Alexander refers to this phenomenon in the South African context as, "English unassailable but unattainable."[80]

Why is it that after 50 or more years of mass education through foreign languages stakeholders fail to recognize that, even for the cleverest of learners, high proficiency is unlikely in contexts in which the language is not widely spoken? It seems apparent that only (or mainly) the elite benefit, due to their inherited cultural and linguistic capital and enhanced opportunities, yet aspirations remain high.[81] Research has shown that dominant languages are of limited usefulness for the poor and marginalized, who will work in the informal sector and rely on local languages.[82] This includes ethnolinguistic minorities, rural dwellers, and girls from nonelite backgrounds, all of whom have difficulty getting to school, much less staying in school long enough to gain the literacy, skills, and knowledge needed to fully participate in society. As Bourdieu explains, "The combined effect of low cultural capital and the associated low propensity to increase it through educational investment condemns the least favoured classes to the negative sanctions of the scholastic market, i.e., exclusion or early self-exclusion induced by lack of success."[83]

What can be done to counteract the false promise of proficiency in dominant languages and to convince stakeholders that L1-based schooling will provide learners with better educational and life opportunities? One important step is to verify whether common perceptions are true; for example, studies in South Africa have found that when given a range of choices, the majority of parents surveyed opt for fully bilingual or semi-bilingual approaches rather than for straight English instruction.[84] Another step is to pilot bilingual programs in contexts in which submersion has been practiced and to improve on short-term bilingual approaches to maximize the positive effects. Both of these practices have demonstrated the effectiveness of L1-based schooling and led to the establishment of bilingual education policies based on demand in countries like Bolivia and Mozambique.[85]

Development agencies have not always raised the language issue with education ministries, using the excuse that it is "too political" or that they only support government initiatives. Those same agencies would be likely to intervene if certain groups were denied access to schools, but denying them access to knowledge somehow slips by. Worse, some donor involvement has created problems for educational systems and for local language initiatives. For example, Clayton[86] has traced the trajectory of English as a second/international language in Cambodia, showing how its displacement of French (a former colonial language) is the result of a conscious, calculated effort on the part of foreign government agencies, nongovernmental organizations (NGOs), and United Nations agencies—virtually the entire relief and development apparatus—to bring about English language hegemony along with sympathy for English-speaking powers in Cambodia and the region. While the state of general literacy was ignored, the discourse of Cambodian "reconstruction and development" focused on promoting English-language proficiency and translation skills. Similarly, our research in Ethiopia[87] found direct links between British assistance to Ethiopia during World War II,[88] British Council promotion of impossibly high English language proficiency standards for all teachers, and negative pressure being applied to Ethiopia's highly successful 8-year L1 medium education policy. A very similar type of negative backwash from English promotion in Tanzania threatens to "wipe out the gains of several decades of Kiswahili medium primary education instead of building on them."[89]

There are, however, organizations that have successfully supported L1-based multilingual education in many parts of the world. UNESCO, the first United Nations agency to stress the importance of "mother tongue" education in 1953,[90] continues to advocate for bi- and multilingual education.[91] UNICEF has also promoted local languages in pre-primary and primary schooling in countries like

Bolivia,[92] where earlier support for experimentation was extended to support for implementation of bilingual intercultural education under the far-reaching education reform of 1994, and Vietnam,[93] where UNICEF has recently partnered with the Ministry of Education to design and implement pilot bilingual schooling in three ethnic minority languages. Another organization that has significantly contributed to bilingual education is the German Agency for Technical Cooperation (GTZ), which has long experience in bilingual teacher training in many parts of Latin America and has worked in materials development in Indigenous languages in a number of African countries.[94] On the linguistic side, SIL International, a faith-based NGO comprised of linguists, anthropologists, and educators, has become a major force in developing writing systems and materials in community languages, as well as influencing policy from the grassroots up.[95] The Netherlands and the Scandinavian countries, all large donors to education sectors in low-income countries, have supported research and development in L1-based education.[96] Finally, the Department for International Development of the United Kingdom (DFID) and the United States Agency for International Development (USAID) have supported bilingual education projects in a range of countries, but as noted by developers of a policy database, "the issue has not received concentrated focus."[97] This could be said for many non-governmental organizations as well, but one milestone came in 2007, when Save the Children published a policy document stating clearly its understanding of the pedagogical desirability of L1 medium schooling.[98] Concentrated focus is indeed needed if schooling systems are to reach all learners equitably with a quality education.

Conclusion

L1-based multilingual education may not be the only way to address educational development issues, but it certainly has the potential to improve access, quality, and equity in systems that currently handicap all but the most privileged learners. Unlike submersion programs that use a foreign medium of instruction, programs in learners' own languages offer them an opportunity to:

- Learn to read and write in a language they understand
- Learn a second (and possibly third) language orally and in writing
- Experience success in learning curricular content
- Feel pride in their home language(s) and culture(s)
- Participate actively in class
- Demonstrate what they have learned
- Get help with schoolwork from their family members
- Become bi(multi)lingual and bi(multi)literate
- Participate productively and equitably in society

The positive effects of L1-based schooling are incontrovertible, yet there is still widespread stakeholder investment in programs that promise competence in a dominant or "international" language, often at the expense of effective learning of and through learners' best languages. This reproductive aspect of schooling needs to be challenged more forcefully and with greater focus. Successful strategies include surveying what stakeholders really want from a range of options, piloting theoretically sound bi- and multilingual programs to demonstrate their potential, raising awareness on the part of policy-makers, and continuing to link research with practice in multilingual contexts. More coordinated and committed policy-making on the part of international organizations would be a giant step forward as recognition grows that the language of instruction is invariably tied to issues of access, quality, and equity in schooling.

Avoiding the kind of mind-numbing foreign language teaching described above in the Mozambican grade 4 lesson, and maximizing the productive interaction of bilingual classrooms such as the Mozambican grade 2 lesson, will go a long way to attracting children to school, keeping them in school, helping them succeed in learning literacy and other curricular content, and giving them an equitable opportunity to participate in society. More children deserve the basic right to be encouraged to write their own thoughts and experiences, and in their own languages.

NOTES

1. Klees, S. (2009, December 10). Message sent to members of the Comparative and International Education Society (by former society president Professor S. Klees), University of Maryland, College Park.
2. Skutnabb-Kangas, T. (2000). *Linguistic genocide in education—or worldwide diversity and human rights?* Mahwah, NJ: Lawrence Erlbaum.
3. López, L. E. (2006). Multilingualism and Indigenous education in Latin America. In O. García, T. Skutnabb-Kangas, & M. Torres-Guzmán (Eds.), *Imagining multilingual schools. Languages in education and globalization* (pp. 238–261). Clevedon, UK: Multilingual Matters.
4. Kosonen, K. (2009). Language-in-education policies in Southeast Asia: An overview. In K. Kosonen, & C. Young (Eds.), *Mother tongue as bridge language of instruction: Policies and experiences in Southeast Asia* (pp. 22–43). Bangkok: Southeast Asian Ministers of Education Organization; World Bank. (2009). *Country social analysis: Ethnicity and development in Vietnam.* Washington, DC: World Bank.
5. Obanya, P. (2002). *Revitalizing education in Africa.* Lagos, Nigeria: Stirling-Horden; Chimbutane, F. (2009). *The purpose and value of bilingual education: A critical, linguistic ethnographic study of two rural primary schools in Mozambique* (pp. 169–170). Unpublished Ph.D. dissertation, School of Education, University of Birmingham, United Kingdom (Translation from Portuguese by Chimbutane).
6. See for extensive review: Ball, J. (2010). *Enhancing learning of children from diverse language backgrounds: Mother tongue-based bilingual or multilingual education in the early years.* Paris: UNESCO.
7. Walter, S. (2008). The language of instruction issue: Framing an empirical perspective. In B. Spolsky, & F. Hult (Eds.), *The handbook of educational linguistics* (pp. 129–146). Malden, MA: Blackwell.

8. Benson, C. (2004). The importance of mother tongue-based schooling for educational quality. Background paper prepared for the *Education for all global monitoring report 2005: The quality imperative*. Paris: UNESCO. Retrieved April 14, 2010, http://unesdoc.unesco.org/images/0014/001466/146632e.pdf; Benson, C. (2005). *Girls, educational equity and mother tongue-based teaching* (Policy document). Bangkok: UNESCO. Retrieved April 14, 2010, http://www.ungei.org/infobycountry/files/unesco_Girls_Edu_mother_tongue.pdf

9. Bentall, C., Peart, E., Carr-Hill, R., & Cox, A. (2000). Language in education. In *Funding agency contributions to education for all. Thematic studies. Education for all assessment* (pp. 46). London: Overseas Development Institute. Retrieved May 18, 2010, http://www.unesco.org/education/efa/global_co/working_group/global_references.shtml

10. This chapter draws on my background paper written for the EFA Global Monitoring Report 2005 (see note 7) focusing on educational quality. The overall report mentioned language of instruction only once or twice, even though I had tried to demonstrate how language issues were involved in nearly all aspects of quality. Recent research reconfirms earlier findings, and governments and international agencies now seem to be paying more attention.

11. Cummins, J. (1996). *Negotiating identities: Education for empowerment in a diverse society*. Ontario, CA: California Association for Bilingual Education; Genesee, F. (1987). *Learning through two languages: Studies of immersion and bilingual education*. New York: Newbury House; Krashen, S. (1985). *The input hypothesis: Issues and implications*. London: Longman; Swain, M., & Johnson, R. (1997). Immersion education: A category within bilingual education. In R. Johnson, & M. Swain (Eds.), *Immersion education: International perspectives* (pp. 1–16). Cambridge, UK: Cambridge University Press.

12. Swain & Johnson. (1997). *Immersion education*; Tucker, G. (1986). Implications of Canadian research for promoting a language competent American society. In J. Fishman (Ed.), *The Fergusonian impact. Sociolinguistics and the sociology of language* Vol. 2 (pp. 361–369). Berlin: Mouton de Gruyter.

13. Benson, C. (2009). Designing effective schooling in multilingual contexts: Going beyond bilingual models. In T. Skutnabb-Kangas, R. Phillipson, A. Mohanty, & M. Panda (Eds.), *Social justice through multilingual education* (pp. 63–81). Clevedon, UK: Multilingual Matters; Heugh, K. (2006). Introduction II—Theory and practice—Language education models in Africa: Research, design, decision-making, outcomes and costs. In H. Alidou, A. Boly, B. Brock-Utne, Y. S. Diallo, K. Heugh, & H. E. Wolff (Eds.), *Optimizing learning and education in Africa–the language factor. A stock-taking research on mother tongue and bilingual education in sub-Saharan Africa* (pp. 31–62). Bamako, Mali: Association for the Development of Education in Africa. Retrieved April 14, 2010, http://www.adeanet.org/biennial-2006/doc/document/B3_1_MTBLE_en.pdf; Bühmann, D., & Trudell, B. (2008). *Mother tongue matters: Local language as a key to effective learning*. Paris: UNESCO; Ouane, A., & Glanz, C. (2010). *Why and how Africa should invest in African languages and multilingual education. An evidence- and practice-based policy advocacy brief*. Hamburg: Association for the Development of Education in Africa (ADEA).

14. Chimbutane. (2009). *The purpose and value of bilingual education*.

15. Ibid.

16. Hornberger, N., & Chick, K. (2001). Co-constructing school safetime: Safetalk practices in Peruvian and South African classrooms. In M. Heller, & M. Martin-Jones (Eds.), *Voices of authority: Education and linguistic difference contemporary studies in linguistics and education* Vol. 1. Stamford, CT: Ablex.

17. Mbatha, T. (2003). *Language practices and pupil performance in rural and urban grade 1 classrooms in Swaziland*. Unpublished Ph.D. dissertation, CALSA, University of Cape Town, Cape Town.

18. Williams, E., & Cooke, J. (2002). Pathways and labyrinths: Language and education in development. *TESOL Quarterly, 36*(3), 307.

19. Benson, C. (1994). *Teaching beginning literacy in the "mother tongue": A study of the experimental Kiriol/Portuguese primary project in Guinea-Bissau* (p. 190). Ph.D. dissertation, University of California, Los Angeles.

20. Ibid.

21. UNESCO. (2000). *The Dakar framework for action. Education for all: Meeting our collective commitments*. Dakar, Senegal: World Education Forum. Retrieved April 14, 2010, http://unesdoc. unesco.org/images/0012/001211/121147e.pdf

22. See e.g., Heugh. (2006). Introduction II—Theory and practice.

23. Benson. (2005). *Girls, educational equity and mother tongue*; Hovens, M. (2002). Bilingual education in West Africa: Does it work? *International Journal of Bilingual Education and Bilingualism, 5*(5), 249–266.

24. UNESCO. (2005). *First language first: Community-based literacy programmes for minority language contexts in Asia*. Bangkok: UNESCO. Retrieved April 14, 2010, http://www2.unescobkk. org/elib/publications/first_language/first_language.pdf

25. Baker, C. (2006). *Foundations of bilingual education and bilingualism* (4th ed.). Clevedon, UK: Multilingual Matters; Hornberger, N. (2003). Multilingual language policies and the continua of biliteracy: An ecological approach. In N. Hornberger (Ed.), *Continua of biliteracy. An ecocultural framework for educational policy, research, and practice in multilingual settings*. Clevedon, UK: Multilingual Matters.

26. Ouane & Glanz. (2010). *Why and how Africa should invest in African languages*, pp. 13–14.

27. Cenoz, J. (2009). *Towards multilingual education. Basque educational research from an international perspective*. Clevedon, UK: Multilingual Matters; Benson, C. (Forthcoming). Curriculum development in multilingual schools. In J. Cenoz, & D. Gorter (Eds.), *Bilingual education: The encyclopedia of applied linguistics*. Hoboken, NJ: Wiley-Blackwell.

28. Benson. (Forthcoming). Curriculum development in multilingual schools.

29. Ramirez, J., Yuen, S., Ramey, D., Pasta, D., & Billings, D. (1991). *Final report: Longitudinal study of structured English immersion strategy, early-exit and late-exit transitional bilingual education programs for language-minority children*. San Mateo, CA: Aguirre International.

30. Thomas, W., & Collier, V. (1997). School effectiveness for language minority students. In *NCBE resource collection series*, no. 9. Washington, DC: National Clearinghouse for Bilingual Education; Thomas, W., & Collier, V. (2002). *A national study of school effectiveness for language minority students' long-term academic achievement*. Santa Cruz, CA: Center for Research on Education, Diversity and Excellence. Retrieved April 14, 2010, http://gse.berkeley.edu/ research/crede/pdf/rb10.pdf

31. Modiano, N. (1973). *Indian education in the Chiapas Highlands*. New York: Holt, Rinehart and Winston.

32. Williams, E. (1998). *Investigating bilingual literacy: Evidence from Malawi and Zambia*. London: DFID Education Research Series.

33. See reviews in: Alidou et al. (2006). *Optimizing learning and education in Africa*; Benson, C. (2000). The primary bilingual education experiment in Mozambique, 1993 to 1997. *International Journal of Bilingual Education and Bilingualism, 3*(3), 149–166.

34. Fafunwa, A., Macauley, J., & Funnso, J. (1989). *Education in mother tongue: The Ife primary education research project (1970–1978)*. Ibadan, Nigeria: Ibadan University Press.

35. Reeves, C., Heugh, K., Prinsloo, C., Macdonald, C., Netshitangani, T., Alidou, H., & Diedericks, G. (2008). *Evaluation of literacy teaching in the primary schools of the Limpopo Province*. Pretoria: Human Sciences Research Council; Heugh, K., Diedericks, G., Prinsloo, C., & Herbst, D. (2007). *Assessment of the language and mathematics skills of grade 8 learners in the Western Cape in 2006*. Pretoria: Human Sciences Research Council.

36. Walter. (2008). The language of instruction issue; Patrinos, H., & Velez, E. (2009). Costs and benefits of bilingual education in Guatemala: A partial analysis. *International Journal of Educational Development, 29*, 594–598.

37. Walter, S., & Davis, P. (2005). *Eritrea national reading survey*. Dallas: SIL International.

38. Heugh, K., Benson, C., Gebre Yohannes, M. A., & Bogale, B. (2010). Multilingual education in Ethiopia: What assessment shows us about what works and what doesn't. In K. Heugh, & T. Skutnabb-Kangas (Eds.), *Multilingual education works: From the periphery to the centre*. New Delhi: Orient BlackSwan.

39. García, O. (2006). *Bilingual education in the 21st century: A global perspective.* Malden, MA: Wiley-Blackwell; Heugh. Introduction II—Theory and practice; Heugh, et al. Multilingual education in Ethiopia; Walter. (2008). The language of instruction issue.

40. Albó, X., & Anaya, A. (2003). *Niños alegres, libres, expresivos: La audacia de la educación intercultural bilingüe en Bolivia [Happy, free, expressive children: The audacity of bilingual intercultural education in Bolivia].* La Paz: UNICEF; Dutcher, N. (1995). *The use of first and second languages in education. A review of international experience.* Pacific Island Discussion Paper Series no.1. Washington, DC: World Bank; Traoré, S. (2001). *La pédagogie convergente: Son expérimentation au Mali et son impact sur le système educatif.* Genève: UNESCO Bureau International d'Education; Bühmann & Trudell. (2008). *Mother tongue matters;* Heugh. (2006). Introduction II—Theory and practice; Ouane & Glanz. (2010). *Why and how Africa should invest in African languages;* Walter. (2008). The language of instruction issue.

41. Benson. (2000). The primary bilingual education experiment, pp. 149–166; Chimbutane. (2009). *The purpose and value of bilingual education.*

42. Benson. (2005). *Girls, educational equity and mother tongue-based teaching;* Hovens. (2002). Bilingual education in West Africa; Ouane & Glanz. (2010). *Why and how Africa should invest in African languages.*

43. Alidou, H., Batiana, A., Damiba, A., Pare, A., & Kinda, E. (2008). *Le continuum d'éducation de base multilingue du Burkina Faso: Une réponse aux exigencies de l'éducation de qualité. Evaluation prospective du programme de consolidation de l'éducation bilingue et plan d'action stratégique opérationnel 2008–2010.* Rapport d'étude, Ouagadougou, Mai 2008; Ball. (2010). *Enhancing learning of children,* pp. 21–22; Trudell, B. (2009). Contesting the default: The impact of local language choice for learning. In C. Stark, (Ed.) *Globalization and languages: Building our rich heritage* (pp. 152–157). Paris: UNESCO.

44. Benson. (2004). The importance of mother tongue-based schooling.

45. Benson, C., Heugh, K., Bogale, B., & Gebre Yohannes, M. A. (2010). Medium of instruction in Ethiopia. In K. Heugh, & T. Skutnabb-Kangas (Eds.), *Multilingual education works: From the periphery to the centre.* New Delhi: Orient BlackSwan; Heugh et al. (2010). Multilingual education in Ethiopia.

46. Similar conclusions have been reached in many other studies, including team research in Eritrea that found that, despite incomplete implementation of a theoretically sound mother L1-based approach, those regions with maximum L1 development have the best potential for achieving Universal Primary Education. See: Ministry of Education Eritrea. (2005). *Eritrea national reading study. September 2002.* Dallas: SIL Academic Books.

47. See e.g., Cummins, J. (2009). Fundamental psycholinguistic and sociological principles underlying educational success for linguistic minority students. In A. Mohanty, M. Panda, R. Phillipson, & T. Skutnabb-Kangas (Eds.), *Multilingual education for social justice: Globalising the local* (pp. 21–35). New Delhi: Orient BlackSwan. Also in Skutnabb-Kangas, T., Phillipson, R., Mohanty, A., & Panda, M. (Eds.). (2009). *Social justice through multilingual education* (pp. 19–35). Clevedon, UK: Multilingual Matters.

48. Bialystock, E. (2001). *Bilingualism in development: Language, literacy and cognition.* Cambridge, UK: Cambridge University Press.

49. Cenoz. (2009). *Towards multilingual education;* see also García. (2008). *Bilingual education in the 21st century* on translanguaging.

50. Kenner, C. (2004). Living in simultaneous worlds: Difference and integration in bilingual script-learning. *International Journal of Bilingual Education and Bilingualism, 7*(1), 43–61.

51. López. (2006). Multilingualism and Indigenous education in Latin America.

52. Gibbons, P. (2002). *Scaffolding language, scaffolding learning. Teaching second language learners in the mainstream classroom.* Portsmouth, NH: Heinemann.

53. Cummins. (2009). Fundamental psycholinguistic and sociological principles; Swain, M., & Lapkin, S. (2005). The evolving socio-political context of immersion education in Canada: Some implications for program development. *International Journal of Applied Linguistics, 15,* 169–186.

54. See reviews in: Alidou et al. (2006). *Optimizing learning and education in Africa*; Baker. (2006). *Foundations of bilingual education and bilingualism*; Benson. (2009). Designing effective schooling in multilingual contexts.

55. Code-switching and code-mixing involve alternation between languages and are common communication strategies in bi- and multilingual contexts. Code alternation functions best when all parties are competent speakers of the languages involved, but in submersion classrooms it is more of a coping strategy than a pedagogical one.

56. Cummins. (2009). Fundamental psycholinguistic and sociological principles; Bialystock. (2001). *Bilingualism in development*.

57. Mbude-Shale, N., Wababa, Z., & Plüddemann, P. (2004). Developmental research: A dual-medium schools pilot project, Cape Town, 1999–2002. In B. Brock-Utne, Z. Desai, & M. Qorro (Eds.), *Researching the language of instruction in Tanzania and South Africa* (pp. 151–168). Cape Town: African Minds.

58. Ibid.

59. Mohanty, A. (2006). Multilingualism of the unequals and predicaments of education in India: Mother tongue or other tongue? In O. García, T. Skutnabb-Kangas, & M. Torres-Guzmán (Eds.), *Imagining multilingual schools. Languages in education and globalization* (pp. 262–283). Clevedon, UK: Multilingual Matters, Clevedon.

60. Heugh. (2006). Introduction II—Theory and practice.

61. Nikiema, N. (2010). Enseignement en context multilingue et formation des enseignants bilingues en Afrique de l'Ouest "francophone": Un état des lieux. In M. Chatry-Komarek (ed.), *Professionaliser les enseignants de classes multilingues en Afrique* (pp. 12–34). Paris: l'Harmattan.

62. SIL International. (n. d.). *Multilingual education*. Dallas: SIL. Retrieved October 29, 2010, http://www.sil.org/literacy/multi.htm; Lewis, M. (Ed.). (2009). *Ethnologue: Languages of the world* (16th ed.). Dallas: SIL. Retrieved October 29, 2010, http://www.ethnologue.com/

63. Malone, S. (2007). *Advocacy kit for promoting multilingual education: Including the excluded*. Bangkok: UNESCO. Retrieved October 29, 2010, http://www.sil.org/literacy/multi_resource-kit.htm; Kosonen, K., Young, C., & Malone, S. (2007). *Promoting literacy in multilingual settings*. Bangkok: UNESCO. Retrieved October 29, 2010, http://www.sil.org/literacy/promo.htm

64. Ah-Vee, A. (2001). The role of a movement in the process of standardization of the orthography of Kreol and in the process of the development of the language: A case-study of Mauritius 1975–1999. In *Textes études et documents* no. 9 (pp. 6–10). Réunion, FR: Ibis Rouge.

65. Wababa, Z., & Diwu, C. (2009, December). *Mathematicking in isiXhosa*. Paper presented at the 3R's Consortium National Policy Dialogue Forum, Johannesburg. (See summary in LEAP News, December 2009). Retrieved October 29, 2010, www.praesa.org.za

66. Benson et al. (2010). Medium of instruction in Ethiopia; Heugh et al. (2010). Multilingual education in Ethiopia.

67. López. (2006). Multilingualism and Indigenous education in Latin America.

68. Chimbutane. (2009). *The purpose and value of bilingual education*.

69. Benson, C., & Kosonen, K. (2010). Language-in-education policy and practice in Southeast Asia in light of the findings from Ethiopia. In K. Heugh, & T. Skutnabb-Kangas (Eds.), *Multilingual education works: From the periphery to the centre*. New Delhi: Orient BlackSwan.

70. Benson. (2004).The importance of mother tongue-based schooling.

71. Benson et al. (2010). Medium of instruction in Ethiopia; Heugh et al. (2010). Multilingual education in Ethiopia.

72. Alidou, H., Garba, M., Halilou, A., Maman, L., & Daddy, A. (2009). *Etude d'élaboration du document de stratégie nationale de generalization de l'enseignement bilingue au Niger*. République du Niger: Ministère de l'éducation nationale de la République du Niger.

73. Ouane & Glanz. (2010). *Why and how Africa should invest in African languages*.

74. Grin, F. (2005). The economics of language policy implementation: Identifying and measuring costs. In N. Alexander (Ed.), *Mother tongue-based bilingual education in Southern Africa*.

The dynamics of implementation (pp. 11–25). Frankfurt: PRAESA; Patrinos & Velez (2009). Costs and benefits of bilingual education in Guatemala; Heugh. (2006). Introduction II—Theory and practice; Ouane & Glanz. (2010). *Why and how Africa should invest in African languages.*

75. Skutnabb-Kangas. (2000). *Linguistic genocide in education.*
76. Kosonen. (2009). Language-in-education policies in Southeast Asia.
77. Bourdieu, P. (1991). *Language and symbolic power.* Cambridge, UK: Cambridge University Press.
78. Mohanty. (2006). Multilingualism of the unequals, p. 270.
79. Rubagumya, C. (2003). English medium primary schools in Tanzania: A new "linguistic market" in education? In B. Brock-Utne, Z. Desai, & M. Qorro (Eds.), *Language of instruction in Tanzania and South Africa (LOITASA)* (pp. 149–169). Dar-es-Salaam, TZ: E and D Limited.
80. Alexander, N. (2000). *English unassailable but unattainable: The dilemma of language policy in South African education.* PRAESA Occasional Papers no. 3. Cape Town: University of Cape Town. Retrieved April 14, 2010, http://web.uct.ac.za/depts/praesa
81. Benson, C. (2008). *Language "choice" in education.* PRAESA Occasional Papers no. 30. Cape Town: University of Cape Town. Retrieved April 14, 2010, http://web.uct.ac.za/depts/praesa
82. Bruthiaux, P. (2002). Hold your courses: Language education, language choice, and economic development. *TESOL Quarterly, 36*(3), 275–296.
83. Bourdieu. (1991). *Language and symbolic power,* p. 62.
84. Heugh, K. (2003). *Language policy and democracy in South Africa. The prospects of equality within rights-based policy and planning* (pp. 182–183). PhD dissertation, Centre for Research on Bilingualism, Stockholm University, Elanders Gotab, Stockholm.
85. Benson. (2004). The importance of mother tongue-based schooling.
86. Clayton, S. (2008). The problem of "choice" and the construction of the demand for English in Cambodia. *Language Policy, 7,* 143–164.
87. Benson et al. (2010). Medium of instruction in Ethiopia; Heugh et al. (2010). Multilingual education in Ethiopia.
88. Negash, T. (1990). The crisis of Ethiopian education: Some implications for nation building. In *Uppsala reports on education* no. 29. Uppsala, SE: Uppsala University.
89. Rubagumya. (2003). English medium primary schools in Tanzania, p. 165.
90. See UNESCO website describing efforts related to languages in education at: http://portal.unesco.org/education/en/ev.php-URL_ID=30871andURL_DO=DO_TOPICandURL_SECTION='201.html (Retrieved May 20, 2010.)
91. See publications by UNESCO Hamburg and UNESCO Bangkok, for example: Ouane, A. (Ed.). (2003). *Towards a multilingual culture of education.* Hamburg: UNESCO Institute for Education, Hamburg. Retrieved April 14, 2010, http://www.unesco.org/education/uie/publications/uiestud41.shtml;Kosonen & Young. (2009). *Mother tongue as bridge language of instruction.*
92. Albó & Anaya. (2003). *Niños alegres, libres, expresivos.*
93. Benson & Kosonen. (2010). Language-in-education policy and practice in Southeast Asia.
94. See GTZ's summary of activities at http://www2.gtz.de/dokumente/bib/07–1268_1.pdf, and its support of research activities such as Alidou, et al. *Optimizing learning and education in Africa.* (Retrieved May 20, 2010.)
95. See bibliography of SIL publications on bilingual education at: http://www.ethnologue.com/show_subject.asp?code=BED (Retrieved May 20, 2010.)
96. See e.g. Iversen, E. (Ed.). (2008). *Mother tongue and bilingual education: A collection of conference papers.* Copenhagen: Danish Education Network. Retrieved May 20, 2010, http://www.uddannelsesnetvaerket.dk/rdb/1205421604.pdf
97. Anís, K., & Tate, S. (2003). *Development of a language of instruction policy database. Final report prepared for basic education and policy support activity.* Washington, DC: United States Agency for International Development; Bentall et al. (2000).Language in education provides a review of organizations working in bi- and multilingual education.

98. Save the Children. (2007). *The use of language in children's education.* London: Save the Children U.K. Retrieved April 14, 2010, http://www.savethechildren.org.uk/en/docs/The_Use_of_Language_in_Education.pdf See also: Pinnock, H. (2009). *Steps towards learning. A guide to overcoming language barriers in children's education.* London: Save the Children U.K. Retrieved April 14, 2010, http://www.savethechildren.org.uk/en/docs/Steps_Towards_Learning_LR.pdf

10

Improving Indigenous Children's Educational Access and Outcomes Through Intercultural Bilingual Education

BRITTANY LAMBERT

The Problem: The Status of Indigenous People in Bolivia and Worldwide

Inequity between Indigenous and non-Indigenous people is a problem worldwide. Throughout history, Indigenous people everywhere have been denied rights to their ancestral properties, languages, cultures, and forms of governance, and have suffered from poor access to basic services and health care.[1] Today, Indigenous people around the world continue to suffer from higher levels of poverty and lower levels of education than do other groups. A 2009 report revealed that the majority of the 101 million children out of school are from minority or Indigenous groups.[2] Belonging to a minority or Indigenous group is one of the greatest obstacles to a quality education, along with being a girl, living in a rural area, and coming from a poor family. Indigenous children often face many of these obstacles at once, compounding their educational disadvantage.[3] In Guatemala, for example, Mayan children of both sexes fare worse than non-Mayan children, and extremely poor Mayan girls have the worst educational outcomes of all. At age 7, only 50% of extremely poor Mayan girls are enrolled in school, compared to 54% of all Mayan girls, 71% of Mayan boys, 75% of Latina girls, and 80% of Latino boys.[4] Dropout rates are also at their highest among extremely poor Mayan girls, with only 10% completing primary education.[5] High dropout rates are common in Indigenous communities worldwide. In the Chittagong Hill Tracts region of eastern Bangladesh, for example, primary school dropout rates among Indigenous students are as high as 60%—double the national average.[6] Indigenous literacy rates are also strikingly low in all the regions of the world. In Vietnam, for example,

Indigenous literacy rates are five times lower than the national average, and in Colombia, they are three times lower than in the rest of the population.[7]

Although Indigenous people are a minority in many countries, they are a majority in Bolivia, accounting for 62% of the population.[8] Despite their majority status, Bolivia's Indigenous people are severely disadvantaged in comparison to Bolivians of European descent. In Bolivia, being Indigenous increases one's likelihood of being poor by 13%.[9] This can be partially explained by the low education levels in Bolivia's Indigenous communities, which keep Indigenous people entrenched in a cycle of poverty. Most Indigenous children attend school at some point in their lives, but often for a year or less.[10] Indigenous children in Bolivia have, on average, 3.7 fewer years of schooling than do their non-Indigenous peers.[11] Repetition and dropout rates are considerably higher among Indigenous students than they are in the rest of the population. By the age of 15, for example, 50% of Quechua[12] Indigenous youth have left school compared to 10% of non-Indigenous students.[13] Studies have also revealed test score gaps between Indigenous and non-Indigenous children in all subject matters across all levels of education.[14]

Education is one of the most important predictors of income level.[15] Identifying the barriers to education for Indigenous youth and designing policies to overcome them should therefore be important priorities. Such policies could help reduce poverty in Indigenous communities and lessen the economic disparities between Indigenous and non-Indigenous Bolivians.

Why Bolivia?

Bolivia is a good setting in which to study policies for reducing discrimination against Indigenous people for several reasons. First, almost two-thirds of Bolivians are Indigenous, making Bolivia the country with the highest proportion of Indigenous people in South America.[16] Although Indigenous people constitute the majority of the Bolivian population, they are significantly disadvantaged compared to the non-Indigenous minority. This means that the majority of the population experiences discrimination and hardship on a daily basis. This reality makes it all the more pressing to study policies and programs that can help reduce inequity in Bolivia. Such programs have the potential to lift a very large proportion of the country's citizens out of poverty.

Not only are Indigenous people disadvantaged within Bolivia, Bolivians are also disadvantaged globally. Bolivia is one of the poorest countries in South America, with 65% of the population living below the national poverty line.[17] Recent studies suggest that ending the marginalization of Indigenous people in Bolivia could help the poverty-stricken country as a whole. A 2002 International Fund for Agricultural Development study found that eliminating the exclusion of Indigenous people could expand Bolivia's national economy by 37%.[18] In this context, policies that improve Indigenous persons' well-being have the potential to effect positive change on an even larger scale.

Intercultural Bilingual Education: A Solution?

Indigenous scholars and leaders have long argued that language is a major barrier to equitable education in Bolivia.[19] Rural Indigenous people use over 30 different languages for everyday communication. Studies conducted in rural areas show that 100% of rural Quechuas and 98.5% of rural Aymaras (Bolivia's two largest Indigenous groups) use their Indigenous languages as their primary modes of communication.[20] For this reason, many Indigenous children speak little or no Spanish by the time they reach school age. Despite this reality, the education system in Bolivia has been highly hispanicized historically. The hispanicization of schools began in the 1950s, when the first rural schools were built under the government of Victor Paz Estenssoro. Estenssoro believed that Indigenous peasants should be incorporated into national life and that the most effective way of incorporating them was through assimilation.[21] In an attempt to homogenize Bolivians, his government implemented an educational reform aimed at hispanicizing the population. Article 115 of the reform stated that Indigenous languages could only be used in the classroom as a vehicle for immediate hispanicization.[22]

Although the education reform aimed to make all Bolivians equal, it had the unintended consequence of increasing inequity between Indigenous and non-Indigenous students. Children who had only ever spoken their home language were forced to attend school in Spanish, a language they did not understand. Indigenous students struggled in this environment. Not only did they have to learn new skills, they also had to learn the language that the skills were being taught in. Moreover, classrooms were often fraught with discrimination. Indigenous students were ridiculed for their accents and chastised by their teachers for their inability to speak proper Spanish. They were made to feel ashamed of their language and culture and began to associate school with feelings of fear and humiliation. All these factors contributed to Indigenous children having poorer grades, lower self-esteem, and higher dropout rates than did non-Indigenous students.[23]

In response to these problems, Indigenous leaders and non-governmental organizations (NGOs) began to fight for the incorporation of Indigenous languages into the education system. They believed that if students were taught in a language they understood, they would be happier, more confident, and more participative. This would keep them interested in school and encourage them to stay enrolled for longer. Experts also believed that if students learned basic skills in a language they were familiar with, they would acquire a solider didactic foundation and that the eventual transition to Spanish would be easier.[24] In this view, children's heritage language is conceived as a building block for the acquisition of a second language and other skills, rather than a hindrance. Studies conducted in other settings have proved that this model is successful. For example, in U.S. schools with large proportions of Hispanics, dual-language instruction was found to be more successful in "enhancing student outcomes and fully closing the achievement gap in second language"[25] (English) than single-language instruction in English.[26]

These ideas were put into action in Bolivia in the late 1980s and early 1990s, when intercultural bilingual education (IBE) was introduced, first as a pilot project and then as a national education policy in 1994. The approach consisted of teaching children to read and write in their home language first, then gradually integrating Spanish. From grades 1 to 3, students were taught in their Indigenous language with Spanish as a subject matter. From grades 4 to 6, students learned in both Spanish and their home language. From grade 7 onward, students learned primarily in Spanish, with their Indigenous language as a subject matter. The program was implemented primarily in rural areas, the areas in which language posed the greatest obstacle to learning.

The international community played a large role in the design and implementation of IBE as there were very few resources for this type of project in Bolivia at the time. UNICEF embraced the idea and provided the Ministry of Education with the financial and technical support necessary to introduce the 5-year pilot project in 1989. The Deutsche Gesellschaft für Technische Zusammenarbeit (GTZ), a federally owned German international cooperation organization, acted in an advisory capacity for Bolivian government ministries, organizations, and universities, and provided pedagogical material in pilot schools.[27] PROEIB Andes, a pan-Andean nonprofit organization created to consolidate IBE in the Andean region, was also involved in the early development of IBE. The 1989 pilot project implemented IBE in 30 school boards across the country, including 14 rural schools and 400 teachers. The pilot project introduced the program in the three most spoken Indigenous languages: Quechua, Aymara, and Guarani.

When the 5-year pilot project came to an end, several evaluations were carried out to assess its impacts.[28] The government was so pleased with the results that, in 1994, it introduced an education reform and made IBE an integral part it. IBE became official state policy and was extended to other, smaller Indigenous linguistic groups.[29] In its first year, the IBE program was applied in the first-grade classes of 300 school boards and approximately 1,500 schools. From that point on, the program was extended to one additional grade every year.[30] Each year, new schools were chosen to apply the bilingual program. By 2002, 2,899 schools were incorporating IBE. This meant that 192,238 students were receiving IBE and 9,028 teachers were teaching it.[31]

Successes

This case study assessed the successes and limitations of Bolivia's IBE Program through 50 semi-structured interviews with government officials, members of

NGOs and teachers' unions, Indigenous leaders, scholars, teachers, principals, and students. The research was based in La Paz and the surrounding area, where most Indigenous people are of Aymara descent. The research revealed interesting and mixed results. This section explores those areas in which IBE was successful. Most notably, the program improved Indigenous children's educational outcomes, increased their levels of participation and engagement in class, and improved the status of Indigenous languages.

In the first few years of its existence, Bolivia's IBE program displayed positive results. In the first decade following the program's implementation, the number of IBE schools grew rapidly. Between 1997 and 2002, school enrollment rates in areas of high Indigenous presence shot up by 13%.[32] Passing rates also rose during this time period, increasing 3 percentage points more in areas of high Indigenous presence than in areas of low Indigenous presence. Dropout rates followed a similar trend, dropping by 4% in areas of high Indigenous presence compared to only 0.2% in areas of low Indigenous presence.[33] These statistics suggest that Indigenous students were the primary beneficiaries of the IBE program and that it succeeded in reaching its target population.

Several evaluations of the program compared math and language test scores in IBE and non-IBE schools. Most of these evaluations were conducted by the Sistema de Mediacion de la Calidad Educativa (SIMECAL), a system created by the government to evaluate students' academic performance and identify the factors that influence it. SIMECAL evaluations showed that Indigenous students in IBE schools generally scored higher on the tests than did Indigenous students in non-IBE schools. For example, a 1997 evaluation revealed that 35% of IBE Indigenous students had achieved a "satisfactory" result, whereas only 19% of non-IBE Indigenous students had. Likewise, only 24% of IBE Indigenous students were classified in the "risk" category, compared to 48% of non-IBE Indigenous students.[34]

Another study, which assessed the academic achievement of 400 Indigenous children between grades 1 and 4, found that IBE Indigenous students did better in most subject matters than did non-IBE Indigenous students. IBE students in grades 2, 3, and 4 did better in math than did students in control schools. In all four grades, IBE students mastered grammar in their home language better than did students in traditional schools.[35] IBE students' Spanish grammar test scores also tended to be higher than those of students attending Spanish schools, supporting the idea that heritage language instruction can facilitate the acquisition of other languages. In most cases, boys continued to score higher than girls, but the contrast was not as great as in control schools.[36]

Several interview participants had positive things to say about IBE. Multiple comments revealed the positive psychological impacts of bilingual education on students. Amaro Tenorio, a linguist and former primary school teacher, explained the difference he noticed in his students when he started teaching in their own language:

I started my teaching career with a grade 1 class in a rural school. My first day of class was a total failure. No one raised their hand to answer my questions. That night, I looked back on my day and tried to understand what had gone wrong. I had a theory and decided to test it the next day. Instead of teaching my class in Spanish, I taught it in Aymara, the children's mother tongue. The change was remarkable. The students seemed happy, engaged, and followed me everywhere for the rest of the day. It was clear to me that the problem had been the language. The students hadn't understood a word I was saying on the first day of school! From that point on, I became committed to bilingual education.[37]

Tenorio's testimony shows how differently children behave when they are placed in an environment in which they feel comfortable. Instruction in the children's home language made it possible for them to participate and be actively engaged in their learning. Participation is an extremely important part of learning. It has not only been empirically linked to increased knowledge acquisition and problem-solving skills,[38] but it also makes it possible for teachers to determine how well students understand concepts.[39] Tenorio's passage also demonstrates the extent to which language can obstruct communication between teachers and students. Since verbal communication is one of the keys to knowledge transmission in a classroom, it is important that such barriers be overcome.

Felix Lopez, president of the Aymara Indigenous Council, agreed that bilingual schools provide a more favorable learning environment for rural Indigenous children. He looked back upon his own childhood and described the trauma of attending school in a foreign language, particularly in an environment fraught with discrimination:

Before starting school, I only spoke Aymara. I did not understand a word of Spanish. All the teachers spoke in Spanish, and the Aymaras in the class didn't understand anything. They would hit us with sticks because we couldn't pronounce Spanish words properly. I would even go as far as saying that we were tortured. These traumas have stayed with us. Fortunately, IBE is changing this.[40]

Once again, this testimony suggests that one of the most important arguments in favor of IBE is psychological. Students who associate school with trauma and hostility are more likely to feel discouraged and to abandon their studies than are students who enjoy school and feel comfortable there.

Xavier Albo, a linguistic anthropologist who has been involved in the evaluation of the IBE program, points out another important benefit of IBE: It raises the status of Indigenous languages. Students' heritage language and culture are recognized and validated in bilingual education programs. Moreover, students learn that being bilingual is something to proud of, not something to be ashamed of. He recounts a testimony by a student he spoke with while monitoring the program:

> I completed my primary education in an IBE school. Now I attend a Spanish intermediate school. My new teachers know that I went to an IBE school and often call me up to the blackboard to write in Aymara. My classmates are surprised that I know how to write Aymara, and they admire me. They think that it's hard to read and write Aymara.[41]

Raising the status of Indigenous languages is an important step toward reducing discrimination against Indigenous people. Throughout history, Indigenous languages have not been regarded as real languages but rather as "peasant dialects." They have been associated with notions of brutishness, savagery, and stupidity. This made Indigenous people feel ashamed of who they were. Many attempted to mask their Indigenous roots by changing their names and denying that they spoke an Indigenous language.[42] Raising the status of Indigenous languages, in contrast, allows Indigenous people to retain their culture and history while being considered equal members of society.

In sum, it is clear that IBE has been successful in several ways. It has had positive pedagogical impacts, increasing enrollment rates, decreasing repetition and dropout rates, and improving educational attainment among Indigenous children. It has also allowed children to be more participative and engaged in their learning. Finally, it has increased the status of Indigenous languages, helping them to be recognized as real languages and not merely peasant dialects.

Shortcomings

Despite the successes described above, Bolivia's IBE program has encountered several obstacles. These challenges can be divided into four categories: management problems, human resource shortages, conceptual issues, and public opinion perceptions. The following subsections will expand on these obstacles. The first two obstacles are quite specific to Bolivia, while the other two—the conceptual issues and the public opinion problems—are relevant in many other countries and settings. Bilingual education programs do not only exist for Indigenous children in countries with a history of colonialism, but are also common in Western countries with high levels of immigration. Issues highlighted in this section may therefore be of interest to policy-makers from a variety of countries struggling to provide equal opportunities to children from different linguistic backgrounds. The conclusion will further explore how these transferable issues play out in different settings worldwide and draw parallels between IBE in Bolivia and elsewhere in the world.

MANAGEMENT PROBLEMS

First, several management issues have prevented IBE from reaching its full poten-tial. One example is the lack of continuity and coherence in Bolivian state policy. Bolivia is an extremely political country characterized by fierce opposition between parties. New leaders are generally reluctant to build on the work of previous gov-ernments, preferring to abolish old policies and create new ones.[43] For this reason, Evo Morales' government offered very little support to the existing IBE program, opting instead to start a new one. Morales' 2005 election campaign was built on strong rhetoric that vehemently opposed the government in power, which had been associated with neo-liberalism and privatization. When Morales came into office, he put an end to most of the former government's programs, arguing that they were tinged with corruption and neo-liberal influence. The IBE program was no exception, despite its solid foundations and positive results. Several interview participants indicated that this was normal behavior for newly elected politicians. Lopez indicated that Morales' rejection of the old education reform was to be expected: "He's Indigenous, he's our brother. But it's normal that he reacted to the old state policy and didn't understand its positive sides. There's always this type of resistance."[44] Morales and his government have designed a new education reform which, after many years of work, was passed in December 2010. Thus, for several years IBE in Bolivia was stuck in a legal vacuum. The original education law that established IBE was no longer valid, but Morales' new education bill had not yet been passed or made official.

Evo Morales is not the only reason that IBE's implementation slowed to a halt. Even in the years leading up to Morales' election, Bolivia's IBE program suffered from mismanagement problems. One reason for this was instability within the Ministry of Education. Julio Vitale, who worked closely with the Ministry of Education during in the 1990s, discussed the impact of this instability on IBE:

> IBE has been in a sort of crisis since 2002, because of continuous changes in authorities, ministers and directors within the Ministry of Education. We had four education ministers in the space of 3 years. All these leaders had vastly different personalities, ideas, and capabilities. These strong changes disrupted the whole structure of the Ministry of Education, and very little progress has been made with regards to IBE since then.[45]

Thus, high turnover rates within IBE's leadership ranks posed another obstacle to IBE's progress prior to 2010.

Another management problem that hindered the IBE program is the lack of monitoring. When IBE was first implemented in the mid-1990s, a monitoring system was put in place. This created a new class of professionals, called peda-gogical consultants. Their main task was to work with teachers and help them implement the education reform. However, there was a great deal of resentment toward them, fueled by the fact that they were paid significantly more than teachers, despite having only received 3 short months of training. Teachers who had been in the field for years felt insulted that these less qualified consultants were telling them what to do and receiving better salaries than they were. Moreover, many pedagogical consultants assumed a stronger leadership role than intended, further offending the teachers. The teachers' unions rose up against them, and the consultant position was eventually abolished. Since then, there has been no official body monitoring the implementation of the IBE program. Lydia Armstrong, an American scholar involved in the training of the pedagogical consultants, described the tense dynamics that characterized schools during the monitoring processes. Her words suggest that their removal marked the moment when IBE began to lose momentum:

> The pedagogical consultants were not supposed to be in a supervisory role, they were not supposed to be directing. They were supposed to be in a complementary, helping role. But a lot of them were former directors and were used to taking the lead. So, there was often conflict between them and the teachers and principals in the schools they were monitoring. The teachers' unions eventually got rid of all the consultants. This was a real watershed moment as far as the government backing off.[46]

Armstrong later suggested that the Ministry of Education could have done several things to handle the consultant situation more effectively. First, they could have given the consultants more training. They could also have paid them more modest salaries. Finally, they could have implemented the reform in teachers' colleges a few years before implementing it in primary schools. That way, some teachers would have received training by the time the pedagogical consultants came along, and the clash between the two may have been less intense.[47] It is clear, then, that mismanagement with regards to program monitoring has been yet another obstacle to successful IBE in Bolivia.

HUMAN RESOURCE SHORTAGES

Another problem plaguing IBE is the ongoing shortage of qualified teachers. Many rural teachers speak their Indigenous language but are unable to read and write it, since they completed their own schooling at a time when Spanish was the only language of instruction. Raul Barrionuevo Ibanez, a rural school principal in the province of La Paz explained the situation at his school: "Our teachers use Aymara orally, to help their students understand the material. But they don't teach written Aymara. The problem is that most of our teachers speak excellent Aymara but don't know how to read and write it."[48] The shortage of qualified teachers makes it difficult to fully implement IBE. It also perpetuates the problem. Barrionuevo explained that, due to the lack of instruction, most students who graduate from his school write very little Aymara. If they go on to become teachers, they too are unable to teach their students to read and write proper Aymara. In Barrionuevo's opinion, the largest challenge for IBE will be training a sufficient number of teachers to fully implement the program.

This is not to say that efforts have not been made to train new teachers to teach IBE. According to a World Bank report, nine of Bolivia's 18 Teacher Training Institutes train IBE teachers.[49] However, these efforts have also been fraught with difficulties. One of the main problems, naturally, has been finding qualified professionals to train teachers. Since Indigenous languages were not taught in Bolivia before IBE was implemented, few Bolivians know how to read and write them. This makes it almost impossible to train large groups of teachers to do so. The few professionals who are able to train teachers are in high demand and require large salaries.[50]

Teachers who do receive IBE training generally do so at specific teacher training colleges over the course of a 2-year program. However, many of them find that 2 years of training is not enough to master grammar in their Indigenous language. Many still write poorly and teach incorrect grammar to their students in the classroom. Others, to avoid teaching mistakes to their students, prefer to teach in Spanish. In response to this situation, several complementary IBE training programs have appeared in universities, giving teachers the opportunity to increase their level of comfort with their Indigenous language and with IBE. These programs cater to teachers who have already started their careers but would like to complement the training they received in teacher's college. Seven rural school teachers in the final year of one such program at a University in La Paz were interviewed. All of them explained that they had felt underqualified to teach in Aymara, despite their formal teacher training. Eustaquio Lanza Mallo, a school teacher and student in the program, is one example. He teaches in a small rural community in the province of La Paz during the week and comes to the university on weekends. He explained his situation: "After graduating from teacher's college, I still made many errors in the written form of Aymara. This caused me problems in the classroom. I am grateful to this university because they have helped me a lot."[51] It is clear that this type of supplementary training is very helpful to teachers and gives them the skills and confidence necessary to implement IBE in the classroom. However, these programs are generally private and most rural Indigenous school teachers do not have the means to enroll. In fact, Mallo was selected by his community to take part in the program and given financial assistance to do so. Even so, he works during the week and attends class on weekends to make ends meet.[52]

As well, many older teachers in the system still do not read and write Indigenous languages at all. In the schools observed, the majority of teachers were older and had never learned to write in their Indigenous language. There is talk of evening and weekend training, but nothing has materialized yet.[53] For all these reasons, there is very little consistency in terms of what is taught to students. For the time being, the language of instruction depends on the abilities and initiative of each individual teacher.

CONCEPTUAL ISSUES

Policy-makers, stakeholders, Indigenous leaders, and parents who are invested in the IBE program are grappling with several conceptual issues. The first, and perhaps most important, relates to the goals of IBE. This has been a major source of contention in the IBE community. There seem to be two different conceptions of what IBE's goal should be. For the people who designed and implemented the original IBE program, the goal was primarily pedagogical. It aimed to ease Indigenous students into the Spanish world more gently, by allowing them to acquire a solid educational foundation in a language they understood. By these standards, the program was successful. It succeeded in keeping Indigenous children in school longer, increased their self-confidence, and improved their performance in most subject matters, including Spanish. However, there is a feeling among many Indigenous leaders that the goal of IBE should be more than just pedagogical. They believe that the use of Indigenous languages in the classroom should be more than just a means to an end; it should be an end of its own. It should value Indigenous languages and cultures because they are valuable, not because they facilitate Indigenous students' transition into the Spanish-speaking world. Interview participants explained that the original IBE program made use of Indigenous languages but continued to portray the world through a Western lens, since this was the world it aimed to ease students into. No effort was made to create an authentically Indigenous curriculum. Several interview participants argued that the original IBE program perpetuated occidental power structures in the Bolivian education system. As Didoro Gomez, an Indigenous leader explained: "It is useless to teach us in our own language if the content of our education is not our own. We do not want to be domesticated in our own language."[54]

Tenorio explained that Indigenous people have their own beliefs and ways of seeing the world and argued that these should be recognized in the curriculum. He explained that Indigenous and European logic systems are fundamentally different and that there is no good reason to privilege a European perspective over an Indigenous one:

> There is no absolute truth. Different people have different ways of seeing things. Let's take the concept of "future," for example. Occidental people believe the future is in front of them. However, Aymara people see it differently. We cannot see the future the way we can see the past. So for us, the future is behind us, behind our backs, where we can't see it. This way of understanding things is just as valuable as the European way. How can the West claim to hold the absolute truth?[55]

This simple example suggests how confusing it must be for Indigenous children to be forced, once they begin school, to understand concepts in ways that are completely counterintuitive to them.

In sum, if the goal of IBE were simply to help students develop a solid didactic foundation, culture would presumably not matter. However, it is clear that the goal of IBE, for many of the people interviewed, should go beyond skills acquisition. In their eyes, the goal of IBE should be to recognize, respect, and make equal different cultures, languages, and worldviews.[56]

Another conceptual issue arises from the fact that Bolivia is incredibly socially and linguistically diverse, making it difficult to establish an IBE program that is adequate for everyone. Different levels of bilingualism exist in rural Indigenous communities. Some students are monolingual Aymara until they start school, whereas others speak mostly Spanish. IBE may make learning easier for monolingual Aymara children, but it makes learning harder for Spanish-speaking children. In such situations, it is a challenge to avoid reverse discrimination. There has been a great deal of disagreement over this question within the parent–teacher community in Bolivia.[57]

Another conceptual question is whether IBE should be implemented in all Indigenous languages. Approximately three dozen Indigenous languages exist in Bolivia, some of which are spoken by millions of people and others that are only spoken by a few hundred. Implementing IBE is expensive, as it involves training new teachers, producing school material in different languages, and paying for monitoring and evaluation. Bolivia is a lower middle income country in which financial resources are stretched at the best of times. Several prominent Bolivian scholars believe that IBE is an inefficient use of resources. Angela Padilla, a university professor and researcher, exemplifies this point of view. She suggests that Bolivia's priorities are backward. Before spending money on the preservation of culture, she argues, the government should focus on feeding its population and creating jobs.

> Most Indigenous nucleuses are extremely small. . . . Yet huge amounts of time and money are spent fighting over the correct translation, accentuation and graphology of these tiny languages. . . . Bolivia's biggest problem is economic. This is not a moral question, but a socioeconomic one. It is impossible to save cultural identity without a material structure.[58]

Padilla's argument resembles Maslow's pyramid of needs, in which survival and safety are the most basic needs. Only once these basic needs have been satisfied can people begin to think about needs related to culture and identity.[59]

Julio Vitale, a UNICEF project director working on Indigenous issues in Bolivia, prefers to look at the question from a rights-based perspective: "I believe that an Indigenous child has the same right to learn in his or her language as any other child in the world. I believe that this right takes precedence over the economic analysis." He also suggests that the economic argument for not extending IBE to all language groups is flawed. He explains that failing to implement IBE may actually have long-term economic consequences. For example, Indigenous children in Spanish schools are more likely to repeat grades or drop out of school. In the long run, these wasted investments can be more expensive than translating educational material. They also have the added disadvantage of leading to a fragmented, poorly educated society.[60] In sum, it is clear that the financial implications of IBE constitute a source of tension within the IBE community. The issue raises important ethical questions with regards to which needs and rights should be prioritized and whether it is acceptable for small languages to die for the greater economic good.

Another conceptual problem that IBE has encountered is the question of how to standardize Indigenous languages. For an IBE program to work, pedagogical material must be produced in Indigenous languages. However, most Indigenous languages are primarily oral and have never had a written form. There have been huge debates about how to standardize these languages properly. Indigenous languages have often been standardized in a very "Spanish" way, with the Spanish alphabet and Spanish phonemics. Many speakers have complained that this type of standardization strips the languages of their Indigenous character. Dozens of Indigenous leaders and linguists have created new, more "Indigenous" versions of the language, hoping that their version will become the official one. Tenorio is an Indigenous scholar who has dedicated himself to such work. He explained the monumental task he faced in trying to create an alphabet that reflected Aymara sensibilities:

> There were more than 22 different Aymara alphabets at the time, but all of them had been created as mediums to help hispanicize Indigenous people. None of them reflected the structure and the phonology of the Aymara language. So I studied each one of these alphabets and looked at why they had been created the way they had. After several months of work, I was able to create an alphabet that, I believe, truly reflects the Andean world.[61]

Tenorio exemplifies the passion many people feel for creating an Indigenous alphabet that retains the character of the oral language. However, this passion has also led to dozens of different alphabets, leaving the government with the difficult task of choosing an official version—and the political implications of each choice. This dilemma is made more difficult by the fact that some languages, such as Quechua, are spoken in different parts of the country. Often, the same word is pronounced slightly differently in two different areas. The government must choose one "correct" version in order to standardize the language.[62] Such a decision becomes very political, as it implies that the version that was not chosen is "incorrect." This is insulting to people who have spoken that way for generations.

Some members of the Indigenous community are against the very notion of standardization. Pilar Mendez, an employee at the Fundacion PROEIB Andes, believes that too much focus on the "correct" and "incorrect" ways of writing words discourages people from using Indigenous languages at all, for fear of making mistakes. This is counterproductive, as the primary objective of standardizing Indigenous languages is to facilitate their use and their spread: "I'm not attached to the benefit of standardization in the case of Indigenous languages. People get caught up in fights about how to standardize these languages and fail to see that standardization is merely a tool for something more."[63] Therefore, it is clear that there are important disagreements about how to correctly standardize Indigenous languages and whether standardization is even desirable. These ongoing debates about standardization have caused delays in the production of scholarly materials, which has made it difficult to implement the IBE program as a whole.

PUBLIC OPINION PERCEPTIONS

A fourth and final obstacle that has limited IBE's success is the opposition it received from different sectors of the population, particularly from parents, teachers, and teachers' unions. One of the reasons for this was the feeling that IBE had been imposed with very little public consultation.[64] These groups felt that the Bolivian people had not been sufficiently involved in the design of the IBE program. The government that introduced the program was strongly associated with neo-liberalism and foreign influence. Moreover, the pillars of the IBE program were designed by international organizations and experts. The IBE program was therefore perceived as an imposition from the outside. Although many of these groups agreed with the concept of IBE, they disagreed with the way it had been implemented. Armstrong, who was involved in the early conceptualization of the IBE program, admitted that Bolivians are correct to associate IBE with foreign influence and NGOs. However, she argued that the program could not have gotten off its feet in any other way. Historically, there had been very little government support for such programs and a serious lack of expertise in Bolivia. Armstrong explained that "they saw IBE as tainted with foreign influence, and it certainly was, because for so long, the government wasn't interested at all! If anyone was going to do IBE, it was going to be foreigners."[65] This raises interesting questions about the advantages and disadvantages of foreign involvement.

One of the main reasons parents resisted IBE was the fear that their children would not learn to speak Spanish properly and would not be able to succeed in a Spanish-speaking society. It was difficult to convince these parents, many of whom had little or no education, that IBE would actually improve their children's Spanish in the long run. Rather, parents focused on the fact that their child's acquisition of Spanish was delayed. Many parents did not understand why their children should receive schooling in a language they already spoke. They believed that school was made for learning Spanish. Most had grown up during a time when speaking an Indigenous language was shameful and was associated with marginalization and discrimination. They did not want their children to have similar experiences. Instead, they wanted their children to learn Spanish because they were convinced that this was the key to success in life. Spanish is a necessary condition for accessing job opportunities and higher education in Bolivia.

Angela Padilla understands parents' resistance to IBE. She explains that the average Indigenous peasant does not identify with the goals of the intercultural bilingual education. Most Indigenous people in Bolivia are poor, rural subsistence farmers. Their priorities are surviving, finding work, and ensuring economic security for their children. All these things, she argues, create a need for Spanish language education, not intercultural bilingual education. She explains that IBE is grounded in righteous and noble ideals, but that most Indigenous peasants are not in a position to be able to prioritize these ideals:

> IBE appears very avant-garde and very revolutionary. It holds a series of important values that I, as an academic, recognize and appreciate. But it does not correspond to the daily reality of Bolivian Indigenous people. Throughout history, Indigenous people have been systematically excluded from society. All they want it to integrate somehow. They know, from their daily experiences, that people who speak English and Spanish are successful, and are full members of society. They want their children to learn English and Spanish.[66]

Padilla recognizes that, from an impoverished Indigenous parent's perspective, IBE may actually be seen as negative because it obstructs one's societal aspirations. Even ardent IBE supporters such as Armstrong and Mendez concede that revitalizing a language is difficult when the community of speakers is economically stressed, especially when the language is historically associated with economic disadvantage. According to Mendez, this is one of the primary obstacles facing IBE today: "The main challenge, I believe, is getting the very speakers of Indigenous languages to see the value in IBE."[67]

Lessons Learned

Many relevant policy lessons can be drawn from Bolivia's experience with intercultural bilingual education. The first is the importance of citizen participation for a program to be accepted by, and respond to the needs of its intended beneficiaries. When Morales was elected, his government began working on a new IBE bill, called the *Ley Avelino Sinani y Elizardo Perez*. Although the bill has many points in common with the old one, it was elaborated with more community participation, which makes it feel more legitimate to the people. German Jimenez, the government's Vice Minister of Primary Education, explains:

> This new law will fundamentally change the things that made the last education reform unpopular. Community organizations, Indigenous wisemen, teachers, and parents have participated directly in its creation. The new curriculum is based on Indigenous knowledge and Indigenous logic systems. None of this was possible during the first education reform, since it was conceived by foreigners.[68]

There was a general sentiment, among most of the people interviewed, that the new law would be more successful and better accepted than the first one.

Increased Indigenous participation in the design of the new bill has allowed for Indigenous voices and perspectives to be heard. One of the things that some Indigenous people have emphasized is that IBE should aim to do more than simply ease students into the Spanish-speaking world. Indigenous-language education should value and revitalize Indigenous languages and customs. Marta Lanza, the IBE director at the Ministry of Education, explains that this has been taken into account in the design of the new bill. As a result, one of the new bill's main pillars is decolonization. Its goal is to value Indigenous languages and cultures for their own sake, instead of making integration into mainstream society the main goal.[69] One example of this new orientation is the bill's emphasis on *productive education*. Productive education is education that respects the Indigenous way of life by acknowledging the importance of work in rural Indigenous communities. Many Indigenous Bolivians are subsistence farmers. Harvest time is intense and requires the participation of the entire family. In the old IBE program, Indigenous children were not excused from school during this time of year. If their parents decided to keep them home during harvest time anyway (as many did), children would fall behind at school. School holidays corresponded to Christian holidays, such as Christmas and Easter—holidays that many Indigenous people do not celebrate. Indigenous Bolivians were angry that their children were given holidays on these occasions rather than at the times when they needed them the most.[70] This notion of productive education is therefore consistent with the goal of decolonization described above. It makes the content of education truly Indigenous, not only from a linguistic point of view but also in terms of the values and worldview reflected in the curriculum and school calendar.

It is important to note, however, that the calls for decolonization and for incorporation of Indigenous values into education have come primarily from Indigenous elites, community leaders, and scholars. They have not come from the more numerous, economically stressed, Indigenous peasants. As discussed throughout this chapter, most rural Indigenous Bolivians are primarily concerned with survival. They want to secure a better future for their children and know that this is best done through integration into mainstream society. Most Bolivian subsistence farmers do not have the luxury of thinking about cultural and linguistic revitalization. In this sense, they may prefer the more pedagogical conception of IBE (which aims to ease students into mainstream society), or no IBE at all. In fact, some of the strongest opposition to IBE has come from rural Indigenous parents. There is, therefore, an important lack of uniformity within the Indigenous community. The desires of Indigenous elites and the desires of regular Indigenous peasants are fundamentally different. The fact that the people intended to benefit from IBE are often those who resist it most raises other difficult questions. What to do when the very people a program seeks to help oppose it? It seems unethical to impose "help" programs on people if they feel they are being hindered rather than helped by such programs. Yet, it is clear that the hispanicized education system that existed in Bolivia prior to the implementation of IBE was not optimal for Indigenous people either.

One possible way to resolve both of these questions may be to enhance poverty reduction efforts in Indigenous communities. If Indigenous peasants were not as worried about day-to-day survival, then they would be in the position to make a real *choice* between integrating into dominant society or resisting it and revitalizing Indigenous cultures and languages. If Indigenous people knew that they would be able to enjoy a reasonable standard of living regardless of the path they chose, then it is likely that more of them would choose the cultural conception of IBE over its merely pedagogical conception, and much of the resistance from parents would disappear. As shown previously, many parents oppose IBE because they are desperately poor and want nothing more for their children than to learn Spanish, move to the city, and get a good job. However, if they were in a better socioeconomic position to begin with, this desire might no longer take precedence over the desire to preserve their language and culture. It is also possible that Indigenous parents simply need more time to see the program's positive results. Improving education and outreach campaigns, and trying to help parents understand that bilingual education may temporarily delay, but will not permanently affect, their children's acquisition of Spanish, may also decrease resistance.

One final policy issue that deserves attention is the question of how far to extend IBE. There is considerable debate about whether it should be extended to all languages, particularly those with only a few hundred speakers. This chapter has highlighted the costs associated with standardizing dozens of oral languages, particularly in lower-income countries such as Bolivia. Many people believe that it is unethical to spend millions of dollars discussing the details of proper accentuation and alphabetization while many Bolivians are hungry and jobless. On the other hand, standardizing these tiny languages and teaching them in school may be one of the only ways to prevent them from dying within a few generations. With the death of a language, a culture and part of the world's rich diversity also dies. The international community may have a role to play in helping these languages survive. Yet, in a world plagued by war, hunger, and disease, language may always be a secondary concern. The ethical dilemmas associated with weighing the relative importance of culture and economics will no doubt continue to be a source of discussion for many years to come.

Successful experiences in other countries may shed some hope on this difficult issue, by showing that there are ways to promote language preservation that do not rely on expensive textbooks and standardization processes. Focusing on political measures that help revitalize languages may be one way to sidestep the economic dilemma and increase the use and prestige of Indigenous languages without standardizing all of them immediately. For example, increasing the power or the rights of an endangered language group within the dominant community can promote language survival. This has been the case with many small language groups in Europe following European Union legislation to ensure basic minority protection standards in all member countries. Increased wealth relative to the dominant community can also revitalize a language. The strong economy in the Catalan region of Spain, for example, has given momentum to the Catalan language.[71]

Conclusion

The residual legacy of colonialism is still very present in Bolivia today. Bolivia's Indigenous people are overwhelmingly poor and do not enjoy the same opportunities as their non-Indigenous counterparts. This situation creates an urgent need for policies that can improve the status of Indigenous people in Bolivia and end their marginalization. IBE may be one such policy. This chapter has offered some preliminary thoughts on the successes, shortcomings, and policy lessons of IBE.

The issues discussed in this chapter are not unique to Bolivia, nor are they unique to countries with high Indigenous populations. Globalization has intensified migration flows worldwide and many countries are grappling with how to manage high levels of cultural and linguistic diversity. Bilingual education is being discussed and debated as a possible measure to accommodate new immigrants in multiple countries, whether it be Mexican immigrants in the United States, Turkish children in the Netherlands, or Moroccan immigrants in Belgium. Much of the controversy surrounding IBE in Bolivia exists in these countries too, particularly around the transferable issues discussed in this chapter: the conceptual issues and the public opinion perceptions. In California, for example, where bilingual education programs for Hispanic children have been implemented, a great deal of debate exists over whether the goal should be to have children learn English as quickly as possible or whether it should be to help them maintain their own culture and language while learning English.[72] There is also significant debate about whether it is even possible for immigrants to become full members of American society if they maintain their own culture and language. And, in much the same way that Bolivian parents worry that IBE may strip their children of economic opportunities, Hispanic parents in California worry that bilingual education will prevent their children from learning proper English and that "their reason for immigrating—to make better lives for their children—will have been thwarted, perversely, by the very programs designed to aid them."[73]

It is clear, then, that the challenges and opportunities of bilingual education will continue to occupy a central spot in the minds of policy-makers and researchers worldwide. The challenging questions highlighted in this chapter provide fertile ground for new research in upcoming years, as we continue to strive toward a fairer, more equal world.

NOTES

1. International Fund for Agricultural Development. (n. d.). *Enhancing the role of Indigenous women in sustainable development: IFAD experience with Indigenous women in Latin America and Asia*. Third Session of the Permanent Forum on Indigenous Issues. Retrieved from http://www.ifad.org/english/Indigenous/pub/documents/IndigenouswomenReport.pdf
2. Taneja, P. (Ed.). (2009). *The state of the world's minorities and Indigenous peoples 2009: Education special*. London: Minority Rights Group International.
3. Ibid.
4. Ibid.
5. Hallman, K., Peracca, S., Catino, J., & Ruiz, M. J. (2007). *Assessing the multiple disadvantages of Mayan girls: The effects of gender, ethnicity, poverty, and residence on education in Guatemala*. New York: Population Council.
6. Taneja. (2009). *The state of the world's minorities and Indigenous peoples 2009*.
7. Ibid.
8. Albo, X. (2004). *Ninos alegres, libres, expresivos: La audacia de la educacion intercultural bilingue en Boliva*. La Paz: CIPCA and UNICEF.
9. Hall, G., & Patrinos, H. A. (Eds.). (2005). *Indigenous peoples, poverty and human development in Latin America: 1994–2004*. Washington, DC: World Bank.
10. U.S. Department of State. (2010). *Background note: Bolivia*. Washington, DC: Bureau of Western Hemisphere Affairs. Retrieved from http://www.state.gov/r/pa/ei/bgn/35751.htm
11. Hall & Patrinos. (2005). *Indigenous peoples, poverty and human development in Latin America*.
12. Quechuas are the largest of Bolivia's approximately three dozen native groups.
13. Ochoa, M., & Bonifaz, A. (2002). *An analysis of disparities in education: The case of primary school completion rates in Bolivia*. Retrieved from http://129.3.20.41/econ-wp/hew/papers/0302/0302001.pdf
14. Hall & Patrinos. (2005). *Indigenous peoples, poverty and human development in Latin America*.
15. Ibid.
16. Department for International Development. (2009). *Bolivia's Indigenous children learn lessons for life*. London: Department for International Development. Retrieved from http://www.dfid.gov.uk/media-room/case-studies/2009/bolivias-Indigenous-children-learn-lessons-for-life/
17. United Nations Development Programme (UNDP). (2009). *Human development report 2009: Population living below the poverty line*. New York: UNDP. Retrieved from http://hdrstats.undp.org/en/indicators/104.html
18. International Fund for Agricultural Development. (2002). *Valuing diversity in sustainable development: IFAD experience with Indigenous peoples in Latin America and Asia*. Johannesburg: International Fund for Agricultural Development. Retrieved from http://www.ifad.org/events/wssd/ip/ip.pdf
19. Lopez, L. E. (2005). *De resquicios a boquerones: La educacion intercultural bilingue en Bolivia*. La Paz: PROEIB Andes y Plural Editores.
20. Ibid.

21. Taylor, S. (2004, February). *Intercultural bilingual education in Bolivia: The challenge of ethnic diversity and national identity*. La Paz: Instituto de Investigaciones Socioeconomicas. Retrieved from http://www.iisec.ucb.edu.bo/papers/2001–2005/iisec-dt-2004–01.pdf

22. Ruiz Martinez, G. (2005). *Analisis critico de la reforma educativa*. Cochabamba: Editorial Univalle.

23. Albo. (2006). *Ninos alegres, libres, expresivos*, pp. 49.

24. D'Emilio, L. (2006). *Voices and processes toward pluralism: Indigenous education in Bolivia*. Education Division documents no. 9. Stockholm: Swedish International Development Cooperation Agency.

25. Collier, V. P., & Thomas, W. P. (2004). The astounding effectiveness of dual language education for all. *NABE Journal of Research and Practice, 2*(1), 1.

26. Ibid.

27. Deutsche Gesellschaft für Technische Zusammenarbeit. (n.d.). *About us*. Retrieved from http://www.gtz.de/en/689.htm

28. U.S. Department of Labor. (n. d.). *Bolivia: Addressing child labor and promoting schooling: Educational alternatives*. Washington, DC: Bureau of International Labor Affairs. Retrieved from http://www.dol.gov/ilab/media/reports/iclp/Advancing1/html/bolivia.htm#268

29. Albo. (2006). *Ninos alegres, libres, expresivos*.

30. Lopez. (2005). *De resquicios a boquerones*.

31. Nucinkis, N. (2006). La IBE en Bolivia. In L. E. Lopez, & C. Roja (Eds.), *La IBE en America Latina bajo examen*. La Paz: Plural Editores.

32. Ibid.

33. Ibid.

34. Albo. (2006). *Ninos alegres, libres, expresivos*.

35. Ibid.

36. Ibid.

37. Tenorio, A. (Linguist and former school teacher). Interview with Brittany Lambert, July 8, 2008. Note: some names used throughout this case study have been changed to protect confidentiality.

38. Murray, H. G., & Lang, M. (1997). Does classroom participation improve student learning? *Teaching and Learning in Higher Education, 20*(February), 7–9. Retrieved from http://www.stlhe.ca/pdf/Does%20classroom%20participation%20improve%20student%20learning.pdf

39. Smithee, M., Greenblatt, S., & Eland, A. (2004). *U.S. culture series: U.S. classroom culture*. New York: NAFSA: Association of International Educators. Retrieved from http://www.auburn.edu/academic/international/oie/iss/prospective/classroom_culture.pdf

40. Lopez, F. (President of the Aymara Indigenous Council). Interview with Brittany Lambert, July 9, 2008.

41. Albo. (2006). *Ninos alegres, libres, expresivos*.

42. Pinaya, N. (NGO worker specializing in education). Interview with Brittany Lambert, August 9, 2008.

43. Armstrong, L. (American academic). Interview with Brittany Lambert, July 16, 2008.

44. Lopez. (President of the Aymara Indigenous Council). Interview with Brittany Lambert, July 9, 2008.

45. Vitale, J. (UNICEF employee). Interview with Brittany Lambert, August 14, 2008.

46. Armstrong (American academic). Interview with Brittany Lambert, July 16, 2008.

47. Ibid.

48. Barrionuevo Ibanez, R. (School principal). Interview with Brittany Lambert, August 20, 2008.

49. World Bank. (2006). *Basic education for Bolivia: Challenges for 2006–2010*. Report no. 35073. Washington, DC: Human Development Department, Bolivia, Ecuador, Peru and Venezuela Country Management Unit.

50. Armstrong (American academic). Interview with Brittany Lambert, July 16, 2008.

51. Lanza Mallo, E. (Teacher and university student). Interview with Brittany Lambert, August 9, 2008.

52. Ibid.
53. Barrionuevo Ibanez (School principal). Interview with Brittany Lambert, August 20, 2008.
54. Gomez, D. (Indigenous leader). Interview with Brittany Lambert, July 1, 2008.
55. Tenorio (Linguist and former school teacher). Interview with Brittany Lambert, July 8, 2008.
56. Nucinkis. (2006). La IBE en Bolivia.
57. Pinaya (NGO worker Specializing in Education). Interview with Brittany Lambert, August 9, 2008.
58. Padilla, A. (Academic working on education policy). Interview with Brittany Lambert, June 30, 2008.
59. Maslow, A. (1943). A theory of human motivation. *Psychological Review, 50*(4), 370–96.
60. Vitale (UNICEF employee). Interview with Brittany Lambert, August 14, 2008.
61. Tenorio (Linguist and Former School Teacher). Interview with Brittany Lambert, July 8, 2008.
62. Mendez, P. (Linguist and employee at the Fundacion PROEIB Andes). Interview with Brittany Lambert, July 17, 2008.
63. Ibid.
64. Jimenez, G. (Vice-Minister of Primary Education). Interview with Brittany Lambert August 13, 2008.
65. Armstrong (American academic). Interview with Brittany Lambert, July 16, 2008.
66. Padilla (Academic working on education policy). Interview with Brittany Lambert, June 30th, 2008.
67. Mendez (Linguist and employee at the Fundacion PROEIB Andes). Interview with Brittany Lambert, July 17, 2008.
68. Jimenez (Vice-Minister of Primary Education). Interview with Brittany Lambert, August 13, 2008.
69. Lanza, M. (IBE director at the Ministry of Education). Interview with Brittany Lambert, August, 22, 2008.
70. Tenorio (Linguist and Former School Teacher). Interview with Brittany Lambert, July 8, 2008.
71. Moseley, C. (Ed.). (1999). *Encyclopedia of the world's endangered languages*. London: RoutledgeCurzon.
72. Leiterman, H. L., Ryan, J. P. (1999). Immigration: A dialogue on policy, law, and values. *Focus on Law Studies, XIV*(2) 1-16.
73. Frerking, B. (1997). *Immigrant parents join campaign against bilingual education*. Houston: Center for Research on Parallel Computation at Rice University. Retrieved from http://www.crpc.rice.edu/newsArchive/nsl_11_16_97.html
74. Kaplan, S. (2006). Making democracy work in Bolivia. *Orbis, 50*(3), 501–517
75. Joubert-Ceci, B. (2005, June 14). Behind the Indigenous-led uprising in Bolivia. *Workers World*. Retrieved from http://www.workers.org/2005/world/bolivia-0623/
76. Rory, C., & Schipani, A. (2008, August 24). Bolivia split in two as the wealthy aim to defy the Morales revolution. *The Observer*. Retrieved from http://www.guardian.co.uk/world/2008/aug/24/bolivia

Appendix 1: Methodology

The research for this case study was done in the context of the Institute for Health and Social Policy's 2007–2008 Policy Fellowship program. The field research was conducted in Bolivia's administrative capital, La Paz, and the surrounding area. When combined with its fast-growing suburb, El Alto, La Paz is the largest and fastest growing city in Bolivia. With over 1.6 million inhabitants, the greater La Paz area is home to nearly 20% of Bolivians.[74] This made it possible to study a large and representative sample of the Bolivian population. In addition to its size, La Paz was chosen for its large Indigenous population. In the city of La Paz, over 60% of the population is Indigenous, and in El Alto, nearly 80% identify as Indigenous Aymara.[75] In contrast, only 38% of the population in Bolivia's second largest city, Santa Cruz, identifies as Indigenous.[76] La Paz was therefore considered the most appropriate place to study questions relating to Indigenous peoples.

Information about the IBE program was gathered through interviews and observations. A total of 50 people were interviewed, including government officials, members of NGOs, Indigenous leaders, scholars, representatives of teachers' unions, teachers, principals, and students. Initial interviewees were found through Internet research and through Canadian academic advisors with research experience in the area. The rest of interviewees were referrals from other interview participants. All interviews were conducted in Spanish and therefore transcribed in Spanish. The quotes in this chapter were translated from Spanish to English.

Appendix 2: List of Interviewees

Government Officials

- One Vice Minister of Primary Education
- One Head of Teacher Training at the Ministry of Education
- One IBE Director at the Ministry of Education

Teachers and Principals

- One Aymara Language Teacher for Adults
- One Aymara Teacher for Adults
- One Teacher and Policy Specialist
- One Urban School Teacher
- Six Rural School Teachers
- Five Rural Teachers and IBE University Students
- One Rural School Teacher and Teacher Union Member
- Two Rural School Principals

Academics and Professors

- One Academic Working on Language Policy
- One American Academic involved in establishing IBE
- One University Professor, Masters Program in IBE
- One University Professor in Cochabamba
- One Professor at a Teacher Training College
- One Academic Director at a Teacher Training College

Others

- One Aymara Indigenous leader
- One President of the Aymara Educational Council
- One Indigenous Scholar and Leader
- One Linguist and Employee at the Fundacion PROEIB Andes
- One Linguist and Former School Teacher
- One UNICEF Project Director
- Two NGO Employees Working on Curriculum Design
- Twelve Mature Rural Students
- One Head of a Teachers' Union
- One General Director at a Teacher Training College
- One Employee Responsible for the Undergraduate Program in IBE at a university in La Paz

Part 4

EARLY CHILDHOOD EDUCATION AND TRANSITIONS

11

Early Childhood Strategies for Closing the Socioeconomic Gap in School Outcomes

CLYDE HERTZMAN, LORI IRWIN, ARJUMAND SIDDIQI, EMILY HERTZMAN, AND ZIBA VAGHRI

The early years are critical for learning, health, and well-being throughout life.[1] Quality early childhood care and education (ECCE) programs, and early child development (ECD) programs more generally, can have a positive impact on children's development and their long-term health and educational attainment. Conversely, socioeconomic inequalities in access to ECCE programs can result in lifelong disparities both inside and out of the classroom. This chapter explores how feasible and effective ECCE strategies can give children from all socioeconomic groups the chance to acquire a foundation for lifelong learning and development.

Between 2000 and 2009, the Canadian province of British Columbia completed three waves of population-based assessments of developmental health, including more than 90% of children in school entry cohorts from across the province each time. Assessments of developmental health were conducted during the kindergarten year using a measure called the Early Development Instrument (EDI), in which kindergarten teachers fill out a detailed checklist for each child in their class based on five scale measures of development: physical well-being, social competence, emotional maturity, language and cognitive development, and communication and general knowledge.[2] *Physical health and well-being* assesses children's gross and fine motor skills, pencil holding, running on the playground, motor coordination, energy levels for classroom activities, independence in looking after own needs, and daily living skills. *Social knowledge and competence* includes items about children's curiosity about the world, eagerness to try new experiences, knowledge of standards of acceptable behavior in a public place, ability to control own behavior, appropriate respect for adult authority, cooperation with others, following rules, and ability to play and work with other children. *Emotional health and maturity* assesses children's abilities to reflect before acting, balance between too fearful and too impulsive, abilities to deal with feelings at age-appropriate levels, and empathic responses to other people's feelings. *Language and cognitive development* includes items designed to tap children's reading awareness, age-appropriate reading and writing skills, age-appropriate numeracy skills, board game performance, abilities to understand similarities and differences, and ability to recite back specific pieces of information from memory. *Communication skills and general knowledge* includes items that assess children's skills to communicate needs and wants in socially appropriate ways, symbolic uses of language, storytelling, and age-appropriate knowledge about the life and world around them. In particular, it identifies communication challenges faced by those whose home language is different from the language of instruction of the class. To date, differential item function analysis by gender and ethnicity has not shown any systematic bias in teacher reporting.[3,4]

The EDI identifies each child as "vulnerable" or "not vulnerable" based on a cutoff score on each of these five scales.[5] Cutoffs for each scale were initially established on samples of children from two Canadian provinces and the far North (among Inuit children). The principal criterion for the cutoffs was the consensus opinion of kindergarten and primary school teachers about the level of competence on the given scale needed to succeed in the primary grades. Thus, EDI vulnerability is interpreted as a state of development wherein the child is at increased risk of not being able to receive full benefit from the school experience.

Although this approach to setting cutoffs was both subjective and approximate, its concurrent and predictive validity has been repeatedly demonstrated in Canada and Australia.[6,7] For example, Figure 11.1 shows the strong predictive

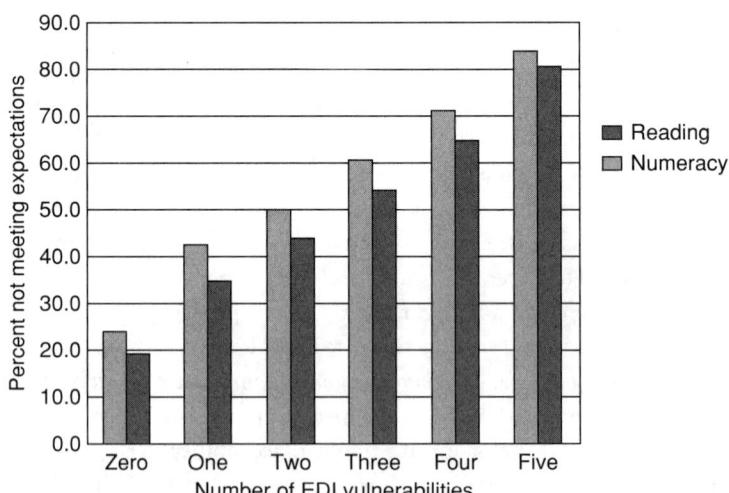

Figure 11.1 Linkage of Early Development Instrument (EDI) to School Success by Grade 4.

power of the state of children's early development, according to the EDI, on school success in the following years in British Columbia. By linking EDI ratings to individual school records, we were able to directly assess the relationship between early child developmental status and performance on standardized reading and arithmetic tests in grade 4. The figure shows that the proportion of children failing the grade 4 tests increases stepwise with the number of scales of the EDI upon which the children were vulnerable. It shows that *all* domains of development seem to contribute to school success, not just language and cognitive skills. Thus, equity of access to education can only take place in a context in which there is equity of access to opportunities to thrive in the preschool years. Quality ECCE programs have long been known to have the capacity to positively influence each of the domains of development on the EDI.

Gradients in Child Development

Vulnerability rates on the EDI are strongly correlated with the socioeconomic position (SEP) of children's families and the neighborhoods where they live. In British Columbia, approximately 50% of the neighborhood variation in vulnerability on the EDI is "explained," in a statistical sense, by neighborhood socioeconomic variables. Moreover, the relationship between EDI and SEP follows a gradient pattern. What does this mean? In virtually every society on earth, regardless of its level of wealth, differences in SEP translate into inequalities in child development.[8] The relationship is much more subtle than solely differentiating rich from poor; rather, each additional step up the family social and economic ladder results, on average, in improved prospects for child development. This step-wise relationship between SEP and child development is called a *gradient effect*. Gradients in developmental outcomes result from the broad array of systematic differences in experiences and environmental conditions that exist across the socioeconomic spectrum. Some of these are intimately connected to the child, and, therefore, readily identifiable (e.g., the quality of time and care provided by parents, and the physical conditions of the child's surroundings), but others are more distal (e.g., whether government policies provide families and communities with sufficient income, health care resources, early childhood education, safe neighborhoods, decent housing, etc.).

Gradients have been demonstrated for infant and child mortality, low birth weight, injuries, dental caries, malnutrition, infectious diseases, and health care services use.[9-14] In the cognitive domain, gradients are found for school enrollment, mathematics and language achievement, literacy, and school success.[15] Across the resource-rich world gradients in physical, social-emotional, and language-cognitive development emerge by school age and predict school success, such that 25% or more of children reach adulthood without the basic literacy and numeracy skills needed to participate in a modern economy. Similar gradients in reading literacy among fourth-graders have been demonstrated in 43 resource-poor countries in the Progress in International Literacy Study (PIRLS).[16] By middle childhood (6–12 years), strong SEP gradients emerge in social-emotional development, particularly for externalizing behaviors.[17,18]

In light of the gradient, societies need to be concerned with those in the lowest SEP—but not solely. Gradients mean that the largest overall burden of adverse outcome is spread, albeit at lower prevalence, across the middle of a society's SEP distribution. In principle, the optimum strategy for improving child development would be to try and flatten the gradient "upward" through spreading the conditions for healthy child development as broadly as possible throughout society. International comparisons of school success show that societies with the flattest gradients do the best. In these societies, the average differences in basic competencies demonstrated by children from the bottom, to the middle, to the top of the SEP spectrum is smaller, in absolute terms, than it is in less successful societies.[19] These findings challenge us to understand how to provide access to factors fundamental to health and development as rights of citizenship, rather than according to socioeconomic privilege.

Early Child Development Policies and Programs

Quality ECD programs and services (herein, "programs") provide effective supports for survival, growth, and development,[20–23] leading to better child[24,25] and adult outcomes.[26,27] Most ECD programs address one or more of the following key issues: breast-feeding, key systems development (i.e., vision, hearing, dental, speech/language), childcare, early childhood education, nutrition, parenting, community strengthening, or institutional capacities such as instructional and training programs. Although all children can benefit from quality ECD programs, disadvantaged groups stand to benefit most: the 40% of children in resource-poor nations who are living in extreme poverty; the 10.5 million children who die from preventable diseases before they are 5 years old; the 20%–25% of children in resource-poor nations who suffer from malnutrition and poor health; and all children who currently do not attend school.[28] Conditions that contribute to poverty, illness, lack of access to schooling, and malnutrition also contribute to intergenerational transmission of poverty,[29] which affects the productivity of future adults and puts an increased burden of cost on the economic resources of a country.

Juxtaposing these insights against the characteristics of the gradient leads to a clear policy corollary. This policy corollary is: Societies need to prioritize the most disadvantaged children while, at the same time, achieving universal coverage of effective programs. Avoidable developmental vulnerability is found everywhere, but it becomes more prevalent as one goes down the socioeconomic spectrum. This pattern is associated with an increasing range and complexity of barriers of access to programs that can help children thrive. Whereas, among the most privileged families, the principal barrier is time pressure on parents, as one goes down the SEP spectrum a range of barriers accumulate, including cost, transportation, time of day offered, language differences with providers, social distance/distrust between provider and family cultures, conflicting expectations between providers and families, and lack of an effective individual champion for the child. It is important to recognize that this list includes barriers (e.g., cost) that could apply to a standardized program, as well as others (e.g., conflicting expectations) that imply that standardized programs may generate their own barriers of access to conditions needed in order for the child to thrive. Thus, to provide de facto universal access to environments that help children thrive, the particularity of these and other barriers need to be addressed in the contexts in which they emerge. When it comes to ECCE, achieving universal access does not mean providing a universally standard experience under standardized terms and conditions. It means that senior policy and funding bodies make available proportionate resources and expertise, as well as flexible rules, to allow generic goals for ECCE to be translated locally to local realities.

Below are three examples of approaches to support the early stages of human development from a diverse group of middle and upper income countries. Each has generated evidence of effectiveness, making its approach worthwhile for other societies to consider.

EXAMPLE ECD1: CONDITIONAL CASH TRANSFERS IN MEXICO: *OPORTUNIDADES*

Many governments have implemented conditional cash transfer (CCT) programs with the goal of improving options for poor families through interventions in health, nutrition, and education. Families enrolled in CCT programs receive cash in exchange for complying with certain conditions: preventive health requirements and nutrition supplementation, education, and monitoring designed to improve health outcomes and promote positive behavior change. In an intervention that began in 1998, in Mexico, more than 500 low-income communities were randomly assigned to be enrolled in a CCT program (*Oportunidades*) immediately or 18 months later. In 2003, 2,449 children aged 24–68 months who had been enrolled in the program their entire lives were assessed. A doubling of cash transfers was associated with higher height-for-age, lower prevalence of stunting, lower body mass index for age percentile, and lower prevalence of being overweight. A doubling of cash transfers was also associated with children doing better on a scale of motor development, three scales of cognitive development, and receptive language—corresponding to the language and cognitive and the physical development scales of the EDI. The investigators concluded that the cash transfer component of *Oportunidades* is associated with better outcomes in child health, growth, and development. Programs similar to this are currently being implemented in five other poor and middle-income countries in Latin America.[30]

EXAMPLE ECD2: KANGAROO CARE: BEGINNINGS IN BOGOTA, COLOMBIA

Kangaroo Care is based on mothers, fathers, and caregivers providing skin-to-skin contact for low-birth-weight infants as part of early stimulation, which has been shown to improve survival rates of the most vulnerable infants. Premature babies (under 2,000 g) born in poorly resourced settings may not have access to incubators and those who do are separated from their mothers. Kangaroo Care was first developed in 1978, to help premature babies with temperature regulation and bonding in Bogota. Mothers, fathers, or caregivers carry/sleep with newborn babies skin to skin in upright positions 24 hours a day. Kangaroo Care has been shown to be at least as effective as traditional care in incubators at a fraction of the cost. It has been shown to deliver ideal conditions for premature infants; reduce costs of caring for premature infants; improve breast-feeding rates; improve bonding; and reduce morbidity and hospital stay. It is a practice with roots in traditional child rearing that has been taken up in many industrialized nations (e.g., France, Sweden, United States, Canada).[31] In EDI terms, benefits would primarily be seen on the physical development scale.

EXAMPLE ECD3: SURE START CHILDREN'S CENTRES, UNITED KINGDOM

Sure Start Children's Centres were developed in the political context of the U.K. Government's commitment following the Acheson Inquiry[32] in 1998, to tackle health inequalities, reduce child poverty, and break cycles of intergenerational transmission of deprivation. They evolved from the Sure Start Local Programs (SSLPs) set up between 1999 and 2003 as area-based initiatives in the 20% most deprived areas in England aimed at providing integrated services to parents and young children and managed by local partnerships. An evaluation of the effects of fully established SSLPs on children and their families showed benefits including improved positive social behavior and independence in children, less negative parenting, and better home learning environments. In EDI terms, these benefits would be seen on the scales of emotional and social development. They conclude that early interventions can improve the life chances of young children living in deprived areas.[33] Sure Start has also been demonstrated to be an effective platform for interventions in families with children at high risk of conduct disorder.[34]

As an example of the principles outlined above regarding de facto universal access, Sure Start Children's Centres in the most disadvantaged areas offer a more comprehensive range of services than those offered in more advantaged areas. Children's Centres in the most disadvantage areas offer good-quality early learning combined with full day care provision for children (minimum 10 hours a day, 5 days a week, 48 weeks a year); good-quality teacher input to lead the development of learning within the center; child and family health services, including antenatal services; parental outreach; family support services; a base for a child-minder network; support for children and parents with special needs; and effective links with "Jobcentre Plus" to support parents and caregivers who wish to consider training or employment.[35]

The Role of Health Care Systems

Health care systems (HCS) are in a preeminent position to contribute to ECD since they are already concerned with the health of individuals and communities, employ trained professionals, provide facilities and services, and, most importantly, are a primary contact for childbearing mothers and children from the very beginning. Worldwide, young children have comparatively more exposure to HCS in their early years than to education systems, which many do not encounter until age 6–8. For example, the World Health Organization (WHO)'s Expanded Program on Immunization (EPI) was originally launched in 1976, at a time when less than 5% of the world's children received immunization against the six most easily preventable diseases: diphtheria, tetanus, pertussis (whooping cough), polio, measles, and tuberculosis. Over the past 30 years, the EPI has increased its coverage to the point where there are now an estimated 500 million immunization contacts with children around the world on an annual basis.

The scale of the WHO's EPI, as well as its near-universal coverage, are now being recognized as potentially valuable opportunities with which to bundle other child health promotion activities. The time at which 90% of the world's children receive immunization, usually within their first 2 years of life, is a potential contact point for other health interventions or monitoring. In some developing countries, HCS are already serving as a platform for ECD information and support to parents through coordination with existing ECD and nutrition/growth monitoring programs, immunization, women's health, or reproductive care.[36] Kenya has been especially proactive in utilizing this early contact point. The Kenyan Ministry of Health has recently decided to collect information about a few developmental indicators during immunization visits as a way of monitoring the progress of ECD in Kenya on a population basis. Immunization visits are also viewed as an opportunity to distribute information about ECD and infant health to parents. Thus, HCS are emerging as an important point of contact that can link ECD programming to children and families who would otherwise have no access, and can often do so for relatively small marginal costs.[37]

Linking ECD programmes and services to HCS has the potential to improve child survival rates, while at the same time fostering ECD. These realities do not mean that the HCS should go it alone, or that they should become the lead agency for ECD. Rather, HCS should serve as a platform of access for a full range of intersectoral initiatives in ECD. The following examples of positive use of HCS platforms are abstracted from the full scientific report of the Global Knowledge Hub on Early Child Development to the WHO Commission on the Social Determinants of Health.[38]

EXAMPLE 1: INTERNATIONAL LEADERSHIP HELPING NATIONALLY AND LOCALLY

The WHO's Integrated Management of Childhood Illness (IMCI) program seeks to reduce childhood mortality, illness, and disability, as well as promote health and development among children aged 0–5 years. IMCI has both preventive and curative aspects, which are implemented at the level of the family, the community, and through the HCS. IMCI prioritizes the proper identification and treatment of childhood illnesses within a variety of settings, including homes and health facilities, but also provides counselling for parents and caregivers, and referral services for severely ill children.

The main implementation involves the following steps:

- Adopting an integrated approach to child health and development in the national health policy
- Adapting the standard IMCI clinical guidelines to the country's needs, policies, available drugs, and to the local foods and language
- Upgrading care in local clinics by training health workers in new methods to examine and treat children, and to counsel parents effectively
- Making upgraded care possible by ensuring a sufficient supply of the right low-cost medicines and simple equipment
- Strengthening care in hospitals for those children too sick to be treated in outpatient clinics
- Developing support mechanisms within communities for preventing disease, for helping families to care for sick children, and for getting children to clinics or hospitals when needed

In partnership with UNICEF, the WHO has developed a special early childhood development component, called the Care for Development, to incorporate into existing IMCI programs. Care for Development aims to enhance parents' and caregivers' awareness of the importance of play and communication with children by providing them with information and instruction during children's clinical visits. Care for Development is considered an effective method of supporting parents' and caregivers' efforts to provide a stimulating environment for their children by building on their existing skills.[39] Health care professionals are encouraged to view children's visits for acute minor illnesses as opportunities to spread the messages of Care for Development, such as the importance of active and responsive feeding to improve children's nutrition and growth, and the importance of play and communication activities to help children move to the next stages in their development.

EXAMPLE 2: INTERNATIONAL AGENCIES SUPPORTING A LOCAL/NATIONAL INITIATIVE

In Thailand, several local and international organizations, for example, UNICEF, Christian Children's Foundation, and Save the Children, in collaboration with the Department of Health in the Ministry of Public Health and local universities, have supported the development of the Integrated Family-Based ECD (IFBECD) project, which has been in effect since 1990. The project operates out of child health centers and involves collaboration between experienced mothers (who volunteer as ambassadors), the HCS, and the broader community (e.g., universities, other educational centers, not-for-profit organizations). Each ambassador works with five families in her neighborhood and provides the mothers with information and advice about child health, nutrition, and development in a range of settings such as in peoples' homes or at a local market. Monthly training sessions (on issues such as family life, child development, infant care, etc.) and meetings are held in local departments of health to update the ambassadors on new information and materials in relation to child health and development. The approach is especially useful because older children frequently provide some care for their younger siblings or neighbors in Thailand. The ambassadors also provide necessary information about the importance of child health, nutrition, and developmental issues to these older children. In one of the more "hands-on" lessons, students in the fifth and sixth grades work with and learn from the ambassador about how to determine the vaccination status and developmental progress of the younger children in their families. All these educational and training initiatives are coordinated through the Ministry of Public Health.

EXAMPLE 3: THE LOCAL HEALTH CARE CLINIC AS THE SITE OF PROGRAM INITIATION

Reach Out and Read (ROR) is an American nonprofit organization that promotes early literacy by giving new books to children and advice about the importance of reading aloud to parents attending pediatric examinations. ROR programs make early literacy a standard part of pediatric primary care. Following the ROR model, physicians and nurses advise parents that reading aloud is the most important thing they can do to help their children love books and to start school ready to learn. Pediatricians and other clinicians are trained in the three-part ROR model in an effort to promote pediatric literacy:

1. At every well-child check-up, doctors and nurses encourage parents to read aloud to their young children, and offer age-appropriate tips and encouragement. Parents who may have difficulty reading are encouraged to invent their own stories to go with picture books and spend time naming objects with their children.
2. Providers give every child between the ages of 6 months and 5 years a new, developmentally appropriate children's book to keep.

3. In literacy-rich waiting room environments, often with volunteer readers, parents and children learn about the pleasures and techniques of looking at books together.

Research findings[40] evaluating the impact of ROR's efforts have been remarkably consistent. Compared to families that have not participated in ROR, parents who have received the ROR intervention are significantly more likely to read to their children and have more children's books in the home. Most importantly, studies examining language in young children found an association between the ROR intervention and statistically significant improvements in preschool language scores, a good predictor of later literacy success. Currently, ROR program sites are located in all 50 states, the District of Columbia, Puerto Rico, the U.S. Virgin Islands, and Guam. ROR programs are housed at hospitals, health centers, and private pediatric practices.

Quality and Sustainability

It is problematic to transfer effective ECD programs from one society to another in standardized fashion because the prospects for program effectiveness are deeply embedded in local conditions. Instead, the international development community has found that it is more useful to think, in generic terms, of three categories of quality in ECD programs: structure, process, and nurturance.[41-43] *Structure* includes staff training and expertise, staff-to-child ratios, group size, and physical characteristics of the space or service, the available materials and resources, and the adherence to health and safety standards. *Process* aspects include staff stability; continuity and job satisfaction; the relationships among services providers, caregivers, and children; and relationships among levels of sponsorship (including community, civil society, government, and multinational donor agencies).[44] *Nurturant* environments are defined as those in which exploration is encouraged, mentoring in basic skills is provided, the child's developmental advances are celebrated, development of new skills on the part of the child is guided and extended (i.e., scaffolding), there is protection from inappropriate punishment and ridicule, and the language environment is rich and responsive to the child.

In developing countries, adding stimulation and care components to nutrition interventions improves child outcomes, including the physical health outcomes associated with the nutritional intervention.[45] By using gender-neutral philosophies, teaching and caregiving practices, and curricula, ECD programs can also promote gender equality, which is linked to improvements in both maternal health and child outcomes.[46] Beyond program quality, there is a separate set of principles for sustainability worldwide. These include cultural sensitivity and awareness; community ownership; a common purpose and consensus about outcomes related to the needs and goals of the community; partnerships among community, providers, and parents; enhancing community capacity through active involvement of families and other stakeholders; and a management plan that facilitates the monitoring of quality, the assessment of program effectiveness, and the potential for institutional growth.[47] These principles of sustainability also relate to quality in that they are associated with improved outcomes for young children.[48]

Scaling Up

Programs can shift the norms of ECD and reduce inequalities if they are universal in coverage and generous. A prime example is Cuba's *Educa a Tu Hijo* (Educating Your Child) program, described below.[49]

HEALTH AND EARLY CHILDHOOD EDUCATION IN CUBA

In Cuba, basic indicators of child health and development (infant mortality and under-5 mortality and low birth weight rates) are comparable to those of North America and Western Europe. Cuban children have high retention rates in primary and secondary education. The First International Comparative Study of Language, Mathematics, and Associated Factors indicated that third- and fourth-grade Cuban students significantly outperform their counterparts in other Latin American countries on tests of mathematics and language.[50] The study also found that Cuban children are less likely than their Latin American counterparts to be engaged in school fights.

Between 1983 and 2003, Cuba phased in a program called *Educa a Tu Hijo* (Educating Your Child), a community-based, family-centered program that integrates health and education services into a single system, prioritizing health, learning, behavior, and life trajectories during prenatal life, infancy, childhood, and adolescence. Child Development services start early, are universal, and are conducted with the participation of different Ministries, social organizations, families, and an extended social network. The network includes 52,000 "Promotres" (teachers, pedagogues, physicians, and other trained professionals), 116,000 "Executors" (teachers, physicians, nurses, retired professionals, students, volunteers), and more than 800,000 families. At the neighborhood level, family doctor and nurse teams assume responsibility for a group of people. At the same time, local self-government units promote social involvement and encourage residents in protecting their own health. All pregnant women in Cuba have at least 12 prenatal medical checks and deliver in a maternity clinic or specialized health center. They are entitled to 18 weeks of maternity leave before the birth and 40 weeks afterward (which can be taken by either parent). Children receive between 104 and 208 stimulation and development monitoring sessions up to the age of 2 years, and between 162 and 324 group sessions from ages 3–5.

A recent follow-up of *Educa a Tu Hijo* showed that 87% of children participating in the program reach school age with satisfactory development in key domains (motor skills, cognition, social-personal, and personal hygiene). As a rough comparison, this implies a vulnerability rate approximately half of that in Canada and Australia, two wealthy countries where population-based EDI data are available. This may well be a key contributor to school success in Cuba.

Remarkably, during the "special economic period" in the early 1990s, when Russia stopped subsidizing the Cuban economy through massive sugar purchases, the central government not only maintained its high investment in early human development, but increased it. It was during this period that *Educa a Tu Hijo* was extended, helping to increase ECD service coverage to 99.8% of children ages 0–5, even while, between 1990 and 1995, daily per capita caloric intake for children dropped 25%. How could this have happened? The answer is simply that mothers and children were recognized by the government to be the top priority in a period of economic emergency, since they represented the country's most important investment in the future. It is hard to imagine such a policy choice emerging from the political dynamics of the liberal democracies.

The Economic Argument

Many economists now argue that, on the basis of the available evidence, investment in early childhood is the most powerful investment a country can make, with returns over the life course many times the size of the original investment. ECD programs foster and promote the quality of human capital: that is, individuals' competencies and skills for participating in society and the workforce.[51] The competencies and skills fostered through ECD programs are *not* limited to cognitive gains, but also include physical, social, and emotional gains, all of which are determinants of health over the life course.[52] Much of the burden of disease worldwide (e.g., cardiovascular disease, obesity, HIV/AIDS, depression) begins in early childhood.[53] Accordingly, ECD programs—which incorporate and link health-promoting measures (e.g., good nutrition, immunization) with nurturance, participation, care, stimulation, and protection—offer the prospect of sustained improvements in physical, social–emotional, and language–cognitive development, while simultaneously reducing the immediate and future burden of disease, especially for those who are most vulnerable and disadvantaged. According to a recent UNESCO Global Monitoring Report, in every country, children from the poorest communities—those most exposed to malnutrition and preventable diseases—are least likely to have access to ECD programs, yet these children would also benefit the most.[54] Early interventions can alter the lifetime trajectories of children who are born poor or are deprived of the opportunities for growth and development available to those more fortunate. ECD programs and services (e.g., childcare for working parents, preschool, access to primary school) have high rates of return, and are an effective route to reduce poverty, and to foster health, productivity, and well-being.

If governments in both resource-rich and -poor societies were to act while children were young, by implementing quality ECD programs and services as part of their broader social protection policies, they would have a reasonable expectation that these investments would pay for themselves many times over.[55,56] In resource-rich countries where the issue has been studied directly, savings come from reduced remedial education and criminal justice costs.[57,58] Economic gains come from improved access of mothers to the labor force[59] and increased economic activity in adulthood among those whose developmental trajectories were improved through intervention.[60] The economic benefits of ECD intervention over the long term have not been directly studied in resource-poor countries. However, a rather robust literature suggests economic growth in resource-poor nations accrues to a variety of outcomes that stem from investments in human capital [61-64] more generally, such as increased school enrolment and improved literacy rates. It is widely understood that the transformation of the "Tiger Economies" of Southeast Asia from resource-poor, low-life-expectancy to resource-rich, high-life-expectancy societies was accomplished primarily through investment in children, from conception to school leaving. During this period, conditions for young children markedly improved, with infant mortality dropping from approximately 140/1,000 in 1946 to less than 5/1,000 in 2000.[65,66] From 1975 to 2002, the average GDP per capita in the Tiger Economies increased from approximately $4,000 to $23,000.[67,68] Thus, the scale of potential economic gain for resource-poor societies in adopting child development as a cornerstone to their development strategies can be measured not just in cost–benefit terms at the microlevel, but in multiples of economic scale.[69,70]

Conclusion

FROM GLOBAL TO LOCAL

In 2005, the United Nations Committee on the Rights of the Child promulgated General Comment No. 7: Implementing Rights in Early Childhood, which recognizes that young children are holders of all rights enshrined in the Convention on the Rights of the Child and that early childhood is a critical time for their realization.[71] General Comment No. 7 holds governments responsible for monitoring both the state of young children's evolving capacities (language/cognitive, social/emotional, and physical) and also whether or not their living conditions support or undermine these evolving capacities. Most importantly, governments are held responsible to take action to create conditions conducive for young children's capacities to evolve.

In 2008, the WHO Commission on the Social Determinants of Health recommended that "governments build universal coverage of a comprehensive package of quality early child development programs and services for children, mothers, and other caregivers, regardless of ability to pay."[72] To achieve this goal, the global community will need to work in new ways, collaborating across sectors at the international level. In particular, the WHO and UNICEF will need to create strengthened interagency mechanisms to ensure policy coherence for early child development such that a comprehensive approach to early child development is implemented.

At the level of individual countries, there is a need to commit to the following activities:

- Incorporating the science of early child development into policy
- Creating an inter-ministerial policy framework for ECD that clearly articulates the roles and responsibilities of each sector and how they will collaborate
- Integrating ECD policy elements into the agendas of each sector to ensure that they are considered routinely in sectoral decision-making
- Adopting social protection policies for the whole household that support an adequate income for all, maternity and pension benefits, and allow parents and caregivers to balance their time spent at home and work
- Putting systems in place to ensure that quality out-of-home community-based childcare relevant to local culture and context is available
- Encouraging international agencies, non-governmental organizations, and national governments to work collaboratively with community leaders to improve the capacity of local communities to develop and implement ECD programs, as well as to effectively participate in monitoring and reviewing ECD policies and programs
- Developing strategies for "scaling up" effective programs from local to national levels, without sacrificing the characteristics of the program that made it effective[73]

As the example of Cuba and the other successes described in this chapter show, these activities do not depend upon high levels of national wealth. Instead, they require a coherent, credible, functioning society willing to give priority to long-term investment in human development right from the start.

NOTES

1. Kuh, D., & Ben-Shlomo, Y. (Eds.). (2004). *A lifecourse approach to chronic disease epidemiology* (2nd ed.). New York: Oxford University Press.
2. Janus, M., & Offord, D. (2007). Development and psychometric properties of the Early Development Instrument (EDI): A measure of children's school readiness. *Canadian Journal of Behavioral Science, 39,* 1–22.
3. The cross-cultural sensitivity of the EDI is a matter of ongoing study and debate. So far, the EDI has been used in 14 high-, middle-, and low-income countries. Moreover, core EDI items have been included in the current version of UNICEF's MICS survey that goes to households

in 43 poor and middle-income countries. This reflects an informal consensus in the international development community that, although different cultures have different ideas of successful early development, the core domains of physical, social-emotional, language-cognitive-communication are common to all. The EDI has been most extensively used in Canada and Australia—countries with high rates of immigration from non-European countries—where up to 3% of the population is Aboriginal. In both countries, work to adapt the EDI to Aboriginal realities is ongoing. These efforts do not involve changing the core questions and domains of the EDI but, instead, include Aboriginal governance of data analysis and reporting (British Columbia), direct Aboriginal participation in data collection (Australia), and supplementary information collection (British Columbia and Australia).

4. Guhn, M., Gadermann, A., Hertzman, C., & Zumbo, B. (2010). Children's development in kindergarten: A multilevel, population-based analysis of ESL and gender effects on socioeconomic gradients. *Child Indicators Research, 3*, 183–203.
5. Janus & Offord. (2007). Development and psychometric properties.
6. Guhn, M., Janus, M., & Hertzman, C. (Eds.). (2007). Special issue: The early development instrument. *Early Education and Development, 18*(3), 427–452.
7. Forget-Dubois, N., Lemelin, J. P., Boivin, M., Dionne, G., Sguin, J. R., Vitaro, F., & Tremblay, R. E. (2007). Predicting early school achievement with the EDI: A longitudinal population-based study. *Early Education and Development, 18*(3), 405–426.
8. Houweling, T. A., Kunst, A. E., Looman C. W., & Mackenbach, J. P. (2005). Determinants of under-5 mortality among the poor and the rich: A cross-national analysis of 43 developing countries. *International Journal of Epidemiology, 34*, 1257–1265.
9. Adler, N. E., Boyce, T., Chesney, M. A., Cohen, S., Folkman, S., Kahn, R. L., & Syme, S. L. (1994). Socioeconomic status and health: The challenge of the gradient. *American Psychologist, 49*, 15–24.
10. Braveman, P., & Tarimo, E. (2002). Social inequalities in health within countries: Not only an issue for affluent nations. *Social Science and Medicine, 54*, 1621–1635.
11. Kunst, A. E., Geurts, J. J., & van den Berg, J. (1995). International variation in socioeconomic inequalities in self reported health. *Journal of Epidemiology and Community Health, 49*, 117–123.
12. Kunst, A. E., & Mackenbach, J. P. (1994). The size of mortality differences associated with educational level in nine industrialized countries. *American Journal of Public Health, 84*, 932–937.
13. van Doorslaer, E., et al. (1997). Income-related inequalities in health: Some international comparisons. *Journal of Health Economics, 16*, 93–112.
14. Houweling, T. A., Kunst, A. E., & Mackenbach, J. P. (2001). World health report 2000: Inequality index and socioeconomic inequalities in mortality. *Lancet, 357*, 1671–1672.
15. Smith, J. R., Brooks-Gunn, J., & Klebanov, P. K. (1997). The consequences of living in poverty for young children's cognitive and verbal ability and early school achievement. In G. J. Duncan, & J. Brooks-Gunn (Eds.), *Consequences of growing up poor.* New York: Russell Sage.
16. Willms, J. D. (2006). *Learning divides: Ten policy questions about the performance and equity of schools and schooling systems* (UIS Working Paper no. 5). Montreal: UNESCO Institute for Statistics.
17. Externalizing behaviors are often characterized by inattentive, impulsive, aggressive, and disruptive conduct (Spielberger, C. [Ed.]. [2004]. *Encyclopedia of applied psychology* Vol. 3. Boston: Elsevier Academic Press).
18. Bradley, R. H., & Corwyn, R. F. (2002). Socioeconomic status and child development. *Annual Review of Psychology, 53*, 371–399.
19. Siddiqi, A., Kawachi, I., Berkman, L., Subramanian, S. V., & Hertzman, C. (2007). Variation of socioeconomic gradients in children's development across advanced capitalist societies: Analysis of 25 OECD nations. *International Journal of Health Services Planning, Administration, Evaluation, 37*, 63–87.
20. UNESCO. (2007). *EFA global monitoring report: Strong foundations, early childhood care and education.* Paris: UNESCO.

21. Anderson, L. M., Shinn, C., Fullilove, M. T., Scrimshaw, S. C., Fielding, J. E., Normand, J., Carande-Kulis, V. G., & the Task Force on Community Preventative Services. (2003). The effectiveness of early childhood development programs. *American Journal of Preventive Medicine, 24*, 32–46.

22. National Institute of Child Health and Human Develoment (NICHD) Early Child Care Network. (1996). Characteristics of infant child care: Factors contributing to positive care-giving. *Early Childhood Research Quarterly, 11*, 269–306.

23. Clifford, D., Peisner-Feinberg, E., Culkin, M., Howes, C., & Kagan, S. L. (1998). Quality child care: Quality care does mean better child outcomes. *National Center for Early Development and Learning, Spotlight Series 2.*

24. Burchinal, M. R., & Cryer, D. (2003). Diversity, child care quality, and developmental outcomes. *Early Childhood Research Quarterly, 18*, 401–426.

25. Palfrey, J. S., Hauser-Cram, P., Bronson, M. B., & Warfield, M. E. (2005). The Brookline early education project: A 25-year follow-up study of a family-centered early health and development intervention. *Pediatrics, 116*, 144–152.

26. Ibid.

27. Temple, J. A., & Reynolds, A. J. (2007). Benefits and costs of investments in preschool education: Evidence from the child–parent centers and related programs. *Economics of Education Review, 26*, 126–144.

28. Grantham-McGregor, S., Cheung, Y. B., Cueto, S., Glewwe, P., Richter, L., & Strupp, B. (2007). Developmental potential in the first 5 years for children in developing countries. *Lancet, 369*, 60–70.

29. Behrman, J., Alderman, H., & Hoddinott, J. (2004). Hunger and malnutrition. In L. Bjorn (Ed.), *Global crises, global solutions.* Cambridge, UK: Cambridge University Press.

30. Fernald, L. C., Gertler, P. J., & Neufeld, L. M. (2008). Role of cash in conditional cash transfer programmes for child health, growth, and development: An analysis of Mexico's *Oportunidades. Lancet, 371*, 828–837.

31. Siddiqi, A., Irwin, L., & Hertzman, C. (2007). *Total environment assessment model for early child development.* Evidence report for the World Health Organization (WHO) Commission on the Social Determinants of Health. Geneva: WHO.

32. Acheson, D. (1998). *Independent inquiry into inequalities in health.* London: The Stationery Office, Government of the United Kingdom.

33. Melhuish, E., Belsky, J., Leyland, A. H., & Barnes, J. (2008). Effects of fully-established Sure Start Local Programmes on 3-year-old children and their families living in England: A quasi-experimental observational study. *Lancet, 372*, 1641–1647.

34. Hutchings, J., Bywater, T., Daley, D., et al. (2007). Parenting intervention in Sure Start services for children at risk of developing conduct disorder: Pragmatic randomised controlled trial. *British Medical Journal, 334*, 678–685.

35. Department for Children, Schools, and Families, Sure Start Children's Centres. (2009). *What's on offer?* Retrieved from http://www.dcsf.gov.uk/everychildmatters/earlyyears/surestart/surestartchildrenscentres/provision/onoffer/

36. Ruiz-Pelaez, J. G., Charpak, N., & Cuervo, L. G. (2004). Kangaroo mother care, an example to follow from developing countries. *British Medical Journal, 329*, 1179–1181.

37. Irwin, L., Siddiqi, A., & Hertzman, C. (2007). *Early child development: A powerful equalizer.* Report to the WHO International Commission on the Social Determinants of Health, Human Early Learning Partnership, Vancouver, Canada.

38. Siddiqi, Irwin, & Hertzman. (2007). *Total environment assessment model.*

39. World Health Organization Maximizing Positive Synergies Collaborative Group. (2009). An assessment of interactions between global health initiatives and country health systems. *Lancet, 373*, 2137–2169.

40. Reach Out and Read. *Reach out and read's evidence base.* Retrieved from http://www.reachoutandread.org/impact/evidencebase.aspx

41. NICHD Early Child Care Network. (1996). Characteristics of infant child care.

42. NICHD Early Child Care Research Network. (2002). Early child care and children's development prior to school entry: Results from the NICHD study of early child care. *American Educational Research Journal, 39*, 133–164.

43. Anderson, L. (2003). The effectiveness of early childhood development programs.

44. Evans, J. L. (1993). Health care: The care required to survive and thrive. Consultative group for early childhood care and development. *Coordinators' Notebook, 13*, 1–30.

45. Engle, P. L., Black, M. M., Behrman, J. R., Cabral de Mello, M., Gertler, P. J., Kapiriri, L., Martorell, R., Young, M. E., & The International Child Development Steering Group. (2007). Strategies to avoid the loss of developmental potential in more than 200 million children in the developing world. *Lancet, 369*, 229–242.

46. UNICEF. (2006). *State of the world's children 2007–women and children: The double dividend of gender equality.* New York: UNICEF. Retrieved from http://www.unicef.org/sowc07/

47. Evans. (1993). Health care.

48. Engle et al. (2007). Strategies to avoid the loss of developmental potential.

49. WHO. (2007). *Civil society report to the commission on the social determinants of health* (pp. 109–112). Geneva: WHO.

50. Casassus, J., Froemel, J. E., Palafox, J. C., & Cusato, S. (1998). *First international comparative study of language, mathematics, and associated factors for third and fourth grade primary school students.* Paris: UNESCO.

51. Knudsen, E. I., Heckman, J. J., Cameron, J. L., & Shonkoff, J. P. (2006). Economic, neurobiological, and behavioural perspectives on building America's future workforce. *Proceedings of the National Academy of Sciences USA, 103*, 10155–10162.

52. Carneiro, P., & Heckman, J. (2003). *Human capital policy.* Discussion Paper Series no. 821, pp. 1–107. Bonn: Institute for the Study of Labour.

53. Marmot, M., & Wilkinson, R. G. (Eds.). (1997). *Social determinants of health.* Oxford, UK: Oxford University Press.

54. UNESCO. (2007). *EFA global monitoring report.*

55. Schweinhart, L. J., Barnes, H. V., & Weikart, D. P. (1993). Significant benefits. The High/Scope Perry preschool study through age 27. In *Monographs of the High/Scope educational research foundation* Vol. 10. Ypsilanti, MI: Highscope Press.

56. Schweinhart, L. J., Montie, J., Xiang, Z., Barnett, W. S., Belfield, C. R., & Nores, M. (2005). Lifetime effects: The High/Scope Perry preschool study through age 40. In *Monographs of the HighScope educational research foundation* Vol. 14. Ypsilanti, MI: High/Scope Press.

57. Schweinhart, Barnes, & Weikart. (1993). Significant benefits.

58. Schweinhart, Montie, Xiang, Barnett, Belfield & Nores. (2005). Lifetime effects.

59. Cleveland, G., & Krushinsky, M. (1998). The benefits and costs of good child care: The economic rationale for public investment in young children—A policy study. In *Monograph no. 1.* Centre for Urban and Community Studies, University of Toronto at Scarborough.

60. Schweinhart, Barnes, & Weikart. (1993). Significant benefits.

61. Baldacci, E., Clements, B., Gupta, S., & Cui, Q. (2004). *Social spending, human capital, and growth in developing countries: Implications for achieving the MDGs* (IMF Working Paper no. WP/04/217). Washington, DC: International Monetary Fund.

62. Romer, P. (1986). Increasing returns and long-run growth. *Journal of Political Economy, 94*, 1002–1037.

63. Ravallion, M., & Chen, S. (1997). What can new survey data tell us about recent changes in distribution and poverty? *World Bank Economic Review, 11*, 357–382.

64. Sen, A. (1999). *Development as freedom.* New York: Knopf.

65. Hertzman, C., & Siddiqi, A. (2000). Health and rapid economic change in the late twentieth century. *Social Science and Medicine, 51*, 809–819.

66. Siddiqi, A., & Hertzman, C. (2001). Economic growth, income equality, and population health among the Asian Tigers. *International Journal of Health Services, 31*, 323–333.

67. Hertzman & Siddiqi. (2000). Health and rapid economic change.

68. Siddiqi & Hertzman. (2001). Economic growth, income equality, and population health.

69. Schady, N. R. (2000). The political economy of expenditures by the Peruvian social fund (FONCODES). *The American Political Science Review, 94*, 289–304.

70. Behrman, J. R., Cheng, Y., & Todd, P. (2004). Evaluating preschool programs when length of exposure to the program varies: A nonparametric approach. *Review of Economics and Statistics, 86*, 108–132.

71. Kikuchi-White, A. (2006). *General Comment 7: Implementing child rights in early childhood: Young children as active social participants.* The Netherlands: Bernard Van Leer Foundation.

72. CSDH. (2008). *Closing the gap in a generation: Health equity through action on the social determinants of health.* Final report of the Commission on Social Determinants of Health. Geneva: World Health Organization.

73. Hutchings, Bywater, & Daley, et al. (2007). Parenting intervention in Sure Start services.

12

Improving Boys' Achievement in Early Childhood and Primary Education

MERLE FROSCHL AND BARBARA SPRUNG

Overview

In many countries around the world, boys are not faring as well as girls academically. Comparative international testing such as the Programme for International Student Assessment (PISA) and the Trends in International Math and Science Study (TIMSS) has allowed governments to measure their students' achievement in comparison to other countries and has led many nations to reexamine their educational systems.[1] In the 2006 PISA tests, girls outperformed boys in reading in all of the Organisation for Economic Co-operation and Development (OECD) countries.[2] In the United States, research from the U.S. Department of Education documents that, by 12th grade, boys score 16 points lower in reading and 24 points lower in writing than girls.[3] A study of over 7,000 middle school students in Beijing, China, found that, although the achievement gap gradually decreased, girls outperformed boys throughout primary and middle school and had a more positive experience at school, and boys had a higher dropout rate by middle school.[4] The researchers found that primary school test scores were the only significant predictor of the gender achievement gap by the end of middle school, indicating that early intervention is necessary.

Countries around the world have varied reactions to the availability of international comparative data of student achievement and their implications for gender and education. For example, Scottish gender policies at the preschool level are much more influenced by the international comparative data and the "travelling discourse of the 'boys underachievement crisis'" that has resulted from it, whereas in Sweden gender equality has been continuously important since the 1970s, and gender policies have been much less influenced by the new data.[5] Smith argues that the result of international testing in the United States and the

United Kingdom is the emergence of a system of unprecedented national testing and target setting to eliminate underachievement.[6] In the United Kingdom, a specific focus has been placed on boys' underachievement as measured on the General Certificate of Secondary Education (GCSE).[7]

This chapter synthesizes research from the United States and from countries around the world that documents both the difficulties boys are experiencing in school and the strategies being employed to remedy the situation. The first part of the chapter discusses the increasingly academic, teacher-directed approach to early childhood education and describes how boys are faring in this environment, particularly in terms of the gap in academic achievement, high rates of expulsion, and disproportionate referral to special education for behavioral issues. A discussion of the particular risks facing African American and Latino boys in the United States is included. The second part of this chapter proposes strategies to reduce the negative educational outcomes that disproportionately affect boys during the early years and beyond. Subsequently, it brings to light programs that nations and states around the world have implemented or are currently implementing. The chapter concludes with recommended actions to improve boys' achievement in early childhood and primary education in the United States.

Impact of High-stakes Testing on Early Learning Environments

The standards movement and its corollary—high-stakes testing—have had an impact on early childhood education in ways that can have a detrimental effect on all children and that appear to affect boys particularly negatively. This trend in early childhood education is commonly referred to as "the push-down" curriculum.

Kindergartners spend an increasing amount of time being taught and tested in literacy and math in preparation for standardized tests. For example, three studies by researchers at the University of California–Los Angeles (UCLA), Sarah Lawrence College, and Long Island University, including surveys of 254 kindergarten teachers in New York City and Los Angeles, show that teacher-directed activities including literacy and math instruction take up most class time, and test preparation is a daily activity, limiting free play to 30 minutes or less a day.[8] In one research study, in half-day preschools, close to 20% of the day was spent on teacher-directed literacy and language activities; in kindergarten, it had increased to 28%; by first grade, it was 60% in the first 3 hours of the day; and by third grade, it was 48% of the entire school day.[9] In these teacher-directed classrooms, attention to developmental needs and principles of child development are sacrificed to raising test scores. In addition, literacy "instruction" often requires leveled reading books, which typically consist of dull stories and illustrations that are unlikely to build a love of reading.

This trend toward an increasingly scripted, standardized kindergarten classroom is in opposition to a growing body of evidence that supports the importance of social-emotional learning and a play-centered early childhood learning environment. A recent report by Miller and Almon maintains that the situation for young children deprived of a play-centered learning environment in early childhood has reached crisis proportions.[10] The report states that, on a typical day, children in all-day kindergartens spend 2–3 hours in literacy, math, and test-prep activities and as little as 30 minutes per day in free/choice time activities. It minces no words:

> Kindergartners are now under great pressure to meet inappropriate expectations, including academic standards that until recently were reserved for first grade. At the same time, they are being denied the benefits of play—a major stress reliever. This double burden, many experts believe, is contributing to a rise in anger and aggression in young children, reflected in increasing reports of severe behavior problems.[11]

A study on anxiety in children reported by Wenner measured how sweaty children's palms were, and showed that those allowed to play were less anxious.[12] The study concluded that children need play to promote physical and emotional health.

To create a learning environment in which social-emotional skill development is a high priority, teachers must be able to take the time and make the effort to reach every child on a relational level. In many early childhood classrooms, however, time and space for relationship-building has been sacrificed to time spent on worksheets and academic mandates that take up most of the school day.

Impact of Early Academic Learning Environments on Boys

ACADEMIC ACHIEVEMENT

Evidence links the increased focus on scripted learning in early childhood education to boys' academic disadvantage. A study following 183 African American children from a low socioeconomic background compared and followed until the fourth grade students who attended three kinds of preschools: academically focused, child-initiated, and both academically focused and child-initiated.[13] The research revealed that the smallest gender gap by the fourth grade was for those boys in the child-initiated preschool class, indicating that those who had the opportunity to be involved in active, self-initiated learning were better able to cope with new demands.

STIGMATIZING AND EXPELLING BOYS EARLY

Boys are disproportionately at risk of expulsion in the early years. During interviews, many teachers were willing to admit that they were unable to handle boys they considered to be overactive or to have behavioral problems. When asked if they had expelled a child from their classroom in the last 12 months, one in ten teachers replied that they had. The resulting report, *Prekindergarteners Left Behind: Expulsion Rates in State Prekindergarten Programs*, documents the alarming rate of expulsions at the preschool level, particularly among African American boys.[14] Studying a sample of almost 5,000 state funded pre-kindergarten classrooms across the United States, Gilliam found that the likelihood of expulsion dropped when the teacher had an ongoing relationship with a classroom-based behavioral consultant. This relationship may also be because of other factors, including greater resources overall; however, the pronounced differences of expulsion rates when consultants are available is significant. Gilliam also found that the likelihood of expulsion increased with larger class sizes.

In 2000, based on 3 years of participant observation research at an elementary school, Ferguson published *Bad Boys: Public School in the Making of Black Masculinity*.[15] The author focused on the situation for African American boys and offered an account of daily interactions between teachers and students to understand why African American males are disproportionately getting in trouble and being suspended from school. On the issue of exclusion, a 2006 study on the instructional and emotional climate in 100 randomly selected Pre-K to K classrooms documented that African American boys were stigmatized as "bad boys" and "troublemakers," made to sit in isolation next to the teacher's desk while other children sat at group tables, and often shunned by other children.[16] The study found that children picked up on the bad boy label, and, once labeled, the stigmatization followed the boy from grade to grade.[17] As one researcher said, "I observed it over and over again. And it wasn't just that it was only boys, it was always, always, black boys."[18]

Once a child is labeled as a troublemaker, the label is passed on from teacher to teacher, and the process of disengagement from school is under way. Why would any child want to stay in a place where he is made to feel ashamed, isolated, and not liked? Expelling a boy from preschool or stigmatizing him as "bad" from the time he enters school is the beginning of the achievement gap that leads to a high school dropout rate that limits the potential of far too many children and deprives society of a vast pool of human talent. Like African American boys, Latino boys are also particularly at risk in this regard: Although the national average for high school completion is 70%, the percentage decreases to 50% for African American, Latino, and Native American populations, and only an estimated 48% of Latino boys graduate on time.[19] In addition, although Latinos make up 19% of school-aged children in the United States, they comprise 40% of high school dropouts.[20] The dropout rate has reached crisis proportions: Schools are not meeting the needs of the fastest growing ethnic group in the United States.[21]

REFERRAL TO SPECIAL EDUCATION

Although there are children for whom special education is beneficial, one way in which teachers deal with "problem" boys is to refer them to special education.[22] The statistics bear this out: Boys comprise two-thirds of the special education population, are two and one half times as likely as girls to be diagnosed with attention-deficit hyperactivity disorder (ADHD),[23] are four times as likely as girls to be referred to a school psychologist,[24] and comprise 80% of children who are diagnosed with emotional disturbance or autism.[25] A disproportionate number of these boys are African American. In 2000–2001, African American boys made up 8.6% of national public school enrollment, but 20% of those classified as mentally retarded, 21% of those classified as emotionally disturbed, 22% of those expelled from school, and 23% of those suspended.[26]

Strategies to Promote Equity in the Early Years

EARLY INTERVENTION

Substantial evidence suggests that early childhood programs can have long-term positive effects that include better educational and social outcomes, particularly for boys from at-risk groups.[27,28] A 15-year follow-up study of the Chicago Child–Parent Centers Program including 989 low-income children in public schools found that children who participated in the preschool intervention had a higher rate of school completion; 49.7% versus 38.5%.[29]

DEVELOPING SOCIAL-EMOTIONAL COMPETENCE

Social-emotional competence is at the core of early childhood education for all children. As defined by the Collaborative for Academic, Social, and Emotional Learning (CASEL), there are five key components to social-emotional competency. They include the ability to calm oneself when angry, initiate friendships, resolve conflicts respectfully, make ethical and safe choices, and contribute constructively to the community.[30] Researchers believe that social-emotional skills such as self-awareness, self-discipline, persistence, and empathy are as vital as cognitive skills measured by IQ and achievement tests.[31] A meta-analysis of 200 research studies conducted by CASEL shows that children who attend programs that focus on social-emotional development do better academically, have higher rates of attendance, and are safer in school.[32]

Recent research documents that teachers of grades K–5 who provide high levels of emotional and instructional support close the achievement gap for at-risk children.[33] In fact, a longitudinal study showed that students who received intervention strategies to help with their social development in grades 1–6 had reduced rates of violence and use of alcohol, were more likely to complete high school, are above the median in socioeconomic status and education by ages 24 and 27, and have fewer mental health and sexual health problems.[34] The differences begin to show up in the teen years, which, in many cases, is a particularly stressful period.

Other research has shown that prosocial behavior in the classroom is connected with positive intellectual outcomes and achievement on standardized tests.[35] Rigorous experimental studies of several programs including PATHS, Second Step, Steps to Respect, and Caring School Communities show reduction in aggression and disruptive behavior, decrease in antisocial behavior and increase in socially competent behavior, and reduction in bullying.[36] In addition, a study on dropout prevention in Quebec, Canada, surveying over 13,000 students found that a focus on the socioemotional learning environment promotes achievement and reduces dropout.[37]

Many guides to implementation exist. In the third edition of NAEYC's *Developmentally Appropriate Practice in Early Childhood Programs*, editors Copple and Bredekamp provide an essential guide to principles of high-quality education for children ages 0 through 8 and for building social-emotional skills in the current educational climate.[38] Their main focus is on a comprehensive, effective curriculum that fosters cognitive, social, emotional, and physical learning based on interrelationships and sequences of ideas differentiated for each child. Copple and Bredekamp also focus on both child- and teacher-guided experiences, including play and planned curriculum.[39] In *Me, You, Us: Social-Emotional Learning in Preschool,* Epstein offers a highly practical approach to addressing the whole range of social-emotional learning, including self-identity, empathy, competence, and community within the school, the home, and the larger community.[40]

The HighScope Research Foundation suggests the following classroom practices to promote social-emotional development in preschool: arrange and equip classrooms for social play, implement predictable schedules and routines, plan transitions, and create opportunities for sociodramatic play. To promote specific social-emotional knowledge and skills, they recommend modeling behavior, coaching children by breaking behavior into sequenced steps, and providing opportunities for practice.[41]

Guidance that begins in preschool is another strategy to help children develop social-emotional skills that make school a more successful experience for them. Strategies include rethinking the physical setup and learning environment of the classroom with children's needs in mind (e.g., modifying the classroom to include indoor/outdoor large motor and whole body experiences, sensory and experimentation experiences, building and construction experiences, and novel dramatic play experiences), as well as rethinking literacy choices. This nonpunitive approach guides teachers toward making classrooms more conducive to active learning. Guidance involves understanding a child from the perspective of child development, teaching nonviolent problem-solving skills, and helping children learn how to express a full range of emotions.[42] Having guidance counselors available in preschool would help to mitigate the issues of expulsion and stigmatization discussed earlier in this chapter.

EMPHASIZING RELATIONAL TEACHING

When pre-K, kindergarten, and primary grade children have warm, caring relationships with their teachers, these relationships foster development and learning.[43] There are four central features of a "trustworthy teaching–learning relationship": the teacher's capacity to be connected to her or his students, the teacher's genuine interest in nurturing students' own ideas, collaborative study on the part of teacher and students, and an environment in which trust can prevail.[44]

Relational teaching involves taking time to know each individual child's strengths and weaknesses, and adapting the curriculum and learning environment to meet his or her needs. It involves talking one-on-one with a child to find out his or her interests, and shaping learning activities around them. It also means knowing a child's family environment and what stressful situations might affect his or her school day. Raider-Roth describes relational teaching as, "knowing their journey." She led a Teaching Boys Study Group through a series of descriptive and associative processes to help teachers examine their relationships with the boys they were teaching and the way in which their relationships shaped boys' learning.[45]

At the preschool level, relationships with adults and peers are at the heart of helping young children learn. Recently, researchers have looked at how the relational life of a classroom shapes social-emotional development and learning, particularly for boys. In 2000, Chu studied the centrality of relationships from the young boy's point of view. In her ethnographic studies of boys, she examined boys' experiences of gender socialization and explored how boys negotiate their senses of self, behaviors, and relationships in light of cultural constructions of masculinity. She concluded that boys learn to anticipate how others will respond to them and accordingly modify their self-expression and styles of relating.[46] In a yearlong study conducted by Raider-Roth, a group of teachers, pre-K through high school, met monthly to describe individual children in their classes using the Descriptive Review process, a process in which teachers take the time to look at something deeply using descriptive rather than evaluative language. In this particular case, the research focused on the teachers' relationship with children and how the notions of gender shaped those relationships. At the end of the study, teachers reported an overall shift in their relationship with the observed students; their understanding of boys had changed.[47]

REVIVING PLAY IN THE EARLY CHILDHOOD CURRICULUM

Early childhood educators are in agreement that reviving play in early childhood classrooms is a strategy that is beneficial to all children. The Alliance for Childhood, the National Association for the Education of Young Children, and renowned child psychologists have been advocating for the return of a more playful and less academic environment in preschool, kindergarten, and even in the early primary grades.[48–50] In "The Importance of Being Playful," Bedrova and Leong draw on the work of Piaget and Vygotsky, early childhood psychologists whose research made clear the connections between play and cognition in young children. Their research revealed that "mature" play, guided by a teacher to help children plan, assign roles, and select props for their scenarios resulted in greater gains in literacy skills and concepts, social skills, and regulation of physical and cognitive behaviors than did activities in classrooms where play was minimal and the focus was on academics.[51] In addition, Pellegrini, an educational psychologist, found that "successful peer interaction at recess was an excellent predictor of success on standardized tests."[52]

FOSTERING EARLY LITERACY

When appealing stories are read to children daily, they become motivated to become literate readers and writers. Paley, a noted early childhood educator, speaks about the importance of children's stories in the development of language. She encourages 2-year-olds to use their limited vocabulary to tell stories, and by the time they are 5, girls and boys in her classrooms weave rich tales and develop plays with multiple characters.[53] In addition, early childhood educators have been urged to move away from the direct instruction and scripted literacy curricula that is now the norm in so many settings, and to refocus on children's natural and spontaneous capacities to engage in sociodramatic play and storytelling as the foundation for literacy.[54]

A number of strategies for elementary and middle school boys have proven successful in terms of promoting literacy. These include, as Daniel Casciato describes, reading groups led by males held in libraries;[55] adults reading to boys while they wait for a turn in the barbershop;[56] and multimedia projects that engage boys in producing videos and music.[57] A 7-year longitudinal study in Clackmannanshire, Scotland, involving 300 children compared a whole language approach, a mixture of whole language and phonics, and a purely phonics approach to reading.[58] The study reported that synthetic phonics was highly effective and led to serious gains in reading for all children, especially boys.

CHANGING CLASSROOM PRACTICE

In 2000, the Educational Equity Center at AED (now Educational Equity Center at FHI 360) began an initiative, The Raising and Educating Healthy Boys Project. As a first step, the Project conducted nine focus groups with pre-K–Grade 3 teachers and parents in both urban and suburban settings to learn about boys' experiences, how boys are perceived, and to explore strategies for change. It became clear that, although parents and teachers were aware that boys are not faring well in school, concerted strategies for change were scattered. In 2004, as a result of the research, the Project issued a report reflecting the consensus that there is a growing crisis in boys' education, and that early childhood, a high-risk time for boys, is an opportune time to intervene.[59]

In 2010, as a direct result of the Project, *Supporting Boys' Learning: Strategies for Teacher Practice Pre-K–Grade 3* was published to address the needs of boys at the early childhood level. Suggested strategies include incorporating classroom practice that intentionally counter prevalent stereotypes about boys, fitting relational teaching into the mandated curriculum, finding books that are of interest to boys and engaging them in language development through play, building physical activities into the mandated curriculum, observing and recording boys' behaviors to ascertain and meet their needs, and building engagement through small group projects based on boys' interests.[60]

Strategies to Promote Equity Beyond the Early Years

Achievement gaps that begin in early childhood often affect achievement later in the course of school life. This section explores strategies to address educational gender gaps that appear in secondary and postsecondary education.

The Maine Boys Network, a statewide group of activists and educators dedicated to promoting school success for all boys, conducted 72 focus groups in 14 of Maine's 16 counties with 541 boys and young men in elementary, middle and high school, and some colleges to hear from boys of all ages and socioeconomic classes about how they view school.[61] The study, part of a statewide effort to understand the gender divide between male and female achievement at all levels of education, showed that the decline in high school graduation is larger for boys than girls and that there is a 10% gap between genders in college attendance. The focus groups were moderated by members of the Maine Boys Network, and in some cases, by male and female college students who were enrolled in a course on boys' development. Ten questions were asked about boys' impressions of school. For example: Why do you think some students don't care about school? How is school different for boys and girls? Are there adults in the building who understand you? What do you think makes a teacher effective?

The study revealed that boys feel under scrutiny from teachers and are disciplined for minor infractions, both male and female teachers were perceived as favoring girls, and some boys felt divided between the push to pursue higher education and the physical labor their fathers did. Based on what they learned from the voices of boys and young men throughout the state of Maine, the following recommendations were made: ensure that every student has at least one teacher that knows him or her well, model appropriate and respectful behaviors, express interest in what matters to boys, provide more choices within the school day, create opportunities for open dialogues about topics of interest to boys, and develop a school-wide culture of trust, acceptance, and support.

In *No Map to Manhood*, Kleinfeld discusses the gender gap in postsecondary enrollment based on interviews conducted with 99 male and female high school seniors. She suggests several strategies to increase the number of young men who go to college, including providing boys with information about the changing job market, since many boys from working class families still think they can get well-paid jobs with a high school diploma, and opening boys' minds up to new and exciting careers in emergency medical services, justice, and law enforcement. She also suggests combining high school courses with courses offered on college campuses to entice young men into higher education. Finally, she suggests making classrooms more boy friendly by allowing more movement and physical activity.[62]

The Schott Foundation, in addition to reporting on the disturbing statistics about disengagement and the appalling school dropout rate of young African American males, has identified and highlighted high schools of excellence that are successful in creating a challenging environment that results in higher graduation rates for African American males. The strategies for success are highly visible arts programs, well-equipped libraries and laboratories, music courses, high expectations for all students, strong curriculum, and an expectation of personal responsibility.[63] Addressing the same issue for Latino boys, Soza of Arizona State University presents best practices nationwide used to combat the status quo, including small learning communities within schools, culturally relevant curriculum including the history and culture of the Latino experience, academic/personal mentoring, manageable school reform focusing on cooperation between the public and charter/alternative schools, and community-school support cooperatives.[64] Rodriguez of Florida State University recommends listening to the "perspectives, experiences, and voices of the students at the center of inquiry," and creating creative pedagogies that bring together traditional curricula and popular culture.[65]

Nation- and State-wide Programs

Thus far, this chapter has reviewed how school systems struggle with gendered achievement gaps and how they have developed a variety of strategies to remedy the situation. In some global instances, action has been taken at the highest levels of government. Policies have been written at the state level and implemented in school districts across Australia, Great Britain, New Zealand, and Belize. These policies address professional development for teachers, curriculum, guidance and counseling, and parent influences, and interventions took place over several years. The research and products from these efforts are now available in books, on CD-ROMs, and online to the next generation of educators.

As an example, in 1997, the Australian government launched Success for Boys,[66] and over 5 years, allocated $27 million to support more than 550 schools throughout the country in the development of effective teaching practices and strategies for boys' success in school. The national government acted as a catalyst for states and local communities to support the program with additional funds. The guiding principles of the program included collecting data, implementing a flexible school-wide approach with a person and team responsible, ensuring good teaching for all students, clarifying and supplying the supports that boys require, catering to different learning styles of boys, recognizing that gender matters and challenging stereotypes, developing positive relationships, providing positive male role models, focusing on literacy, and using information and communication technologies as a valuable learning tool.[67]

In Great Britain, the Raising Boys' Achievement Project[68] was a 4-year study (2000–2004) that focused on apparent differential academic achievement of boys and girls at key stages in their education. The study, undertaken by the National Department for Education and Skills, focused on literacy in primary schools and intervention strategies aimed at reading, writing, speaking, and listening. As in Australia, the British study engaged in a whole-school systemic approach and, in some cases, single-sex classes raised student achievement for both boys and girls. Intervention strategies were grouped around the following: pedagogic, classroom-based approaches centered on teaching and learning; individual approaches, including target-setting and mentoring; organized learning at the whole-school level; and sociocultural learning environments in which boys and girls felt able to work with, rather than against, the aims and aspirations of the school. The project also addressed "laddish masculinity" and "ladettish femininity," British terms for gender stereotypical attitudes and behaviors.

In the United States, efforts have taken place at both the grassroots and state levels. The RULER Approach is a comprehensive, school-wide, evidence-based program to teach social-emotional literacy to elementary school students. RULER is an acronym for Recognizing, Understanding, Labeling, Expressing, and Regulating emotion. Stakeholders include students, teachers, special service providers, support staff, school leaders, and families. Developed by researchers at Yale University, the RULER approach makes social-emotional learning central to success in school.[69]

Alaska has a statewide effort that has been duplicated in the state of Maine. Based at the University of Alaska, The Boys' Project[70] defines five strategies for connecting boys to schools. The project seeks to educate teachers on gender differences in development and learning; start school at a later age for slower developing boys; create "focus schools" offering nurturing, personalized education; connect boys in groups with caring adults; and respect boys.

Project GRAD (Graduation Really Achieves Dreams)[71] is another comprehensive effort to close the achievement gap for low-income minority students, with a focus on males. GRAD sites exist in several states including New Jersey, Ohio, Tennessee, Georgia, and Texas. The GRAD program requires all teachers to vote on accepting the program, and trains them on their particular approach to teaching reading, mathematics, and classroom management to be used for all grades, starting in preschool. GRAD focuses on basic skills as a foundation for high academic standards in the arts, humanities, social sciences, sciences, and technology.[72] An evaluation of Project GRAD by the MDRC found that the most value added was in districts that have low achievement and high levels of disadvantaged and minority students.[73]

Recommended Actions

This chapter has documented that boys, particularly African American and Latino boys, are not faring as well as girls in school and society. Research demonstrates that they are disengaged from school, often beginning in early childhood, and the disengagement grows throughout elementary school, middle school, high school and college. Although there are excellent efforts taking place in the United States to address issues such as high school dropout rates and declining college enrollment at higher levels of education, we believe that efforts must begin at the early childhood level and that they must be systemic in nature. The following are recommended actions:

EARLY CHILDHOOD EDUCATION

- Return to a focus on social-emotional skill development and a play-centered learning environment that includes ample opportunities for relational and active learning. The research has clearly demonstrated that this approach is most beneficial for all young children and may be particularly effective in reducing the negative educational outcomes that boys are facing.
- Provide guidance. Early childhood teachers need access to guidance professionals who can help them develop strategies for addressing the needs of every child. Having access to this process would mitigate the expulsion of children from preschool and the stigmatization of boys with behavioral problems.

TEACHER EDUCATION INSTITUTIONS

- Require teacher education institutions to include coursework on gender issues to better understand the needs of boys and girls. At present, gender issues are included at the discretion of individual professors.
- Provide textbooks addressing boys' and girls' needs at every level.
- Require in-service education courses that focus on gender issues to be an ongoing part of professional development for classroom teachers.

CLOSING THE LITERACY GAP

- Create a national effort to turn research on boys' literacy development into practice.

- Require teacher education institutions to incorporate studies about what boys as well as girls *do* like to read, how to use mixed media to engage all children, and the importance of providing male role models who read for pleasure and information. In addition to phonics, whole language, word recognition, and all the other aspects of teaching literacy, teacher education institutions and providers of in-service courses need to develop teachers who convey their love of reading by reading stories to children in every grade.

SCALING UP

- Use the Maine Boys Network as a model for statewide initiatives to address boys' educational needs, with funding (state and/or federal) available to carry out activities.
- Hold a White House conference on boys to highlight the need for national efforts.
- Create a National Boys' Task Force using federal funding streams.

EDUCATIONAL POLICY

- Replace the high-stakes testing movement with a system of assessment that evaluates progress in various ways to capture student performance. Teacher insights and portfolios of student work should be employed along with testing to provide a rounded picture that takes into account the talents, special interests, and learning style of each individual child.

Conclusion

The lack of success that young boys are experiencing is a gender equity issue, and it calls for the intentional focus and concerted effort that worked so well over the past several decades to address gender issues in girls' education. For example, in the early 1970s, researchers, policy-makers, teachers, and parents began to question why girls in general did not seem interested or adept in the areas of science and math, and weren't engaged in strenuous physical activity or playing sports. They concluded that it wasn't because girls weren't capable in all those areas, but that because of socialization practices, teacher and parental expectations, and media messages, girls learned that these areas "were not for them." When educators at all levels became aware that girls were not developing their potential in large areas of the curriculum, they created and implemented intervention strategies, including nonbiased curriculum; terminology that was inclusive of males and females; provision of role models and mentors; professional development workshops and in-service courses on how to avoid sex role stereotyping; media campaigns that advocated for gender inclusion and a more positive view of women and girls; and legislation, such as Title IX, prohibiting gender-bias in education. Girls now have higher high school grade point averages, are more widely represented as school valedictorians, and attend and graduate from college in greater numbers than do boys.[74] Although much more remains to be done, changes for girls occurred because attention was paid.

The focus of this chapter is the negative effect of current early learning environments on the educational experiences and outcomes of boys. And, as it was for girls, attention must be paid. The research makes it clear that boys are not faring well in school, from preschool through postsecondary education. The lag in literacy and writing that grows larger as the school years go by makes it difficult to do college level work; lack of success is followed by disengagement from school, and disengagement leads to dropping out for too many boys, particularly African American and Latino boys. Dropping out of school as the world moves from an industrial to an information-based economy results in unemployment, underemployment, or jobs at the lowest pay scales.

In the United States, grassroots efforts are admirable but scattered; statewide and district-level efforts are excellent, but too few. Advocacy and years of work led to federal legislation such as Title IX and the Women's Educational Equity Act that opened up new avenues of opportunity for girls. Advocacy is needed at the national level for policies and scaled-up programs that address boys' well-being and success in school.

Acknowledgements

The authors would like to thank Leslie Suss, Research Assistant, for her keen insight and excellent research skills which contributed immeasurably to this chapter.

NOTES

1. Smith, E. (2010). Underachievement, failing youth and moral panics. *Evaluation & Research in Education, 23*(1), 37.
2. Watson, A., Kehler, M., & Martino, W. (2010). 'The problem of boys' literacy underachievement: Raising some questions. *Journal of Adolescent and Adult Literacy, 53*(5), 356.
3. U.S. Department of Education. (2004). *Trends in educational equity of girls and women.* Washington, DC: U.S. Department of Education—Institute of Education Sciences NCES.
4. Lai, F. (2010). Are boys left behind? The evolution of the gender achievement gap in Beijing's middle schools. *Economics of Education Review, 29*(3), 383.
5. Edström, C. (2009). Preschool as an arena of gender policies: The examples of Sweden and Scotland. *European Education Research Journal, 8*(4), 534.
6. Smith. (2010). Underachievement, failing youth and moral panics.
7. Ibid.
8. Miller, E., & Almon, J. (2009). *Crisis in the kindergarten: Why children need to play in school.* College Park, MD: Alliance for Childhood.

9. Hamre, B., & Pianta, R. C. (2007). Learning opportunities in preschool & early elementary classrooms. In R. C. Pianta, M. J. Cox, & K. S. Snow (Eds.), *School readiness and the transition to kindergarten in the era of accountability*. Baltimore: Paul H. Brookes Publishing.

10. Miller & Almon. (2009). *Crisis in the kindergarten*.

11. Ibid., p. 11.

12. Wenner, M. (2009). The serious need for play. *Scientific American Mind, 20*(1), 22.

13. Marcon, R. A. (2002). Moving up the grades: Relationship between preschool model and later school success. *Early Childhood Research and Practice, 4*(1), 1.

14. Gilliam, W. S. (2005). *Prekindergarteners left behind: Expulsion rates in state prekindergarten programs*. Policy Brief, Series no. 3. New York: Foundation for Child Development.

15. Ferguson, A. A. (2000). *Bad boys: Public school in the making of black masculinity*. Ann Arbor, MI: University of Michigan Press.

16. Barbarin, O., & Crawford, G. M. (2006). Acknowledging and reducing stigmatization of African American boys. *Young Children, 61*(6), 79.

17. Ibid.

18. Ibid., p. 80.

19. Bridgeland et al. (2006) and Levin (2009), as reported in Hudock, M. (2009). Review of *Latino dropouts in rural America: Realities and possibilities*, by C. Hondo, M. E. Gardiner, & Y. Sapien. *Journal of Education Students Placed At Risk (JESPAR), 14*(3), 275.

20. Ibid.

21. Soza, R. A. (2007). *Pathways to prevention: The Latino male dropout crisis*. Phoenix: Arizona State University's Center for Community Development and Civil Rights.

22. Haggerty, J. J. (2009). Gender disparity: Boys v. girls in special education. Unpublished paper. Retrieved August 10, 2010, http://works.bepress.com/jennifer_haggerty/1

23. Conference on Minorities in Special Education, Harvard Civil Rights Project, March 2001.

24. U.S. Department of Education. (2003). *25th Annual report to congress*. Washington, DC: U.S. Department of Education. Office of Special Education Programs.

25. Kindlon, D. & Thompson, M. (1999). *Raising Cain: Protecting the emotional life of boys*. New York: Ballantine Books.

26. Smith, R. A. (2002). Black boys: The litmus test for "No Child Left Behind". *Education Week, 22*(9), 40.

27. Reynolds, A. J., Temple, J. A., Robertson, D. L., & Mann, E. A. (2001). Long-term effects of an early childhood on educational achievement and juvenile arrest: A 15-year follow-up of low-income children in public schools. *Journal of the American Medical Association, 285*(18), 2339.

28. Barnett, W. S. (1995). Long-term effects of early childhood programs on cognitive and school outcomes. The Future of Children, *5*(3), 25-50; Campbell, F. A., Helms, R., Sparling, J. J., & Ramey, C. T. (1998). Early childhood programs and success in school. In S. Barnett & S. Boocock (Eds.), *Early childhood care and education for Children in Poverty*. Albany, NY: State University of New York Press; Reynolds, A. J., Temple, J. A., Robertson, D. L., & Mann, E. A. (2001). Long-term effects of an early childhood intervention on educational achievement and juvenile arrest: A 15-year follow-up of low-income children in public schools, Journal of American Medical Association *285*, 2339–2346, as reported in Ou, S. R. (2005). Pathways of long-term effects of an early intervention program on educational attainment: Findings from the Chicago longitudinal study. *Applied Developmental Psychology, 26*, 578.

29. Ibid.

30. Collaborative for Academic, Social, and Emotional Learning (CASEL). (2007). *Background on social and emotional learning*. CASEL briefs. Chicago: CASEL.

31. Goleman, D. (1995). *Emotional intelligence: Why it can happen*. New York: Bantam Books.

32. Payton, J., et al. (2008). *The positive impact of social and emotional learning for kindergarten to eighth-grade students*. Chicago: CASEL. Retrieved February 17, 2010, http://www.casel.org/pub/reports.php

33. Pianta, Cox, & Snow. (2007). *School readiness and the transition to kindergarten*.

34. Hawkins, J. D., Kosterman, R., Catalano, R. F., Hill, K. G., & Abbott, R. D. (2005). Promoting positive adult functioning through social development intervention in childhood. *American Medical Association, Archives of Pediatrics & Adolescent Medicine, 159*(1).

35. Zins, J. E., Bloodworth, M. R., Weissberg, R. P., & Walberg, H. J. (2007). The scientific base linking social and emotional learning to school success. *Journal of Educational and Psychological Consultation, 17*(2), 191.

36. Osher, D., Bear, G. G., Sprague, J. R., & Doyle, W. (2010). How can we improve school discipline? *Educational Researcher, 39*(1), 48.

37. Archambault, I., Janosz, M., Morizot, J., & Pagani, L. (2009). Adolescent behavioral, affective, and cognitive engagement in school: Relationship to dropout. *Journal of School Health, 79*(9), 408.

38. Copple, C., & Bredekamp, S. (Eds.). (2009). *Developmentally appropriate practice in early childhood programs: Serving children from birth through age 8*. Washington, DC: National Association for the Education of Young Children.

39. Ibid.

40. Epstein, A. S. (2009). *Me, you, us: Social-emotional learning in preschool*. Ypsilanti, MI: HighScope Press.

41. Ibid.

42. Gartrell, D. (2004). *The power of guidance: Teaching social-emotional skills in early childhood classrooms*. Clifton Park, NY: Thompson Delmar Learning.

43. Pianta, Cox, & Snow. (2007). *School readiness and the transition to kindergarten.*

44. Raider-Roth, M. B. (2005). *Trusting what you know: The high stakes of classroom relationships*. San Francisco: Jossey-Boss.

45. Raider-Roth, M. (2003, April). *Knowing their journey: Understanding the complexities of teaching boys: A documentary account*. Presentation at American Educational Research Association annual conference, Chicago, IL.

46. Chu, J. Y. (2000). *Learning what boys know: An observational and interview study with six four-year-old boys*. Unpublished doctoral dissertation, Harvard University, Cambridge, Massachusetts.

47. Raider-Roth. (2005). *Trusting what you know.*

48. Miller & Almon. (2009). *Crisis in the kindergarten.*

49. Copple & Bredekamp. (2009). *Developmentally appropriate practice in early childhood programs.*

50. Elkind, D. (2006). *The power of play: How spontaneous, imaginative activities lead to happier, healthier children*. Cambridge, MA: DeCapo Press.

51. Bedrova, E., & Leong, D. J. (2003). The importance of being playful. *Educational Leadership, 60*(7), 50.

52. Tyre, P. (2008). *The trouble with boys: A surprising report card on our sons, their problems at schools, and what parents and educators must do* (p. 105). New York: Crown Publishers.

53. Paley, V. G. (1997). *The girl with the brown crayon: How children use stories to shape their lives*. Cambridge, MA: Harvard University Press.

54. Genishi, C., & Dyson, A. H. (2009). *Children, language and literacy: Diverse learners in diverse times*. New York: Teachers College Press.

55. Casciato, D. (2005, October 27). Group aims to make reading a guy thing. *Pittsburgh Tribune-Review*. Retrieved December 21, 2010, http://www.pittsburghlive.com/x/pittsburghtrib/s_387390.html

56. Brinson, S. A. (2007). Boys booked on barbershops: A cutting-edge literacy program. *Young Children, 62*, 42–48.

57. Hull, G. A., Kenney, N. L., Marple, S., & Forman-Schneider, A. (2006). Many versions of masculine: An exploration of boys' identity formation through digital storytelling in an after-school program. *Afterschool Matters, 6*(Occasional Paper Series).

58. Ellis, S. (2007). Policy and research: Lessons from the Clackmannanshire synthetic phonics initiative. *Journal of Early Childhood Literacy, 7*(3), 281.

59. Froschl, M., & Sprung, B. (2005). *Raising and educating healthy boys: A report on the growing crisis in boys' education*. New York: Educational Equity Center at AED.

60. Sprung, B., Froschl, M. & Gropper, N. (2010). *Supporting boys' learning: Strategies for teacher practice, pre-K–grade 3*. New York: Teachers College Press.

61. Maine Boys Network. (2008). *The gender divide in academic engagement—Perspectives from Maine boys and young men*. A Maine Boys Network report. Portland: Maine Boys Network.

62. Kleinfeld, J. (2009). No map to manhood: Male and female mindsets behind the college gender gap. *Gender Issues, 26*, 171.
63. Holzman, M. (2006). *The 2006 state report card, public education & black male students.* Boston: Schott Foundation for Public Education.
64. Ibid.
65. Rodriguez, L. E. (2008). Latino school dropout and popular culture: Envisioning solutions to a pervasive problem. *Journal of Latino's and Education, 7*(3), 262.
66. Australian Government Department of Education. *Employment and workplace relations.* Retrieved August 10, 2010, http://www.deewr.gov.au/Schooling/BoysEducation/Pages/success_for_boys.aspx
67. A planning guide and four modules are now available online at http://catalogue.nla.gov.au/Record/3772868.
68. Cambridge University Faculty of Education. *Raising boys achievement.* Retrieved August 10, 2010, http://www-rba.educ.cam.ac.uk
69. Emotionally Literate Schools. *The RULER approach to social and emotional learning.* Retrieved August 23, 2010, www.therulerapproach.org
70. The Boys Project. *The boys project home.* Retrieved from www.boysproject.net, 2010.
71. Project GRAD USA. *Our model.* Retrieved August 17, 2010, http://www.projectgrad.org/site/pp.asp?c=fuLTJeMUKrH&b=365977, 2010.
72. Ibid.
73. Snipes, J. C., Holton, G. I., & Doolittle, F. (2006). *Charting a path to graduation: The effect of project GRAD on elementary school student outcomes in four urban school districts.* New York: MDRC.
74. Sadowski, M. (2010). Putting the "boy crisis" in context. *Harvard Education Letter, 26*(4).

13

Equity for Indigenous Children in Early Childhood Education

JESSICA BALL

Globally, Indigenous and ethnic-minority populations and the children of immigrants are less likely to participate in early childhood care and education (ECCE) than is the average child in their country. These disparities persist despite increased recognition of the benefits of ECCE for all children and its equalizing impact for those who are disadvantaged.[1,2] This chapter explores how early childhood initiatives provided to Indigenous young children can enhance opportunities for early learning and foster a sense of identity and belonging, while equalizing readiness for formal schooling. The chapter suggests ways that key actors can work more systematically to ensure access to quality ECCE for Indigenous children, and highlights the need to bring Indigenous parents and community representatives into decision-making about the goals for ECCE and preferred avenues for achieving them.

An estimated 370 million Indigenous people live in the world.[3] Indigenous populations tend to have a young demographic, due to high birth rates combined with comparatively short life expectancies. Indigenous young children are arguably the most socially excluded population in the world today, and their quality of life very often provides suboptimal conditions for health, development, and early learning. In addition to conditions such as historical trauma and ongoing colonial incursions that sometimes involve sudden, forced relocations from homelands, many Indigenous children experience a combination of the most significant risk factors for educational attainment, namely: minority status, poverty, rural location, minority language, and having a disability or being raised by a parent with a disability.[4]

Although specific information on Indigenous children's participation in schooling and preschool is almost completely lacking, unequal opportunities for Indigenous children are widely acknowledged. According to John Henriksen, the Chairperson-Rapporteur of the UN Expert Mechanism on the Rights of Indigenous Peoples, "The full enjoyment of the right to education as recognized in international human rights law is far from reality for most Indigenous peoples. Deprivation of access to quality education is a major factor contributing towards their social marginalization, poverty and dispossession."[5] Similarly, UNESCO reports that "Indigenous communities are frequently denied access to education. . . . Among the main needs to be met in order for Indigenous children to have access to good quality education are appropriate and accessible schooling opportunities, adequate resources in schools and the cultural relevance of the education offered."[6] Increasing the number of Indigenous people who complete secondary school is a low-hanging fruit for government investment, with far-reaching economic and social benefits for a country as a whole.[7]

Many development strategies, such as the Millennium Development Goals and UNESCO's Education for All initiative[8] center on expanding access to schooling as a priority for promoting equity for Indigenous children and other marginalized groups. However, enrollment in school does not imply school readiness, guarantee attendance, or ensure the kind of active engagement needed for learning. Although Indigenous youngsters may enroll in primary school, they appear to be more likely to have high rates of absenteeism, early learning challenges, failure, and premature school leaving.

Several issues besides access to schooling must therefore be addressed to reduce educational inequities among Indigenous children. First, life conditions for Indigenous children must be improved through structural reforms and infrastructure developments that reduce poverty, food insecurity, lack of all-weather transportation access to programs and services, exposure to racism, and other social exclusions. Second, many Indigenous children lack access to adequate nutrition and conditions for health, as well as timely identification and intervention for emerging health problems or developmental delays. As a result, many Indigenous children experience a higher prevalence of a range of health problems that affect school attendance, engagement in school, and learning outcomes. For example, in Canada, Indigenous children suffer significantly higher rates of early hearing loss, fetal alcohol spectrum disorder, early-onset diabetes, respiratory disorders, and accidental injury.[9] Third, only a minority of Indigenous children have access to any early childhood development program, and few of their parents experienced early childhood as a period of stimulating language development and acquiring a drive for learning.[10] Fourth, when Indigenous children attend school, expectations for parents' involvement tend to be low, and the language of instruction, teaching methods, and curriculum content may be linguistically and culturally incongruent and hold little interest.

Among these, early childhood care and education plays a central role. Quality ECCE programs have been shown to be a "powerful equalizer" in nurturing children's social adjustment and the communication skills needed for schooling, promoting excitement about learning, and engendering a sense of themselves as capable learners.[11] Studies of the developing brain, the human genome, and the impact of early childhood experiences on later learning, behavior, and health have converged to create a compelling argument for investing in programs to provide optimal conditions for children's growth and development before formal schooling.[12] Consequently, policy-makers around the world increasingly recognize the importance of improving the quality of ECCE in addition to improving access.

Early experiences of feeling prepared for the demands of school and academic success are pivotal in engendering children's high self-esteem, engagement in schooling, and bonding with the school environment. In contrast, experiences of being unable to handle learning challenges are associated with low self-esteem, poor academic performance, and early school leaving.[13] Research on transitions to school also show that children who feel socially accepted and a sense of belonging when they encounter their classmates, teachers, and curriculum content at school are more likely to become engaged.[14] Indigenous children entering school with little or no understanding of the language of instruction, however, face monumental challenges for their engagement and for parents' involvement in supporting their children's successful transition to school.[15]

This chapter emphasizes the potential for targeted investments in culturally based, family-involving ECCE to increase Indigenous children's readiness for sustained and successful engagement in education. Research findings and promising ECCE practices are highlighted. As an example, the Canadian government's long-term investment in the Aboriginal Head Start program is described as a successful demonstration of the kind of flexible, community-driven, holistic approach that enjoys high demand and involvement from Indigenous parents and appears to increase Indigenous children's educational engagement in the first years of schooling. The need to strengthen Indigenous community capacities to design, deliver, evaluate, and expand quality ECCE is identified as a first step in creating the infrastructure for community-based ECCE. Recommended steps emphasize interministerial coordination and collaborative partnerships between governments and Indigenous organizations to enable Indigenous families and communities to improve conditions for their children's health, nutrition, and development, and to implement culturally based approaches to early learning and school readiness.

Initiatives That Promote Equity for Indigenous Children

THE SCOPE OF EARLY CHILDHOOD CARE AND DEVELOPMENT PROGRAMS

Initiatives to support young children's health, development, and learning include (but are not limited to) prenatal nutrition and education programs focused on mothers; home visiting programs that help mothers, fathers, and other family caregivers to stimulate children's cognitive development; early learning programs based in community settings; preschool and kindergarten programs colocated with schools; and community-wide programs for environmental safety and family recreation. Considerable evidence obtained in high-income countries supports the potential cognitive benefits of out-of-home (often called center-based) early childhood programs for children 3 years of age and older if these programs are of high quality and congruent with children's language and culture.[16] Although little research has focused specifically on Indigenous children, studies show that families who are impoverished, face high stress, and/or lack access to safe, reliable, nurturing care for infants and young children are most likely to benefit from such programs.[17] In the majority of the world, although a wide variety of ECCE initiatives have been described in program literature, little research has evaluated the effectiveness of programs for meeting various needs in various circumstances. Research is especially lacking on home-based programs that focus on parents as children's first teachers, in contrast to the amount of research focused on the child in out-of-home program contexts.

MULTILEVEL INTERVENTIONS

Although most investments in early childhood development in high-income countries go toward center-based programs, a synthesis of research on early childhood development concludes that "nurturant qualities of the environments where children grow, live, and learn—parents, caregivers, family, and community—will have the most significant impact on their development."[18] Research linking early experiences with neurobiological development suggests that environmental conditions in the early years literally "sculpt" the developing brain.[19] Poverty, with its attendant risk factors of poor nutrition, high stress, and high stigma, has a particularly strong impact on early development. A plethora of studies shows that up to 50% of the variance in early childhood outcomes is significantly associated with socioeconomic status.[20] Education deficits of Indigenous children can thus be understood to reflect the cumulative effects of pervasive poverty and social exclusion.[21]

Ensuring access to quality ECCE experiences—whether home- or community-based—as well as to early intervention services as needed, can contribute in important ways to the overall experience of a nurturant environment. However, the early environment also includes a broad range of inputs, from food quality and security, to government policies determining birth registration and availability of transportation to access services and resources, to macrolevel societal values affecting experiences such as racism, social exclusion of children with disabilities, and so on. Strategies at any of these levels can affect the quality of the learning environment for infants and young children, as well as their long-term educational attainment, quality of life, health, and life expectancy.[22] One thing is abundantly clear: Interventions at only one or two of these levels—early learning programs without provisions for health and nutrition or family income generation, for example—will not likely yield measurable gains in educational equity for young Indigenous children.[23] This reality calls for focused, persistent efforts among sector leaders within countries to collaborate to create multisectoral solutions.

THE CULTURAL NATURE OF QUALITY EARLY CHILDHOOD CARE AND EDUCATION PROVISION

Culture is embodied in the ways children are raised and the proximal ecological system in which they grow and develop.[24] It follows that no singular approach to ECCE initiatives will fit all parents and children. Although it is generally acknowledged that goals and approaches to early childhood development are grounded in culture, there is a great deal more rhetoric about responding to cultural diversity than there is evidence of time taken to consider cultural values and the goals of children's primary caregivers, and to incorporate cultural activities and local language preferences into early learning.

A conspicuous example of the contradictions between rhetoric about cultural congruence and community development and what is actually supported by donor agencies and national governments is the transfer of so-called best practices from high-income to low-income countries. This practice is frequently seen in the promotion and implementation of brand-name programs and the steady march toward standardization and homogenization of ECCE training, early learning progress measurement, and program evaluation, often based on persuasive program promotion by originators of the early learning tool, toy, or technique.[25] It is common to hear that, where no locally developed tools or programs appear to exist, there is no need to "reinvent the wheel" when a Euro-Western tool or program model can be adopted or adapted. Yet, few peer-reviewed research reports substantiate claims of "best" in controlled comparative studies or standardized school readiness measurement tools transported from one setting to another. A similar paucity of evidence-based program models developed by and for local communities should provide impetus for efforts to implement and evaluate locally driven program models, rather than be seen as a vacuum to be filled with imported programs.

Exporting Euro-Western early learning programs to Indigenous communities can interrupt the transmission of locally valued cultural knowledge and practices and undermine the diversity of voices, knowledge sources, ways of life, and supports for raising children in local conditions.[26] Why does this matter? First, these assets constitute the very resources that community development programs aim to preserve and capitalize on to support children's learning and development.[27] Programs built on these local assets are likely to garner high participation from parents, grandparents, and local leaders, and are most likely to fit and be sustainable in local conditions.[28] Second, imported standards and programs that reproduce prescribed Euro-Western parenting behaviors and child development outcomes often erode the cultural, linguistic, and social heterogeneity of societies around the world.[29] Third, when measurement tools and programs are marketed as best practice and terms like "the science of early childhood development" (as if there is only one) are invoked to justify this proliferation, it can undermine efforts by Indigenous community leaders and scholars to establish the legitimacy of local perspectives on important curriculum content and appropriate pedagogical approaches.

Universal access to learning opportunities does not imply universal models, which is often assumed when funders plan to take a program to scale. Similarly, equitable opportunities does not mean that all programs must offer the same curriculum content, language of instruction, and format to all children according to a standardized model.[30] Further, universal access does not guarantee universal provision: Some parents will enroll their children in a program and ensure their attendance, whereas others will not. Universal provision therefore requires actively working with parents to establish what kinds of programs interest them and what locations, hours, content, and demands on them will work for their families.

LOCALLY DETERMINED EARLY LEARNING SETTINGS AND GOALS

Although some countries and states are encouraging the downward expansion of public schools to encompass more programs for preschoolers, centralizing programs for young children in public schools is not necessarily the most promising approach to improve access for many Indigenous children. Government-operated schools have yet to prove that they can grasp and effectively address the historically, socially, and economically conditioned needs and goals of Indigenous families and ensure their cultural safety and dignity. Programs operated by public school districts tend to reproduce dominant cultural understandings of what children and parents need and should be doing to promote children's school readiness and success. The corresponding emphasis on measuring school readiness using standardized tools created in North America has generated alarm among some Indigenous peoples who are concerned that pressures for preschoolers to develop numeracy and communication skills in the dominant language will overshadow the holistic learning goals at the heart of many Indigenous-based approaches to raising young children.[31] These approaches often include Indigenous language acquisition, teaching and learning through intergenerational relationships, participation in family and community activities that often yield functional life skills, a literacy of the land, and spiritual development.[32] Unlike school-based programs, early learning programs that are community based and community driven have the potential to serve the dual purpose of improving conditions for Indigenous children's health, development, and learning, while also contributing to Indigenous peoples' capacity for self-determination and the maintenance or revitalization of their cultural knowledges and languages.

The first step in implementing quality ECCE programs that are culturally meaningful, accessible, and well-subscribed is to include Indigenous parents in deliberations about promising approaches. In most countries, Indigenous populations wield less economic and political power than other populations and are consequently less able to influence policies and institutions that affect them. They are likely to be more affected by the interests of (non-Indigenous) dominant cultural groups, and there is often an expectation or demand for them to acculturate to mainstream society. In an educational context, this often means that pressure is placed on parents to yield their home language,[33] cultural values, and ways of life in favor of those of the dominant group for their child's early learning, and to accept mainstream forms of teaching and learning and relinquish decision-making about choices of knowledge and skills for children to master before they start school. This power differential means that those in privileged positions in civic organizations, non-governmental organizations (NGOs), and policy sectors need to support Indigenous people in advocating for their right, codified in the UN Convention on the Rights of the Child, to set and pursue their own goals and approaches in promoting their children's early education.

MEANINGFUL PARENT AND COMMUNITY INVOLVEMENT

Engaging parents and other caregivers more actively in supporting their children's early learning, and working with linguistically and culturally diverse children are two areas identified as lagging in education sectors.[34] It is generally accepted that engaging parents begins with showing respect, listening, and communicating about their central roles in their children's early education and transition to schooling, and about their beliefs, goals, needs, and ideas for supporting their child's early learning. Parent involvement must be a funded aspect of ECCE initiatives and of the broader agenda for schooling. ECCE practitioners and decision-makers must work to raise parents' awareness of the importance of ECCE, encourage their participation in program planning, and create flexible opportunities for parent involvement through, for example, assisting with language translation or enhancing the curriculum with local songs, games, and stories.

Research consistently shows that the primary caregivers' nurturing and teaching style has the strongest influence on children's motivation and learning. Parents' interest in their children's education and their involvement with their children in learning activities, from talking about school experiences, to assisting with homework, to participating in after-school activities such as culture and athletic clubs, can have a tremendous positive impact on children's academic success and retention in school.[35] Programs must also include education and activities for parents to learn about promoting their child's nutrition, health, development, and early learning in ways that are culturally congruent and feasible.

Involving parents and other community members has worked effectively in many instances to produce locally relevant resource materials and teaching strategies, as well as to garner parents' enthusiasm and support. In Canada, for example, Inuit Elders and ECCE practitioners worked together to create books in the local language (Inutittut), illustrated by community members with familiar objects and home and community scenes, telling stories that the community wanted to pass on to their children.[36] In the remote Kyrgyz Mountain areas of Kyrgyzstan, a project called Reading for Children provides opportunities for family members to introduce young children to illustrated books and stories in their own languages. The project worked with Kyrgyz writers and illustrators to create books in local languages.[37] Community members were trained as facilitators of parent–child reading, and they delivered workshops for parents of 3- to 10-year-old children. In Papua New Guinea, the national government has been able to implement home-language-based multilingual early education in hundreds of local languages partly by involving communities in the development of materials.[38] These examples also illustrate the need to consider the language(s) used in ECCE initiatives.

LANGUAGE OF INSTRUCTION IN EARLY CHILDHOOD CARE AND EDUCATION

Most Indigenous parents have to face the fact that if their child attends formal schooling, he or she will be taught in a language other than their Indigenous language. For many Indigenous children, this means starting school in an unfamiliar language. Children who speak a vernacular of the majority language may have been socialized at home to use language in particular ways that make them seem resistant or almost phobic about participating in typical whole-classroom discourse.[39]

Learning in a language not one's own presents a double challenge. One must learn a new language *and* new knowledge contained in that language. Furthermore, young children can perceive that languages are valued differently.[40] When a linguistic and cultural discontinuity exists between home and preschool or primary school, Indigenous and other minority-language children may perceive that their language and culture are not valued—a perception that lowers their self-confidence and self-esteem and interferes with their learning.[41] These challenges exacerbate the risks to Indigenous children's attendance, engagement in learning tasks, and retention in the first years of school, and may create insurmountable obstacles to garnering parents' interest and involvement in their child's education.

Studies show that home-language-based instruction can increase a child's self-esteem and cultural pride and promote a smooth transition between home and school, thus fostering an emotional stability that translates to cognitive stability.[42] Benson, a leading scholar in the field of bi- and multilingual education, contends that, worldwide, children's home language has been established as the most efficient language for early literacy and content area instruction.[43] Dutcher, drawing on extensive involvement in early education in majority world contexts, also concludes that young children develop literacy and cognitive skills and master content material most easily when they are taught in a familiar language.[44] Several robust studies show that cognitive and academic language skills, once developed, and subject knowledge, once acquired, transfer readily from one language to another.[45] These findings are consistent with anecdotal reports of the benefits of home-language-based instruction in ECCE programs in Mali, Papua New Guinea, and Peru, as reported by UNESCO.[46]

Language is not only a tool for communication and knowledge but also a fundamental attribute of cultural identity and empowerment, both for individuals and groups. It is said that the home language symbolizes a deep, abiding, even cord-like connection between speakers and their cultural identity.[47] Indigenous scholars in Canada,[48] the United States,[49] and Aotearoa New Zealand[50] make frequent reference to connections between language, community, place, and time. Although most parents want their children to get a good education, they also hope they will love and respect their heritage language and culture and their home community. As one parent in a home-language-based education program in the North Solomons Province of Papua New Guinea said: "It is important to teach our children to read and write, but it is more important to teach them to be proud of themselves and of us."[51] At the very least, early education should not separate the child culturally or linguistically from his or her family or culture of origin. This may mean delivering ECCE and primary school materials in an Indigenous language only, in an Indigenous language plus a language that is more broadly used, or in one or more non-Indigenous languages.

In many countries, language rights, including schooling in home languages, are among the first claims that Indigenous peoples and other minorities voice in situations of political change and evolution. Over the past half-century, Indigenous peoples have worked to reclaim their languages and to promote language transmission to young children through a variety of strategies[52] including curriculum development[53]; teacher training[54]; and the development of print, multimedia, and online resources.[55] Indigenous people have explored a range of delivery models, including several examples of Indigenous language immersion in early childhood programs.[56]

A host of UN declarations and conventions affirm the rights of minorities, including Indigenous peoples, to learn and/or to have instruction in their "mother tongue."[57] Key documents include the 1989 Convention on the Rights of the Child and the 2007 UN Declaration on the Rights of Indigenous Peoples. According to UNESCO, "It is increasingly obvious that the language of instruction at the beginning of one's education at such a crucial moment for future learning should be the mother tongue."[58]

Regardless of Indigenous claims and international agreements, however, decisions about which languages will serve as the medium of instruction, and the treatment of children's home languages in the education system[59] frequently exemplify the exercise of power, the manufacture of marginalization and minoritization, and the unfulfilled promise of children's rights. The political and socioeconomic marginalization of Indigenous peoples goes hand in hand with their linguistic marginalization from their earliest experiences of education, and the former can be seen as a consequence of the latter.

Language-in-education policies are often motivated by an explicit or hidden curriculum of assimilation. Political, social, and technical considerations often collide in policy-makers' decisions on language medium, schooling, and curriculum. Considerations include, but go beyond, questions of resources, teacher training, and subjects to be studied. Other crucial factors include the political will of local, regional, and national governments; the relationships between countries and their former colonizers; the understanding and patience of international donors; and parents' hopes and anxieties about which languages their children will need to secure employment and participate with dignity in their social, legal, and economic worlds. Although the broader political ramifications of language-in-education policies and practices are beyond the scope of this chapter, Blommaert,[60] Golding and Harris,[61] and Rampton[62] provide excellent analyses of these issues.

The dominant language or dominant cultural model of ECCE is not always imposed on families. In some contexts, parents express a clear preference for their children to receive early education in the dominant language or language of schooling, rather than in their home language(s). Parents often have good reasons for this choice, and tensions must be addressed between respecting parents' preferences and providing education for them to understand the long-term contribution of their child's academic proficiency in their home language to their learning and social outcomes.

Additional tensions and trade-offs are related to home-language schooling. In many situations, a single program serves families with different home languages, and difficult decisions must be made about which language(s) to support in an ECCE program. Resolving these dilemmas requires careful mapping of community assets, needs, and goals that would support alternative pathways to providing quality ECCE, and mutual learning on the parts of funders/decision-makers and community members about the potential outcomes for children of alternative approaches. One set of principles will not yield the most advantageous and practical approach in all settings.

BILINGUAL PROGRAMS

Many Indigenous children grow up with a language used in the home and one or more other languages used more widely in the community or in public media. Home-language-based bilingual and multilingual ECCE and primary school programs may be effective for these children. UNESCO recommends that, whenever possible, a child's home language should be the primary language of instruction, and that children should be offered additional instruction in one or more additional languages that have socioeconomic advantage, such as the language of local commerce or an international language.[63] The relationship between the language(s) used for instruction in school and children's ultimate academic achievement is complex and beyond the scope of the current discussion. However, it is important to note the convergence of findings from investigators on this topic indicating the critical importance of providing continuity in the primary language of the home through ECCE programs and throughout primary school, until children are proficient readers of academic subject matter.[64] During this time, children should not be compelled to transition from learning in their primary language to learning in a secondary language.[65] Reports on home-language-based programs, in which children may learn another language only as a subject of study, conclude that children who learn in their primary language for the first 6 to 8 years of formal schooling have better academic performance and self-esteem than do those who receive instruction exclusively in the official language or those who transition too early from the home language to the official language.[66]

Although home-language-based bilingual ECCE programs have been established in many minority language communities around the world, they are far from common and research on them is scarce.[67] In general, bilingual programs need to provide children with opportunities to interact with fluent speakers of the languages. For Indigenous children whose ancestral language is not spoken either in the home or in the community, the situation is complicated. There is insufficient evidence to support heritage-language-only immersion programs unless fluent speakers are available to deliver the program. However, given the groundswell of demand among Indigenous parents for heritage-language immersion ECCE programs, including Hawaiian and Navajo in the United States, Mi'kmaq in Canada, and Maori in Aotearoa New Zealand, there is a need for pilot projects with methodologically sound outcome research.

COMMUNITY-DRIVEN PROGRAMS

In many contexts, the current upsurge of resistance to colonialism among Indigenous peoples can encourage community engagement in early learning initiatives that afford priority to home languages and local cultural knowledge. Indigenous parents' demand for culturally based, home-language-based ECCE was the impetus for both the Aha Pūnana Leo program in Hawaii[68] and the Kaugel First Language First education program in the Western Highlands Province of Papua New Guinea.[69] In both instances, grassroots demand was met by political will on the part of local governments. The Kaugel program was created in response to the Kaugel people's concern that their children, who spoke only their Kaugel language, were doing poorly in the English-only education system. They established a program in which children learn to read and write in their own language before they enter primary school. After children become proficient in reading and writing in Kaugel, they continue their education in the English school system.

Hawaiian immersion preschools with a high level of parent involvement have yielded impressive academic results. In the 1960s and 1970s, as part of a broader reform of civil rights, a Hawaiian renaissance took root. In 1978, Hawaiian and English were designated co-official languages in the new state constitution, which also mandated the promotion of Hawaiian language, culture, and history.[70] Parents and language activists established Aha Pūnana Leo community-operated pre-schools delivered entirely in Hawaiian.[71] Parents successfully lobbied the state government for Hawaiian-medium tracks in primary and secondary schools, which in turn generated a need for ongoing recruitment and development of native-language teachers and materials. Hawaiian-based education now serves approximately 2,000 students. Hawaiian-based bilingual high schools boast 100% graduation and college attendance among students, who are mostly Indigenous.[72] A similarly successful program of Maori language nurseries, preschools, and schools was established through a grassroots Indigenous language revitalization movement in Aotearoa New Zealand in the 1980s.[73]

Such well-established programs are promising practices that could be explored with other Indigenous populations when there is parent demand and enough fluent speakers to support program delivery. These programs were only able to get started through the participation of parents and other community members who were passionate about seeing the programs succeed, both in order to preserve their Indigenous cultures and languages and to turn around the high failure rate among their children in schools where they were being educated in a language they did not know. These programs have grown exponentially over two decades and continue to be governed in part by parents and local community leaders.

INDIGENOUS CAPACITY BUILDING

Teacher characteristics are a key ingredient in student engagement and performance. Although research has not conclusively identified characteristics of good teachers, a call is consistently heard among Indigenous peoples for more Indigenous teachers and other professionals to work with children and families.[74] Moreover, a national policy allowing and supporting home-language-based early childhood programs must invest in training Indigenous candidates who are fluent in the home language of the target population and have some knowledge of their culture. A need exists for ECCE training opportunities that provide scope for communities' particular cultures, languages, goals, and needs to be considered by trainees through the training program. Further, training needs to be readily accessible through innovative approaches that integrate on-the-job training and mentoring, independent study, peer learning circles, and blended course delivery, including virtual classrooms and tele-education. A targeted, coordinated approach that fosters partnerships between Indigenous organizations and postsecondary institutions could expand the number of qualified Indigenous ECCE practitioners.

One model with documented success in strengthening Indigenous capacity for ECCE and for leadership in policy and program decision-making that affects Indigenous education is the First Nations Partnership Program offered for

20 years by the University of Victoria in Canada.[75] The program was instigated by the Meadow Lake Tribal Council (MLTC) in the province of Saskatchewan in 1989. Aiming to provide ECCE training for Cree and Dene community members, MLTC could not find an existing program with room for culturally specific knowledge to come into the students' course work, and no universities or colleges were prepared to deliver postsecondary courses in the community or involve community members, including Elders, in the teaching and learning process. The MLTC applied successfully for federal funds through Human Resources Development Canada and entered into a partnership with the University of Victoria's School of Child and Youth Care to create a career-laddered program of course work. The courses developed a "generative curriculum" approach that incorporated, in equal measure, university- and community-generated content. Twenty co-scripted courses were delivered in the partnering First Nation communities, enabling Elders to teach alongside locally recruited, university-appointed instructors. Participation by community members in all aspects of the training program contributed significantly to program success. Community-based delivery also enabled students to undertake practica in local settings and allowed community members and service staff in local agencies to observe and be involved in the students' learning journeys.

Evaluation of the program after seven partnerships found that it was the most successful postsecondary education program in Canada in terms of Indigenous students' completion of a 1-year certificate and 2-year diploma program. Over a total of ten 2-year partnerships, the program supported completion of Early Childhood Education (ECE) credentials by 151 Indigenous graduates. Ninety-five percent of these graduates remained in their communities; 65% introduced new programs for children, youth, and families; 21.5% joined the staff of existing programs; and 11.5% continued on the education ladder toward a university degree.[76] A career-laddered approach provided access to accredited postsecondary education, enabling students first to obtain preparatory training to ensure their success in postsecondary courses; second, to complete an ECE certificate; third, to upgrade certification with additional course work in special needs and infant and toddler care, which are separate levels of certification in some jurisdictions; fourth, to complete a diploma in ECE or a related field such as child and youth care; and finally, to apply to postsecondary institutions to continue with third- and fourth-year bachelor-level studies in ECCE or a related field.

Following the program's pilot delivery, the MLTC passed their co-ownership of the program to Saskatchewan Indian Institutes of Technology, which currently carries on the traditions of community-based, cohort-driven delivery of the career-laddered program through partnerships that incorporate Indigenous as well as Euro-Western–based curricula. Recognized by UNESCO as an exemplary approach to training that incorporates Indigenous knowledge, the program has been adapted in other culturally specific education programs around the world, not only in ECE but in other professional fields as well.[77]

Key Gaps in Evidence on Effective Supports for Indigenous Children's Early Learning

DISAGGREGATED DATA ON INDIGENOUS CHILDREN'S ENGAGEMENT

Despite promising developments in community-based ECCE provision in different regions, much remains to be learned. Indigenous and other minority children are often the hardest to reach due to their socially marginalized status and, often, their rural or remote locations. There is therefore a need for disaggregated data to track the extent to which ECCE initiatives—which may be delivering gains with the majority population of youngsters—are actually reaching this population. There is also a need for research to develop understandings of what kinds of ECCE strategies generate the most demand by Indigenous parents for their boys and for their girls, and which strategies are most effective in promoting girls' and boys' educational participation and early learning in different kinds of circumstances.

MEASURING PROGRAM UPTAKE AND EFFECTIVENESS

Educational researchers' overwhelming focus has been on teaching children over 7 years of age. Experimentation and evaluation are a key missing aspect of policymaking and program development in most countries and in the ECCE field as a whole. ECCE is distinct from primary education in its emphases on supporting the care and development of the whole child in the context of his or her family and on doing, speaking, and listening more than on reading, writing, and numeracy. The current lack of performance measurement—even as basic as tracking Indigenous children's subsequent grade-level completion—focused on Indigenous children makes it impossible to know which policies, program delivery approaches, program elements, and staff characteristics are working or where reforms are most needed.

LANGUAGE OF PROGRAM DELIVERY

Only a handful of research studies describe long-term outcomes of home-language-based ECCE programs; most studies are limited to early outcomes of innovations during and at the end of primary school.[78] Although decades of research in psychology and linguistics have focused on how children learn their first language, almost no research highlights the conditions that support young children to learn more than one language in the early years. Many scholars point to the need for more research to identify the most effective approaches to supporting second language acquisition and delivering bilingual curriculum in early childhood programs.[79] Few guidelines exist to support parents in raising their children to be bi- or multilingual, or to continue to develop their home language while participating in early childhood programs or primary school delivered in a different language. Given the priority many Indigenous communities place on sustaining or strengthening Indigenous language transmission to the youngest generation, these are critical areas for research and program innovation.

EARLY LEARNING MEASUREMENT CHALLENGES

Early learning programs and measurement tools created by national governments or international bodies can enable regional and cross-national comparisons. When a common curriculum exists, there is the potential for children to develop a common set of skills that are thought to prepare them for success in primary school. However, a growing number of investigators express concern that developmental norms and expectations for early learning and school readiness may not be appropriate for all Indigenous and other minority children.[80] Standardized developmental assessment and program evaluation tools are associated with standardized program goals and approaches, many of which are based on research with North American and European children. Transporting these externally developed monitoring and evaluation technologies and standardized curricula to Indigenous communities seems to directly contradict the common rhetoric about supporting cultural diversity, linguistic rights, and locally meaningful learning targets.[81] As the foregoing discussion has emphasized, uniformity in early learning programs and performance measurement can complicate the challenges inherent in creating ECCE programs that are meaningful to parents and children and that will ultimately secure their long-term engagement in education.

There is much at stake in these tradeoffs. One study in Canada found that many Indigenous parents and some non-Indigenous ECCE practitioners were concerned that standardized tools for measuring speech and language development and school readiness contributed to misinterpreting speech and language differences, such as Indigenous English dialects or vernaculars, as evidence of deficits. Low scores on tests that are assumed to be universally valid likely contribute to the alarmingly high rates of diagnosis of Indigenous children as cognitively or linguistically delayed or impaired.[82] New information-gathering strategies to monitor and measure program effectiveness are needed to build the business case for long-term investments in locally designed ECCE that produces educational equity for Indigenous children.

LEARNING DISABILITIES AND EARLY INTERVENTION

Data on special needs affecting the early learning outcomes of Indigenous children are generally not available. However, it is generally perceived that, due to many suboptimal conditions for their health and development, Indigenous children are at far greater risk of starting school with one or more undetected disability. When Indigenous children do attend school, an alarmingly high number are excluded from the mainstream curriculum due to apparent learning impairments.[83] Developmental delays and handicaps may be detected by community practitioners, such as community health workers, through direct observation, conversations with parents about their children's developmental milestones, or simple developmental checklists. However, a lack of early intervention services is a common barrier to secondary prevention, especially for children in rural and remote areas. Information gaps about prevalence rates, access, uptake, and effectiveness of early intervention services need to be considered in plans to equalize readiness for formal schooling.

The Aboriginal Head Start Program in Canada

In Canada, Indigenous peoples, known as "Aboriginal," make up 4% of the population.[84] The Aboriginal population is much younger than the average, with a median age in 2006 of 26.5 years, compared to 39.5 years for all Canadians. The 2006 Census enumerated 131,000 Aboriginal children under the age of 6, with about 40,000 living on reserve lands and 91,000 living off-reserve.[85] The Aboriginal population will maintain its high growth rate and remain significantly younger relative to the non-Aboriginal population for at least the next 20 years.[86,87]

With Aboriginal children making up an increasing proportion of all children in Canada, there is growing recognition of persisting failures of the formal education system to drive Indigenous peoples' recovery from the devastations of past colonial policies that excluded them from mainstream education.[88,89] Aboriginal leaders and organizations argue that poor-quality education, lack of cultural relevance, and inappropriate assessment tools frequently result in serious negative consequences for Aboriginal children.[90] Problems include over- and under-recognition of children with developmental challenges; early intervention services introduced too late; undermining Indigenous language and cultural goals for development through an overvaluing of standard urban English and of monolingualism; cultural alienation; low levels of school readiness; and high rates of early school failure and premature school leaving.

Indicators of developmental challenges and negative educational outcomes experienced by many Aboriginal children, combined with their high rates of health problems, are so alarming that in 2004, the Council of Ministers of Education stated:

> There is recognition in all educational jurisdictions that the achievement rates of Aboriginal children, including the completion of secondary school, must be improved. Studies have shown that some of the factors contributing to this low level of academic achievement are that Aboriginals in Canada have the lowest income and thus the highest rates of poverty, the highest rate of drop-outs from formal education, and the lowest health indicators of any group.[91,92]

Furthermore, given that attainment of a high school diploma or higher has been shown to improve labor market outcomes for Aboriginal people,[93] clear incentives exist for the Canadian government to make Aboriginal education a priority. This should be enough to make poverty reduction, family supports, and intersectoral approaches to ECCE for Aboriginal children a priority for federal, provincial, and territorial governments, given the demonstrated influence of these factors on education outcomes. However, unlike most high-income countries, Canada lacks a national strategy to ensure access to quality programs to promote optimal early development and learning either for all children or for children in an identified risk category. Although the current "catch-as-catch-can" collection of ECCE programs increases many children's vulnerability, the situation is vastly bleaker for Aboriginal children,[94] less than 18% of whom have access to any early childhood care or development program.[95]

Amid these shortfalls, one exception is long-term federal investment, beginning in 1995, in Aboriginal Head Start (AHS). This initiative was a federal response to calls by Aboriginal community representatives, leaders, and practitioners for an adequately resourced, sustained, and culturally based national strategy to improve supports for Aboriginal young children's health, development, and early learning.

In 1990, the Native Council of Canada undertook the first national effort to define Indigenous child care and the meaning of cultural appropriateness with respect to the delivery of early childhood care and development services.[96] The Council's report, entitled *The Circle of Care*, conceptualized a direct link between culturally relevant child care services that are controlled by First Nations, the preservation of First Nations culture, and improved developmental outcomes for children. They called for these supports to be delivered within the contexts of children's families and cultural communities through community-driven programs operated by qualified Aboriginal practitioners. A report by the Royal Commission on Aboriginal Peoples recommended that federal, provincial, and territorial governments cooperate to support an integrated early childhood funding strategy that (a) extends early childhood education to all Aboriginal children regardless of residence; (b) encourages programs that foster the physical, social, intellectual, and spiritual development of children, thus reducing distinctions between child care, prevention, and education; (c) maximizes Aboriginal control over service design and administration; (d) offers one-stop accessible funding; and (e) promotes parental involvement and choice in early childhood education options.[97] In 1995, federal funding was committed by Health Canada to implement AHS in First Nations on reserves, and in 1998, federal funding was committed through the Public Health Agency of Canada to implement AHS for First Nations, Métis, and Inuit children living in urban and northern communities.

When funding was committed, a fundamental principle was for Aboriginal people to direct, design, and deliver services in their communities—an unprecedented recognition by the federal government of the inherent right of Aboriginal peoples to make decisions respecting their children. A corresponding key feature of AHS is that an Aboriginal host agency or community leadership council that successfully applies to host the program receives funding to deliver it, in consultation with mandatory parent advisory committees. Thus, the nature of each program varies from one community to another, including criteria for children to enroll. Most children with special needs are eligible to participate in AHS, depending upon staff qualifications and facilities that can accommodate their needs. Many programs require parents to volunteer time or make a monetary contribution. Most programs operate on a part-time basis 3 or 4 days a week. The majority of staff is Aboriginal.

Approximately 140 AHS programs serving about 4,500 Aboriginal children in urban centers and northern communities are operated by the Public Health Agency of Canada. Aboriginal Head Start programs serving about 9,100 Aboriginal children living on reserves are operated by Health Canada. It is currently estimated that 8% of Aboriginal preschool children between ages 3 and 5 attend AHS.[98] In 2001, a survey of Aboriginal parents living in urban and northern centers showed that the proportion of Aboriginal children living in nonreserve areas who were attending early childhood programs specifically designed for them had increased fourfold over an 8-year period, reflecting in large measure the federal investment in AHS. Sixteen percent of Aboriginal children entering first grade had participated in Aboriginal-specific programs during their preschool years, compared to only 4% of children who turned 14 the same year.[99]

AHS in Canada differs from the Head Start approach pioneered in the United States.[100] Although both programs prepare children for successful transition from home to school learning environments, the emphasis in Canada is on culturally fitting, community-specific elaborations of six program components shown in Figure 13.1: culture and language, education and school readiness, health promotion, nutrition, social support, and parent/family involvement.

Local control of AHS programs allows for innovation to find the best curricula and staff for each community and child. Staff trained in early childhood education work with Elders, Indigenous language specialists, cultural teachers, and parents to enhance child development, cultural pride, and school readiness. Although some programs primarily use an Indigenous language, most operate in English or French with some exposure to one or more Indigenous language. This situation reflects the severe attenuation of most Indigenous languages in Canada such that, with the exception of the Inutittut, Cree, and Ojibway languages, few host communities could support a significant commitment to an Indigenous language medium.

Although management evaluations of AHS are conducted annually, effectiveness evaluations have been fraught with difficulties, partly due to a lack of widely accepted tools to measure Aboriginal children's development in ways that are amenable to standardized scoring and composite analysis. Efforts to collect qualitative data across several program sites have also encountered problems with

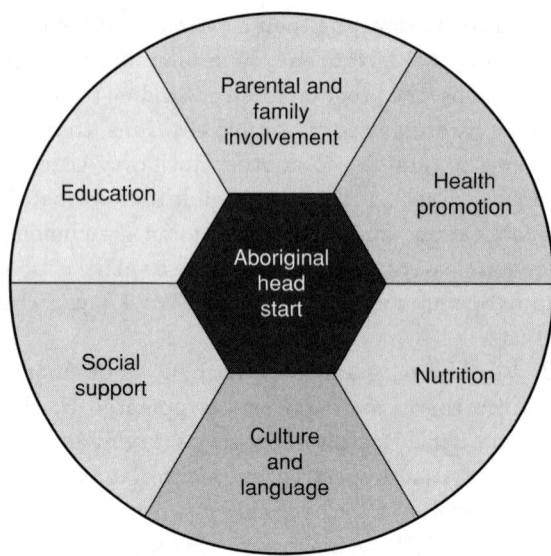

Figure 13.1 Integrated program components in Aboriginal Head Start (AHS), Canada.

consistency. No studies include control comparisons with randomization of children to programs. Despite these difficulties, a few studies yield positive evidence of benefits to children's cultural knowledge, confidence, physical health, language and literacy skills, social skills, and kindergarten readiness, as well as benefits to parents.[101] Furthermore, a nationwide survey of Aboriginal parents found that participation in at least 1 year of AHS reduced the risk that a child would repeat a grade in elementary school.[102] A recent critical assessment of health services for Canadian children conducted by the federal Ministry of Health called for an expansion of AHS to achieve 25% coverage of Aboriginal children.[103]

Although more work is needed to establish the effectiveness of AHS, the program has a number of promising features that are highly congruent with principles advocated by many Indigenous organizations beyond Canada:

- Aboriginal Head Start provides safe, supervised, stimulating environments for young children. This is especially important for children whose home environments may be crowded, chaotic, or contaminated. Many programs provide nutrition supplementation, cognitive stimulation, socialization with Aboriginal peers, adult role models and Elders, and exposure to Indigenous language and spirituality.
- Aboriginal Head Start supports families during the early stages of family formation, when parents—many of them very young and with few resources—need social support and practical assistance.
- Aboriginal Head Start has been a timely and effective vehicle to enable communities to deliver ECCE programs in culturally fitting ways to children who need them most.

- Aboriginal Head Start is increasing the numbers of Aboriginal people across the country who are skilled in delivering programs and playing various supportive roles for Aboriginal children and families. Each site employs community members who receive pre- and in-service training through a number of training workshops convened annually by regional and national AHS offices.

- Aboriginal Head Start programs provide resources within marginalized communities that may otherwise lack the hard and soft infrastructure to ensure early learning, nutrition, health, and intervention services for children. Some AHS programs have been described as reducing the high rates of removal of children from their families and communities to government care, and others have played a role in reuniting parents and children. This is a uniquely promising aspect of AHS: One of the challenges for ensuring Aboriginal children's access to needed supports and services is that they often do not make it as far as the entry point in mainstream service delivery systems set up to meet the needs of families who have ready access to transportation and know how service systems work and how to advocate to get their child's needs met. A study conducted in three Aboriginal communities in Canada documented how AHS and other community-based ECCE programs can function as "hooks" to involve young children and their parents in early learning and then evolve to become community hubs providing streamlined access to other kinds of developmental and family programs and services, as illustrated in Figure 13.2.[104] When a family enrolls their young child in a program, such as an infant development program or preschool, they become known to community-based staff who can increase family members' awareness of a range of other program options and connect them to other services offered in the community center or beyond. In the example illustrated in Figure 13.2, the community reached out to parents of newborns, offering them a parent–child music and play program, followed by a laddered sequence of programs appropriate for their child as they grew older. Health information, education about nutrition, speech and language stimulation programs, and opportunities to participate in cultural events were offered concurrently. When specific needs arose, families could access early intervention services, patient navigator services to assist them in dealings with government health care services, and advocacy and accompaniment supports for dealings with the child welfare system, family court, the formal school system, and so on.

Recommended Actions and Lessons to Be Drawn from Model Programs

Steps that policy-makers can take to improve equity of opportunities for young Indigenous children to succeed in education include the following:

- Raise awareness among policy-makers in every sector about the importance of supporting young Indigenous children's meaningful and successful

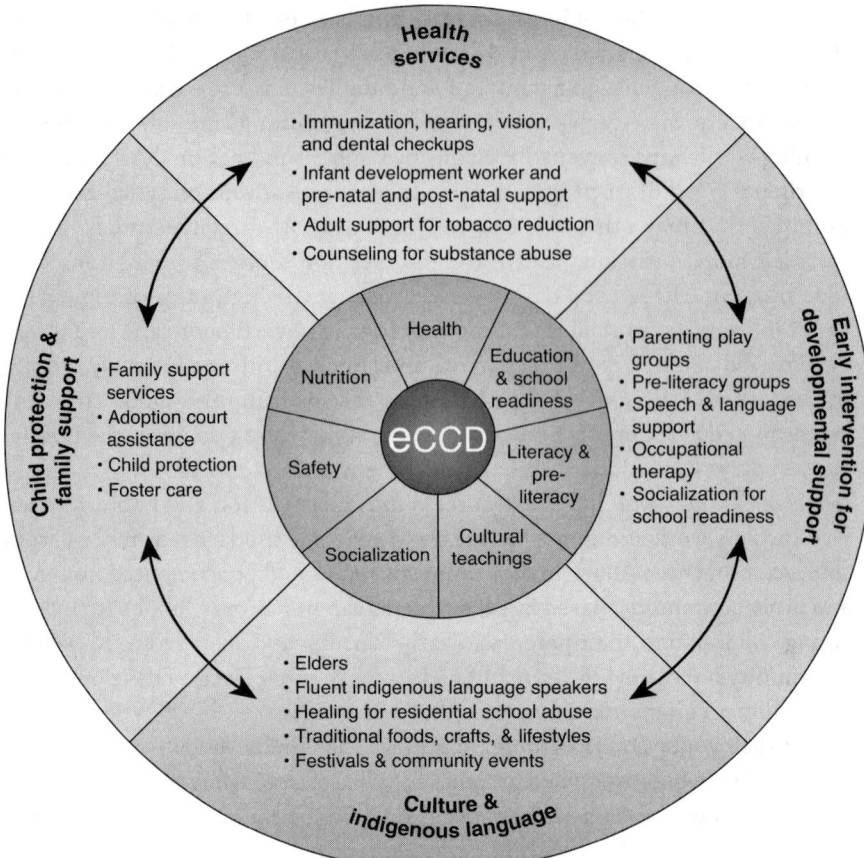

Figure 13.2 "Hook and Hub": Intersectoral coordination of programs with early childhood care and development (ECCD) as a central organizing starting point.

participation in education as a right codified by international agreements and a wise investment, with a goal of generating political will among various parties to become engaged in developing solutions.

- Work to remove bureaucratic barriers to intersectoral collaboration needed to reduce poverty and improve quality of life for Indigenous children and to provide health, nutrition, education, and social components of a comprehensive ECCE strategy.

- Educate the public about the challenges Indigenous children face in gaining equitable access to life opportunities, with the goal of generating a broad base of civic support for initiatives and social inclusion for Indigenous children and families.

- Make quality ECCE programs that fit the needs of Indigenous families available to all Indigenous children from birth through a transitional year in primary school.

- Create opportunities, through linkages between postsecondary institutions and Indigenous community organizations, for culturally relevant, career-laddered, accessible education for Indigenous people to become qualified ECCE practitioners and decision leaders.
- Provide opportunities for Indigenous parents to participate—in their communities, with NGOs, and with policy-makers—in decision-making about priorities for investments to improve educational equity for their children and about how investments in ECCE will be materialized.
- Commission holistic, controlled, longitudinal evaluations of ECCE programs by early development researchers.

The research and programs reviewed in this chapter show how family-focused, culturally responsive policies, funding, and evaluation frameworks can encourage community initiative and involvement in young Indigenous children's learning. Funding allocations and program quality indicators need not be tied to preschools that follow a prescribed curriculum.[105] "One size does *not* fit all" has been a recurrent learning point across health, education, community development, and other sectors over the past decade. Equity for Indigenous children requires a shift beyond a Eurocentric developmental paradigm to embrace culturally embedded approaches informed by communities. This chapter highlights some successful movements away from the standardized application of universalist principles toward a dialogical approach that encompasses parents' values, goals, and resources as well as locally meaningful teaching and learning strategies and content. Aboriginal Head Start illustrates a centrally funded program that is designed and managed in a decentralized way. Rather than being a prescriptive, cookie-cutter model of the kind often associated with brand-name programs, the several hundred AHS programs are as highly varied as the cultural communities that operate them.

The illusion that best practices exist that could be dropped into any setting is gradually giving way to a search for what can be learned from *promising* practices in particular settings. Dialogue with communities of parents can illuminate how to combine knowledge and tools from research on early learning with local knowledge and approaches to address culturally defined goals for young children's early learning and development. Several examples document participatory approaches to Indigenous ECCE program development.[106] Monitoring and evaluation of community-driven programs can draw upon the enormous capacity that has developed in health, social sciences, and education in the past decade for collaborative approaches to research (variously called community-based research, community-engaged scholarship, and community-university partnerships).

A critical policy focus in the education sector must include investments in meaningful early learning opportunities for Indigenous children from infancy and throughout the early years through home- or community-based ECCE programs. Quality early childhood care and development programs should not focus narrowly on cognitive skill development, but perhaps most importantly on building self-esteem and a sense of social, cultural, and linguistic belonging, which are precursors to developing an identity as a capable learner with a rightful place in a school community. Although the need for equitable and stable funding for flexible early learning initiatives is a key factor, it is not the only requirement. Collaboration across sectors is also needed to create lasting policy and program solutions that improve the conditions for learning and life for Indigenous children.

Conclusion

Indigenous populations in many countries are in crisis. Improving the social and economic well-being of Indigenous children while protecting the world's repository of languages and cultural knowledges is not only a moral imperative, it is a sound investment that will pay significant dividends in the coming decades. Investing in disadvantaged children is one of the important public policy opportunities that has no equity-efficiency tradeoff. Increasing the educational attainment level of Indigenous children will benefit not only Indigenous children, families, and communities, but also government and businesses, and, by extension, the entire population.

Lack of political will is the biggest obstacle to planning and acting on a comprehensive agenda of policy reforms and program investments targeting educational equity for young Indigenous children. The problem of educational inequities for Indigenous children is a circular one: Without political will to create and implement policies prioritizing equity and dignity for Indigenous children, the human resource capacity, curriculum and learning resources, and popular demand for these programs will be lacking. To increase demand and enhance Indigenous self-determination in regards to educational equity, it is important to support greater Indigenous representation in key political positions and/or to provide enhanced structures and venues for Indigenous peoples to voice and exercise their political will about educational equity, including the need for more access to quality, appropriate ECCE. The key step is to formulate an enabling national policy and a funded action program supporting a range of community-driven ECCE initiatives.

Many education programs around the world struggle to embody core principles of building on local assets and responding to cultural diversity, such as customization of curricula to meet community-specific needs and goals and integration of typically fragmented infrastructure for nutrition, health, education, and social welfare. Reflecting on the lack of local relevance or meaning in what Indigenous children are asked to learn in many kindergartens and primary schools in Canada, an Indigenous community leader asked: "Has anything changed since the government first designed their education systems to take the Indian out of the child?"[107] There is no doubt about the added complexities of creating policies that permit flexibility of program design and locally defined goals and indicators for children's early learning. However, providing community-driven, culturally relevant programs—and monitoring program quality and outcomes—upholds the rights of Indigenous and other minority parents and children, and is probably the most effective way to secure young children's engagement in education. Equity of educational provision must include consideration of the language(s) in which ECCE programs and primary schooling are delivered.

Having a national goal of providing universal access to quality ECCE is not antithetical to allowing local choice and control of program staffing, scheduling, curriculum content, pedagogy, and dimensions for program evaluation. Evidence from a few majority world countries shows the positive effects of government funding, local autonomy, and community involvement in education at the primary and secondary school levels.[108] The example of AHS programs in Canada demonstrates that it is feasible for a government to invest in an ECCE program that not only allows but depends upon local autonomy in the design and delivery of programs that are holistic, family centered, and informed by each local community's internally identified needs and vision for equalizing young children's chances for educational success and quality of life.

NOTES

1. Grantham-McGregor, D., Cheung, Y., Cueto, S., Glee, P., Richter, L., & Strupp, B. (2007). Developmental potential in the first five years for children in developing countries. *The Lancet, 369*(9555), 60–70; Jolly, R. (2007). Early childhood development: The global challenge. *The Lancet, 369*(9555), 8–9; Magnuson, K. E., Ruhm, C., & Waldfogel, J. (2006). The persistence of preschool effects: Do subsequent classroom experiences matter? *Early Childhood Research Quarterly, 22*(1), 18–38.

2. The acronyms ECCD, ECCE, and ECE are used by various funding, service, and training agencies to refer to research, policy, and practice addressing the health, development, and education of children from conception to 8 years of age. Early childhood care and development (ECCD) is preferred by the author and her Indigenous community partners since it emphasizes the care environment and the broad scope of child development, which subsumes early learning and education. This book has adopted the term early childhood care and education (ECCE), which places special emphasis on education. The term ECE is typically used in reference to the professional credential required in Canada and some other countries for staff delivering programs to young children.

3. UNESCO. (2011). *Indigenous people*. Paris: UNESCO. Retrieved from http://www.unesco.org/en/inclusive-education/Indigenous-people/

4. UNESCO. (2009). Summary: Overcoming inequality: Why governance matters. In *EFA global monitoring report*. Paris: UNESCO.

5. Henriksen, J. B. (2009). Foreword. In *State of the world's minorities and Indigenous peoples 2009* (p. 10). New York: Minority Rights Group International and UNICEF.

6. UNESCO. (2009). *Inclusive dimensions of the right to education: Normative bases*. Concept Paper, 8th and 9th Meetings of the Joint Expert Group UNESCO on the Monitoring of the Right to Education (p. 14). Paris: UNESCO.

7. Sharpe, A., & Arsenault, J. F. (2009). *Investing in Aboriginal education in Canada: An economic perspective*. Ottawa, ON: Canadian Policy Research Networks.

8. UNESCO. (2000). *The Dakar framework for action. Education for all: Meeting our collective commitments*. Paris: UNESCO.

9. Kohen, D., Uppal, S., & Guevremont, A. (2007). *Children with disabilities and the educational system: A provincial perspective.* Education Matters, Catalogue 81–004, no. 4.1. Ottawa, ON: Statistics Canada; Smylie, J., & Adomako, P. (2009). *Indigenous children's health report: Health assessment in action.* Toronto: Saint Michaels Hospital. Retrieved from http://www.stmichaelshopital.com/crich/Indigenous_childrens_health_report.php

10. Bennett, J. (2003). *Early childhood education and care policy: Canada, country note.* OECD Directorate for Education. Retrieved from http://www.oecd.org/dataoecd/42/34/33850725.pdf

11. Heckman, J. J. (2006). Skill formation and the economics of investing in disadvantaged children. *Science, 312*(5782), 1900–1902; Irwin, L. G., Siddiqi, A., & Hertzman, J. J. (2009). The equalizing power of early child development: From the commission on social determinants of health to action. *Child Health and Education, 1*(3), 146–161.

12. Shonkoff, J., & Phillips, D. (Eds.). (2000). *From neurons to neighborhoods: The science of early childhood development.* Washington, DC: National Academy Press.

13. Audas, R. P., & Willms, J. D. (2007). *Engagement and dropping out of school: A life-course perspective.* Ottawa, ON: Applied Research Branch, Strategic Policy, Human Resources Development Canada; Lee, V. E., & Burkam, D. T. (2003). Dropping out of high school: The role of social organization and structure. *American Educational Research Journal, 40*(2), 353–93.

14. Myers, R. (1992). *The twelve who survive.* London: Routledge.

15. Wright, S. C., & Taylor, D. M. (1995). Identity and the language of the classroom: Investigating the impact of heritage versus second language instruction on personal and collective self-esteem. *Journal of Educational Psychology, 87*(2), 241–252.

16. Calman, L. J., & Tarr-Whelan, L. (2005). *Early childhood education for all: A wise investment.* Recommendations arising from The Economic Impacts of Child Care and Early Education: Financing Solutions for the Future conference, Legal Momentum, New York; Heckman. Skill formation and the economics; Lynch, R. G. (2004). *Exceptional returns: Economic, fiscal, and social benefits of investment in early childhood development.* Washington, DC: Economic Policy Institute.

17. Jolly. (2007). Early childhood development.

18. Irwin, L. G., Siddiqi, A., & Hertzman, C. (2010). The Equalizing Power of Early Child Development: From the Commission on Social Determinants of Health to *Action. Child Health and Education, 2*(1), 3–18.

19. DiPietro, J. A. (2000). Baby and the brain: Advances in child development. *Annual Review of Public Health, 21,* 455–471.

20. Canada Council on Learning. (2007). *State of learning in Canada: No time for complacency. Report on learning in Canada 2007.* Ottawa, ON: Canada Council on Learning; Case, A., Lubotsky, D., & Paxson, C. (2002). Economic status and health in childhood: The origins of the gradient. *The American Economic Review, 92*(5), 1308–1334; Dearing, E. (2007). Psychological costs of growing up poor. *Annals of the New York Academy of Sciences, 10,* 1196–1425; Raver, C. C., Gershoff, E. T., & Aber, J. L. (2007). Testing equivalence of mediating models of income, parenting, and school readiness for White, Black, and Hispanic children in a national sample. *Child Development, 78*(1), 96–115; Weitzman, M. (2003). Low income and its impact on psychosocial child development. In *Encyclopedia on Early Childhood Development* (pp. 1–8). Montreal: Centre of Excellence for Early Childhood Development.

21. Smylie & Adomako. (2009). *Indigenous children's health report;* UNESCO. (2009). *Inclusive dimensions of the right to education.*

22. Evans, J. L., Myers, R., & Ilfeld, E. (2000). *Early childhood counts: A programming guide on early childhood care for development.* Washington, DC: World Bank.

23. Engle, P., Black, M. M., Behrman, J. R., Cabral de Mello, M., Gertler, P. J., International Child Development Steering Group, et al. (2007). Strategies to avoid the loss of developmental potential in more than 200 million children in the developing world. *The Lancet, 369*(9557), 229–242; UNICEF. (1993). *Towards a comprehensive strategy for the development of the young child. Inter-agency policy review.* New York: UNICEF.

24. Cole, M. (1998). Culture in development. In M. Woodhead, D. Faulkner, & K. Littleton (Eds.), *Cultural worlds of early childhood* (pp. 11–33). London: Open University Press; Greenfield, P. M., & Suzuki, L. K. (1998). Culture and human development: Implications for parenting, education, pediatrics, and mental health. In W. Damon (Ed.), and I. E. Sigel, & K. A. Rennigner (Vol. Eds.), *Handbook of child psychology: Vol. 4, Child psychology in practice* (5th ed., pp. 1059–1109). New York: Wiley; Harkness, S., & Super, C. M. (1996). *Parents' cultural belief systems: Their origins, expressions, and consequences.* New York: The Guilford Press; LeVine, R. A., & New, R. S. (Eds.). (2008). *Anthropology and child development: A cross-cultural reader.* New York: Blackwell; Rogoff, B. (2003). *The cultural nature of human development.* New York: Oxford University Press.

25. Dahlberg, G., Moss, P., & Pence, A. (2007). *Beyond quality in early childhood education and care: The languages of evaluation.* London: Falmer Press; Fuller, B. (2007). *Standardized childhood: The political and cultural struggle over early education.* Palo Alto, CA: Stanford University Press; MacNaughton, G. (2007). *Doing Foucault in early childhood studies: Applying poststructural ideas.* New York: Routledge; Olfman, S. (2003). Pathogenic trends in early childhood education. In S. Olfman (Ed.), *All work and no play . . . How educational reforms are harming our preschoolers* (pp. 193–211). Westport, CT: Praeger.

26. Stairs, A. H., Bernhard, J. K., & the Aboriginal Colleagues. (2002). Considerations for evaluating "good care" in Canadian Aboriginal early childhood settings. *McGill Journal of Education, 37*(3), 309–330.

27. Nsamenang, A. B. (2008). (Mis)understanding ECD in Africa: The force of local and imposed motives. In M. Garcia, A. Pence, & J. Evans (Eds.), *Africa's future, Africa's challenge: Early childhood care and development in sub-Saharan Africa* (pp. 135–149). Washington, DC: World Bank.

28. UNESCO. (2008). *Mother tongue matters: Local language as a key to effective learning.* Paris: UNESCO.

29. Kincheloe, J. L. (2000). Certifying the damage: Mainstream educational psychology and the oppression of children. In L. D. Soto (Ed.), *The politics of early childhood education* (pp. 75–84). New York: Peter Lang; Lubeck, S. (1998). Is developmentally appropriate practice for everyone? *Childhood Education, 74*(5), 283–292.

30. Ryan, S., & Grieshaber, S. (2005). Shifting from developmental to postmodern practices in early childhood teacher education. *Journal of Teacher Education, 56*(1), 34–45.

31. Li, J., D'Angiulli, A., & Kendall, G. E. (2007). The early development index and children from culturally and linguistically diverse backgrounds. *Early Years: An International Journal of Research and Development, 27*(3), 221–235.

32. Eickelkamp, U. (2008). "I don't talk story like that": On the social meaning of children's sand stories at Ernabella. In J. Simpson & G. Wigglesworth (Eds.), *Children's language and multilingualism* (pp. 79–102). London: Continuum; Greenwood, M., & Ngaroimata Fraser, T. (2005). Ways of knowing and being: Indigenous early childhood care and education. In A. Pence, & V. Pacini-Ketchabaw (Eds.), *Research connections Canada* (pp. 41–58). Ottawa, ON: Canadian Child Care Federation; Little Bear, L. (2000). Jagged worldviews colliding. In M. Battiste (Ed.), *Reclaiming Indigenous voice and vision* (pp. 77–86). Vancouver: UBC Press.

33. The term *home language* may refer to several different situations. Definitions often include the following elements: the language(s) that one has learned first; the language(s) one identifies with or is identified as a native speaker of by others; the language(s) one knows best; and the language(s) one uses most. *Home language* may also be referred to as the *primary language, first language,* or *mother tongue.*

34. UNESCO. (2006). *Strong foundations: Early childhood care and education,* Summary: EFA Global Monitoring Report 2007. Paris: UNESCO. Retrieved from http://www.unesco.org/en/education/efareport/reports/2007-early-childhood/

35. Audas & Willms. (2007). *Engagement and dropping out of school*; Ensminger, M. E., & Slusarcick, A. L. (1992). Paths to high school graduation or dropout: A longitudinal study of first-grade cohort. *Sociology of Education, 65*(2), 95–113.

36. Avataq Cultural Institute. (2006). *Unikkaangualaurtaa (Let's tell a story).* Westmount, QC: Avataq Cultural Institute; Rowan, M.C. (2010). Disrupting colonial power through literacy:

A story about creating Inuttitut language children's books. In V. Pacini-Ketchabaw (Ed.), *Flows, rhythms, and intensities of early childhood education curriculum* (pp. 155–176). New York: Peter Lang.

37. Aga Khan Foundation. (2008). *Reading for children: A project in Kyrgyz mountain areas*. Retrieved from http://ismailimail.wordpress.com/2008/05/29/aga-khan-foundation-opens-first-central-kindergarten-of-kyzyleshme-village-in-chonalay/

38. Klaus, D. (2003). The use of Indigenous languages in early basic education in Papua New Guinea: A model for elsewhere? *Language and Education, 17*(2), 105–111.

39. Ball, J., & Bernhardt, B. M. (2008). First Nations English dialects in Canada: Implications for speech-language pathology. *Clinical Linguistics and Phonetics, 22*(8), 570–588; Moses, K., & Wigglesworth, G. (2008). The silence of the frogs: Dysfunctional discourse in the "English-only" Aboriginal classroom. In J. Simpson & G. Wigglesworth (Eds.), *Children's language and multilingualism: Indigenous language use at home and school* (pp. 129–153). London: Continuum.

40. Rubio, M.-N. (2007). Mother tongue plus two: Can pluralingualism become the norm? *Children in Europe* (12), 2–3.

41. Baker, C., & Prys Jones, S. P. (1998). *Encyclopedia of bilingualism and bilingual education*. Clevedon, UK: Multilingual Matters; Covington, M. V. (1989). Self-esteem and failure at school: Analysis and policy implications. In A. M. Mecca, N. J. Smelser, & J. Vasconcellos (Eds.), *The social importance of self-esteem* (pp. 72–124). Berkeley, CA: University of California Press.

42. Kioko, A., Mutiga, J., Muthwii, M., Schroeder, L., Inyega, H., & Trudell, B. (2008). *Language and education in Africa: Answering the questions*. Nairobi: Multilingual Education Network of Eastern Africa; Wright & Taylor. (1995). Identity and the language of the classroom.

43. Benson, C. (2002). Real and potential benefits of bilingual progammes in developing countries. *International Journal of Bilingual Education and Bilingualism, 5*(6), 303–317.

44. Dutcher, N., & Tucker, G. R. (1994). *The use of first and second languages in education: A review of international experience*. Pacific Island Discussion Paper Series no. 1. Washington, DC: World Bank.

45. Ibid.; Cummins, J. (2000). *Language, power and pedagogy*. Clevedon, UK: Multilingual Matters.

46. UNESCO. (2008). *Mother tongue matters*.

47. McCarty, T. L. (2008). Native American languages as heritage mother tongues. *Language, Culture and Curriculum, 21*(3), 201–225.

48. Kirkness, V. (2002). The preservation and use of our languages: Respecting the natural order of the creator. In B. Burnaby, & J. A. Reyhner (Eds.), *Indigenous languages across the community* (pp. 17–23). Flagstaff, AZ: Northern Arizona University Center for Excellence in Education.

49. Greymorning, S. (2007). Going beyond words: The Arapaho immersion program. In J. Reyhner (Ed.), *Teaching Indigenous languages* (pp. 22–30). Flagstaff, AZ: Northern Arizona University Center for Excellence in Education.

50. Harrison, B., & Papa, R. (2005). The development of an Indigenous knowledge program in a New Zealand Maori-language immersion school. *Anthropology and Education Quarterly, 36*(1), 57–72.

51. Delpit, L. D., & Kemelfield, G. (1985). *An evaluation of the Viles Tok Ples Skul scheme in the North Solomons province*. ERU Report no. 51, University of Papua New Guinea, Waigani, Papua New Guinea.

52. Hornberger, N. H. (Ed.). (1996). *Indigenous literacies in the Americas: Language planning from the bottom up*. Berlin: Mouton de Gruyter; Hornberger, N. H. (2002). Multilingual language policies and the continua of biliteracy: An ecological approach. *Language Policy, 1*(1), 27–51; Hornberger, N. H. (2005). Opening and filling up implementational and ideological spaces in heritage language education. *Modern Language Journal, 89*(4), 605–609; McCarty, T. L., Watahomigie, L. J., & Yamamoto, A. Y. (guest Eds.). (1999). Reversing language shift in Indigenous America–collaborations and views from the field. [Special Issue.] *Practicing Anthropology, 20*(2), 1–47.

53. Kirkness. (2002). The preservation and use of our languages.
54. Johns, A., & Mazurkewich, I. (2001). The role of the university in the training of native language teachers: Labrador. In L. Hinton, & K. Hale (Eds.), *The green book of language revitalization in practice* (pp. 355–366). San Diego: Academic Press; Suina, J. H. (2004). Native language teachers in a struggle for language and cultural survival. *Anthropology and Education Quarterly, 35*(3), 281–302.
55. Morrison, S., & Peterson, L. (2003). *Using technology to teach Native American languages.* Retrieved from http://www.cal.org/ericcll/langlink/feb03feature.html; Wilson, W. H., Kamanā, K., & Rawlins, N. (2006). Nawahi Hawaiian laboratory school. *Journal of American Indian Education, 45*(2), 42–44.
56. King, J. (2001). Te Kohanga Reo: Maori language revitalization. In L. Hinton, & K. Hale (Eds.), *The green book of language revitalization in practice* (pp. 119–128). San Diego: Academic Press; McKinley, R. (2003). *Aboriginal language: When it's gone, that's it. No more Indians.* Retrieved from http://ammsa.com/classroom/CLASS4language.htm; Wilson, W. H., & Kamanā, K. (2001). Mai loko mai O ka 'I'ini: Proceeding from a dream–The 'aha Punana Leo connection in Hawaiian language revitalization. In L. Hinton & K. Hale (Eds.), *The green book of language revitalization in practice* (pp. 147–176). San Diego: Academic Press.
57. Home language instruction generally refers to use of the learners' home language (sometimes referred to as mother tongue) as the medium of instruction.
58. UNESCO. (2001). *International conference on education 46th session: Final report* (p. 11). Paris: UNESCO.
59. The language of instruction in or out of school refers to the language used for teaching the basic curriculum of an educational system. The choice of language or indeed the languages of instruction (educational policy might recommend the use of several languages of instruction) is a recurrent challenge in the development of quality education. Although some countries opt for one language of instruction, often the official or majority language, others have chosen to use educational strategies that give national or local languages an important place in schooling.
60. Blommaert, J. (Ed.). (1999). *Language ideological debates.* London: Mouton de Gruyter.
61. Golding, P., & Harris, P. (Eds.). (1997). *Beyond cultural imperialism: Globalization, communication and the new international order.* London: Sage.
62. Rampton, B. (1995). *Crossing: Language and ethnicity among adolescents.* Longman, UK: Harlow.
63. Baker, C. (1996). *Foundations of bilingual education and bilingualism* (2nd ed.). Clevedon, UK: Multilingual Matters.
64. Cummins, J. (1986). Empowering minority students: A framework for intervention. *Harvard Educational Review, 56*(1), 18–36.
65. UNESCO. (2007). *Advocacy kit for promoting multilingual education: Including the excluded.* Bangkok: UNESCO/Bangkok.
66. Benson. (2002). Real and potential benefits of bilingual progammes; Cummins. (1986). Empowering minority students.
67. Benson, C. (2009). Designing effective schooling in multilingual contexts: The strengths and limitations of bilingual "models." In A. Mohanty, M. Panda, R. Phillipson, & T. Skutnabb-Kangas (Eds.), *Multilingual education for social justice: Globalising the local.* New Delhi: Orient Blackswan.
68. Wilson & Kamanā. (2001). Mai loko mai O ka 'I'ini.
69. UNESCO. (2007). *Advocacy kit for promoting multilingual education.*
70. Warner, S. (2001). The movement to revitalize Hawaiian language and culture. In L. Hinton & K. Hale (Eds.), *The green book of language revitalization in practice* (pp. 134–144). San Diego: Academic Press.
71. Wilson & Kamanā. (2001). Mai loko mai O ka 'I'ini.
72. Wilson, Kamanā, & Rawlins. (2006). Nawahi Hawaiian laboratory school.
73. King. (2001). Te Kohanga Reo: Maori language revitalization; McClutchie Mita, D. (2007). Maori language revitalization: A vision for the future. *Canadian Journal of Native Education, 30*(1), 101–107.

74. Ball, J., & Simpkins, M. (2004). The community within the child: Integration of Indigenous knowledge into First Nations childcare process and practice. *American Indian Quarterly, 28*(3–4), 480–498; Bernard, J., Lefebvre, M. L., Kilbride, K. M., Chud, G., & Lange, R. (1998). Troubled relationships in early childhood education: Parent-teacher interactions in ethnoculturally diverse child care settings. *Early Education and Development, 9*(1), 5–28.

75. Ball, J., & Pence, A. (2006). *Supporting Indigenous children's development: Community-university partnerships.* Vancouver: UBC Press.

76. Ibid.

77. UNESCO/MOST. (2002). *Best practices using Indigenous knowledge.* The Hague: UNESCO/MOST.

78. UNESCO. (2008). *Mother tongue instruction in early childhood education: A selected bibliography.* Paris: UNESCO.

79. Bellar, S. (2008). *Fostering language acquisition in daycare settings: What does the research tell us?* Working Papers in Early Childhood Development. The Hague: Bernard van Leer Foundation; Nicholas, H., & Lightbown, P. M. (2008). Defining child second language acquisition, defining roles for L2 instruction. In J. Philp, R. Oliver, & R. Mackey (Eds.), *Second language acquisition and the younger learner* (pp. 27–51). Amsterdam: John Benjamins.

80. Fuller. (2007). *Standardized childhood*; Kincheloe. (2000). *Certifying the damage*; MacNaughton. (2007). *Doing Foucault in early childhood studies*; Nsamenang. (2008). *(Mis)understanding ECD in Africa.*

81. Cummins, J. (1986). Psychological assessment of minority students: Out of context, out of focus, out of control? In A.C. Willig, & H.F. Greenberg (Eds.), *Bilingualism and Learning Disabilities* (pp. 3–13). Chicago: American Library; Stairs, Bernhard, & Colleagues. Considerations for evaluating "good care."

82. Ball & Bernhardt. (2008). First Nations English dialects in Canada.

83. Canada Council on Learning. (2007). *State of learning in Canada.*

84. In Canada, the 1982 Constitution Act recognizes three separate peoples as original inhabitants: Inuit, Métis, and North American Indian (more commonly known as First Nations).

85. A reserve is land set apart and designated for the use and occupancy of an Indian group or band—as such, the terms "on-reserve" or "off-reserve" are generally not applicable to Métis or Inuit.

86. Indian and Northern Affairs Canada and Canadian Mortgage and Housing Corporation. (2007). *Aboriginal demography: Population, household and family projections, 2001–2026.* Ottawa, ON: INAC and CMHC.

87. The population of Aboriginal children entering schools in Canada has been increasing, particularly in the Yukon, Northwest Territories, and Nunavut, and in the provinces of Saskatchewan and Manitoba. For example, in 2006, in Saskatchewan, Aboriginal children made up 20% of all children under 6 years old. According to the 2006 census, there were approximately 7,000 Inuit, 35,000 Métis, and 47,000 off-reserve First Nations children under the age of 6 across Canada See Statistics Canada. (2006). *Census of the population 2006.* Ottawa, ON: Statistics Canada.

88. Battiste, M. (2000). Maintaining aboriginal identity, language, and culture in modern society. In M. Battiste (Ed.), *Reclaiming Indigenous voice and vision* (pp. 192–208). Vancouver: UBC Press; Mendelson, M. (2006). *Aboriginal peoples and postsecondary education in Canada.* Ottawa, ON: Caledon Institute of Social Policy.

89. Until recently, Indigenous peoples were excluded from educational opportunities equivalent to those offered to nonIndigenous peoples. Most options for postsecondary education were closed to them until the 1960s. Most parents and grandparents of Aboriginal children today were forced to attend Indian residential schools (or occasionally day schools) where the curricula prepared students for nonacademic roles including manual and domestic labor. The last of these schools closed in 1996. See Fournier, S., & Crey, E. (1997). *Stolen from our embrace: The abduction of First Nations children and the restoration of Aboriginal communities.* Vancouver: Douglas and McIntyre.

90. Canadian Centre for Justice. (2001). *Aboriginal peoples in Canada. Statistics profile series.* Ottawa, ON: Minister of Industry; First Nations Child and Family Caring Society of Canada.

Wen: De: We are coming to the light of day. Retrieved from http://www.fncfcs.com/docs/WendeReport.pdf

91. Council of Ministers of Education. *Quality education for all young people: Challenges* (para. 22). Retrieved from http://www.cmec.ca/international/ice/47_ICE_report.en.pdf

92. For example, in 2003, the Ministry of Education in British Columbia found that Aboriginal students in grade 4 were "not meeting expectations" at a rate 16% higher than non-Aboriginal students. In grade 7, this rose to 21%. Between 40% and 50% of Aboriginal students failed to meet the requirements of grades 4, 7, and 10 literacy tests. See Bell, D., with Anderson, K., Fortin, T., Ottoman, J., Rose, S., Simard, L., & Spencer, K. (2004). *Sharing our success: Ten case studies in Aboriginal schooling.* Kelowna, BC: Society for the Advancement of Excellence in Education. Retrieved from http://www.artssmarts.ca/media/fr/sharingoursuccess.pdf. Among Canadian children enrolled in school, the proportion of Indigenous people who have not attained a high school diploma is approximately 2.5 times greater than the proportion of non-Aboriginal Canadians, accounting for nearly half of Aboriginal youth leaving secondary school early (see Mendelson. (2006). *Aboriginal peoples and postsecondary education.*). The gap in high school attainment is highest for Inuit (3.6 times higher than the Canadian average). One of the primary reasons Inuit students now state for leaving high school is to care for a child. See Government of Nunavut and Nunavut Tunngavik, Inc. (2004). *Background paper submitted to the Canada-Aboriginal peoples roundtable.* Iqaluit, ON: Government of Nunavut and Nunavut Tunngavik, Inc.

93. Sharpe & Arsenault. (2009). *Investing in Aboriginal education in Canada.*

94. Bennett. (2003). *Early childhood education and care policy.*

95. Leitch, K. K. (2008). *Reaching for the top: A report by the advisor on healthy children and youth.* Ottawa, ON: Health Canada.

96. Native Council of Canada. (1990). *Native child care: The circle of care.* Ottawa, ON: Native Council of Canada.

97. Royal Commission on Aboriginal Peoples. (1996). *Report of the royal commission on Aboriginal peoples* Vols. 1 and 3. Ottawa, ON: Minister of Supply and Services Canada.

98. Indian and Northern Affairs Canada. (2007). *Early childhood development: Programs and initiatives.* Retrieved from http://www.ainc-inac.gc.ca/hb/sp/ecd/index-eng.asp

99. Statistics Canada. (2006). *Aboriginal peoples' survey 2001–initial findings: Well-being of the non-reserve Aboriginal population.* Retrieved from http://www.statcan.gc.ca/pub/89–589-x/index-eng.htm

100. Zigler, E., & Valentine, A. (Eds.). (1979). *Project Head Start: A legacy of the war on poverty.* New York: Free Press.

101. Minister of Public Works and Government Services. *Aboriginal Head Start in urban and northern communities: Program and participants 2001.* Retrieved from http://www.hc-sc.gc.ca/hppb/childhoodyouth/acy/ahs.html; Western Arctic Aboriginal Head Start Council. (2006). *Ten years of Aboriginal Head Start in the Northwest Territories 1996 to 2006.* Yellowknife, NWT: Western Arctic Aboriginal Head Start Council.

102. First Nations Centre. (2005). *First Nations regional longitudinal health survey 2002/03: Results for adults, youth and children living in First Nations communities.* Ottawa, ON: Assembly of First Nations/First Nations Information Governance Committee. Retrieved from http://www.naho.ca/firstnations/english/regional_health.php

103. Leitch. (2008). *Reaching for the top.*

104. Ball, J. (2005). Early childhood care and development programs as hook and hub for inter-sectoral service delivery in Indigenous communities. *Journal of Aboriginal Health, 2*(1), 36–49.

105. Fuller. (2007). *Standardized childhood.*

106. May, H., & Carr, M. (2000). Empowering children to learn and grow–Te Whariki: The New Zealand early childhood national curriculum. In J. Hayden (Ed.), *Landscapes in early childhood education: Cross-national perspectives on empowerment–a guide for the new millennium* (pp. 153–169). New York: Peter Lang; Reeders, E. (2008). The collaborative construction of knowledge in a traditional context. In J. Simpson, & G. Wigglesworth (Eds.), *Children's*

language and multilingualism: Indigenous language use at home and school (pp. 103–128). London: Continuum; Tagataga, Inc. (2007). *Inuit early childhood education and care: Present successes–promising directions*. Prepared for Inuit Tapiriit Kanatami; Wilson, Kamanā, & Rawlins. (2006). Nawahi Hawaiian laboratory school.

107. Ball, J. (2005). "Nothing about us without us": Restorative research partnerships involving Indigenous children and communities in Canada. In A. Farrell (Ed.), *Exploring ethical research with children* (pp. 81–96). London: Open University Press/McGraw-Hill Education.

108. Hanushek, E. A., & Wolfmann, L. (2007). *Education quality and economic growth*. Washington, DC: World Bank.

Part 5

APPLYING LESSONS
ACROSS GEOGRAPHY

14

Adapting Innovations Across Borders to Close Equity Gaps in Education

FERNANDO REIMERS, NORTH COOC, AND JODUT HASHMI

Over the last 60 years, the world has witnessed a remarkable transformation in educational opportunity. The inclusion of education as one of the fundamental rights in the Universal Declaration of Human Rights, adopted in 1948, and the ensuing creation of a global architecture to support the achievement of this right, transformed humanity. Whereas, 60 years ago, the vast majority of the world's children did not have the opportunity to set foot in a school, today most of them do. The most dramatic expansion took place in the developing world, since early industrialized nations had long been working to universalize schooling.

Despite this progress, the objective of providing all children in the world access to a primary education has not been reached. According to official statistics, which may underestimate the problem significantly, 72 million children of primary school age are not currently enrolled in school, and approximately 759 million adults lack literacy skills. One in four children who begin elementary school in developing countries drops out before being able to read and write. Almost one in five adolescents, nearly 71 million in all, were out of school in 2007.[1] The children and youth most excluded from education are typically from subdominant groups: the poor, females, and members of ethnic and linguistic minorities.

Three alternative explanations for this global failure in educating all children are a lack of political commitment at the national and global level, deficient approaches to achieve the goal of providing all children a quality education, and implementation failures. Given the abundant national and international pronouncements and legislation in support of universal basic education, it would be hard to argue that these problems reflect a lack of professed interest or shared global commitment to educating all children. There is certainly evidence that serious implementation challenges are faced by programs trying to achieve this goal. To a great extent, however, this global failure reflects the absence of effective

315

approaches to doing what most countries around the world have expressed an interest in and a commitment to doing: *educating all children*. As a result, in spite of the remarkable progress in access to school achieved during the 20th century, existing evidence suggests that many children learn too little of the intended curriculum, that there are serious inequalities in what is learned by children of different social groups, and that too often what is learned in school has limited potential to alter the social chances of educated people or to expand their freedoms.

As our aspirations about including all children in schools have increased, so has demand for knowledge about what works. Such demand outstrips by far the output of specific research and evaluation in each of the specific contexts in which such knowledge is necessary. As a result, there is a growing demand for *knowledge transfer* about what practices "work" from one education context to another. With this growing demand also come growing concerns about the limitations of *transfer* to support effective policy and a greater need for understanding how to transfer appropriately from one context to another. The awareness of the limitations with the transfer of education practices has led many educators and policy-makers interested in educating all children to another path to innovation—to try to innovate without attention to what has worked elsewhere. This trial-and-error approach is a very expensive way to discover how best to deliver on the global aspirations of the last 60 years.

This chapter problematizes the question of precisely what knowledge is helpful to innovate in order to promote equity in education. We argue that effective innovation to educate all children requires not innovation and creativity unburdened by the careful understanding of the facts, innovation based on naïve transfer, or innovation based on a complete indigenous research and development infrastructure, but innovation supported by *contextualized transfer* of education policies and practices.

Contextualized transfer is the process of adapting practices that have demonstrated effectiveness in one context to another while examining the way in which various policy interventions relate to policy outcomes across national contexts, analyzing the dependency of those relationships on characteristics of the context, and determining how differences among these contexts might limit the transferability of policy effects. At the core of this concept of contextualized transfer is an understanding of quality education as the product of a system, rather than the product of a single policy intervention, where context is a core element of this system.

To be useful, transfer of ideas and practices about "what works" need to stimulate educational innovation in the context into which such ideas are "imported"; to do this well, the transfer of ideas about "what works" in one context needs to be not just about which practices have proven to be effective in certain contexts to achieve particular education objectives, but also why they have been effective in that context, as well as what adaptations are necessary in order to be able to obtain similar results, given differences in context. The mere transfer of practices that have worked in one context to another, without the additional analysis just described will, more often than not, lead not to sustainable innovation, but to disappointing results and to implementation failures.

Educational Innovations and Knowledge Transfer

Much of the progress that has been made in advancing educational equity globally has been the result of a series of innovations and of transfer and borrowing of such innovations. First, the very innovative idea produced by Jon Amos Comenius in the mid-1600s, that all persons should be educated, was an idea that travelled in time and across geographies. Comenius, who lived through a protracted period of religious-based intolerance, thought that at the root of such violence lay deficient skills and knowledge for people to understand one another and work out their differences peacefully. It would take another two centuries until another innovation, the Lancasterian method of instruction, produced an approach to educate large numbers of children at low cost. This method was transferred to Prussia, where another innovation of the 19th century, a public and universal education system, served as a model that inspired reformers in other contexts. John Quincy Adams, for example, as U.S. Minister in Berlin, described with admiration the education system of Silesia in 1804 to his fellow citizens back home.[2] In 1871, a Japanese delegation traveled to the United States and Europe to borrow educational practices that would help to modernize Japan.[3]

More recent examples of the transfer of the idea that all should be educated include the leading role played by UNESCO in the early 1950s, by convening meetings of ministers of education and of finance in different regions of the world to set quantitative targets and milestones to universalize basic education. UNESCO and other development organizations continue to facilitate the exchange of experience and practice to achieve this goal through regional conferences, publications, training programs, and the advice provided by education advisors mobilized through cooperative programs. In addition, member organizations such as the Organisation for Economic Co-operation and Development (OECD) provide countries with expert teams that analyze the effectiveness of education policies and propose reform strategies. By design, these teams are composed of experts from a range of countries with the aim of informing their analyses and recommendations with the lessons of comparative experience.

The ideas and practices that have been transferred through this infrastructure include ideas about what to teach, how to teach it, how to organize school systems, how to support the professional development of teachers, how to develop education plans, and how to monitor the performance of education systems. Some of the ideas that were transferred to support the expansion of education included the creation of "double shifts" in schools, through which the same school buildings would be used to serve two groups of children; the establishment of "multigraded schools" in rural areas, which tasked a teacher or two with the instruction of several grades of elementary education; and the creation of "school clusters" through which small rural schools were grouped around a more resourced "nucleus" school, which served as a center of professional development for the teachers of the affiliated schools. More recent practices that have been borrowed and transferred to support equity in education include specific curricula and instructional programs, approaches to teacher professional development, scholarships to support school attendance of marginalized children, or the creation of national evaluation systems to assess student knowledge and skills.

The practice of borrowing and transferring educational ideas and practices from one context to another is therefore joined at the hip with the history of educational expansion. Some of the ideas transferred have produced great educational progress. For example the creation of double shifts in the same school buildings to rapidly expand access to school, given limitations in the financial capacity to invest in infrastructure during the 1950s and 1960s, was central to the significant increase in enrollment rates in the developing world during this period. The Centers of Excellence for Teacher Training (CETT), for instance, have improved the quality of literacy instruction in Latin America since 2001 by adopting and transferring best practices from the International Reading Association and successful programs like Reading Is Fundamental.[4] Another example of successful contextualized transfer is INJAZ Al-Arab, a program that has modeled itself after the Junior Achievement Worldwide, which provides high school students and recent high school graduates with business, entrepreneurship, and life skills to address unemployment in the Middle East-North Africa (MENA) region.[5] Many other educational ideas and practices, however, have not travelled well across cultural contexts. For example, in 1997, South Africa reformed the curriculum of instruction following an approach called *outcomes-based education* (OBE). Several scholars have described how OBE failed to improve educational practice in South Africa, largely because of a lack of attention to differences in teacher knowledge and skills.[6] Another example is the documented case of failure to transfer new math curricula from Australia to Papua New Guinea because the transfer did not take into account differences in teacher quality between the two contexts.[7] Similarly, the import of a whole-language curriculum to support literacy instruction in Malawi has failed to produce conditions that enable most children to learn to read, arguably as a result of the much larger class sizes and deficient general preparation of teachers.[8]

Although concern over the limitations of educational transfer and of policy borrowing is not new, systematic scholarship studying this process is more recent. In 1970, in the golden age of educational expansion in developing countries, and with much participation of the international development community, Beeby stated "those who are responsible for education in developing countries know that, through lack of books, lack of equipment, and lack of adequately trained teachers, they will, over the next few years, be driven to importing educational ideas that are really irrelevant to their needs."[9] Most contemporary scholarly study of the process of policy transfer focuses on its consequences and how those relate to the political conditions under which transfer takes place, or to the actors and institutions that participate in the process and their motivations.[10-13]

Although it is generally possible to describe ex-post when educational transfer succeeds or fails, it is an altogether different issue to do this ex-ante. This is because, while the problematic nature of the relationship between transfer and context has been recognized by comparative education scholars, relatively less attention has gone to producing analytic devices to increase the effectiveness of transfer. This leads policy reformers to recognize the risks of transfer without the tools to manage those risks. This chapter presents an analytic approach, in the form of a five-step conceptual framework, to facilitating the transfer of education practices to stimulate educational innovation to close equity gaps in education.

What Do We Need to Know to Close Equity Gaps in Education?

To close equity gaps in education, we need to know what those gaps are, what causes them, and what could work in closing them. To know this in any given context, we need to take stock of what is known, carry out specific research, and transfer knowledge and best practices from other contexts.

There are four broad areas in which further knowledge is essential to inform action in expanding educational opportunity. First, we need to know how educational institutions relate to other social institutions. This includes understanding how a society and various groups within the society value education, and what the continuities and discontinuities are between how schools conduct their work and the values, expectations, and norms of families and communities. Understanding educational institutions also includes knowing what broad purposes they serve, in addition to the stated purpose of educating children. For example, in some societies, public education systems are used to reward political loyalty and support political parties or groups. In some societies, educational institutions are one of the mechanisms through which various forms of segregation are practiced along socioeconomic, political, ethnic, racial or religious divides. In some societies, different forms of bribes and gifts are extracted from students and parents for access to the best schools or teachers, or to obtain special attention from teachers. Knowledge about the pervasiveness of these practices and their consequences in sorting different students into different education streams is very important if we are to understand how educational institutions relate to other institutions and cultures. It is essential to know what different groups in the society expect of schools and how satisfied they are with the way in which schools function at present.

Second, we also need to know how educational institutions function and what is learned in them. Who teaches, in what way, with what technology, with what pedagogy, with what governance, as well as what is taught, to which students, at what cost, and who pays. We also need to know how effective schools are at developing cognitive, social, and emotional competencies; what learning environments are like; and how students are treated by their peers, by teachers, and by others in the school. Other relevant considerations include how children engage with schools and the process of school learning, and how school learning fits with other aspects of students' lives.

Third, attention to quality of education requires a focus on the intended purposes of instruction, as well as on the processes that help teachers achieve those purposes. Thus, the concern with educational opportunity in middle- and low-income countries should go much further than the current emphasis on access and completion of a basic education. It should focus as well on how teachers can help students develop capabilities that expand their options in life. To achieve this, we need knowledge to support instructional improvement, including the instructional core—the daily interactions among students, teachers, curriculum, and instructional resources. Additional dimensions of instructional improvement are time, consistency, and alignment. It takes time to learn and to teach, and in general the more engaged learning time students and teachers have available, the more students will learn. It is also important that consistency be maintained in instructional quality throughout the learning trajectories of students. It is not much help to have a great teacher in one subject only in one year of one's life. Curriculum, instruction, resources, and assessment should be aligned within and across grades, so that students' educational experiences are coherent, cumulative, and synergistic.

Fourth, based on a good understanding of the relationship of educational institutions to their social context and of their functioning and effectiveness, we need to know the impact of interventions deliberately designed to improve the effectiveness of schools. The goal of this form of evaluation should be more than establishing program impact; it should be to contribute to the development of program theory. To do this, evaluations need to examine the process, the actual mechanism through which certain interventions produce particular results.

Finally, we need knowledge about the process of change itself, and about the role of leadership and professional development in initiating and sustaining change. The purpose of educational leadership is to support efforts at the school level that bring high-quality teachers to schools; that provide them with excellent preparation at the beginning of and throughout their careers; that guide their work with relevant, authentic, high-quality, and intellectually challenging and engaging purposes and curriculum; and that support extended engaged learning time, with consistency and alignment. We need more knowledge about how to select, prepare, and sustain such leadership, especially in low-income countries.

How Do We Generate the Knowledge Necessary to Close Equity Gaps?

The transfer of innovative ideas about education purposes and practices has been, historically and globally, the principal mechanism through which equity gaps in access to education have been closed. The facilitation of this form of transfer of educational practices has been one of the functions of the global architecture that was specifically developed over the second half of the 20th century to support the achievement of the right to education. Occasionally, some of the practices that travel through the networks that form the global education architecture have been systematically evaluated in particular contexts, but this has not been the norm nor has it proved a necessary condition for their diffusion or adoption in the form of innovation in new contexts.

The problem of innovating based on the naïve transfer of educational practices is that educational institutions are complex systems whose performance is the result of the interdependencies of the components of the system. One of those components is *context*, an abbreviation for the set of norms and practices that characterize a specific culture, society, and set of institutional practices. The fact that an educational practice, such as a particular approach to math education, has proven to be effective in country A does not mean that it will also be effective in country B, where the levels of teacher capacity, parental support for instruction, or availability of instructional resources to support teaching may be different. Strictly speaking, knowledge about the effectiveness of education practices should not be generalized outside the boundaries in which these practices have been scientifically examined. These boundaries include the outcomes in which such effects have been tested, the grade levels and particular student populations in which they have been studied, the particular set of social and economic circumstances in which they were studied, and the characteristics of the educational institutions in which they were studied. For example, the results of research on the impact of class size on student achievement conducted in countries where class size ranges from 18 to 45 students tell us little about the impact of class size in contexts in which class sizes range from 50 to 300 students. In turn, class size is a dimension of context that mediates the impact of other educational practices. Current research on literacy instruction in the United States emphasizes the importance of providing individualized attention to "struggling readers." Doing this assumes methods for the identification of such readers and conditions through which teachers or other reading specialists can dedicate time to these students with reading difficulties. But the translation of these practices, which have been adopted in education systems that can afford relatively small classes, to contexts in which first-grade teachers have classes that include hundreds of students, as is the case in Malawi for example, presents a significant challenge to implementation, with the result that the kind of practices that allow attention to struggling readers in countries with small class sizes are unlikely to be practical in contexts where class sizes are much larger.

One way to respond to this limitation of research-based knowledge is to argue for the replication of studies evaluating the impact of such practices across a wide range of contexts. This replication would, over time, help discern knowledge about policy–outcome relationships that generalize well across a range of contexts from the specific to particular. We could, in the example just mentioned, empirically assess how class size impacts student achievement in contexts where such size reaches over 100 students. This has been done in replicating experimental studies of the impact of conditional cash transfer (CCT) programs in several countries. However, the investment in evaluation resources necessary to build this body of knowledge exceeds by several orders of magnitude the level of resources devoted to educational research and evaluation. This underscores, of course, the importance of investing in those resources, as well as the importance of having a strategy to guide how to invest in them. It is clearly impossible to replicate a study about the effects of a particular education practice in every conceivable context. A strategy should help determine which replications are most likely to advance a theory and help decide when to discontinue replications. But these limitations stemming from the unfeasibility of conducting endless studies underscores also the urgency to find alternatives to generate a knowledge base.

Because generating an indigenous knowledge base to support innovation is expensive and time-consuming, those who need to make immediate decisions about increasing educational access, quality, and relevance for marginalized groups typically innovate based on ideas about good practice, no matter where these ideas have been generated. In other words, they naïvely transfer ideas about "what works" without much attention to the particular aspects of context in which such effects have been established.

The limitations of naïvely transferring educational practices, the challenges to developing an indigenous knowledge base, and the limitations of replicating studies of policy effectiveness account in part for the persistent challenges to achieving educational equity. As a result, many education policies are not based on evidence, or at least on evidence that is relevant to the pertinent context. Innovation is obviously necessary, but based on what knowledge?

Contextualized Transfer: A Framework

Contextualized transfer is a pragmatic approach to support and discipline the process of educational innovation, making the best possible use of scientifically based knowledge about what works in education, in the realistic time frame in which policy-makers and program designers need to make decisions about ways to move forward, and within the limitations of resources to support decision-making that are typical of most policy settings. Contextualized transfer of knowledge about policies and practices to close equity gaps is a five-step process that involves (1) a clear identification of needs translated into a tractable problem, (2) a thorough analysis of the context in which the problem exists, (3) taking stock of existing research on the determinants of the problem at hand and on the best practices to address it in other contexts, (4) an analysis of the gaps between the extant research and the context, and (5) the design of innovation or transfer of practices to close the gap. This basic five-step framework can extend into an additional step, if resources and time permit it—the evaluation of a pilot of the innovation based on transfer in the importing context.

This five-step sequence makes transparent the process of adaptation of practices from one context to another and, as such, it is very different from the naïve transfer of policy where, at best, such formal analysis is implicit. In so doing, contextualized transfer makes the adaptation subject to the same processes of public scrutiny and verifiability that inform the intersubjective agreements on which scientific knowledge is based. The knowledge base that informs transfer is thus *falsifiable* in the very same way that all positive knowledge is falsifiable, and therefore scientifically true.[14]

IDENTIFYING NEEDS

The first step in a process to establish what evidence is relevant to inform how to close equity gaps is to establish what the gaps and needs are in a particular context, as perceived by the various groups that have an interest in the education enterprise. It is possible to use social science methods in assessing those needs systematically.

The definition of what problems are important in a particular society or community should be informed by a direct analysis of that reality, not by the advocacy or interest of those working on those problems in other contexts. Too often, through the networks that form the global education architecture, travel not just ideas about solutions to real and perceived problems, but also ideas about what problems are worth treating and should receive priority. Because the global architecture includes industries and interest groups that provide services to treat education problems, there is an inherent conflict of interest in having those institutions, external to the localities in which educational equity needs to improve, establish the priority of the problems that call for their particular forms of expertise or services. Many of the education priorities of the international development community are the result of the well-organized efforts of global advocacy coalitions, with limited accountability to the communities and beneficiaries they try to serve. Although these global coalitions can and have played a very valuable role in expanding educational opportunity, it is imperative to tap more directly the knowledge of those closer to the problems to determine which of their education needs should receive priority attention and to establish possible promising options to address them.

Three unique characteristics of education institutions are relevant to the identification of needs and priorities. The first is that numerous stakeholders are affected by the outcomes of these institutions. The students themselves are obviously a most important group, but during the earlier part of their educational trajectories, the students are represented by adults, including parents and caregivers, who make decisions for them. Other stakeholders include teachers, members of communities, and society at large, all of whom are affected by the outcomes of education.

A second unique characteristic of education institutions is that they have multiple outcomes, short- and long-term, which can be valued differently by different constituencies and different societies. Schools can offer a relative level of safety for children during part of the day, providing shelter, care, and often nutrition. They can offer the possibility of engagement in activities valued by society, a social role for children, and the opportunity for positive social, emotional, and cognitive engagement. They can prepare students for subsequent education, and provide knowledge and skills that are helpful to assuming adult roles. Some of the outcomes societies care most about, such as helping people live fulfilling lives and be productive and engaged members of society, unfold over a long lifespan. It is very hard to predict ex-ante the social context in which people will live their lives, which makes it difficult to determine how best to prepare people for an uncertain future. Since different groups in society may place different value on these outcomes, achieving consensus on reform strategies is difficult.

A third characteristic of education institutions is that they operate as a system whose scale and complexity makes identification, coordination, and alignment of interventions to meet needs challenging. Good education is the result of the alignment and synergies among the components of such a system: good curriculum, qualified teachers, school principals and school supervisors supporting the work of teachers, and a good research and development system to continue to support innovation in schools. There is no educational equivalent of oral rehydration therapy, contraceptives, malaria nets, vaccines, drug cures, or other silver bullets in which a single input has significant effects independent of other conditions in the education system. In part, this is because cognitive, emotional, and social development is a long-term process and as such it requires sustained, high-quality support. The multidimensional nature of human development also requires rich and broad opportunities to foster it.

These three characteristics of education institutions make the use of evidence to promote equity challenging. For some of the relevant questions, obtaining evidence is itself very challenging, for instance, on the long-term effects of education policies, programs, or practices, or on their effects over a broad range of outcomes.

One example depicting how challenging it can be to define the needs and priorities of education institutions is the question of whether *Madrassas* are effective options to expand access to education. *Madrassas* are educational institutions that have a variety of goals and have come to the attention of many, as they are perceived as spreading Islamic extremism. But to truly judge whether *Madrassas* are effective options for increasing educational opportunity, especially in areas such as Pakistan and Afghanistan, it is important to examine the needs and priorities of these communities and of this institution, and to balance the potential risk for some students against the benefits that this form of education provides a great many students.

Madrassas affect a variety of stakeholders. A *Madrassa* is a "school" in Arabic, and many were developed along the Afghanistan and Pakistani borders in the late 1970s to provide an education to the rural communities there when no other educational institution was available. Since *Madrassas* are often funded by the religious alms that Muslims are required to provide, *Madrassas* provide housing and meals to the students who attend them, making them all the more attractive to low-income families and students. They also expanded education for girls along the two nations' borders. Thus, the *Madrassa* was able to increase access for a great number of students who did not formerly attend school.

They also have a variety of outcomes. Islam emphasizes two types of knowledge: the "revealed"—which is given directly by God—and the "earthly"—that which humans must discover.[15] *Madrassas* are meant to provide both forms of knowledge to prepare students for the life they lead in the present and for the afterlife. Different entities, such as leaders, funders, and nations, may choose which to emphasize. Fundamentalist leaders may emphasize the "revealed" knowledge, whereas a more secular government or leadership may emphasize a more balanced knowledge within the *Madrassa*. And finally, *Madrassas* operate as a system in interdependency with other social institutions, including government. So, regardless of the purposes of the *Madrassas*, the content that is chosen is a result of the synergies among components of the system rather than intrinsic to this educational modality itself. If, as in Afghanistan, the Taliban come to power, a more "revealed" form of knowledge may be emphasized, or different elements of the "revealed" knowledge may be taught (but the same could happen in secular schools under the same regime). When government changes, or when school leadership changes as a result of the interactions of those within the system, the focus of the *Madrassa* may be completely different.

Given these complexities, there is no easy and simple answer to the question of whether *Madrassas* are a good option to expand access: It all depends on the context. Social science methods, such as surveys or focus groups among students, parents, teachers, and members of the community, can be very effective in helping to characterize the specific context, identify what the children who are excluded from school identify as their needs, and assess the relative merits of various options to serve those needs.

ANALYZING CONTEXT

A second step in the process of contextualizing the transfer of education policies is to analyze the demographic, geographic, cultural, historical, economic, political, and social dimensions of the context in which schools are embedded, the institutional context of schools themselves, and to the extent possible, future trends. For example, an analysis of the demographic structure of the population and of the predictable trends in that structure, can help to identify current gaps in access and the institutional and human resources necessary to meet future educational needs as the school-aged population expands or its composition shifts. An analysis of the economic context will help explain how education is contributing, and can contribute, to economic development and to the employment and productivity of the labor force. Institutional analysis will establish the degree of capacity to support various types of activity and reform. Against the backdrop of this contextual analysis, it will be possible to discern which research about how to address particular education needs is most relevant, and it may be possible to make adaptations to what is known from extant research in other contexts.

For example, when trying to create a policy or an evaluation to address educational access and opportunities for minorities, such as Muslims in India, it would be necessary to examine all of the relevant dimensions of the context in which schools are embedded. Muslims compose 13% of India's population, the second-largest religious community, or the largest religious minority in the country. Regions such as Jammu and Kashmir, Punjab, and Bengal have concentrated Muslim populations, and the Muslim population is not evenly distributed through different areas. Although there are large numbers of Muslims in India, however, Muslims are considered minorities, and they remain politically, socially, economically, and educationally marginalized.

Politically, Muslims have often been at odds with the Hindu majority in India as a result of the partition of India in 1947 into the Republic of India and the Islamic Republic of Pakistan. Currently, there is inadequate Muslim representation in government, and many believe this leads to oppositional behavior on the part of some Muslim youth in India. Although the economic situation for Muslims varies by region, unemployment among Muslim graduates is one of the highest among all socioeconomic groups, and Muslims are one of the poorest groups in India. As many as 25% of Muslim youth between the ages of 6 and 14 have never been to school or have dropped out. Despite an increase in primary school enrollments, Muslim enrollment rates lag behind the national average. Finally, the literacy rate for Muslims is far below the national average.[16]

Understanding this context in which Muslim youth live in India is essential to develop effective policy or program initiatives to provide them educational opportunities. A likely consequence of this situation is the alienation of Muslim youth from traditional schools, which may make innovative education programs, perhaps managed by private institutions, or public-private partnerships, more promising options to overcome some of the likely obstacles to incorporating these youth through the expansion of established public schools.

TAKING STOCK OF EXTANT RESEARCH INCLUDING EVALUATION AND OTHER APPLIED RESEARCH

The study of what is already known about the needs and problems that a particular policy is attempting to address is a valuable step in providing some discipline to the logical analysis of how to increase educational equity. What does research say about this topic? What are the regularities across different studies, what findings are sufficiently robust that they are consistent across contexts, what findings vary with particular contexts, and what conclusions can be drawn from examining that variation of results as it relates to variation in contexts?

In learning from what is already known about the educational needs under study it makes sense to look broadly. Looking at contexts different from the particular context at hand is one way to do this. But one can also look at research with different populations, with different educational outcomes, and so on. It may even be helpful to look at research and practices in domains other than education. The main purpose of this step is heuristic, to generate hypotheses that will then be scrutinized systematically to support the design of policy interventions.

It is especially useful to examine applied research and analysis, including in-depth study of national and subnational education systems; historical research; ethnographic studies of schools, classrooms, students, and communities; school effectiveness research; and program evaluation, as well as comparative knowledge of these topics across countries. Such analysis will also need to include evaluation research and other forms of inquiry that may not make it into scholarly publications, but that constitute a fugitive literature that documents the life of programs and policies. The knowledge base to support effective education reform needs to be multidimensional, helping to inform a comprehensive and systemic view of educational institutions and of how they change.

The design and innovation necessary to support educational action will also need to draw on other forms of knowledge and development, not simply on studies of what has been done in the past. For example, the development of new telecommunications technologies, particularly cell phones, computers, and instantaneous translation technologies, offers much potential to engineer innovations for some education challenges, including administering educational institutions as well as enriching pedagogy, supporting teacher professional development, or providing more personalized support for learning directly to students.

For example, facing high rates of grade retention in early grades in a particular country, it makes sense to look at cross-national reviews of studies of grade retention in other settings.[17,18] Most of these posit that early grade retention is associated with reading difficulties in young learners.[19] Based on this finding, one can look for evidence to test the hypotheses that there are indeed problems with early literacy acquisition in the relevant context. If such evidence exists, one can then productively examine the international literature on literacy instruction and use this body of knowledge as a foundation to drive systematic examination of the practice of literacy instruction in the country in question. As discussed earlier, however, systematic translation of lessons from comparative research requires also that we compare how the various contexts differ, for instance in terms of class size, teacher qualifications, or parental support for literacy.

ANALYZING GAPS IN CONTEXT

After systematically analyzing the context in which the educational equity needs have been identified and reviewing the research that exists about those needs and the interventions to address them, it is necessary to identify the gaps between the context in which this research has been conducted and the context under examination.

For example, much of the U.S.-based literature on literacy acquisition emphasizes the importance of balanced instruction, integrating the development of phonological awareness, reading comprehension, decoding skills, and motivation to read. But, in using this literature to address similar reading difficulties in various contexts, one should also examine the differences in the correspondence of sound to script across the languages under comparison, what resources exist to support literacy instruction, and how instruction is constrained by how children are grouped and the size of those groups. In Malawi, for example, primary school teachers teach 85 students on average, a very different number from that found in U.S. classrooms.[20] Basic infrastructure and instructional materials, including blackboards, chairs, pencils, notebooks, or books, are often lacking in many low-income countries, and the level of teacher capacity can vary significantly across contexts, an important factor in transferring approaches to professional development.

Similarly, constraints can be rooted in the culture of pedagogy. In China, for example, learning has been primarily teacher-centered for centuries. If research from other countries proposes educational benefits to student-centered learning, then a gap has been identified in pedagogy. In addition to the identification of this gap, it is important to analyze issues surrounding the gap, such as cost-effectiveness of student-centered learning, expectations of stakeholders such as parents and administrators regarding the roles of teachers and of students, and other complex issues such as changing the purposes of education from being knowledge-based to skills-based.

GENERATING INNOVATIONS AND TRANSFER OF BEST PRACTICES

In response to a clear analysis of the differences between the contexts in which research has been conducted and the context under consideration, it will be possible to establish which practices can be transferred and which innovative modifications are necessary to adapt them to local context. It is a rare practice that is transferred whole from one context to another, and adaptations to fit varying institutional settings and capacity are common and necessary. The result of this process is the recreation of particular instances of innovation, within a general class of interventions, in ways that best fit a particular local context.

An example is the generation of innovation and transfer to address girls' access to education in Afghanistan. Only 20% of girls in Afghanistan are enrolled in school.[21] Attempts to address these equity gaps through the transfer of practices from other regions that have similar challenges would lead us to consider constructing more schools closer to girls' homes, training more female teachers, training teachers in the use of girl-friendly pedagogies, using CCTs to persuade families to send their girls to school, and conducting community workshops to educate families about the importance of girls' education.

Some of these policies may be more applicable to the context of Afghanistan than others, or to particular regions of Afghanistan, and a rigorous analysis of these contextual differences and similarities is essential in deciding which practices might be transferred or how they should be adapted. For instance, the documented high levels of corruption in public administration in this country make the use of scholarships potentially wasteful; evidence that parents did send their daughters to school while they were in refugee camps suggests that improving the supply of education for girls and reducing the distance between home and school should receive priority over demand-based interventions. In regions where there are serious risks to girls who travel from home to school, options for safe travel to school should be assessed against options to support learning at home via various technologies. Fundamentally, best international practices can provide a checklist against evidence of the specific causes of the equity gap and the particular characteristics of the context that would make some of these options better bets than others.

Applying the Framework: Two Case Studies

We illustrate the application of this approach of contextualized educational transfer with two equity challenges: providing education to populations affected by conflict and emergencies, and providing opportunities to learn to read to marginalized populations.

Boys' Access to Education in Post-conflict Armenia

Education can work to serve the needs of families in Armenia, many of which have fallen apart as a result of the significant number of male deaths after the Nagorno-Karabakh (1988-1994) war between Azerbaijan and Armenia. Access to a quality education can provide these children, particularly boys, with tools to succeed in the economy and an avenue to remain free from criminal behavior. Finally, in the long term, improvements in educational access can lift Armenia out of low-income country status and propel the market economy to which it has attempted to transition since the post-Soviet era.

IDENTIFYING NEEDS

In Armenia, education has the potential to benefit both boys and girls who might be inclined to work by providing them instead with the tools to be successful in the workforce when they complete their schooling. Boys in Armenia perform at lower levels on international assessments of student learning compared to girls. Boys also face significant challenges in accessing basic education. As a result, their enrollment in upper secondary and tertiary education has declined and continues to do so. Societal pressure to work while in school causes many boys to leave school to support their families. They are consequently much more likely to be absent from and drop out of school compared to girls. Few programs and policies address these increasing challenges faced by boys in Armenia.

Many supply-side factors can contribute to transforming the education system to meet its goals and to effectively prepare both boys and girls for success in the labor market. These factors can include: qualified teachers, high-quality schools, low schooling costs, federal and local government support for education, school materials, and low opportunity costs to attendance.

ANALYZING CONTEXT

Armenia, a former Soviet republic and a low-income nation, has experienced many political, industrial, and social reforms over the last 15 years as it transformed into a market economy, while its education system, along with other public services, has deteriorated. Resources were devoted to the Nagorno-Karabakh war, and education budgets were subsequently reduced. Low public expenditure on education has made it difficult for communities to maintain quality schools in good condition. Education has become mainly a private system. Schools are now more expensive, exacerbating the financial barriers children face to access and complete school. Schools located in rural and border areas, where many minorities live, have been most impacted by such budgetary shortfalls.[22]

Child poverty also affected students' ability to attend higher levels of education. Students who need to work to support families cannot go on to access higher education. Voluntary military service and the government's conscription of males between the ages of 18 to 45 affected the makeup of many families, leaving them with no central male figure. This has had an impact on the societal expectations of boys, creating additional pressure for them to leave school and find jobs to support their families. Consequently, child labor has become a great barrier to schooling, especially for those from poorer communities.[23]

Communities that prioritize labor in Armenia may affect boys disproportionately because of cultural expectations that assign men to the manual labor associated with agricultural work.[24] Therefore, absenteeism, repetition, and dropout rates for all children in refugee- and minority-populated areas are much higher than the national average.[25] Even teachers in many minority areas are involved in farming and therefore tend to be absent.

TAKING STOCK OF EXTANT RESEARCH INCLUDING EVALUATION AND OTHER APPLIED RESEARCH

A variety of studies have documented the deterioration of boys' schooling in different parts of the world. Research on the effect of child labor on boys' education is particularly extensive and helpful. Discrimination in schools exists toward students who combine work and school, students who are poor or disabled, and students who were formerly child laborers.[26] Many children become disabled because of the work they do, and this prevents them from participating in formal education settings because of a lack of special education support, as in Armenia. Research has also shown that teachers treat disabled students differently, making them feel uncomfortable in the classroom. Former child laborers are often older than their peers, and age differences in the classroom can negatively impact the teacher's ability to teach all students. Child laborers also face peer discrimination, and the combination of institutional discrimination and peer discrimination discourages former child laborers from attending school.[27]

Boys' anti-schooling attitudes and male juvenile crimes have been attributed to the limited number of male role models in Armenian society. The presence of male role models is important for the young male population, but they may not exist within families due to the Nagorno-Karabakh war. Boys are also unlikely to find male role models in school because research shows that Armenian schools are primarily staffed by females.[28] Research from Australia, Lesotho, and Guyana demonstrates that boys value male teachers as role models.[29]

ANALYZING GAPS BETWEEN RESEARCH AND CONTEXT

Although there is limited research on what to do about the problem of boys' underparticipation and underachievement, there is much that provides guidance about antischooling behaviors of boys, and there is evidence on how the post-conflict situation in Armenia has exacerbated these issues. In the context of Armenia, all of the problems that have caused the deterioration in boys' schooling are related. The lack of resources for education in the post-Soviet era has contributed to both the poor quality of and declining access to education. This was even more problematized by the Nagorno-Karabakh war, during which many males died, leaving their families to support themselves. In addition to high absenteeism and dropout among boys, the lack of male role models in schools, gender stereotyping of subjects, the inability to see a relationship between school and the labor market, and the problems associated with re-enrolling in school after having been a child laborer are all associated with the declining access to education for boys. Unless these particular issues, which have been extensively examined in other nations, are addressed using a combination of solutions, or innovations are developed to address specific challenges in the various regions of Armenia, we are unlikely to experience a reversal in the declining trend of access to education for Armenian boys.

GENERATION OF INNOVATION AND TRANSFER OF BEST PRACTICES

Considering the research on child labor, what has been written about boys' anti-schooling attitudes, and the gaps existent in Armenia, some best practices from other areas of the world where these topics have been researched heavily are listed below. Although some have been applied to different groups in varying parts of the world—some quite different from Armenia—they provide an overview of what best practices exist. These practices could serve a heuristic purpose to inform the development of innovative practices in Armenia to educate boys:

- Attract more male teachers, male teaching assistants, and male mentors to expose young boys to positive male role models in society, as has been done to enhance male enrollment in other parts of the world[30]
- Improve current teacher training programs to minimize gender stereotyping in education and to better engage boys in learning[31]
- Emphasize cooperation, confidence-building, and conflict resolution in teaching pedagogy to improve boys' academic performance[32]
- Create a compensatory intervention program, such as a CCT program similar to Mexico's Progresa Program, that is geared toward males in the upper secondary grades, when they are most likely to drop out
- Allocate funds for textbooks, uniforms, and school construction
- Monitor boys who are absent or drop out to join the workforce, and develop interventions to help boys return to school[33]
- Make specialization part of school: education, specialization, and work can be combined so that students can relate education to their line of work[34]

Literacy and Educational Access in Laos

The *Education for All: Global Monitoring Report 2006* (EFA) indicates that investing in education and literacy provides numerous benefits to individuals and nations. Education raises self-esteem and empowers marginalized individuals, such as women and minorities, to voice their opinions and participate in civil society. Greater political participation often translates in turn into quality public policies that can address the needs of disadvantaged groups.[35] In addition, educated individuals can foster the promotion and preservation of cultural values, which is particularly important in an ethnically and linguistically diverse nation like the Lao People's Democratic Republic (PDR).

IDENTIFYING NEEDS

The Lao PDR is a nation of 6 million people. Literacy and enrollment rates indicate a gap in learning and education access for many ethnic minorities in Lao, a problem that affects half the country. The national literacy rate for males is 80% and 60% for females, but rates are lower by ethnic group and region.[36] For example, female literacy rates are below 20% for minority groups like the Hmong, Katang, Makong, and Kor. On the other hand, the Hmong male literacy rate is 60% in Saysomboune province but only 30% in Oudomxay.[37] Educational access is related to literacy and learning. The net enrollment rate of the country is near 80% but in provinces that consist of 90% or more ethnic minorities, the rate drops closer to 50%.[38]

Literacy can clearly play a key role in developing and sustaining economic growth in an agricultural country like the Lao PDR. Studies show that "literacy and numeracy enable farm households to adopt innovations more easily, to better cope with risk, and respond to market signals and other information."[39] The UN Development Programme (UNDP) notes that 4 to 6 years of schooling is the minimum threshold necessary for increases in agricultural productivity. Without upgrading the skills and education of the current labor force, the country's transition from a natural resource–based economy to a human resource–based economy may be delayed for another generation.[40]

ANALYZING CONTEXT

The current state of the Lao PDR reflects political and economic changes of the past 30 years. These changes include the communist Pathet Lao's ascendance to power in 1975 and the transition from a centralized government to the beginnings of a market economy. Although many of these transformations under the Pathet Lao cultivated high annual growth rates in gross domestic product, the confluence of recession in Asia during the mid-1990s, limited natural resources, and dependence on agriculture continues to limit foreign investment and economic growth.[41] Furthermore, not all segments of the population benefited from these economic developments.

The government officially recognizes 47 ethnic groups, but the population is classified into three main categories by topography: *Lao Loum* (Lowland Lao), *Lao Thueng* (Midland Lao), and *Lao Soung* (Highland Lao).[42] The ethnic Lao majority resides primarily in the lowlands and Vientiane municipality and forms much of the ruling political elite in the capital, whereas most ethnic minorities populate the highlands. Although the Constitution of the Lao PDR explicitly states that "the state will provide a policy of unity and equality between different ethnic groups," ethnic minorities report less access to public services such as health and schooling.[43]

Indeed, poverty affects disproportionately those in provinces with high proportions of ethnic minorities. Whereas only 12% of Vientiane residents in 1999 fell below the poverty line, more than 50% in Oudomxay, Phongsaly, and Luangnamtha lived in poverty. Even in provinces with a low ethnic minority population, such as Champasack, the poverty rate is more than one-third. It should be noted that although poverty generally declined from 1993 to 1998, the rate of decline was lower in ethnic minority provinces. Some provinces, such as Oudomxay, actually witnessed a significant increase (51% to 73%) in poverty between those years. Overall, the UNDP reports that 38.6% of the population live below the poverty line, but of this number, 93% are ethnic minorities.[44]

A key barrier to schooling and literacy for many ethnic minorities is the absence of schools in their communities. In provinces that are predominately settled by ethnic minorities (over 90%), nearly half of the villages lack schools.[45] For those who do enroll in school, teacher quality is a major issue. Many teachers are unaware of the curriculum statement and have little knowledge of its contents. More importantly, only half of the 47 ethnic groups speak the national and instructional language of Lao as their native tongue. According to the Asian Development Bank "Children from homes where Lao is not spoken enter schools with a significant handicap, a condition partly accounting for the high dropout rate."[46] Despite the initial language barrier that many ethnic minority children face in learning, few teachers come from these communities or speak the language.[47] Many of the ethnic minority languages also lack a written component. The lack of access to early childhood education compounds these difficulties.

TAKING STOCK OF EXTANT RESEARCH INCLUDING EVALUATION AND OTHER APPLIED RESEARCH

In situations in which students must acquire literacy in a second language, the research emphasizes the importance of developing proficiency in the first language. According to Snow, Burns, and Griffin, "being able to read and write in two languages confers numerous intellectual, cultural, economic, and social benefits."[48] More importantly, their research indicates that instruction in the student's first language can aid the acquisition of literacy in the second language. That is, cognitive skills like letter and sound recognition and phonological awareness that enhance literacy development are transferable across languages. Even students who come to school speaking languages without a written component can still increase phonological and phonemic awareness by improving oral proficiency. Finally, research also shows that these skills serve as a foundation for literacy in both alphabetic and nonalphabetic languages, like Lao.[49]

The educational context in Laos indicates that any intervention to improve literacy should address access to schools that facilitate learning for non-Lao speakers.

However, research shows that investing in adult literacy can also produce high social returns and improve the literacy of children, since parental literacy contributes to child literacy. Evidence from the EFA Global Monitoring Report suggests that the private returns to adult literacy programs are comparable to, if not higher than for primary education. Although these returns are difficult to measure, the EFA concludes that "what people learn from these literacy programmes does help them raise their incomes and move out of poverty."[50] Moreover, the research of Aram with preschoolers in Jaffa demonstrates the impact of adult literacy on children.[51] In a study of two common early literacy programs for children, storybook reading and alphabet skills training, Aram finds that children who are read to develop the phonological awareness and name writing skills often seen in successful readers. In addition, storybook reading stimulates verbal interaction while enhancing vocabulary development and the relationship between print and sound. Aram's research suggests that failure to develop these critical skills early on and even before formal schooling can lead to reading difficulties.

Other research points to specific reading strategies for young learners that can boost literacy in the classroom. Willingham identified three important factors of reading comprehension that effective strategies address: the ability to monitor one's comprehension, relating sentences to one another, and relating sentences to what the reader already knows.[52] Strategies targeting these areas can be learned quickly and appear to provide a boost in literacy for readers in primary school.

ANALYZING GAPS BETWEEN RESEARCH AND CONTEXT

The key gap between the Lao educational context and extant research, aside from the assumption of financial capacity, is human capital. Most literacy experts would emphasize the importance of utilizing the students' linguistic resources when the language of instruction is different from the first language. In provinces that consist primarily of ethnic minorities, sensible classroom policy would entail integration of both the Lao national language and the students' home languages. Examples of effective bilingual models exist in the United States and around the world. The problem, however, is that these models require high levels of teacher capacity. In many of these Lao provinces, the teacher comes from outside the community and lacks fluency in the local language.[53] Building more schools and increasing educational access can improve literacy chances for students, but a major issue is improving school capacity to address the linguistic diversity of the community. Thus, merely transferring a bilingual model from abroad fails to address teacher quality.

Complicating the issue is that many of the ethnic minority languages lack a written component. The research shows that being able to read and write in two languages confers numerous developmental and cognitive benefits for students. Less clear is to what extent these benefits carry over when knowledge of the first language is limited to the spoken form. Similarly, although readers of any language must learn decoding and comprehension skills, there is likely variation between alphabetic and nonalphabetic languages.

GENERATION OF INNOVATION AND TRANSFER OF BEST PRACTICES

Based on the research and current state of education in Laos, improving literacy will require changes at different levels of the institution. Some of these changes, like building more schools and expanding access, are clear inputs that demand more financial capital. Addressing literacy at the classroom and student level, however, means improving teacher quality. The current problem is that many ethnic minorities struggle with the language of instruction, and few teachers understand the languages in these communities. The current dearth of female and ethnic minority teachers suggests that local governments should raise wages or subsidize living costs for potential teachers.

The use of inducements has been implemented with mixed success in the United States to attract more candidates to the teaching profession. Researchers found in Massachusetts that a financial bonus attracted more teachers but few remained in the profession after 3 years, citing poor working conditions and limited professional growth.[54] The Massachusetts experience made clear the importance of ongoing attention to working conditions and professional development. Given local conditions, rather than a monetary bonus, the Lao government may establish a rice coupon system as an additional incentive to prospective teachers since evidence suggests that many often worry about their rice supply. Provision of child care and adequate accommodations may help address the insufficient supply of female teachers. Once teachers from the community are recruited into the profession, it is important to provide regular in-service training on pedagogy and how to use the students' first language while teaching the national language. One key finding in the Massachusetts study was that a proportion of the bonus should have been used to support induction and professional development for new teachers. Similar workshops and training should be provided to current teachers to improve instructional practice and understanding of the languages and learning difficulties of minority students.

Conclusion

The central question of this chapter, "How do we know what works to promote educational equity?" is deceptively simple. It invites us to reflect on the relationship between knowledge and action. How is knowledge useful to action? What knowledge is useful to act? How do we generate that knowledge? How do we use it?

Despite its limitations, research-based knowledge has a role to play in sustaining educational practices to advance equality of educational opportunity.

Evidence-based knowledge can help to inform the consideration of alternative ways to achieve education objectives, once those objectives, and possible tradeoffs between objectives, have been established through the political process. Evidence-based knowledge can also inform the political deliberations about education and the process of agenda setting, as well as policy and program design.

This role for research recognizes that the establishment of education objectives is not a function of research and that the creation and implementation of programs to advance educational opportunity requires as much in terms of creation, design, and invention, as it does from research and evaluation. The search for what works must use research and theory to create and design practical and scalable approaches to helping students learn. We must transfer knowledge about what works from some contexts to others, as we have always done since the global experiment to educate all children began a few centuries ago, and began in earnest for most of the world six decades ago. To increase the odds that knowledge transfer is effective, we must do it methodically, examining the relationship of education practices to context, and comparing not only practices but contexts. In comparing carefully in order to transfer sensibly lies much potential to accelerate the process of expansion of educational opportunity and of closing the equity gaps that still remain.

NOTES

1. Cohen, J., & Bloom, D. (2005). Cultivating minds. *Finance and Development, 42*(2).
2. UNESCO. (2009). *Education for all global monitoring report 2010: Reaching the marginalized.* Retrieved December 24, 2010, http://unesdoc.unesco.org/images/0018/001866/186606E.pdf
3. Ibid., p. 1069.
4. Centers of Excellence for Teacher Training. Retrieved December 24, 2010, http://www.readingforallchildren.org
5. INJAZ Al-Arab. Retrieved December 24, 2010, http://www.injazalarab.org/en
6. Jansen, J. (2004). Importing outcomes-based education into South Africa: Policy borrowing in a post Communist world. In D. Phillips, & K. Ochs (Eds.), *Educational policy borrowing: Historical perspectives.* Didcot, UK: Symposium.
7. O'Donoghue, T. (1994). Transnational knowledge transfer and the need to take cognizance of contextual realities. *Educational Review, 46*(1), 73–89.
8. Wiener, K. A. (2011). *Effective literacy instruction in southern Malawi: Teachers' beliefs and consequences for reform.* Unpublished doctoral dissertation, Harvard Graduate School of Education.
9. Beeby, C. E. (1970). Curriculum planning. In G. Howson (Ed.), *Developing a new curriculum.* London: Heinemann.
10. Phillips, D., & Ochs, D. (Eds.). (2004). *Educational Policy Borrowing: Historical Perspectives.* Oxford: Symposium Books, Oxford.
11. Phillips, D. (2004). Aspects of educational transfer. In R. Cowen, & A. M. Kazamias (Eds.), *International handbook of comparative education* (pp. 1061–1077). New York: Springer.
12. Steiner-Khamsi, G. (2002). Re-framing educational policy borrowing as a policy strategy. In M. Caruso, & H. Tenorth (Eds.), *Internationalisierung: Semantik und bildungssystem in vergleichender perspektive* (pp. 57–89). New York: Lang.
13. Steiner-Khamsi, G. (Ed.). (2004). *The global politics of educational borrowing and lending.* New York: Teachers College Press.

14. Popper, K. (1959). *The logic of scientific discovery.* New York: Basic Books.
15. McClure, K. (2009). Madrasas and Pakistan's education agenda: Western media misrepresentation and policy recommendations. *International Journal of Educational Development, 29*(4), 334–341.
16. Basant, R., & Shariff, A. (Eds.). (2010). *Handbook of Muslims in India: Empirical and policy perspectives.* New Delhi: Oxford University Press.
17. Eisemon, T. (1998). *Reducing repetition. Issues and strategies.* Paris: International Institute for Educational Planning.
18. McGinn, N., et al. (1992). *Why do children repeat grades? A study of rural primary schools in Honduras.* Cambridge, MA: Harvard Institute for International Development.
19. Snow, C. E., Burns, M. S., & Griffin, P. (1998). *Preventing reading difficulties in young children.* Washington, DC: National Academy Press.
20. UNESCO. (2010). *Education reports: UNESCO institute for statistics.* Paris: UNESCO. Retrieved March 15, 2010, http://stats.uis.unesco.org/ReportFolders/reportfolders.aspx
21. Sigsgaard, M. (2009). *Education and fragility in Afghanistan: A situational Analysis.* Paris: International Institute for Educational Planning. Retrieved December 14, 2010, http://unesdoc.unesco.org/images/0018/001840/184038e.pdf
22. UNICEF. *Education in Armenia. Country profile 2008.* New York: UNICEF. Retrieved December 14, 2010, http://www.unicef.org/ceecis/Armenia.pdf
23. Ibid.
24. UNICEF. (2005). *Armenia: The status of school education of ethnic minorities in Armenia.* New York: UNICEF.
25. Ibid.
26. Committee on the Rights of the Child (CRC). *The impact of discrimination on working children and on the phenomenon of child labor 2002.* Retrieved December 14, 2010, http://www.antislavery.org/homepage/resources/Discriminationpaper.pdf
27. Ibid.
28. Ibid.
29. Jha, J., & Kelleher, F. (2007). *Boys' underachievement in education.* London: Commonwealth Secretariat.
30. Banerjee, A., & Kremer, M. (2002). *Teacher-student ratios and school performance in Udaipur, India: A prospective evaluation.* Cambridge, MA: Mimeo, Harvard University.
31. Jha & Kelleher. (2007). *Boys' underachievement in education.*
32. Ibid.
33. UNICEF. *Armenia: Child labour in the Republic of Armenia 2008.* New York: UNICEF. Retrieved December 14, 2010, http://www.unicef.org/armenia/resources.html
34. Ibid.
35. UNESCO. (2006). *Education for all global monitoring report 2006: Literacy for life.* Paris: UNESCO Publishing.
36. Ibid.
37. Asian Development Bank. (2000). *Lao People's Democratic Republic: Education sector development report.* Manila, Philippines: Asian Development Bank.
38. Ibid.
39. United Nations Development Programme (UNDP). (2006). *National human development report: International trade and human development Lao PDR* (p. 7). Vientiane, Laos: National Statistics Centre. Retrieved December 24, 2010, http://hdr.undp.org/en/reports/nationalreports/asiathepacific/lao/LAO_2006_en.pdf
40. Ibid.
41. Asian Development Bank. (2000). *Lao People's Democratic Republic.*
42. UNESCO. (2000). *Education for all country report: Lao PDR.* Paris: UNESCO Publishing. Retrieved February 8, 2010, http://www2.unesco.org/wef/countryreports/laos/contents.html
43. World Bank. (2005). *Ethnic groups, gender, and poverty reduction: Case study from a Khmoue Lue community in Oudomxay Province.* Washington, DC: World Bank.

44. UNDP. (2001). *National human development report Lao PDR.*
45. UNESCO. (2000). *Education for all country report.*
46. Asian Development Bank. (2000). *Lao People's Democratic Republic,* p. 3.
47. UNESCO. (2000). *Education for all country report.*
48. Snow et al. (1998). *Preventing reading difficulties in young children.*
49. Shen, H., & Bear, D. (2000). Development of orthographic skills in Chinese children. *Reading and Writing: An Interdisciplinary Journal, 13,* 197–236.
50. UNESCO. (2006). *Education for all global monitoring report 2006.*
51. Aram, D. (2006). Early literacy interventions: The relative roles of storybook reading, alphabetic activities, and their combination. *Reading and Writing, 19,* 489–515.
52. Willingham, D. T. (2007). *The usefulness of brief instruction in reading comprehension strategies.* Washington, DC: American Educator. Retrieved February 8, 2010, http://archive.aft.org/pubs-reports/american_educator/issues/winter06–07/CogSci.pdf
53. UNESCO. (2000). *Education for all country report: Lao PDR.*
54. Liu, E., Johnson, S. M., & Peske, H. G. (2004). New teachers and the Massachusetts signing bonus: The limits of inducements. *Educational Evaluation and Policy Analysis, 26,* 217–236.

Index

Page numbers followed by "*f*", "*t*", or "*n*" denote figures, tables, or notes, respectively